TESI GREGORIANA

Serie Spiritualità

——————————— 3 ———————

T0126745

BARTHOLOMEW WINTERS

PRIEST AS LEADER
The Process of the Inculturation
of a Spiritual-Theological Theme
of Priesthood in a United States Context

EDITRICE PONTIFICIA UNIVERSITÀ GREGORIANA
Roma 1997

Vidimus et approbamus ad normam Statutorum Universitatis

Romae, ex Pontificia Universitate Gregoriana
die 8 mensis novembris anni 1995

R.P. Prof. HERBERT ALPHONSO, S.J.
R.P. Prof. ROBERT FARICY, S.J.

ISBN 88-7652-733-8

© Iura editionis et versionis reservantur
PRINTED IN ITALY

GREGORIAN UNIVERSITY PRESS
Piazza della Pilotta, 35 – 00187 Rome, Italy

ACKNOWLEDGMENTS

During the course of my doctoral studies, my bishop, Joseph Cardinal Bernardin, endured two severe crises: an attack on his integrity and reputation, and the onset of a terminal illness. His response to both of these crises, showed Cardinal Bernardin to be a man of unfaltering courage, dignity, and faith, standing as an inspiration to countless people, and consistently reflecting and embodying the pastoral charity of Christ, the Good Shepherd. In deep gratitude for his leadership, example, encouragement, and support, I dedicate this work to him. *Requiescat in pace.*

I would like to acknowledge and thank the many people who supported me in this project, especially my family, both immediate and extended. My father, my brothers and their wives — John and Terri, Willie and Kerry, Mark and Rita — as well as many aunts, uncles, and cousins offered me unfailing love and encouragement throughout the duration of the project. I also want to acknowledge the support of Bishop Gerald Kicanas, Father John Canary, and the faculty of Mundelein Seminary. Additional thanks goes to Monsignor Charles Elmer and the priests at the Casa Santa Maria in Rome, especially Jim Fox, Michael Kesicki, Michael O'Connell, and Kevin Quirk.

My deep gratitude goes to Fathers Tom Hickey, Jim Heneghan, Joe Kornoski, Tom Nestor, and Stephen Rooney for their friendship, encouragement, and support. Father Louis Cameli gave much in the way of time and energy in offering helpful suggestions and in proofreading the document. I am most grateful to him for his critical eye, expert advice, and invaluable support and friendship during all stages of the project, from beginning to end. Thanks also to Jain Simmons for her helpful advice on writing, as well as her friendship and kind words of encouragement, to Jim and Deb Daniel for their help in printing the dissertation, and especially to Mr. Robert Boyle and Mr. Joseph Spurgeon for their advice during the early stages of the project and for transforming the dissertation manuscript into the publication format and style required by the Pontifical Gregorian Press.

Finally, my deepest gratitude goes to Father Herbert Alphonso, S.J., the director of the thesis, whose ready availability, steadfast support, scholarly expertise, and personal concern were of such importance in assisting me to see this project through to its completion. I am deeply grateful to have had him as a mentor and friend in this process.

INTRODUCTION

In November, 1992, the general membership of the United States National Conference of Catholic Bishops approved the fourth edition of the *Program of Priestly Formation* (*PPF* IV). Chapter One of the document focuses on the foundations of priestly formation, with particular emphasis on priestly identity, mission, and spirituality, making a number of references to the priest in terms of leadership. Alluding to the Second Vatican Council's «Decree on the Ministry and Life of Priests», *Presbyterorum Ordinis*, the *PPF* IV states that «[...] priests act with a spiritual authority that enables them to lead the people of God along the right paths»[1]. Later it states, «Priests provide pastoral leadership in the community of faith», a leadership that implies «[...] a continuing relationship of collaboration and mutual respect»[2]. In the very next section this leadership is described in general terms: «As leaders of the faith community, priests exercise a significant dimension of their shepherding role through the support they offer the laity. As they encourage others to perform the tasks which are theirs by virtue of baptism, priests are called to provide vision, direction, and leadership»[3].

These references to priests as functioning in a leadership capacity demonstrate concern on the part of the U.S. Bishops that the ministerial priesthood be understood, at least in part, in terms of leadership. The meaning and content of this leadership, however, is vague, undefined, and raises a number of questions: Where do priests obtain this spiritual authority that «[...] enables them to lead people along the right paths»? Is such leadership simply rooted in certain skills, or is it a fundamental aspect of the sacrament of Holy Orders? How do priests lead the people of God? What does such leadership look like and how is it to be

---

[1] *PPF* IV, 9; Cf. *PO* 6.
[2] *PPF* IV, 10-11.
[3] *PPF* IV, 11.

understood? To say that the priest is a leader can also be said about lay
persons in the Church. How is the leadership of the priest different from
that offered by a lay person?

In addressing the spiritual life of diocesan priests, the *PPF* IV raises
the topic of leadership again, this time associating such leadership
with the third dimension of the threefold ministry of priest, prophet, and
king. The document describes the threefold ministry as «[...] preaching,
sanctifying, and pastoral leadership», stressing that «[...] to teach, sanctify, and lead is central to the spirituality of priests»[4]. In this context the
document's treatment of priestly leadership offers more specificity, but
raises its own set of problems. First, is it legitimate to identify the kingly
office exclusively with leadership? Second, is the priest's leadership,
then, limited to one office? What about the priestly and prophetic offices:
is leadership associated with them? Third, what is «pastoral leadership»: a
matter of management skills for coordinating the activities of a parish?
Although it is clear that the U.S. Bishops associate the notion of leadership with the ministerial priesthood, as it is to be lived out in the context
of the United States, it is not completely clear what such leadership entails
and how it is to be understood. The purpose of this dissertation, then, is
to examine the meaning of priest as leader in a U.S. cultural context.

Because the topic of leadership in relation to priesthood emerges
explicitly in the *PPF* IV, a document of the United States Bishops, and
because it is largely absent in universal Church teaching on priesthood,
the issue of inculturation must be addressed. The faith of the Church does
not exist as a disembodied reality but is enfleshed in the lives of people
who live in particular cultures. Faith and culture, therefore, encounter
each other and are influenced by one another. The goal of faith, relative
to culture, is to penetrate it with the Gospel so that the culture is transformed by it. But in the process the Church is also affected by the
exchange when the culture begins to influence the Church.

The ministerial priesthood, as part of the structure of the Church, does
not escape from this process. Although primarily a faith reality, it too is
enfleshed in the lives of people and is influenced by their cultures. Such
is the case in the correlation of priesthood and leadership. To say that the
ministerial priest is a leader brings two epistemologically distinct realities
into play: priesthood (theological) and leadership (cultural). Before
examining these two categories in order to understand how they relate to
and differ from each other, it is necessary to examine the process of

---

4 *PPF* IV, 13.

inculturation itself, which will provide a framework and methodology for uncovering both the limits and the possibilities inherent in identifying the priest as leader. Chapter One will examine the Church's teaching on inculturation, establishing a methodology for proceeding with the study of priesthood and leadership.

Having delineated a methodology for examining the ministerial priest as leader, the study can proceed to its next step which is to examine the Church's teaching on the ministerial priesthood, specifically as it relates to leadership. A general description of leadership will be used as a key for the thematic examination of Church teaching on the priesthood. This step of the study entails two parts. First, Chapter Two will examine the conciliar document *Presbyterorum Ordinis* which articulates the Second Vatican Council's central teaching on the ministerial priesthood, along with examination of supplementary conciliar and post-conciliar documents which deal with the topic of priesthood, such as *Lumen Gentium* 10 and 28, *Optatam Totius, Christus Dominus*, and the 1971 synodal document, *The Ministerial Priesthood*. Together with *Presbyterorum Ordinis*, these documents articulate important teachings on the ministerial priesthood and will be examined thematically from the perspective of leadership. The second part of the examination of the Church's teaching on priesthood in terms of leadership will unfold in Chapter Three, a study of the Apostolic Exhortation *Pastores Dabo Vobis* of Pope John Paul II. Although a document specifically written on the topic of priestly formation, *Pastores Dabo Vobis* has much to say about the identity, mission, and spirituality of the ministerial priesthood and will be explored from this perspective, particularly with an eye to filling out an understanding of the ministerial priest as leader.

An inherent danger in such a thematic approach to a topic is to read into the texts meanings they do not necessarily intend. The examination of the documents using a general description of leadership as a key must respect the integrity of the texts and allow them to yield their own intrinsic meaning. The leadership reading key, therefore, is not intended to impose an extraneous interpretation but to unlock the teachings of the texts regarding the ministerial priest as leader. Based on the study of the conciliar and post-conciliar Church teaching on the ministerial priesthood, a preliminary description of the priest as leader can be articulated.

Having examined the ministerial priesthood from the perspective of leadership in Chapters Two and Three, the study will proceed in Chapter Four to its next step: an examination of the concept of leadership as it is understood in a U.S. cultural context. «Leadership» is an enormously complicated field of study and has generated a vast amount of writing;

thus certain limits are needed. Because of their widespread popularity, certain authors have had an influence on how leadership is generally understood in the U.S. Chapter Four will examine some of the writings of selected influential U.S. authors, explore their salient themes, and offer a synthesis of their understanding of leadership.

Chapter Five of the study will examine the various editions of the U.S. Bishops' *Program of Priestly Formation*, with particular emphasis on the *PPF* IV, in order to highlight the Bishops' concern for leadership relative to the ministerial priesthood, as well as their concern that the U.S. cultural context be taken into consideration in seminary training. This will set the stage for the final chapter in which the various elements of the study will be brought into interaction and the process of inculturation will be demonstrated.

In Chapter Six, following the methodology of inculturation established in Chapter One, the research from Chapters Two and Three, on the ministerial priesthood from the perspective of leadership, will be brought into correlation and critical dialogue with the research from Chapter Four, on the U.S. cultural understanding of leadership. The adequacies and inadequacies of such a correlation will be demonstrated, but more importantly, the critical dialogue will culminate in a moment of resonance or inculturation: a spirituality of priest as leader in a U.S. context. Additionally, some of the implications and challenges that such a spirituality have for seminary formation will be spelled out.

Although studies of the ministerial priesthood from the perspective of leadership have been done before[5], a generalized understanding of leadership was assumed. This study contends that the particular cultural context influences how leadership is understood and practiced, and thus how the ministerial priest as leader is understood in that context. The unique contribution of this work is using the matrix of inculturation to demonstrate that the articulation of the priest as leader, as it emerges in the U.S. Bishops' *PPF* IV, represents an instance of inculturation, showing how such an understanding can be faithful to Church teaching and adequate to a particular cultural context. The study makes a further contribution to seminary formation in the United States because it examines a specific, and important, spiritual-theological theme of priesthood, in terms of its fidelity to the Church's tradition and its adequacy to U. S. culture. The clarity achieved in such a study contributes to the efforts to

---

[5] See, for example, R. M. SCHWARTZ, *Servant Leaders of the People of God*; W. KASPER, «A New Dogmatic Outlook on the Priestly Ministry», 20-33.

prepare priests who will be both faithful to the Church and effective in their ministry in a particular cultural context. Additionally, the study makes a contribution in its examination of two relatively recent Church documents on priestly formation: *Pastores Dabo Vobis* (1992), and the fourth edition of the U.S. Bishops' *Program of Priestly Formation* (1993). In studying and analyzing these two documents the dissertation helps to unlock their potential for contributing to the efforts of seminary formation in the United States.

Finally, the study contributes in its articulation of some components of a spirituality that will serve the ministerial priest as he endeavors to minister and live in a U.S. cultural context. Spirituality has been described as «[...] an attempt through the use of various resources and especially theological ones to capture the Christian experience in its particular facets and its totality with a view towards entering into the experience and living it more deeply and authentically»[6]. Among these «various resources» the human sciences, insofar as they lead to a deeper understanding of human nature and its vital dynamism, are helpful tools in the operation of Spiritual Theology[7]. The present study is rooted in the discipline of Spiritual Theology in that it considers the description of a Christian experience, that is, priest as leader as articulated in the *PPF* IV, critically reflecting on the experience in the light of Church doctrine, principally *Presbyterorum Ordinis* and *Pastores Dabo Vobis*. In addition to theological resources, this study uses the resources of the social sciences, U.S. studies on leadership, to broaden and deepen the understanding of the experience. Having critically reflected upon priesthood and leadership from the respective perspectives of theology and the social sciences, the study returns to the experience as articulated in the *PPF* IV, and through the matrix of inculturation, offers indications for living the experience more fully and authentically; in other words, it offers an articulation of a spirituality of priest as leader in a U.S. context.

---

[6] L. J. CAMELI, *Ministerial Consciousness*, 4.

[7] Cf. C. A. BERNARD, *Teologia spirituale*, 97. Sandra Schneiders notes that «[...] while theology is the most important single discipline in the service of spirituality, it is by no means the only one. The spiritual life [...] embraces the whole of human experience within the horizon of ultimate concern. Consequently, the personality sciences, the social sciences, literary and aesthetic disciplines, history, comparative religion, and a variety of other fields of study are important to the understanding and to the living of the Christian religious experience», S. M. SCHNEIDERS, «Theology and Spirituality», 271.

CHAPTER I

Inculturation and Its Process

1. The Church's Concern for Faith and Culture

1.1 *Conciliar and Postconciliar Teaching*

The conciliar and postconciliar teaching on the relationship between Church and culture sets the context for exploring the doctrine of inculturation. One of the Church's core issues at Vatican II and in subsequent years has been that of the relationship between faith and culture[1]. It can be said without exaggeration that the Council marked a moment of reorientation of the Church vis-à-vis its own concept of culture and its relationship with the plurality of cultures in the world. This reorientation was no less than a «[...] new attitude of mind, both theological and anthropological, that progressively grew within the Fathers of the Council as they investigated the meaning of the Church for contemporary men and women»[2]. The significance of this «new attitude of mind» can be grasped most fully when seen against a backdrop of the Church's previous, almost exclusively esthetic understanding of culture. Cultural analysis as an anthropological operation was almost unheard of; thus its introduction in conciliar documents marks a development in the Church's approach to theology and to the world[3]. Before examining the concept and process of inculturation itself, therefore, a brief review of the development of the Church's conciliar and postconciliar teaching on the relationship between faith and culture will be helpful to set the context.

---

[1] For a discussion of the significance of Vatican II on the Church's approach to and understanding of culture, see H. CARRIER, «Vatican II et la culture», 371-383.

[2] H. CARRIER, *Evangelizing the Culture of Modernity*, 8.

[3] Cf. H. CARRIER, *Evangelizing the Culture of Modernity*, 11.

1.2 *The Second Vatican Council*

The document that best illustrates the Church's attitude shift toward culture is the «Pastoral Constitution on the Church in the Modern World», *Gaudium et Spes*, especially Part Two, Chapter Two, «The Proper Development of Culture» (*GS* 53-62)[4], which offered an important description of culture[5]:

> The word "culture" in its general sense indicates all those factors by which man refines and unfolds his manifold spiritual and bodily qualities. It means his effort to bring the world itself under his control by his knowledge and labor. It includes the fact that by improving customs and institutions he renders social life more human both within the family and in the civic community. Finally, it is a feature of culture that throughout the course of time man expresses, communicates, and conserves in his works great spiritual experiences and desires, so that these may be of advantage to the progress of many, even of the whole human family. Hence it follows that culture necessarily has a historical and social aspect and that the word "culture" often takes on a sociological and ethnological sense. It is in this sense that we speak of a plurality of cultures. Various conditions of community living, as well as various patterns for organizing the goods of life, arise from diverse ways of using things, of laboring, of expressing oneself, of practicing religion, of forming customs, of establishing laws and juridical institutions, of advancing the arts and sciences, and of promoting beauty (*GS* 53)[6].

Such an understanding of culture combines both the classical and anthropological approaches to the concept and clearly marks a development in the Church's understanding of the term[7].

---

[4] Cf. D. LANE, «The Challenge of Inculturation», 7.

[5] Carrier observes the parallels between *GS* 53's definition of culture and that adopted by UNESCO in 1983: «Culture may now be said to be the whole complex distinctive, spiritual, material, intellectual and emotional features that characterize a society or a group. It includes not only the arts and letters, but also modes of life, the fundamental rights of human beings, value systems, traditions, and beliefs; it is culture that gives man the ability to reflect upon himself. It is culture that makes us specifically human, rational beings, endowed with a critical judgment and a sense of moral commitment. It is through culture that we discern values and make choices. It is through culture that man expresses himself, becomes aware of himself, recognizes his incompleteness, questions his own achievements, seeks untiringly for new meanings and creates works through which he transcends his limitations», H. CARRIER, *Evangelizing the Culture of Modernity*, 152-153, n. 15.

[6] All references to the documents of Vatican II are taken from M. ABBOTT, gen. ed., J. GALLAGHER, tr. ed., *The Documents of Vatican II.*

[7] Cf. H. CARRIER, *Gospel Message and Human Cultures*, 8. Carrier notes that culture «[...] understood in the older, classic sense, generally has a normative connotation: culture alludes to an ideal that is to be attained. Culture understood in the more

In addition to moving from a classicist to an empiricist understanding of culture[8], *Gaudium et Spes* explicitly acknowledged a positive relationship between the Church and the world[9], between faith and culture[10], advocating «[...] a listening, dialogical attitude with culture, both traditional and modern»[11]. *GS* 58 has been described as «the key passage of the entire document»[12] because of the affirmations it makes regarding the relationship between the Gospel and culture:

> There are many links between the message of salvation and human culture. For God [...] has spoken according to the culture proper to different ages. Living in various circumstances during the course of time, the Church, too, has used in her preaching the discoveries of the different cultures to spread and explain the message of Christ to all nations. [...] the Church, sent to all peoples of every time and place, is not bound exclusively and indissolubly to any race or nation, nor to any particular way of life or any customary pattern of living, ancient or recent. Faithful to her own tradition [...] she can enter into communion with various cultural modes, to her own enrichment and theirs too (*GS* 58).

Although the document did not use the term, it certainly hinted at and laid the foundations for what would come to be known as «inculturation». The affirmations and principles in *Gaudium et Spes* are all the

---

modern anthropological sense, on the other hand, is primarily a descriptive notion: culture describes a socio-historical or socio-cultural situation which, like every human reality, embodies both positive and negative elements vis-à-vis the ideal norm or the loftiest culture of humanity», ID., *Gospel Message and Human Cultures*, 5.

[8] A. Shorter notes that «[...] the Church's understanding of culture has evolved, together with that of humanity at large. Originally, culture was conceived as a single, universal, normative criterion, according to which human beings were adjudged "cultured" or "uncultured". This is what Bernard Lonergan called the "classicist assumption". Christianity was deemed to be the perfection of this culture of humanity, and the Church was thus identified with the world as such. Evangelization was characterized by a Eurocentric monoculturalism. At the theoretical level [...] monoculturalism has now been displaced by the empirical, pluralistic understanding of culture», A. SHORTER, *Evangelization and Culture*, 30. For a description of the evolution from a classicist to a modern understanding of culture, see ID., *Toward a Theology of Inculturation*, especially Chapter Two, «Evolution of the Church's Understanding of Culture», 17-30.

[9] M. de Carvalho Azevedo maintains that *Gaudium et Spes* both «[...] explicates and reinforces especially the relationship between the Church and the world. It does so above all through the analytical and hermeneutical key that is culture», M. DE CARVALHO AZEVEDO, «Inculturation: I. The Problem», 505.

[10] D. Lane describes the positive relationship between faith and culture as a «New Pentecost», D. LANE, «The Challenge of Inculturation», 7.

[11] P. SCHINELLER, *A Handbook on Inculturation*, 40.

[12] A. SHORTER, *Toward a Theology of Inculturation*, 201.

more striking when seen against the backdrop of the Church's previous *fuga mundi* stance toward the world and culture[13]; they reveal a Church moving into a stance of engagement and dialogue with the modern world and its cultures[14].

Another conciliar document instrumental in developing the Church's understanding of and relationship to culture is the «Decree on the Church's Missionary Activity», *Ad Gentes*[15]. In describing the relationship of the Church to the world, the document made two important affirmations regarding culture that would have important ramifications for developing the doctrine of inculturation. The first affirmation is in reference to the Incarnation as the paradigm[16] for the Church's interaction with particular cultures:

> In order to be able to offer to all of them [human beings] the mystery of salvation and the life brought by God, the Church must become part of all these groups for the same motive which led Christ to bind Himself, in virtue of his Incarnation, to the definite social and cultural conditions of those human beings among whom he dwelt (*AG* 10).

The second affirmation is in reference to the seeds of the Word that are already present within particular cultures:

> That they may be able to give this witness to Christ fruitfully, let them [Christians] be joined to those men by esteem and love, and acknowledge themselves to be members of the group of men among whom they live. Let them share in cultural and social life by the various exchanges and enterprises of human living. Let them be familiar with their national and religious traditions, gladly and reverently laying bare the seeds of the Word which lie hidden in them (*AG* 11).

In both of these examples the Council envisioned «[...] an interior transformation of cultures»[17], which indicates that the proper relation of the Church to cultures is one of respect, engagement, and dialogue.

Conciliar concern for culture is further expressed in such documents as «The Decree on the Apostolate of the Laity», *Apostolicam Actuositatem*, wherein lay people are called to the task of «renewal of the

---

[13] Cf. D. LANE, «The Challenge of Inculturation», 6.

[14] Cf. D. LANE, «The Challenge of Inculturation», 7.

[15] Shorter maintains that «[...] it is difficult to exaggerate the importance of *Ad Gentes* for the development of modern missionary theology», A. SHORTER, *Toward a Theology of Inculturation*, 195.

[16] Cf. P. SCHINELLER, A *Handbook on Inculturation*, 41.

[17] A. SHORTER, *Toward a Theology of Inculturation*, 196.

temporal order» (*AA* 7), the elements of which are «[...] the good things of life and the prosperity of the family, culture, economic affairs, the arts and professions, political institutions, international relations, and other matters of this kind» (*AA* 7) — all described as having their own intrinsic value and goodness[18], which are imbued with an even greater dignity because of their relationship to humanity (cf. *AA* 7).

Another document that must be consulted in examining the Church's relation to culture is «The Constitution on the Sacred Liturgy», *Sacrosanctum Concilium*. Because it was the first conciliar document to be approved and promulgated, *Sacrosanctum Concilium* has been described as «ecclesiologically immature»[19]; it did not enjoy the benefits of the conciliar discussions that led to a renewed ecclesiology and understanding of culture and was, therefore, «[...] out of step with the Church's thinking on evangelization and culture»[20]. Despite this gap, the document was not negative in its approach to culture:

> [The Church] respects and fosters the spiritual adornments and gifts of the various races and peoples. Anything in their way of life that is not indissolubly bound up with superstition and error she studies with sympathy and, if possible, preserves intact. Sometimes in fact she admits such things into the liturgy itself, as long as they harmonize with its true and authentic spirit (*SC* 37).

Although the document insisted on «the substantial unity of the Roman rite» (*SC* 38) in adapting the liturgy to local conditions, and did not envision the creation of new rites according to the modes of expression of the various local cultures[21], even here the Council was nevertheless positive in its approach to cultures and expressed a desire that the Church be enriched by the cultures in which it was incarnated[22].

The final document to be noted in this brief survey of conciliar approaches to culture is the «Declaration on the Relationship of the Church to Non-Christian Religions», *Nostra Aetate*. The Church shows its respect for non-Christian religions and the cultures to which they are bound by exhorting Christians to acknowledge, preserve, and affirm the spiritual, moral, social, and cultural values which are found in non-Christian religions. In keeping with the conciliar emphasis on

---

[18] Cf. H. CARRIER, *Gospel Message and Human Cultures*, 12.

[19] A. SHORTER, *Toward a Theology of Inculturation*, 203.

[20] A. SHORTER, *Toward a Theology of Inculturation*, 191.

[21] Cf. A. SHORTER, *Toward a Theology of Inculturation*, 192.

[22] Cf. H. CARRIER, «Inculturation», 513.

engagement and dialogue with cultures, the document encouraged Christians to participate in «[...] dialogue and collaboration with the followers of other religions» (*NA* 2).

The Second Vatican Council can be said to have been represented by two poles of thinking: one pole is the Church's reflection upon itself and the other is its reflection upon its relationship with the modern world[23]. Regarding this latter pole, the Church made a distinct shift at the Council which is perhaps best captured by the word *aggiornamento*. At the Council the Church «[...] tried to open its windows to the modern world, with its joys and sorrows, hopes and anxieties»[24], and «[...] made the historic choice of sharing with all men and women of this planet the challenges of our time»[25]. The cultural and anthropological focus of the Council is probably one of its most original and unique elements[26], establishing the foundation for the development of the Church's post-conciliar teaching on the relationship of faith and culture, which eventually led to the articulation of its teaching on inculturation.

1.3 *Pope Paul VI*

The issue of how to relate faith and culture was of major concern to Pope Paul VI, who recognized the central role of cultures in shaping how the two are linked[27]. Although at times this relationship was marked by tension, and at other times by creative interaction, Paul VI's «large theological vision» held them together and set the direction for their interaction in the years immediately following the Council[28]. Two documents of Paul VI that are of particular importance in developing the Church's reflection on the relationship between faith and culture are his speech at the closing of the first plenary assembly of the Symposium of Episcopal Conferences of Africa and Madagascar on 31 July 1969, the «Kampala Address»[29], and his «Apostolic Exhortation on Evangelization in the Modern World», *Evangelii Nuntiandi*[30].

---

[23] Cf. M. DE CARVALHO AZEVEDO, «Inculturation and the Challenges of Modernity», 1.24.

[24] P. SCHINELLER, A *Handbook on Inculturation*, 40.

[25] M. DE CARVALHO AZEVEDO, «Inculturation and the Challenges of Modernity», 24.

[26] Cf. H. CARRIER, *Evangelizing the Culture of Modernity*, 24.

[27] Cf. M. DE CARVALHO AZEVEDO, «Inculturation and the World Church», 123.

[28] Cf. D. LANE, «The Challenge of Inculturation», 7.

[29] Cf. *AAS* 61 (1969) 573-578.

[30] *EN*, *AAS* 68 (1976) 5-76.

The second part of the «Kampala Address» directly deals with the problem of the relationship between faith and culture, and particularly the cultural expression of the faith[31]. There Paul VI affirmed two important principles that would have direct implications for the problem of inculturation. First, he asserted that the Church, in whatever land it is incarnated «[...] must be entirely founded upon the identical, essential, constitutional patrimony of the self-same teaching of Christ, as professed by the authentic and authoritative tradition of the one true Church. This condition is fundamental and indisputable. [...] We are not the inventors of our Faith; we are its custodians»[32]. Although the Pope affirmed that the revealed doctrine of the Church cannot be altered, such an assertion does not rule out a «certain pluralism» in the expression of the faith. This sets the context for his second principle regarding pluralism:

> The expression, that is, the language and mode of manifesting this one Faith, may be manifold; hence, it may be original, suited to the tongue, the style, the character, the genius, and the culture, of the one who professes this one Faith. From this point of view, a certain pluralism is not only legitimate, but desirable. An adaptation of the Christian life in the fields of pastoral, ritual, didactic and spiritual activities is not only possible, it is even favoured by the Church[33].

In this speech Paul VI not only continues the spirit of dialogue and engagement between the Church and cultures which was begun at the Council, but he even goes further and implies a reciprocity in the relationship between the two. In other words, not only is the faith a source of enrichment and growth for the culture, but the culture is able to make a contribution to the faith[34]. This positive consideration of culture is evidence that the Church, since the Council, has become more sensitive to the connection between the needs and aspirations of humanity on the one hand, and its own evangelizing mission on the other. The Church is thus in a position to shape its mission in the light of the concrete

---

[31] Cf. A. SHORTER, *Toward a Theology of Inculturation*, 208.

[32] PAUL VI, «Kampala Address», 576.

[33] PAUL VI, «Kampala Address», 577.

[34] Shorter notes the significance of one sentence of the speech in which the Pope affirms that the Church in Africa possesses «[...] "forms of culture which can rise up to perfection such as to find *in* Christianity, and *for* Christianity, a true superior fullness, and prove to be capable of a richness of expression all its own, and genuinely African" [emphases not in the original]», A. SHORTER, *Toward a Theology of Inculturation*, 210. According to Shorter, the two prepositions, «in» and «for», are crucial and indicate that Paul VI expected a positive contribution to Christianity from African culture. Cf. PAUL VI, «Kampala Address», 577.

circumstances of the world and to use the means and methods of social analysis in the service of articulating and promoting its mission[35].

The second document of Paul VI, crucial for the development of the doctrine of inculturation, is *Evangelii Nuntiandi*. A seminal document for addressing the area of faith and culture[36], *Evangelii Nuntiandi* drew its inspiration from the Second Vatican Council and added needed clarity and direction for translating the Council's teaching on the Church and culture into more practical guidelines[37].

At the beginning of the document the Pope asked three important questions: 1) «[...] what has happened to the hidden energy of the Good News [...] ?»; 2) «To what extent and in what way is that evangelical force capable of really transforming the people of this century?»; 3) «What methods should be followed in order that the power of the Gospel may have its effect?» (*EN* 4). In seeking to answer these questions the document offered a holistic rather than a fragmentary approach to evangelization, an approach that acknowledges both the richness and complexity of the dynamic of evangelization, which includes proclamation, penetration of all levels of society, and permeation of cultures[38]. Acknowledging that the «[...] split between the Gospel and culture is without a doubt the drama of our times» (*EN* 20), the Pope called for an evangelization of cultures:

> what matters is to evangelize man's culture and cultures (not in a purely decorative way as it were by applying a thin veneer, but in a vital way, in depth and right to their very roots), [...] always taking the person as one's starting point and always coming back to the relationships of peoples among themselves and with God (*EN* 20).

In calling for this penetrating interaction between faith and culture, Paul VI was careful to maintain the Gospel's uniqueness and independence of any and all cultures. Such independence, however, does not imply an incompatibility, nor does it obscure the fact that the Kingdom, which the Gospel proclaims, «[...] is lived by men who are profoundly linked to a culture, and the building up of the Kingdom cannot avoid

---

[35] Cf. L. RICHARD, «Mission and Inculturation», 105.

[36] Lane, for example, refers to *EN* as «[...] probably the best treatment to date of faith and culture in a Church document», D. LANE, «The Challenge of Inculturation», 7. Shorter refers to it as «unrivaled» in its treatment of the issues, A. SHORTER, *Toward a Theology of Inculturation*, 215. Carrier refers to *EN* as «[...] a true charter for the evangelization of cultures», H. CARRIER, *Evangelizing the Culture of Modernity*, 26.

[37] Cf. H. CARRIER, *Evangelizing the Culture of Modernity*, 26.

[38] Cf. L. RICHARD, «Mission and Inculturation», 101.

borrowing the elements of human culture or cultures» (*EN* 20). The task of evangelization is to permeate these cultures with the Gospel in such a way that it does not become subject to or compromised by them[39].

In another crucial passage Paul VI articulated the «hermeneutical challenge» of evangelization today[40], a challenge which laid out what would become three phases of the process of inculturation: assimilation, transposition, and proclamation[41]:

> The individual Churches, intimately built up not only of people but also of aspirations, of riches and limitations, of ways of praying, of loving, of looking at life and the world which distinguish this or that human gathering, have the task of assimilating the essence of the Gospel message and of transposing it, without the slightest betrayal of its essential truth, into the language that these particular people understand, then of proclaiming it in this language (*EN* 63).

In addition to delineating the process of inculturation, Paul VI identified the fields in which the process is applied: liturgy, catechesis, theological formulation, secondary ecclesial structures, and ministries (cf. *EN* 63). He also made use of a cultural anthropological category when he referred to the word «language» in a manner «[...] which one may call anthropological and cultural» (*EN* 63)[42].

Although some authors note certain deficiencies[43], *Evangelii Nuntiandi* marked a notable advance in the Church's teaching on culture. It concretized the process of evangelization by stressing the need «[...] to take into consideration the actual people to whom it is addressed», and

---

[39] L. Richard, citing *EN* 19 and 36, points out that Paul VI's conception of culture does not simply refer to political and social structures, but «[...] to the common understanding and valuing of a specific group of people, although such shared understanding may cut across groups. Culture in this sense is made up of patterns or structures of perceiving and valuing and is handed down from generation to generation in traditions», L. RICHARD, «Mission and Inculturation», 102. Such an understanding of culture, therefore, includes the hearts and minds of the people who make up the culture.

[40] Cf. D. LANE, «The Challenge of Inculturation», 8.

[41] Cf. A. SHORTER, *Toward a Theology of Inculturation*, 217.

[42] Cf. A. A. ROEST CROLLIUS, «What Is So New about Inculturation?», 721-738.

[43] Shorter, for example, affirms that *Evangelii Nuntiandi* offered an advanced theology of a multicultural Church which was unsurpassed by any other official Church statement on the topic, but also notes a number of weaknesses: the Pope's reluctance «[...] to admit the extent to which the process of evangelization is dependent on culture»; the impression that the Gospel emerges from a world of essences; the impression that evangelization means that the Church is doing things for people; and the lack of biblical references in *EN* 63. A. SHORTER, *Toward a Theology of Inculturation*, 215-219.

warned that it loses its force and effectiveness «[...] if it does not use their language, their signs and symbols, if it does not answer the questions they ask, and if it does not have an impact on their concrete life» (*EN* 63). Even though he did not use the word itself, Paul VI laid out the process of inculturation and paved the way for subsequent theological reflection on the topic[44].

1.4 *Pope John Paul II*

Like his predecessor, Paul VI, Pope John Paul II has shown in his teachings a genuine interest in the relationship between Church and culture[45], and because of his widespread travels and vast amount of teaching required by encounters with various peoples, has dealt with the topic of culture on numerous occasions[46]. A few important comments on this topic will be considered here, in order to fill out this survey of the Church's concern for the relationship between faith and culture and its implications for understanding the process of inculturation.

The first document to be considered is his Apostolic Exhortation, *Catechesi Tradendae*[47], which was the fruit of the 1977 Synod of Bishops on catechesis, at which numerous interventions were made on the topic of faith and culture, particularly on the topic of inculturation[48]. This document is significant because John Paul II used the word «inculturation» to describe the relationship between faith and culture[49]:

---

[44] Cf. A. SHORTER, *Toward a Theology of Inculturation*, 219.

[45] Shorter observes that John Paul II's interest in culture is rooted in his interest in «the human phenomenon» as well as in his experience of the struggle between his culture and that of Marxist atheism. A. SHORTER, *Toward a Theology of Inculturation*, 223.

[46] Shorter comments that as a result of his enormous output of teaching, John Paul II «[...] cannot avoid a great amount of repetition. Even the most superficial acquaintance with his teachings shows that there are recurring themes which are repeatedly adapted to different audiences», A. SHORTER, *Toward a Theology of Inculturation*, 222.

[47] *CT, AAS* 71 (1979) 1277-1340. References are from the English translation, «Apostolic Exhortation *Catechesi Tradendae*».

[48] Cf. D. LANE, «The Challenge of Inculturation», 8. Shorter notes that Cardinal Jaime Sin of the Philippines emphasized «[...] the Church's recognition of cultural pluralism and the shift in salvation theology», and that Fr. Pedro Arrupe, S.J. «[...] used the actual term "inculturation" in the *aula* and spoke of the necessity of a balanced pluralism in the Church», A. SHORTER, *Toward a Theology of Inculturation*, 219.

[49] In the first sentence of this quotation, the Pope quotes a statement he had made to the Pontifical Biblical Commission earlier the same year: «Le terme "acculturation", ou "inculturation" a beau être un néologisme, il exprime fort bien l'une des composantes du grand mystère de l'Incarnation», *AAS* 71 (1979) 607. According to Shorter, this state-

"The term *acculturation* or *inculturation* may be a neologism, but it expresses very well one factor of the great mystery of the Incarnation". We can say of catechesis, as well as of evangelization in general, that it is called to bring the power of the Gospel into the very heart of culture and cultures. For this purpose, catechesis will seek to know these cultures and their essential components; it will learn their most significant expressions; it will respect their particular values and riches. In this manner it will be able to offer these cultures the knowledge of the hidden mystery and help them to bring forth from their own living tradition original expressions of Christian life, celebration and thought (*CT* 53).

The Pope's use of the words «inculturation» and «acculturation» (the meanings of which will be explored below) is somewhat unclear and it is not certain whether he was using the terms interchangeably or simply alluding to the intrinsic relationship between them[50]. This passage is significant, however, in that it began the articulation of John Paul II's teaching on the relation between faith and culture, which is best expressed by the concept of inculturation.

In a striking illustration of his deep concern for the problem of faith and culture, John Paul II established in 1982 the Pontifical Council for Culture[51]. Consisting of an international membership of laity, priests, bishops, and religious, the Council was established to give witness to the Church's concern for the progress of culture and to further the dialogue between the Church and cultures[52]. In his letter to Cardinal Casaroli establishing the Council, the Pope affirmed the intrinsic, reciprocal link between faith and culture: «the synthesis between culture and faith is not just a demand of culture, but also of faith. A faith which does not become culture is a faith which has not been fully received, not thoroughly thought through, not fully lived out»[53]. This statement has been described as «characteristic of John Paul II's social and historical realism» because in it he expresses the relationship between faith and culture more clearly than his predecessors[54].

The Pope singled out Saints Cyril and Methodius as missionaries who formed and shaped Slavic culture in the process of their evangelizing

---

ment to the Biblical Commission was the first time a papal document used the word «inculturation». Cf. A. SHORTER, *Toward a Theology of Inculturation*, 223.

[50] Cf. A. SHORTER, *Toward a Theology of Inculturation*, 223.

[51] Cf. «Letter to Cardinal Casaroli for the Foundation of the Pontifical Council for Culture», *AAS* 74 (1982) 683-688.

[52] Cf. P. SCHINELLER, *A Handbook on Inculturation*, 43-44.

[53] JOHN PAUL II, «John Paul II Institutes Council for Culture».

[54] Cf. A. SHORTER, *Toward a Theology of Inculturation*, 231.

activities in his fourth encyclical, *Slavorum Apostoli*[55]. Because of their profound impact on both the development of the faith and the shaping of Slavic culture they are proposed as models of inculturation:

> The work of evangelization which they carried out [...] contains both a model of what today is called "inculturation" — the incarnation of the Gospel in native cultures — and also the introduction of these cultures into the life of the Church. By incarnating the Gospel in the native culture of the peoples which they were evangelizing, Saints Cyril and Methodius were especially meritorious for the formation and development of that same culture, or rather of many cultures (*SA* 21).

Later in the same encyclical he spoke of the urgency for the Church today to evangelize by inculturating the faith, proposing the two saints as models of this process because they «[...] not only carried out their mission with full respect for the culture already existing among the Slav peoples, but together with religion they eminently and unceasingly promoted and extended that culture» (*SA* 26)[56].

In Chapter Five of his encyclical, *Redemptoris Missio*[57], John Paul II featured inculturation as one of the Church's «paths of mission». Quoting the «Final Report» of the Extraordinary Synod of 1985[58], he made a clear distinction between inculturation and adaptation:

> The process of the Church's insertion into peoples' cultures is a lengthy one. It is not a matter of purely external adaptation, for inculturation "means the intimate transformation of authentic cultural values through their integration into Christianity and the insertion of Christianity in the various human cultures". The process is thus a profound and all-embracing one, which involves the Christian message and also the Church's reflection and practice (*RM* 52).

The Pope emphasized the reciprocal relationship between faith and culture, because through the process of inculturation the «[...] Church transmits to them [cultures] her own values», while renewing from within «the good elements» that already exist in them. (*RM* 52).

Pope John Paul II's 1991 encyclical, *Centesimus Annus*[59], without using the term «inculturation», affirmed the role of evangelization in the

---

[55] *SA, AAS* 77 (1985) 779-813.

[56] Shorter asserts that *SA* exemplifies John Paul II's conception of culture: «The most exalted form of culture is that which is permeated and developed by the Gospel», A. SHORTER, *Toward a Theology of Inculturation*, 232-233.

[57] *RM, AAS* 83 (1991) 249-340.

[58] Cf. SYNOD OF BISHOPS, «Final Report», 450.

[59] *CA, AAS* 83 (1991) 793-867.

development of cultures as that of «[...] sustaining culture in its progress towards the truth, and assisting in the work of its purification and enrichment» (*CA* 50). The Church best engages in this kind of evangelizing activity by engaging the whole person on the level of his or her «creativity, intelligence, and knowledge». Because «[...] the first and most important task is accomplished within man's heart», and because «[...] the way in which he is involved in building his own future depends on the understanding he has of himself and his own destiny», «[...] it is on this level that *the Church's specific and decisive contribution to culture* is to be found» (*CA* 51) [emphasis in original][60]. Evangelization and inculturation, then, are not simply systemic operations involving impersonal institutions, but rather processes in which the Gospel, Church teaching, and human beings interact on the level of the heart and have an impact upon the larger systems of Church and culture.

1.5 *The International Theological Commission*

Review of the Church's concern about faith and culture would not be complete without reference to the International Theological Commission's 1988 document, «Faith and Inculturation»[61]. Rooted in a Christian anthropology characterized by the interrelationship of nature, culture, and grace[62], the Commission offers a definition of inculturation:

> The process of inculturation may be defined as the Church's efforts to make the message of Christ penetrate a given socio-cultural milieu, calling on the latter to grow according to all its particular values as long as these values are compatible with the Gospel[63].

Citing a previous encyclical that described inculturation as «[...] the incarnation of the Gospel in native cultures and also the introduction

---

[60] In describing Pope John Paul II's understanding of the evangelization of cultures, the International Theological Commission explains it is grounded in «[...] an anthropological conception firmly rooted in Christian thought since the Fathers of the Church. Since culture, when pure, reveals and strengthens the nature of man, the Christian impregnation presupposes the surpassing of all historicism and relativism in the conception of what is human. The evangelization of cultures should therefore be inspired by the love of man in himself and for himself, especially in those aspects of his being and of his culture which are being attacked or are under threat», ITC, «Faith and Inculturation», 801.

[61] Cf. ITC, «Faith and Inculturation», 800-807.

[62] For a description of this anthropological foundation see ITC, «Faith and Inculturation», 801-802.

[63] ITC, «Faith and Inculturation», 802.

of these cultures into the life of the Church»[64], the Commission's document emphasized the mutual process of growth and enrichment for both the Church and for the culture involved in the process.

Having described the foundations and the process of inculturation, the document then examined the process of inculturation at work in the history of salvation: «[...] in ancient Israel, in the life and work of Jesus and in the early Church»[65]. It then explored present day problems associated with the inculturation process, particularly from the perspective of faith's encounter with popular piety, non-Christian religions, cultural traditions in young Churches, and modernity in its many aspects. Quoting John Paul II, the document concluded by stressing the necessity for the Church, which must «[...] "make itself all things for all men, bringing today's cultures together with sympathy"», to continue in the long and arduous process of inculturation in order that the Gospel may penetrate and transform all cultures[66].

This brief survey of conciliar and postconciliar concern for the problem of faith and culture reveals an evolution, both in thought and in praxis. From the Second Vatican Council, marked by its emphasis on the Church's mission to the world and the centrality of culture in human affairs, to Paul VI's affirmation «[...] that culture must be the chief concern of the Church's missionary activity»[67] (cf. *EN* 20), to John Paul II's emphasis on the necessity of inculturation as an integral part of the Church's evangelization, the Church has committed itself to engagement and dialogue with the world's cultures, convinced that «[...] a faith which does not become culture is a faith not fully received, not thoroughly thought through, not fully lived out»[68]. In this context, inculturation and its theological underpinnings, can be examined.

2. Inculturation: Its Development and Theological Foundations

In an important article Rosette Crollius described inculturation as a concept «[...] situated in the borderlands between anthropological sciences and theology», thus, «[...] heavy with implications from both

---

[64] ITC, «Faith and Inculturation», quoting *SA*, 21.

[65] ITC, «Faith and Inculturation», 801.

[66] Cf. ITC, «Faith and Inculturation», 807; JOHN PAUL II, «Discourse to the Pontifical Council for Culture», *AAS* 75 (1983) 383-389.

[67] L. RICHARD, «Inculturation», 482.

[68] JOHN PAUL II, «John Paul II Institutes Council for Culture», 7.

these areas of knowledge»[69]. Because it is a new word in the Church's theology[70], there is need to give further precision to the evolution of the concept, its present meaning, and its implications for the Church. Before considering the theological foundations of inculturation, therefore, the influence of cultural anthropology will be considered, with particular reference to three key terms: *culture, enculturation,* and *acculturation.*

2.1 *Culture*

As noted, the very concept of culture is problematic[71] because there is little consensus on its meaning[72]. It has already been shown that the Church's understanding of culture has evolved from a classical notion to one that is more influenced by the field of cultural anthropology, as in *Gaudium et Spes* 53, which combines a traditional concept of culture, classically understood, with a more modern view emphasizing «[...] the anthropological life experience and the typical mentality of each human group»[73]. Anthropological understanding is in need of further clarification[74], as indicated by the following varied descriptions of culture:

---

[69] A. A. ROEST CROLLIUS, «What Is So New about Inculturation?», 1-2.

[70] As noted above, Pope John Paul II referred to inculturation as a neologism in his Apostolic Exhortation, *CT* 53. There is, however, some disagreement as to when the word was first used as a theological concept. Carrier notes that, although the word «inculturation» is recent in official Church documents, it «[...] has been in use for over fifty years among Catholics», H. CARRIER, *Evangelizing the Culture of Modernity*, 64. Roest Crollius, however, credits P. B. Segura with the first use of the term in a theological sense. Segura viewed it as a work of discernment and adaptation with a view to freeing cultural values which might be used in the work of evangelization. Cf. P. B. SEGURA, «L'initiation, valeur permanente en vue de l'inculturation», 219, cited in A. A. ROEST CROLLIUS, *Teologia dell'inculturazione*, 31. Shorter cites Fr. Joseph Masson's use of the concept in a 1962 article in which he referred to the «[...] urgent need for a Catholicism that is inculturated in a variety of forms (d'une façon polymorphe)», A. SHORTER, *Toward a Theology of Inculturation*, 10. Cf. J. MASSON, «L'Église ouverte sur le monde», 1032-1043. Shorter also cites an article by Charles Chossonnery which «[...] quotes Meinrad Hebga's assertion that the term was invented by the anthropologist Melville Herskovits in the 1970's», A. SHORTER *Evangelization and Culture*, 51, n. 18. Cf. C. CHOSSONNERY, «Toute Église est en inculturation permanente», 134.

[71] Cf. P. SCHINELLER, *A Handbook on Inculturation*, 22.

[72] Cf. A. A. ROEST CROLLIUS, «Inculturation and the Meaning of Culture», 33. Thomas Clarke observes that «[...] culture is a term with a thousand definitions and no definition», T. CLARKE, «To Make Peace, Evangelize Cultures», 414.

[73] H. CARRIER, *Evangelizing the Culture of Modernity*, 17.

[74] Roest Crollius maintains that because the discourse on the topic of inculturation is of a theological nature, the understanding of culture «[...] should be such as to possess a

that complex whole which includes knowledge, belief, art, morals, law, custom and any other capabilities and habits acquired by man as a member of society[75]; [...] a system of inherited conceptions expressed in symbolic forms by means of which human beings communicate, perpetuate and develop their knowledge about, and their attitudes towards, life[76]; [...] a dynamic system of socially acquired and socially shared ideas according to which an interacting group of human beings is to adapt itself to its physical, social, and ideational environment[77]; [...] a way of life for a given time and place, replete with values symbols and meanings, reaching out with hopes and dreams, often struggling for a better world[78]; [...] a transmitted pattern of meanings embodied in symbols, a pattern capable of development and change [... which ...] belongs to the concept of humanness itself[79].

What is clear from the above sampling of descriptions is that the concept of culture includes both behavioral and cognitional aspects. Operating out of preconceived mental patterns, people interact with each other and then reflect on the interactions. Culture is thus about both behavior and ideas[80]. It is at once the context and the product of human creative activity, distinguishing groups from each other and establishing how they conceive and interpret the fundamental aspects of their lives[81]. The «[...] deepest code to reveal a human, social group and to make it understandable»[82], culture is a process continually taking shape and moving into the future, (while remaining rooted in the past), influencing and

---

basic openness for a fulfillment in theological anthropology», A. A. ROEST CROLLIUS, «Inculturation and the Meaning of Culture», 38.

[75] E. B. TYLOR, *Primitive Culture*, vol. 1, 1, quoted in A. SHORTER, *Toward a Theology of Inculturation*, 4.

[76] C. GEERTZ, *The Interpretation of Cultures*, 89.

[77] L. J. LUZBETAK, *The Church and Cultures*, 74. Luzbetak identifies three levels of culture: the surface level, or symbols as such; the middle level, or the meanings of the symbols; the deepest level, or the basic assumptions, values, psychology. It is on the second and third levels, or on culture as a dynamic, systemic whole that inculturation is focused. Cf. ID., *The Church and Cultures*, 74-78.

[78] R. R. SCHREITER, *Constructing Local Theologies*, 21.

[79] A. SHORTER, *Toward a Theology of Inculturation*, 5.

[80] Cf. A. SHORTER, *Toward a Theology of Inculturation*, 4. For a description of the cognitional aspect of culture which refers to «[...] *what* in fact people of different cultures do think, the received wisdom of a community going about its daily routines, the shared understanding and values without which communal living would be impossible», see G. A. DENAPOLI, «Inculturation as Communication», 72-73.

[81] Cf. L. RICHARD, «Mission and Inculturation», 94.

[82] M. DE CARVALHO AZEVEDO, «Inculturation and the Challenges of Modernity», 10.

shaping the people who belong to it[83]. Because of «[...] the power and energy that reside there»[84], culture and cultures are therefore crucial to the Church's mission of evangelization, and thus an integral component of the process of inculturation.

2.2 *Enculturation*

A sociological concept used analogously to describe the theological notion of inculturation[85], enculturation is a technical term denoting «[...] the process by which an individual becomes inserted into his culture»[86]. Another way to describe enculturation is the socialization process of an individual[87], whereby one «[...] achieves competence in his own culture»[88]. An important aspect of enculturation is that it is an ongoing process that continues throughout a person's life[89]. Although it includes formal aspects of learning, it is largely an informal, even unconscious experience by which a person learns the images and symbols of a culture[90]. The enculturation process can be said to have two stages which correspond with and contribute to cultural stability and cultural change. The first stage is a «conditioning process» by which the person learns the various signs and norms of a group by conforming «to the norms of the social group» and by becoming «assimilated to the culture of his surroundings»[91]. This initial stage or conditioning process transmits the given culture and contributes to the stability of a given social group. When the individual has been shaped by the culture and learns how to function in it, he or she has greater freedom when faced with new forms of culture. Such maturity is essential for the second stage, that of cultural change[92]. The enculturation process thus entails both stability and change: when individuals are rooted in a given culture, it is then that they have the potential to introduce development and change. Such a process is ongoing and lifelong. It will be demonstrated

---

83 Cf. L. RICHARD, «Mission and Inculturation», 94.

84 T. CLARKE, «To Make Peace, Evangelize Culture», 414.

85 Cf. A. SHORTER, *Toward a Theology of Inculturation*, 5.

86 A. A. ROEST CROLLIUS, «What Is So New about Inculturation?», 5.

87 Cf. P. SCHINELLER, *A Handbook on Inculturation*, 22.

88 M. J. HERSKOVITS, *Man and His Works*, 39, as quoted in A. A. ROEST CROLLIUS, «What Is So New about Inculturation?», 8.

89 Cf. A. A. ROEST CROLLIUS, «What Is So New about Inculturation?», 10.

90 Cf. A. SHORTER, *Toward a Theology of Inculturation*, 5.

91 A. A. ROEST CROLLIUS, «What Is So New about Inculturation?», 11.

92 Cf. A. A. ROEST CROLLIUS, «What Is So New about Inculturation?», 12.

below how this cultural-anthropological operation can be understood to analogously describe the theological process of inculturation.

2.3 *Acculturation*

Acculturation is also a term borrowed from cultural anthropology, denoting the interaction between two cultures and the changes[93] that result. Because it has been so closely associated with the theological concept of inculturation, it is sometimes used interchangeably with it[94]. In order to avoid confusion, however, acculturation is best considered in its distinct anthropological sense, even though it is a necessary condition of inculturation. From what was said earlier about culture including behavioral and cognitive aspects, it follows that in the process of acculturation changes will occur on the level of behaviors and ideas. Acculturation, the encounter between cultures, is thus a dynamic process whose «[...] consequences can be discerned *post factum* at the conscious level», while the process itself may at times be unprogrammed and unreflective[95]. Understood as the mutually respectful and tolerant interaction between cultures, acculturation is a necessary operation in the life of the Church if it is to retain its catholicity. The faith that the Church holds and seeks to spread must be able to transcend cultures; it must be passed from culture to culture down through history. In order for this to happen, the Church must be open to the process of acculturation, the encounter with other cultures[96].

2.4 *Inculturation: Anthropological Underpinnings*

Having briefly considered the cultural-anthropological concepts of culture, enculturation and acculturation, the theological concept of inculturation can now be introduced and explicated. It has already been noted

---

[93] Cf. A. A. ROEST CROLLIUS, «What Is So New about Inculturation?», 4.

[94] See, for example, JOHN PAUL II, *CT* 53: «The term *acculturation* or *inculturation* may be a neologism [...]».

[95] A. SHORTER, *Toward a Theology of Inculturation*, 7.

[96] Cf. A. SHORTER, *Toward a Theology of Inculturation*, 8. It is to be noted, however, that the Church is not simply another culture, but has its own special characteristics, mission, and nature. It is not enough, therefore, to say that the Church engages in a simple process of acculturation; evangelization requires not only contact with another culture, but insertion into that culture. Cultural anthropological operations, although helpful, are not adequate to express this process. The theological concept of inculturation, which includes elements of acculturation, is the more adequate concept to describe it. Cf. P. SCHINELLER, *A Handbook on Inculturation*, 22.

that the word «inculturation» began appearing in papal documents, most notably with *Catechesi Tradendae* in 1979, and has since become a «common-place in contemporary theology»[97]. Roest Crollius observes that the choice of the term «inculturation» is an obvious one because it is a «[...] contraction of the expression, "insertion in a culture"»[98]. The simplicity of the word, however, masks the complexity and richness of the process, which entails no less than the Church sinking its roots in a culture, permeating it with the Gospel, and in the process taking on aspects of the culture[99].

Shorter observes that the popularization of the term «inculturation» is largely due to the influence of members of the Society of Jesus[100]; in fact the following description of inculturation given by the late Pedro Arrupe, S.J., the Father General of the Society of Jesus, is considered classic[101]:

---

[97] A. SHORTER, *Evangelization and Culture*, 32. In the evolution of the Church's understanding of evangelization, less adequate words have been used to describe the process: «imposition», the forcing of alien religious customs on a culture; «translation», a necessary starting point but inadequate as an entire process because it remains superficial; «adaptation», an accepted form of evangelical method for many years but now seen as too extrinsic and superficial. Similarly, «indigenization» and «incarnation» have been rejected as terms to describe the dynamic at work between faith and culture because their respective meanings are too restrictive. «Contextualization» is particularly popular in Protestant circles and is also used by some Catholic scholars. Its benefit is that it emphasizes greater awareness of the particularity of contexts, but it is criticized as lacking constancy and not adding clarity to the discourse on the relation between faith and culture. For a description of the less than adequate concepts for describing the processes of evangelization, see P. SCHINELLER, *A Handbook on Inculturation*, 14-21; A. A. ROEST CROLLIUS, «What Is So New about Inculturation?», 3-4. For a description of contextualization, see M. L. STACKHOUSE, «Contextualization, Contextuality, and Contextualism», 3-13. Luzbetak describes three major models of mission: ethnocentric, accomodational, and contextual. Opting for the contextual model, he equates it with inculturation, seeing it as the process «[...] by which a local Church integrates the Gospel message (the "text") with its local culture (the "context")», L. J. LUZBETAK, *The Church and Cultures*, 69.

[98] A. A. ROEST CROLLIUS, «What Is So New about Inculturation?», 4. He also notes that «[...] the adoption of the form "inculturation" at the time of the 32nd General Congregation of the Society of Jesus, may be explained by the fact that this international gathering used Latin as a common language for papers and in discussions. In Latin, however ill-treated by some of those who manipulate it in the 20th century, only the form *inculturation* is possible. Thus it was the form with "in-" that stuck», A. A ROEST CROLLIUS, «What Is So New about Inculturation?», 5-6, n. 14. Cf. G. A. DeNAPOLI, «Inculturation as Communication», 71-72, n. 1.

[99] Cf. *EN*, 20.

[100] Cf. A. SHORTER, *Toward a Theology of Inculturation*, 10.

[101] Cf. M. AMALADOSS, «Inculturation and Ignatian Spirituality», 39.

Inculturation can be looked at from many viewpoints and seen at different levels, which must be distinguished but cannot be separated. Yet, amid the multiple formulations of the problem which we have to reckon with, the fundamental and constantly valid principle is that *inculturation is the incarnation of Christian life and of the Christian message in a particular cultural context, in such a way that this experience not only finds expression through elements proper to the culture in question (this alone would be no more than a superficial adaptation), but becomes a principle that animates, directs and unifies the culture, transforming and remaking it so as to bring about "a new creation"*[102] [emphasis added].

Amaladoss notes that Arrupe's description evokes three paradigms: incarnation, paschal mystery (transforming), and Pentecost (remaking); it also articulates three interrelated activities: «[...] building up the local church as a particular cultural manifestation of the Word», calling the culture to conversion in the light of the Gospel, and the associated effort to bring about a new creation, an alternative culture[103].

In order to clarify inculturation as an operation or process of evangelization, the analogous use of the anthropological concepts of enculturation and acculturation, described above, can be illuminating[104]. As an individual is inserted or socialized into a given culture (anthropological process of enculturation), so is the Church inserted into a given culture (theological process of inculturation). Similarly, because the Church exists in cultural form, it enters the process of inculturation already imbued with elements and characteristics of another culture. From an anthropological point of view, therefore, the process of

---

102 P. ARRUPE, «Father General's Letter on Inculturation to the Whole Society», 181-182.

103 Cf. M. AMALADOSS, «Inculturation and Ignatian Spirituality», 39-40. Both Amaladoss and Shorter have reported that, at a 1993 meeting of the Bishops' chairmen of the Theological Commission of Asian Bishops Conferences in Hong Kong, Cardinal Ratzinger urged that the term «interculturation» should replace «inculturation». «Interculturation» suggests an encounter between cultures, one embodying the Gospel and the other the recipient. Shorter observes: «The cardinal pointed out quite correctly that missionary evangelization takes place through a meeting of cultures, but he ruled out the possibility of one culture dominating the other. He went on to imply that the Christian faith is communicated through Western culture and to say that this culture is "fused" with the evangelized culture. [...] His approach is close to that of Pius XII and the pre-conciliar Church, which favored the idea of a monolithic hybrid Christian culture, in which the cultural matrix was Western», A. SHORTER, *Evangelization and Culture*, 90. Cf. M. AMALADOSS, «Inculturation and Ignatian Spirituality», 39.

104 Roest Crollius asserts that the principle of analogy allows an understanding of the «[...] transposition from the anthropological "enculturation" to the missiological "inculturation"», A. A. ROEST CROLLIUS, «What Is So New about Inculturation?», 7.

inculturation has some of the characteristics associated with the process of acculturation, the encounter of two cultures[105].

Continuing with the analogy of enculturation, a number of important observations can be made about the process of inculturation. First, just as the process of enculturation entails the growth of a person into his own culture, so inculturation «[...] refers primarily to the dynamic relation between the local Church and "its own culture", i.e. the culture of its own people»[106]. This is not to be understood, however, in an exclusive sense, because the goal of the local Church is not only to establish communion among the people in which it is incarnated, but also to enrich the entire Church[107]. Second, just as the process of enculturation described above continues throughout the life of a person, so the process of inculturation continues throughout the life of the local Church. Because a culture is an exceedingly complex, living reality in a continuous process of growth and change, the Church is always faced with new challenges and opportunities to insert itself more deeply into a given culture in the light of that culture's evolution[108]. Such an understanding of inculturation as an ongoing process has significant ramifications for local Churches which have been long-established; it emphasizes that inculturation is not a once-and-for-all event but an ongoing challenge and demand in the life of every local Church. Third, and related to the preceding point, just as the enculturation process of an individual

---

105 Cf. A. A. ROEST CROLLIUS, «What Is So New about Inculturation?», 7. Shorter observes that although «[...] the Christian faith cannot exist except in a cultural form», and that «[...] when we speak of Christian faith or Christian life, we are necessarily speaking of a cultural phenomenon», nonetheless, the process of inculturation «[...] transcends mere acculturation». Inculturation implies a «[...] dialogue between a culture and the faith in a cultural form», but this transcends and exceeds acculturation, because in the inculturation process the «[...] culture is enlivened by the Gospel from within», A. SHORTER, *Toward a Theology of Inculturation*, 12.

106 A. A. ROEST CROLLIUS, «What Is so New about Inculturation?», 9. Cf. *EN* 63: «The individual Churches [...] have the task of assimilating the Gospel message and of transposing it, without the slightest betrayal of its essential truth, into the language that these particular people understand, then of proclaiming it in this language». As noted above, Paul VI used the word «language» in a cultural and anthropological sense.

107 Cf. *LG* 23: «In and from such individual Churches there comes into being the one and only Catholic Church». Luzbetak observes that «as in apostolic times, so today, the local Church, although the primary agent of inculturation responsible for initiative and action, must nevertheless always be in communication with the universal Church and must ultimately submit itself to the judgment of the communion of Churches». L. J. LUZBETAK, *The Church and Cultures*, 72.

108 Cf. A. A. ROEST CROLLIUS, «What Is So New about Inculturation?», 10.

includes two stages related to cultural stability and change, so there are two aspects of the inculturation process that must be considered. The first stage is «[...] akin to the conditioning process of enculturation», in that the Church must «[...] assimilate the language and symbols of the local culture and [...] learn how to function according to the basic cultural patterns of the surrounding society»[109]. Analogously, in the second stage the Church, having learned the «language» of the local culture, can more freely begin to deliberately influence the culture, attempting to reorient it along the lines of the Gospel message[110].

Having considered inculturation in the light of the anthropological processes of enculturation and acculturation, it is possible to identify three distinct, yet interrelated and concomitant stages: translation, assimilation, and transformation[111]. The first stage, translation, corresponds with the acculturation process in which the agents of evangelization interact with the local culture, leading to various changes and developments; both the evangelizers and the evangelized begin the process of assimilating each other's cultures. The second stage, that of assimilation, is when real inculturation begins, because it is the stage in which the local Church begins to sink its roots in the surrounding culture, achieving a certain level of comfort and «at-homeness» in the culture[112]. The third stage, that of transformation, refers to the active role that the Church, having become assimilated, can take in transforming the local culture[113].

As the three stages imply, «[...] a true process of inculturation demands an ongoing and living exchange between the Church, which is also a specific culture, and other cultures»[114]. This process is reciprocal and critical[115]. It is reciprocal in that it is a mutual dialogue between the Church and culture; such dialogue is necessary if it is to be authentic inculturation[116]. In other words, as the Council emphasized, the Church

---

[109] A. A. ROEST CROLLIUS, «What Is So New about Inculturation?», 13.

[110] Cf. A. A. ROEST CROLLIUS, «What Is So New about Inculturation?», 13.

[111] Cf. A. A. ROEST CROLLIUS, «What Is So New about Inculturation?», 14.

[112] Citing *AG* 19, Roest Crollius observes, «One of the characteristics of the local Church [...] is precisely that it is "already rooted in social life and considerably adapted to the local culture"», A. A. ROEST CROLLIUS, «What Is So New about Inculturation?», 8.

[113] Cf. A. A. ROEST CROLLIUS, «What Is So New about Inculturation?», 14.

[114] L. RICHARD, «Inculturation», 483.

[115] Cf. A. SHORTER, *Toward a Theology of Inculturation*, 13.

[116] Cf. L. RICHARD, «Mission and Inculturation», 110. Richard describes dialogue as «[...] concern, respect, and hospitality toward the other; acceptance of the other's identity, modes of expression, and values. True dialogue does not invade; it does not

must approach the various cultures, «[...] gladly and reverently laying bare the seeds of the Word which lie hidden in them» (AG 11). In such a dialogical stance not only is the culture changed by its encounter with the Gospel, the Church itself is open to transformation by the «seeds of the Word» it encounters in the local culture. In addition to being reciprocal, the process is critical in the sense that the Church does not blindly assume the characteristics of the local culture but rather calls «[...] on the latter to grow according to all its particular values as long as these values are compatible with the Gospel»[117]. There is a certain discernment and discrimination in the process of dialogue[118]. Through the reciprocal and critical interaction of the Church and culture, then, culture is transformed by its encounter with the Gospel, and the Church itself is enriched and transformed by its encounter with the given culture[119]. Having considered an initial description of inculturation, its anthropological background, and some of its operational dynamics, a more complete definition of inculturation can now be offered:

> [Inculturation] is the integration of the Christian experience of a local Church into the culture of its people, in such a way that this experience not only expresses itself in elements of this culture, but becomes a force that animates, orients and innovates this culture so as to create a new unity and communion, not only within the culture in question but also as an enrichment of the Church universal[120].

Incorporating the same elements as this definition, Shorter defines inculturation more tersely as «[...] the presentation and re-expression of the Gospel in forms and terms proper to a culture, processes which result in the reinterpretation of both, without being unfaithful to either»[121].

---

manipulate, for there can be no such thing as dialogical manipulation», L. RICHARD, «Inculturation», 483. Cf. AG 12 and EN 63.

[117] ITC, «Faith and Inculturation», 802.

[118] Carrier emphasizes the importance of discerning the local culture's ethos and its cultural patterns: «[...] evangelizing means detecting, criticizing, and even denouncing the aspects of a culture that contradict the Gospel message and represent an attack on the dignity of the human being. For their part, Christians are convinced that their faith can have a real impact on every sector of individual and collective life. [...] faith can really change the mind, conscience, and heart of human beings, bringing about new ways of thinking, feeling, and behaving in persons and in the whole society. New cultural patterns are thus inspired by Christian faith, and the Gospel becomes a ferment, changing mentalities and lifestyles», H. CARRIER, Evangelizing the Culture of Modernity, 70-71. Cf. CT 53.

[119] Cf. A. SHORTER, Toward a Theology of Inculturation, 13.

[120] A. A. ROEST CROLLIUS, «What Is So New about Inculturation?», 15-16.

[121] A. SHORTER, Evangelization and Culture, 32.

Although both examples are of rather balanced descriptions, there is a
tendency in defining inculturation to emphasize one or the other term of
the equation: either to emphasize the Gospel at the expense of culture or
to emphasize culture at the expense of the Gospel[122]. This points to the
risk involved in the inculturation process: if inculturation is not taken
seriously and if the Church does not engage the culture in dialogue, then
it will be addressing irrelevant issues from the past. Or if the Church
uncritically enters into dialogue, accepting even those cultural elements
which are incompatible with the Gospel, there is the danger of collapsing
the faith into exclusively cultural categories[123]. The challenge, then, is to
address and transform the present, concrete culture without compromis-
ing the truth and newness of the faith.

2.5 *Inculturation: Theological Underpinnings*

Having now considered the anthropological aspects of the inculturation
dynamic, its theological underpinnings will be examined. D.S. Amalorpavadass has identified four essential theological components that are
foundational in the process of inculturation: 1) creation and history;
2) Incarnation and Paschal Mystery; 3) the Church's universal mission;
4) authentic Tradition and the ordinary magisterium[124].

2.5.1 Creation and History

As already noted, the Council's «Decree on the Church's Missionary
Activity», *Ad Gentes*, stressed that Christians should be «[...] familiar
with their national and religious traditions, gladly and reverently laying
bare the seeds of the Word which lie hidden in them» (*AG* 11). This
emphasis on the hidden «seeds of the Word», or *semina Verbi*, introduced an important concept originally articulated by St. Justin Martyr
(d. 165 CE.)[125]. For St. Justin, the «Spermatic Logos», or seed-bearing
Word, was the cosmic principle of rationality, God's agent in creation,
implanted in the heart of every human culture[126], thus enabling the

---

[122] Cf. A. SHORTER, *Evangelization and Culture*, 32.

[123] Cf. D. LANE, «The Challenge of Inculturation», 9.

[124] Cf. D. S. AMALORPAVADASS, «Réflexions théologiques sur l'inculturation»,
61: «Quatre points de départ peuvent ici être envisagés: 1. Une vue chrétienne de la
création et de l'histoire; 2. l'Incarnation rédemptrice et le mystère pascal; 3. la mission
universelle de l'Église; 4. la Tradition authentique et le magistère ordinaire».

[125] Cf. A. SHORTER, *Toward a Theology of Inculturation*, 75.

[126] Cf. A. SHORTER, *Evangelization and Culture*, 34.

people of every culture to have «a dim glimpse of the truth»[127]. Before taking on flesh in the Incarnation, the Logos, in the form of *semina Verbi,* was already implanted in creation, although not yet fully known[128]. St. Justin's conception of the Logos offers a hopeful image for the relationship between the Church and cultures, between Christianity and non-Christianity, because it holds out the possibility that, through their dynamic interaction in the proclamation of the Gospel, the seeds of the Word, already present in the culture, will grow to fruition. Seen in this light, the proclamation of the Gospel, leading to the conversion of a culture, is simply another stage, albeit crucial and necessary, in the unfolding of God's espousal of that particular culture[129].

The International Theological Commission took up this theme in its document on inculturation when it affirmed the Church's wish to «[...] animate from the inside [...] these resources of truth and love which God has placed, as *semina Verbi,* into his creation. The Word of God does not come into a creation which is foreign to it»[130]. Such an affirmation means that for cultures to become Christian they do not have to renounce their own heritage (except for those values and meanings which are inimical to or irreconcilable with the Gospel) and take on foreign cultural patterns. Rather, the task of the local Church, under the guidance of the Gospel and Christian Tradition, is to uncover and

---

[127] SAINT JUSTIN MARTYR, «The Second Apology», 134: «Indeed, all writers, by means of the engrafted seed of the Word which was implanted in them, had a dim glimpse of the truth. For the seed of something and its imitation, given in proportion to one's capacity, is one thing, but the thing itself, which is shared and imitated according to His grace, is quite another».

[128] Cf. A. SHORTER, *Toward a Theology of Inculturation,* 75-79; ID., *Evangelization and Culture,* 34-36.

[129] Cf. E.-J. PÉNOUKOU, *Églises d'Afrique: propositions pour l'avenir,* as cited in A. SHORTER, *Evangelization and Culture,* 53, n. 42. Commenting on Pénoukou's theology of inculturation, Shorter stresses that Pénoukou «[...] gives full weight to the conversion that must follow upon the proclamation of the Gospel. Human cultural traditions must be converted to Christ. They are not absolute, but God-in-Christ is. The reason that cultural facts must be interrogated in the light of God's call of love and of Christ's cross is precisely because the implicit dialogue of Logos and culture is continued explicitly after the Incarnation. It is one and the same process, intensified by the Christ-event, the Word becoming flesh. The Logos was always challenging human cultural traditions. After the Incarnation the challenge became a definitive and crucial challenge. [...] The Christ-event issues a clarion-call to culture to be true to itself and to evolve creatively towards the *pleroma*», A. SHORTER, *Toward a Theology of Inculturation,* 79.

[130] ITC, «Faith and Inculturation», 804.

articulate the theological orientation and ultimate meaning of its own culture[131], allowing the *semina Verbi* already present to blossom[132].

The importance of the theological principle of *semina Verbi* for inculturation can be readily seen. First of all, it affirms that the process does not unfold in a godless context, but rather on «[...] holy ground, insofar as God is already in contact with a given context even if in imperfect and hidden ways»[133]. Secondly, it affirms that creation and history are the *loci* of revelation. Since God's self-communication takes place within the context of concrete cultures, the particular context or culture must be taken seriously as a vehicle of revelation. This means that other religions and other parts of the temporal order are implanted with seeds of the Word and that the task of inculturation is not simply to impose an extrinsic message, but in announcing the Gospel, to identify and release the seeds of the Word already within the culture, and to call to conversion those elements that are not compatible with the Gospel[134].

2.5.2 Incarnation and Paschal Mystery

In seeking both to understand and articulate the Church's relationship to culture, particularly its insertion into particular cultures, the Council opted to use the analogy of the Incarnation of Jesus Christ:

> In order to be able to offer all of them the mystery of salvation and the life brought by God, the Church must become part of all these groups for the

---

[131] Cf. M. DE CARVALHO AZEVEDO, «Inculturation and the Challenges of Modernity», 27.

[132] In a recent document on biblical interpretation, the Pontifical Biblical Commission devoted a section to inculturation. In this section it affirms, «Every authentic culture is, in fact, in its own way the bearer of universal values established by God. The theological foundation of inculturation is the conviction of faith that the Word of God transcends the cultures in which it has found expression and has the capability of being spread in other cultures, in such a way as to be able to reach all human beings in the cultural context in which they live», PBC, *The Interpretation of the Bible in the Church*, 117.

[133] P. SCHINELLER, *A Handbook on Inculturation*, 46.

[134] Amalorpavadass observes, «Ce que le Christ a d'unique parmi d'autres est son caractère universel. S'il en est ainsi, sa révélation et sa présence salvifique peuvent être reconnues dans les diverses religions. [...] Aussi la culture est-elle, avec tous ses éléments, le résultat de l'action de Dieu dans un peuple au cours d'histoire. Alors que Dieu s'est, dans le Christ, engagé envers l'humanité de manière totale, inconditionnelle, définitive et irrévocable, en une période particulière de l'histoire et en un lieu et une culture données, néanmoins la présence historique du Verbe créateur et sa présence incarnationnelle s'étendent à toutes les nations. L'histoire de l'événement christique doit être en interaction avec la signification de l'histoire des peuples et des nations [...]», D. S. AMALORPAVADASS, «Réflexions théologiques sur l'inculturation», 63-64.

same motive which led Christ to bind Himself, in virtue of His Incarnation, to the definite social and cultural conditions of those human beings among whom he dwelt (*AG* 10). [...] in imitation of the plan of the Incarnation, the young Churches, rooted in Christ and built up on the foundation of the apostles, take to themselves in a wonderful exchange all the riches of the nations which were given to Christ as an inheritance (*AG* 22). There are many links between the message of salvation and human culture. For God, revealing Himself to His people to the extent of a full manifestation of Himself in His Incarnate Son, has spoken according to the culture proper to different ages. Living in various circumstances during the course of time, the Church, too, has used in her preaching the discoveries of different cultures to spread and explain the message of Christ to all nations, to probe it and more deeply understand it, and to give it better expression in liturgical celebrations and in the life of the diversified community of the faithful (*GS* 58).

Following the lead of the Council, Fr. Arrupe affirmed the Incarnation as the paradigm for inculturation[135]: «The Incarnation of the Son is the primary motivation and perfect pattern for inculturation»[136]. Similarly, Pope John Paul II referred to inculturation as «[...] the incarnation of the Gospel in native cultures — and also the introduction of these cultures into the life of the Church»[137]. The International Theological Commission explained, «[...] since it was fully and historically realized, the Incarnation of the Son of God was a cultural incarnation»[138], implying that the interaction of the Church with the world must reflect the culturally specific dynamic of the Incarnation.

The Church's embrace of the Incarnation as the basic paradigm for the process of inculturation has many positive aspects to recommend it but also some potential limitations if understood too narrowly. Among its more positive aspects are the following: 1) The paradigm of the Incarnation affirms that the subject matter of inculturation is Jesus Christ himself[139]. In Jesus of Nazareth can be seen «[...] the appearance of the universal within the particular, the entry of the absolute into the relative, the manifestation of the eternal within the temporal, the revelation of the

---

135 Shorter points out that «"Incarnation" was used in the decade following the Council as a popular substitute for the less favoured "adaptation" until it was supplanted by the term "inculturation". Indeed, it had much to do with the introduction of the later term», A. SHORTER, *Evangelization and Culture*, 34.

136 P. ARRUPE, «Father General's Letter on Inculturation», 193.

137 JOHN PAUL II, *SA* 21. Cf. ITC, «Faith and Inculturation», 802.

138 ITC, «Faith and Inculturation», 803.

139 Cf. A. SHORTER, *Toward a Theology of Inculturation*, 80.

Infinite within the finite»[140]. The implication of this for the process of inculturation is that the faith of the Church[141] can only be embodied in concrete cultures, in all their unique and particular forms and expressions. Just as Jesus needed to adopt the cultural «language»[142] of his hearers in order to perform his ministry, so does the Church need to express itself through human cultures. 2) Just as the dynamic of the Incarnation involves a double movement of «[...] God becoming human and the human becoming God in Jesus», hence acting as a paradigm for divine-human interaction, so the process of inculturation has a transformative dynamic, bringing out what is best and enabling a culture to realize its potential[143]. 3) Because in the Incarnation God established a new relationship with the world, that is to say because the transcendent God becomes immanent and is transhistorically present throughout all creation and throughout humanity, human culture, a sacrament of God, is able to be a mediator of grace[144]. The process of inculturation, then, is a two-way dialogue, with faith and culture reciprocally contributing to each other[145].

Understood in a restricted sense, the analogy of Incarnation has certain inadequacies and limitations. First, if seen only as the socialization of Jesus into his culture, then analogously, inculturation will be equated with only the initial insertion of the Gospel into a culture, thus short-circuiting the permanent process of conversion[146]. Second, if the Incar-

---

[140] D. LANE, «The Challenge of Inculturation», 10.

[141] Shorter discusses the Christian term of inculturation: the «what» of inculturation is described in varying ways as the Christian faith, the Christian message, the Gospel, or the essence of the Gospel. The goal of evangelization, however, «[...] is to enable the one who is evangelized to recognize the presence of Jesus Christ in his or her own life, both individual and communal». Thus, «[...] it can be truthfully said that what is inculturated is Jesus Christ himself. He is the subject-matter of inculturation, the Christian term of the inculturation equation. It is he who enters into dialogue with human culture», A. SHORTER, *Toward a Theology of Inculturation*, 61.

[142] Cf. PAUL VI, *EN* 63: «The word "language" should be understood here less in the semantic or literary sense than in the sense which one may call anthropological and cultural».

[143] Cf. D. LANE, «The Challenge of Inculturation», 10-11.

[144] Thomas Groome points out that «[...] Christian missionaries do not "bring God" to anyone, since God is already present ahead of them. To say otherwise would deny two central aspects of Catholic Christian faith, namely the universality of God's love and the principle of sacramentality», T. GROOME, «Inculturation: How to Proceed in a Pastoral Context», 123.

[145] Cf. D. LANE, «The Challenge of Inculturation», 11.

[146] Cf. A. SHORTER, *Toward a Theology of Inculturation*, 81.

nation is understood in such a way that Jesus' divinity eclipses his full
humanity[147], it gives the impression «[...] that the Gospel, like the divine
pre-existence of Christ, comes to the evangelized culture in a culturally
disembodied form»[148]. Third, the Incarnation analogy, if it concentrates
only on Jesus' assumption and acceptance of his particular culture, fails
to consider his critique and challenge of his culture, which were
important dimensions of his life and ministry[149].

Because of these potential limitations and inadequacies, the Incarnation must be understood in its full sense which includes the reality of
the Paschal Mystery; such an understanding includes not only Jesus'
socialization into his particular culture, but also his ministry, passion,
death, and resurrection[150]. Shorter points out that inculturation is linked
both «[...] causally and analogically to the Paschal Mystery»[151]. It is
linked causally because it is through his passion, death, and resurrection
that Jesus Christ became accessible as Lord to people of every culture. It
is linked analogically because a genuine process of inculturation must
follow a similar pattern of conversion:

> The Gospel invites people to reappraise their cultures in the light of radically
> new values — values that turn human thinking upside-down. Cultures are
> to be evangelized and to undergo *metanoia* or conversion at their

---

147 Cf. L. RICHARD, «Mission and Inculturation», 108.

148 A. SHORTER, *Evangelization and Culture*, 35. Cf. L. RICHARD, «Mission and
Inculturation», 109. Francesco Rossi De Gasperis states, «Christian inculturation is
not nor can it be the unceasing reincarnation of a nucleus of divine truths and realities
as if they were taken out of history and abstractly isolated into a pure state and applied
to always new historical cultural contexts. Inculturation does not move from a
world of essences to history but *from history to history*, from Jerusalem to the ends
of the earth», F. ROSSI DE GASPERIS, «Continuity and Newness in the Faith of the
Mother Church of Jerusalem», 60.

149 Cf. A. SHORTER, *Toward a Theology of Inculturation*, 82; ID., *Evangelization
and Culture*, 35.

150 Roest Crollius states, «Il Verbo di Dio non si è fatto uomo in un senso astratto
e generale, ma, Figlio della Vergine, è divenuto Ebreo, con la cultura di una classe
sociale e di un'epoca particolare. Per la sua vita ha sanctificato, nel suo ministero ha
purificato, e nella sua morte e risurrezione ha rinnovato anche i valori umani di lingua
e cultura di cui egli era il portatore. La Rivelazione, che ha raggiunto la sua pienezza in
Cristo, è il fondamento e modello di ogni inculturazione», A. A. ROEST CROLLIUS,
«Inculturazione», 281-282. It is in this full sense of Revelation, which includes the entire
Paschal Mystery, that Incarnation must be understood if it is to be an adequate analogue
for the inculturation process.

151 A. SHORTER, *Evangelization and Culture*, 35. For a discussion of the Paschal
Mystery as the more complete analogy for the process of inculturation, see ID., *Toward a
Theology of Inculturation*, 83-87.

profoundest level. They must "die" to all that is not worthy of humanity in their traditions, all that is a consequence of accumulated guilt and social sin. If human structures can be vitiated by sin, then human cultures can be similarly vitiated. [...] Faced by the challenge of the One who died and rose again, cultures are called upon to die in order to rise to a greater splendour[152].

It must not be assumed, however, that this process of dying in order to rise to new life affects only the evangelized culture. As Divarkar has stressed, it also affects both the evangelizer and the message itself:

There is already a self-annihilation in the Incarnation, the kenosis in which the Son of God empties himself, taking the form of a servant; but having become like us in all things, he humbled himself yet more, submitting to death on the cross; and it is in being raised up by the Father's will and power that Jesus is constituted Lord of the Universe and of human destiny. [...] It is this mystery that is at the heart of the Good News that the Gospel proclaims and that the messenger of the Gospel must carry to the ends of the earth. *But in this process both the messenger and the message itself must not only become incarnate in the lives of the people to whom Christ brings new life; they must also die and rise in these people* [emphasis added][153].

To be an adequate analogue for inculturation, then, Incarnation must be understood in its fullest sense, which is to say that it must be understood to include the reality of the Paschal Mystery[154]. The Paschal Mystery, in turn, must be seen as the primary pattern for both evangelizer and evangelized[155]. In this way the process of inculturation is properly seen as a permanent process of cultural conversion and growth in Christ on the part of all participating in the process[156].

---

[152] A. SHORTER, *Toward a Theology of Inculturation*, 83-84.

[153] P. R. DIVARKAR, «*Evangelii Nuntiandi* and the Problem of Inculturation», 10.

[154] Shorter points out that «[...] in fairness to some theologians, it must be noted that the word "incarnation" is sometimes used as shorthand for the whole mystery of Christ which the Incarnation inaugurated», A. SHORTER, *Toward a Theology of Inculturation*, 82.

[155] Divarkar points out that «[...] what comes to us today as a fresh realization is the startling truth that in some mysterious way the Gospel itself must die as Christ died: the word of God, like good seed falling on good ground, must die that it may bear good fruit. No formulation in human terms of God's message is exhaustive or even adequate; hence this message, which ultimately is Christ himself, must constantly find new expression in the language and life of man; this is the mystery of the Church, which is "the fullness of him who fills the whole creation" (1Eph 23)», P. R. DIVARKAR, «*Evangelii Nuntiandi* and the Problem of Inculturation», 10.

[156] Amalorpavadass delineates three stages in this process: «Un tel processus se déroule en trois étapes: a) Incarnation: Tout l'humain est assumé en vue d'être sauvé.

2.5.3 The Church's Universal Mission

Having examined some of the christological foundations of incultura-tion, the ecclesiological dimensions can now be briefly considered[157]. Because the mission of the Church, which is essentially the mission of Christ, includes not only people, but also their cultures and religions[158], the Church can be said to have «[...] a culturally redemptive pre-sence»[159]. In order to fulfill its mission, the Church is to serve «[...] as a leaven and as a kind of soul for human society as it is to be renewed in Christ and transformed into God's family» (GS 40). This mission is carried out in the context of the local Church, a teaching which Shorter has identified as one of the Second Vatican Council's most important insights[160]. If the culture is to be transformed in the process of incultur-ation, as the Incarnation-Paschal Mystery analogue demands, then this transformation process will only take place through the Church's encounter with particular cultures, which necessarily takes place in the context of the local Church[161]. These local Churches, in turn, exist in a relation of communion with each other: «In and from such individual Churches there comes into being the one and only Catholic Church» (LG 23). Such communion prevents the local Churches from being exclusive entities, closed in upon themselves, and ensures that they exist for the good of the whole Church, enriching it with their own unique contributions which are intimately related to their cultures[162].

---

b) Mort: Tout ce qui a besoin d'être racheté passe par le mystère pascal. c) Résurrec-tion: Toutes choses vont être renouvelées et atteindre leur accomplissement», D. S. AMALORPAVADASS, «Réflexions théologiques sur l'inculturation», 61.

[157] Shorter cites Amalorpavadass' four starting-points for a theology of inculturation, and identifies the first two — creation/history and incarnation/paschal mystery — as christological, and the last two — the Church's universal mission and authentic tradition/ordinary magisterium — as ecclesiological. A. SHORTER, Evangelization and Culture, 34-38.

[158] Cf. D. S. AMALORPAVADASS, «Réflexions théologiques sur l'inculturation», 61.

[159] L. RICHARD, «Mission and Inculturation», 97; Cf. GS 58.

[160] Cf. A. SHORTER, Toward a Theology of Inculturation, 68: «The Catholic Church is not a kind of multinational corporation with local branches or subsidiaries. It is a communion of particular Churches. These particular Churches are Church insofar as they are open towards, and in communion with, one another. They are the Catholic Church in a particular place».

[161] For a discussion of the local Church and the process of conversion and trans-formation of a culture, see L. RICHARD, «Mission and Inculturation», 97-99.

[162] Cf. A. SHORTER, Toward a Theology of Inculturation, 68.

It was noted earlier that there is a reciprocal quality to the process of
inculturation in that not only is the culture transformed by the redemptive presence of the Church, but the Church itself is affected by its
encounter with culture. This is not to deny that the Church already
possesses the Revelation of God in Christ and the means to salvation
for all people; nor is it to say that the Church needs to «borrow» elements from cultures in order to «make up» for what is lacking in its
fullness[163]. Rather, it is to say that the Church, in order to be faithful to
its catholicity, must seek to recognize, embrace, and integrate those traditions, moral goods, and spiritual values of various peoples and their
cultures[164].

> the Church, sent to all peoples of every time and place, is not bound
> exclusively and indissolubly to any race or nation, nor to any particular way
> of life or any customary pattern of living, ancient or recent. Faithful to her
> own tradition and at the same time conscious of her universal mission, she
> can enter into communion with various cultural modes, to her own enrich-
> ment and theirs too (*GS* 58).

Schineller has observed that, in the context of inculturation, the four
marks of the Church — one, holy, catholic, and apostolic — receive a
different emphasis or nuance. Although these four marks characterize the
Church, as gifts of the Spirit to the Church they are also understood as a
challenge and task for the Church to be open, adaptable, and receptive in
all cultures — which implies a permanent process of interaction and
transformation[165].

---

[163] Amalorpavadass maintains, «Dans une Église locale l'Esprit ecclésialise une
culture: c'est dire que l'inculturation constitue une nécessité, nonobstant l'opinion selon
laquelle l'Église, du fait qu'elle a déjà la révélation et les moyens de salut et n'a besoin de
rien emprunter en dehors d'elle-même», D. S. AMALORPAVADASS, «Réflexions
théologiques sur l'inculturation», 61.

[164] Cf. D. S. AMALORPAVADASS, «Réflexions théologiques sur l'inculturation»,
61: «[...] dans une recherche permanente et avec des efforts persévérants, dans un
mouvement dynamique constant, l'Église doit tout embrasser, reconnaître toutes choses
comme siennes et intégrer dans sa catholicité toutes les traditions, les biens moraux et les
valeurs spirituelles des différents peuples et de leurs cultures».

[165] Cf. P. SCHINELLER, *A Handbook on Inculturation*, 50. Shorter points out that
catholicity «[...] implies an experiential and ecumenical dynamic, a true communication
of meaning. Since language is closely tied to culture, the meeting with others in their
otherness demands a sensitivity to language. The language of faith can be no other than
the language of the evangelized culture. There can be no universal or standardized
language in a truly Catholic Church», A. SHORTER, *Evangelization and Culture*, 37.

2.5.4 Authentic Tradition and the Ordinary Magisterium

Amalorpavadass asserts that the respective values of the various Church traditions must be discerned and that such ecclesial pluralism calls for various forms of inculturation[166]. The key question then becomes one of determining what is the authentic Christian Tradition that all the local churches must embrace in order to remain in communion with the Universal Church. It has already been pointed out that because the Church does not move from the realm of essences into a culture, but necessarily contains cultural elements itself, the process of inculturation includes elements of acculturation. In the light of this it is crucial to discern both the irreducible elements of Tradition and those that are merely accidental and culture-bound. This complex, thorny question, which does not admit of simple answers, forms a backdrop or a context that must be taken into consideration when involved with the process of inculturation.

In attempting to address this aspect of the inculturation process, Shorter makes the distinction between Sacred Tradition and the «cultural patrimony» of the Church[167]. According to Shorter, Jesus and his disciples bequeathed a «[...] trajectory of meaning within which subsequent interpretation by the Christian community was to take place and which would be augmented in succeeding generations and cultures»[168]. This

---

166 Cf. D. S. AMALORPAVADASS, «Réflexions théologiques sur l'inculturation», 62: «Il y a lieu de discerner la valeur respective des différentes traditions dans l'Église, et par ailleurs le pluralisme ecclésial appelle à des formes diversifiées d'inculturation».

167 Cf. A. SHORTER, *Toward a Theology of Inculturation*, 64-67; ID., *Evangelization and Culture*, 36-38.

168 A. SHORTER, *Toward a Theology of Inculturation*, 64. Raymond Brown insists that «[...] a doctrinal trajectory should be traceable from the NT outlook to the later dogma, even if the connection between the two goes beyond pure logic». Citing Pope John XXIII, who in his opening speech to the Second Vatican Council pointed out the difference between the substance of the doctrine of the faith and how it is presented, Brown holds that the refutation of Hans Küng's challenge to infallibility, by the Congregation for the Doctrine of the Faith, articulates the principle of the historical conditioning of dogma: «(1) The meaning of the pronouncements of faith depends partly on the expressive power of the language used at a certain point in time and in particular circumstances; (2) sometimes dogmatic truth is first expressed incompletely (but not falsely), and at a later date receives a fuller and more perfect expression; (3) the Church usually has the intention of solving certain questions or removing certain errors, and these things have to be taken into account in order that the pronouncements may be properly interpreted; (4) sometimes the truths enunciated by the Church's magisterium are in terms that bear the traces of the changeable conceptions of a given topic», R. BROWN, *Biblical Exegesis and Church Doctrine*, 28-29.

«trajectory of meaning» was the context for the development of Sacred Tradition which, according to Shorter, «[...] concerns the truth about Jesus. It is the testimony to that truth which is preserved in unwritten form and in the inspired writings of Scripture, and which is the subject matter of the dialogue with culture»[169]. Shorter stresses that this Sacred Tradition makes progress in the Church, leading to the development of insight and understanding of the realities being passed on.

On the other hand, the «cultural patrimony» of the Church, although related to Sacred Tradition, refers to the «[...] more or less contingent cultural elements of diverse origin» which accumulate over time and are passed from one inculturated form of Christianity to another[170]. Although such a patrimony is a sign of Catholicism's traditional openness «[...] to the richness and variety of symbols and signs that point to and embody the divine»[171], it should be neither equated nor confused with Sacred Tradition. The challenge of inculturation is to decode and make intelligible the Sacred Tradition[172], articulating it in the cultural language of the local Church.

This brief overview of the theological underpinnings has highlighted two important christological principles and two important ecclesiological principles at play in any genuine operation of inculturation. First, the teaching on the *semina Verbi* emphasizes that even before the proclamation of the Gospel, God is already present and at work in the world, including the world's cultures. Inculturation is a necessary operation that

---

[169] A. SHORTER, *Toward a Theology of Inculturation*, 65.

[170] A. SHORTER, *Evangelization and Culture*, 38. Shorter explains that this cultural patrimony is «[...] a changing and varied phenomenon. Not only does it include culturally conditioned dogmatic formulation, it also comprises forms of devotion, traditions of spirituality, schools of liturgical art and even such trivia as styles of ecclesiastical dress. The priest's biretta vanished with the appearance of the new Roman Missal. The General Instruction of 1969 does not list it among the various vestments to be worn, and its passing has not been generally lamented. While priests gladly consigned their birettas to the dustbin, bishops and cardinals clung tenaciously to their more exotically coloured specimens. That a purple biretta still forms part of episcopal choir-dress possibly means that this piece of European sixteenth century academic headgear is an external symbol of Catholic hierarchy. If such a justification were outweighed by local cultural considerations, the thing should be jettisoned without regret. [...] Other elements in the Church's cultural patrimony are more important, but not all are irreducible in the sense of providing a necessary symbolic and conceptual link with Christ», A. SHORTER, *Toward a Theology of Inculturation*, 66. Shorter cites devotional practices and doctrinal formulations as examples of such patrimony.

[171] P. SCHINELLER, *A Handbook on Inculturation*, 52.

[172] Cf. J.-B. METZ, «Unity and Diversity», 86.

allows the presence of God to unfold to its fullest, transforming the culture in the process. Second, the Incarnation, understood in its full sense as including the Paschal Mystery, is the central paradigm for the process of inculturation. It emphasizes that inculturation is basically a process of conversion and transformation that affects both the evangelized and the evangelizer, the culture and the Church, both locally and universally. Third, although the Universal Church is responsible for carrying out Christ's mission, this takes place in the context of the local Church. While the Universal Church is made up of the communion of local Churches, its catholicity does not mean uniformity, but rather it signifies unity-in-diversity. The Church remains authentically Catholic as long as it continues to embrace the diversity of cultures in the world. Its catholicity is thus both a gift and a challenge. Finally, in embracing the various cultures and growing organically within their particular contexts, the challenge for the Church is to remain true to its authentic Sacred Tradition, expressed in the languages of the particular cultures, but not confusing it with its cultural patrimony, rich as it may be. The challenge is to remain faithful to authentic Sacred Tradition and to the local culture, giving birth to a genuinely inculturated local Church.

2.6 *Criteria For Inculturation Process*

Because the inculturation process involves two distinct orders of reality with their own laws and processes, namely faith and culture, because the process of their interaction is freighted with complexity and challenge, and because this process is so critical for the life of both the Church and of cultures, some guidelines or criteria are necessary for its successful implementation. Carrier offers four such criteria: 1) distinguish faith's proper role; 2) build the Church according to its identity; 3) reconcile unity and pluralism; 4) promote discernment and investigation[173].

1) Although the process of inculturation emphasizes that the Gospel itself is a product of a particular culture or cultures and that the task of the Church is to penetrate all cultures with this culturally conditioned, albeit inspired, Gospel, there is nevertheless a radical distinction between the Gospel and any given culture, a distinction that precludes an exclusive identification of the Gospel with a culture (cf. *EN* 20). This radical distinction, however, is not the equivalent of separation or

---

[173] Cf. H. CARRIER, *Evangelizing the Culture of Modernity*, 73-81; ID., «Inculturation de l'évangile», 199-202.

dissociation. As Paul VI emphasized, the Gospel is not incompatible with cultures, but rather is «[...] capable of impregnating all cultures without becoming enslaved to any» (*EN* 20). On the other hand, culture also has an active role to play in the process. John Paul II has noted that «[...] culture is not only a subject of redemption and elevation; it can also play a role of mediation and collaboration»[174]. The task of inculturation is to encourage the creative interaction between faith and culture without confusing or collapsing the two[175].

2) Although the importance of distinguishing between the Church's Sacred Tradition and its cultural patrimony has been pointed out, this distinction is neither clear and simple nor hard and fast; thus the «cultural patrimony» must not be disregarded or discarded precipitously. As a living organism the Church grows «[...] out of the same roots and the same common stem that link it historically to its beginnings»[176]. Composed of many vital parts which contribute to the Church's identity, both in its unity and catholicity, the Church is enriched by the various cultural expressions of the faith that have been contributed down through the centuries, whether in the form of theology, spirituality, liturgy, art, law, etc.[177]. Such culture-bound expression «[...] does not nullify the perduring value and basic meaning of dogmatic formulations and ways of conceptualizing the faith, of basic sacramental and liturgical structures»[178]. Each local Church, because it is part of a larger communion, must therefore harmonize its own unique cultural experience with that of the Universal Church so that the one Church may grow according to its own nature in the diverse cultures. In this way both the unity and catholicity of the Church will be preserved and fostered[179].

3) Out of the previous criterion comes the challenge to reconcile unity and pluralism. This tension between unity and pluralism is held together by an understanding of the Church as communion[180]. Pluralism, properly understood, creates communion. The 1985 Extraordinary Synod of Bishops stated that «[...] because the Church is

---

174 JOHN PAUL II, «Address to the University of Coimbra, Portugal», cited in H. CARRIER, *Evangelizing the Culture of Modernity*, 75.

175 Cf. H. CARRIER, *Evangelizing the Culture of Modernity*, 73-75.

176 H. CARRIER, *Evangelizing the Culture of Modernity*, 77.

177 Cf. JOHN PAUL II to the Roman Curia, *AAS* 76 (1984) 477-487, cited in H. CARRIER, *Evangelizing the Culture of Modernity*, 77.

178 H. CARRIER, *Evangelizing the Culture of Modernity*, 77.

179 Cf. H. CARRIER, *Evangelizing the Culture of Modernity*, 75-77.

180 Cf. *LG* 13.

communion, which joins diversity and unity in being present throughout the world, it takes from every culture all that it encounters of positive value»[181]. Cultural differences are thus integrated into the communion of the Church. Such integration affirms Paul VI's insight that «[...] a pluralism of expression in the unity of substance is legitimate and even desirable when it comes to professing a common faith in one and the same Jesus Christ»[182]. The task of inculturation, then, not only includes a deep respect for the differences but also an integration of these into the communion of the Church[183].

4) In order to implement the three criteria mentioned, —that is, to distinguish faith's proper role, build the Church according to its identity, and reconcile unity with pluralism — a fourth criterion, the practice of discernment and investigation, is necessary. Discernment and investigation necessarily include practical judgment and methodological reflection. As has been demonstrated, such a process is inevitably complex and difficult because it involves two different orders of reality: faith and culture[184]. And even on these basic terms of the process, there is not necessarily agreement. Schreiter has observed that «[...] when trying to mediate the question of the inculturation of faith or the identification with culture, we must be aware not only of how we define faith and culture, but also of how those definitions carry with them implications that shape the direction of the inculturation process»[185]. Discernment and investigation, both in the area of faith and in the area of culture, are necessary for the inculturation process to unfold in a way that is adequate to both terms of the equation. The process is fraught with complexity and

---

181 SYNOD OF BISHOPS, «The Final Report», 450.

182 PAUL VI, «Address to the Bishops of Asia», *AAS* 63, 21-27, cited in H. CARRIER, *Evangelizing the Culture of Modernity*, 78.

183 Cf. H. CARRIER, *Evangelizing the Culture of Modernity*, 77-79.

184 Robert Schreiter has contrasted two positions relative to the inculturation process. One emphasizes the faith as the starting point and the other emphasizes the dynamics of culture as a starting point. Schreiter articulates the challenges which these positions pose to inculturation: «How would one go about mediating between these two positions? Each affirms an important point: the transcendence of the gospel and the complexity of human cultures. And each position acknowledges the validity of the other's concerns. But neither position has been able to answer the objection of the other: just how does the first position assure that its approach to inculturation is not a form of cultural domination? How does it answer the objection that much so-called Christianization has really been a Westernization? And when will the second position articulate criteria that will assure that close identification with the culture does not end in a false inculturation of the Gospel?», R. SCHREITER, «Inculturation of Faith or Identification with Culture?», 17.

185 R. SCHREITER, «Inculturation of Faith or Identification with Culture?», 19.

challenge, but it is the only proper, satisfactory way for the encounter of
faith and culture to unfold. Based on solid theological discernment and
cultural investigation and analysis, the process of inculturation will benefit both the local Churches and the universal Church[186].

Having considered the Church's concern for the interaction of faith
and culture since the Second Vatican Council, the general dynamics of
the process of inculturation, its theological underpinnings, and criteria
for guiding the process, the methodology for delineating the actual
process of inculturating specific aspects or themes of the faith into a
culture can now be considered.

3. Methodology

Lane has observed that, although the conciliar documents do not map
out an explicit methodology of inculturation, they do point to the beginnings of one[187]. Such a methodology would include a critical correlation
between faith and culture, principles of good conversation and dialogue
(hermeneutics), and the need for a liberating praxis[188]. Schineller has
offered a similar methodology of inculturation through employment of a
«hermeneutical circle»[189], which is a pedagogical tool that consists of
three elements: the situation (pole 1); the Christian message (pole 2); and
the pastoral agent or minister (pole 3). His methodology echoes that of

---

[186] Cf. A. CARRIER, *Evangelizing the Culture of Modernity*, 79-81.

[187] Lane cites *GS* 5 which «[...] speaks of the duty of the Church in terms of
"scrutinizing the signs of the times and of interpreting them in the light of the Gospel"»;
Unitatis Redintegratio which «[...] recognizes the ecclesial reality of other churches»; and
Nostra Aetate which «[...] acknowledges the presence of truths and values in other major
world religions», D. LANE, «The Challenge of Inculturation», 12.

[188] Cf. D. LANE, «The Challenge of Inculturation», 11-14. The «[...] mutually
critical correlation between human experience and Christian tradition», the first step of
Lane's methodology, is a correlation that takes place within the guidelines of certain
hermeneutical principles (second step) which allow an honest, free-flowing conversation
between the various components of the inculturation process to take place. Such a
hermeneutical framework «[...] seeks to provide a way forward beyond the impasse of
objectivism and relativism as well as the ever-increasing welter of pluralism, difference
and otherness», by allowing the various interpreters' presuppositions and prejudices to
emerge; such honesty is a prerequisite for real conversation. Such conversation leads to
the third moment of Lane's model, that of «liberating praxis», a necessary step lest the
impression be given that faith and culture have at their disposal disembodied truths
coming from the world of essences. Conversation must lead to a real reshaping and
realignment of the elements involved in the inculturation process, thus to «a more human
and just society». Cf. D. LANE, «The Challenge of Inculturation», 13.

[189] Cf. P. SCHINELLER, «A Method for Christian Ministry», 137-144; ID., «Ten
Summary Statements», 55-56; ID., *A Handbook on Inculturation*, 61-73.

Lane in that it includes Tillich's method of correlation[190] and affirms
the importance of hermeneutics; Schineller, however, also emphasizes the
importance of the agent of inculturation who facilitates the process[191].
Although he does not employ «liberating praxis» as a category in his
methodology, it is clear that, in his understanding, the process of interaction among the three poles is to lead to a moment of truth or resonance which is then the basis for action[192]. Schreiter offers a map to
demonstrate the complexity of the interaction of the Gospel, the Church,
and cultures, suggesting that the issues raised by this interaction of
the three realities admit of various questions, thus various answers[193].
De Carvalho Azevedo suggests caution with regard to epistemological
considerations because faith and culture are two different subjects that
require two different approaches. Although they are not necessarily
opposed to one another, they are different from each other and this
difference must be kept in mind in any attempt to analyze or explore
the relationship between the two[194], which of course is the focus of the
operation of inculturation.

3.1 Methodological Considerations for the Present Study

The methodological elements mentioned above — correlation, conversation, praxis, Church, Gospel, culture, epistemological concerns — are
important «pieces» in the operation of inculturation that come together in
a comprehensive manner in a methodology articulated by Drilling, who
takes inculturation as a methodological presupposition for developing

---

190 Cf. P. TILLICH, *Systematic Theology*, 59-66, as cited by P. SCHINELLER,
A Handbook on Inculturation, 63.

191 Cf. P. SCHINELLER, *A Handbook on Inculturation*, 68-70.

192 Cf. P. SCHINELLER, *A Handbook on Inculturation*, 71.

193 Schreiter notes that «[...] the Gospel raises questions about the community
context» — the quality of its praxis, worship, and other forms of action; the Church
raises questions about tradition and the interaction of the local Church with the universal Church: culture questions about identity and social change. R. SCHREITER,
Constructing Local Theologies, 22-39.

194 Regarding the operations of faith and anthropology/sociology, which proceed
from different premises, Azevedo states, «There does not have to be a necessary
opposition between the two approaches, but there is a *different epistemological discourse*
and, consequently, a diverse *methodological* instrument. Because of the nature of our
subject matter — Christian message and culture — the reader should be aware of
these methodological peculiarities». Such awareness of the cultural anthropological
and theological approaches, which may at times be interwoven into a text, will prevent
«[...] epistemological confusion between the two standpoints», M. DE CARVALHO
AZEVEDO, «Inculturation and the Challenges of Modernity», 13, n. 4.

a theology of ministry[195]. Insofar as it entails an interaction between faith and culture, such a methodology roughly follows the dynamics of inculturation already described; it demands, however, more than mere conversation:

> It is not theologically acceptable simply to acknowledge and observe that the Gospel influences cultures and that cultures influence the Gospel. It is required that the mutual influence be critically examined. For since inculturation is a joint endeavor of the living Spirit of Jesus and human members of the Church who are limited in their abilities and truncated by their sin, mistakes will accompany the enterprise of rooting the Gospel in a culture. Sometimes it happens that the culture co-opts the Gospel [...] and sometimes those who preach the Gospel fail to respect what is true and good in the culture[196].

Because the methodology of inculturation requires such critical examination, it will be most effective and comprehensive if it focuses on relevant data, asks questions to deepen understanding, reflects critically on such understanding, and evaluates every instance of inculturation to determine its faithfulness to the gospel and to authentic cultural values[197]. The elements of methodology used in this study can now be articulated, keeping in mind the basic dynamics of attentiveness to the data, critical reflection, evaluation and verification, and responsible choice. Such a process allows the operation of inculturation to be assessed in terms of its fidelity to the gospel and its respect for cultural values.

The present study seeks to explore the theme of priest as leader in a United States context. The genesis of the project is rooted in a document approved in 1992 by the Roman Catholic Bishops of the United States, *The Program of Priestly Formation*, fourth edition [*PPF* IV], which uses the language of leadership in referring to priests: «Priests provide pastoral leadership in the community of faith. [...] As leaders of the faith community, priests exercise a significant dimension of their shepherding role through the support they offer to the laity. [...] priests are called to provide vision, direction and leadership»[198]. Describing priestly spirituality, the bishops affirm that, along with teaching and sanctifying,

---

[195] Cf. P. J. DRILLING, *Trinity and Ministry*, 1-21.

[196] P. J. DRILLING, *Trinity and Ministry*, 20.

[197] Cf. P. J. DRILLING, *Trinity and Ministry*, 21: «Critical investigation from the methodological perspective of inculturation yields transcultural, as well as more limited cultural, truth in ministry, its practice, doctrine, and theology. It also uncovers mistakes».

[198] NCCB, *PPF* IV, 10-11.

leadership «[...] is central to the spirituality of priests because it enters so deeply and powerfully into their own personal lives, [...] Leadership without the witness of holiness, asceticism and personal integrity lacks authenticity»[199].

Before attempting to explore the meaning of these statements regarding priestly leadership, a number of preliminary observations might be helpful. First, the *PPF* IV itself is written by Roman Catholic Bishops of the United States in order to guide the formation of priests for service in the United States, a factor that immediately points to the interaction of Church and culture. That the universal Church is concerned about priestly formation throughout the world is well documented[200]. Because such formation must take place in a variety of cultural contexts, there is a need for the various Episcopal Conferences around the world to draw up programs that are both faithful to the universal Church teachings and guidelines regarding priestly formation, while at the same time cognizant and respectful of the cultural context in which such formation takes place. Second, the *PPF* brings together two different realities or categories — Roman Catholic priesthood (an ecclesial reality) and leadership (a culturally-conditioned reality) — which, although epistemologically distinct, are not mutually exclusive. The challenge is to examine these categories, respecting their own methodological peculiarities; to explore how they interact with each other; and to offer a description of priest as leader that is faithful to the Church's teaching on priesthood and adequate to a U.S. cultural understanding of leadership.

In the light of these considerations the following process will be used as a methodology for exploring the priest as leader in a U.S. context:

1) The ordained, ministerial priesthood is a transcultural, ecclesial reality that is rooted in the Church's tradition and articulated in its teachings. Of particular importance for understanding the ministerial priesthood are the Second Vatican Council's «Decree on the Ministry and Life of Priests», *Presbyterorum Ordinis*, and Pope John Paul II's Post-Synodal Apostolic Exhortation, *Pastores Dabo Vobis*. These and related documents will be examined and analyzed from the perspective of leadership in order to yield a particular understanding of the universal Church's teaching on priesthood.

---

199 NCCB, *PPF* IV, 13.

200 See, for example, NCCB, *NPF*, vols. 1 and 2, a compendium, in English translation, of 24 official Church documents related to priestly formation, beginning with those of the Second Vatican Council and including subsequent documents issued by various dicasteries of the Holy See.

2) Next, the concept of leadership will be explored. Because the particular cultural context exerts a strong influence on how leadership is understood and practiced, it will be approached from a United States cultural context. An exploration of some widely popular works of various U.S. authors writing in the leadership field will yield an understanding of how the dynamics, qualities, characteristics, and expressions of leadership are widely understood in U.S culture today.

3) Returning to the *PPF*, which posited the assertion of priest-as-leader in the first place, the two pieces of research — the theological/spiritual exploration of the Roman Catholic priesthood from the perspective of leadership, and the cultural examination of leadership — will be placed in critical dialogue and interaction with each other. The result of such an interaction will be threefold: a) clarity regarding the spiritual-theological term of the equation, namely ordained ministerial priesthood; b) clarity regarding the cultural term of the equation, namely leadership; c) clarity regarding a specific instance of inculturation that is faithful to the ecclesial understanding of priesthood and adequate to the cultural understanding of leadership. Additionally, such a critical interaction will lead to a moment of resonance: an articulation of a spirituality of priest as leader in a U.S. cultural context.

The methodology offers a critical examination of cultural and spiritual-theological data by analyzing and correlating them, placing them in dialogue, and determining their fidelity to Church tradition and adequacy to cultural realities. The two terms of the inculturation equation, faith tradition (ministerial priesthood) and culture (leadership), are brought into play; the mutual penetration of the two is shown; adequacies and inadequacies are highlighted; and direction is offered for a more effective living out of priesthood that is faithful to the Gospel and tradition and adequate to the cultural understanding of leadership.

3.2 *Inculturation and Spirituality*

A final word on methodology concerns the relationship of inculturation to the theological discipline of Spirituality. Sudbrack has described spirituality as «[...] a general science that cuts across all the rest and bridges all subjects relevant to theology. Always directly flowing from the font of revelation in Christ, it brings all such subjects into the life of the individual. Therefore it naturally arranges the other disciplines according to their bearing on actual Christian existence»[201]. Bernard defines spirituality as «[...] a theological discipline that, founded on the principles of revelation, studies Christian spiritual experience, describes its progressive development and makes known its structures

---

[201] J. SUDBRACK, «Spirituality, I», 151.

and laws»[202]. Cameli combines some of the elements of these definitions and offers a comprehensive definition of spirituality as «[...] an attempt through the use of various resources and especially theological ones to capture the Christian experience in its particular facets and its totality with a view towards entering into the experience and living it more deeply and authentically»[203]. These definitions point to the interdisciplinary character of the operation of spirituality insofar as it includes both specifically theological resources and the data of human experience[204], bringing the two into conversation with each other.

Because the Church's teaching on inculturation is a recent development[205], the concern for its relation to spirituality is also relatively new[206]. Like other dimensions of Church life, however, spirituality «[...] is a cultural phenomenon and it needs to be studied within the context of its interrelationship with the society in which it is found»[207]. The methodology described above is thus a valid one for a study in spirituality because it takes a concrete human experience, namely that of priest as leader, and seeks to understand that experience in all its complexity, both from a spiritual-theological perspective and from a cultural perspective. Such analysis will lead to a deeper understanding and fuller grasp of the experience, offering some directions and indications for entering and living the experience more authentically.

---

[202] Cf. C. A. BERNARD, *Teologia Spirituale*, 70: «La teologia spirituale è una disciplina teologica che, fondata sui principi della rivelazione, studia l'esperienza spirituale cristiana, ne descrive lo sviluppo progressivo e ne fa conoscere le strutture e le leggi».

[203] L. J. CAMELI, *Ministerial Consciousness*, 4.

[204] For a description of the fonts of spiritual theology, see C. A. BERNARD, *Teologia Spirituale*, 92-97.

[205] Cf. W. REISER, «Inculturation and Doctrinal Development», 135-148.

[206] D. J. Fasching notes that «[...] to ask about the relation between spirituality and culture is to ask a very "modern" question», D. J. FASCHING, «Culture», 242.

[207] A. RUSSELL, «Sociology and the Study of Spirituality», 38.

CHAPTER II

Priest as Leader in *Presbyterorum Ordinis* and Related Documents

1. Contextual Considerations

In the past thirty years, Church teaching on priestly ministry has been explored in many documents, thus the nature of our reflections on the priest as leader demands some focus. Vatican II's «Decree on the Ministry and Life of Priests», *Presbyterorum Ordinis (PO)*, expresses the most authoritative teaching on the priesthood, has provided the basis for subsequent teaching, and will therefore provide the needed focus and point of reference for a synthesis of Church teaching. Other documents, conciliar and postconciliar, also make important contributions to a fuller understanding of the priesthood and will be included in the considerations of this chapter. Among conciliar documents to be consulted are the «Dogmatic Constitution on the Church», *Lumen Gentium (LG)*, particularly 10 and 28; the «Decree on Priestly Formation», *Optatam Totius (OT)*; and the «Decree on the Bishops' Pastoral Office in the Church», *Christus Dominus (CD)*. The document from the 1971 Synod of Bishops, *The Ministerial Priesthood (MP)*, will additionally be consulted at certain points in order to deepen an understanding of priest as leader[1].

---

[1] *AAS* 63 (1971) 898-922. References are taken from the English translation, «The Ministerial Priesthood», NCCB, *NPF*, vol. 1, 293-313. For commentaries on the documents related to priesthood see the following. M. CAPRIOLI, *Il Decreto Conciliare «Presbyterorum Ordinis»*. P. J. CORDES, *Inviati a servire*. J. FRISQUE et Y. CONGAR, eds., *Les Prêtres*. A. GRILLMEIER in *CDV*, vol. 1: «The Mystery of the Church, Art. 2»,138-152; «The People of God, Art. 10»,153-185; «The Hierarchical Structure of the Church, Art. 28», 218-226. R. F. HARVANEK, «Decree on the Training of Priests», 91-108. D. E. HURLEY, «Bishops, Presbyterate and the Training of Priests

1.1 *Historical Perspective*

An authentic understanding of the development of Church teaching on priestly ministry must necessarily identify its historical and theological contexts[2]. Historically, it is important to understand the context in which the postconciliar teaching on the ministerial priesthood was formulated and received, a context dominated by what has come to be known as a priestly «identity crisis». Even as early as 1968, Paul VI alluded to such a crisis:

> [He spoke of] the violent waves of questions, doubts, denials, and open-ended new ideas that are crashing against the ministerial priesthood in other countries. [...] Problems are being raised about its true nature and primary function, about its proper place, and about its original, authentic reality. Assailed by these doubts, the priest begins to ask himself questions, and to wonder about his vocation[3].

Although the roots of the crisis were primarily theological, its consequences were to be manifest in sociological, psychological, spiritual, and pastoral dimensions.

Castellucci traces this crisis to the years prior to the Council when theologians were considering two significant issues: the increasing secularization occurring in many parts of the world, and the sacramentality of episcopal consecration[4]. The Council closely scrutinized both themes. Although unrelated, both contributed significantly to ecclesiological formulations that radically reshaped the Church's self-awareness. The reality of secularization led to a new theological perspective on the laity: in virtue of their baptism they were recognized as an essential component of the missionary structure of the Church. At the same time, the episcopal office was understood as the primary ministerial office and guarantor

---

(*Christus Dominus*; *Presbyterorum Ordinis*; *Optatam Totius*)», 141-150. A. LAPLANTE, *La formation des prêtres*. J. LÉCUYER, «Decree on the Ministry and Life of Priests», vol. 4, 183-210. J. NEUNER, «Decree on Priestly Formation», 371-404. T. E. O'CONNELL, «Decree on the Ministry and Life of Priests», 197-215. G. PHILIPS, «Dogmatic Constitution on the Church», vol. 1, 105-137. R. A. TARTRE, *The Postconciliar Priest*. D. WUERL, «The Third Synod of Bishops on the Priesthood», 50-87. ID., «Recent Theological Conclusions on the Priesthood», 246-278. ID., *The Catholic Priesthood Today*. F. WULF et al., «Commentary on the Decree», vol. 4, 210-297.

[2] For an analysis of the historical and theological contexts of the conciliar and postconciliar teaching on priesthood, see E. CASTELLUCCI, «L'identità del presbitero», 92-139.

[3] PAUL VI, «Counsels for the City Priest», 115. Cf. *AAS* 60, 216.

[4] Cf. E. CASTELLUCCI, «L'identità del presbitero», 93-97.

of ecclesial communion. Although this renewed understanding of the laity and the episcopacy represented significant ecclesiological developments, prior to the Council neither had any immediate, direct impact on the understanding of the ministerial priesthood which remained firmly fixed in its Tridentine, cultic foundation[5].

During the Council, a renewed, dynamic ecclesiology that highlighted the role of the laity and the centrality of episcopal office revealed the inadequacies of the rather static understanding of the ministerial priesthood. A renewed ecclesiology, therefore, motivated conciliar thinking on the priesthood. The document on the priesthood, developed over the length of the entire Council[6], benefited from the Council's reflection on the Church, and reveals conciliar ecclesiology in its contents.

Because the language of «crisis» often accompanies postconciliar discussions about the ministerial priesthood, it is important to note that the development of the conciliar teaching on priesthood did not take place in a context of crisis. Its development was rather stimulated by the necessity of harmonizing the new, conciliar understanding of the Church with the articulation of its various aspects and components[7]. Thus the Council focused on the laity and the bishops, so developing new ecclesiological perspectives, which in turn provided the lens for the conciliar treatment of the ministerial priesthood.

The priestly «crisis» took place after the Council, when the ministerial priesthood was approached from the hermeneutic of a renewed ecclesiology. The ecclesiological re-reading of the priesthood, and the «crisis» connected to it, prompted the Synod of 1971 to adopt the ministerial priesthood as one of its principal foci. Unlike the Council, which took place in a relatively serene atmosphere, the Synod of 1971, a mere six years after the close of the Council, was characterized by an atmosphere of urgency to resolve the priestly identity crisis that was manifest in many parts of the world. The main focus of the Synod, relative to priestly identity, shifted the emphasis on priesthood from an ecclesiological to a christological perspective[8].

Three notable problems contributed to the crisis that began in the postconciliar years: 1) the question of the democratization of the Church;

---

5 Cf. E. CASTELLUCCI, «L'identità del presbitero», 94.

6 Cf. J. FRISQUE, «Le décret "Presbyterorum Ordinis"», 126.

7 Cf. E. CASTELLUCCI, «L'identità del presbitero», 95; B. KLOPPENBURG, *Ecclesiology of Vatican II*, 263-265.

8 Cf. E. CASTELLUCCI, «L'identità del presbitero», 95; D. WUERL, «Third Synod of Bishops», especially 56-63.

2) ecumenical endeavors; 3) the decline of priestly vocations[9]. The first problem, the perceived democratization of the Church, resulted from a misreading of the conciliar ecclesiology, especially the designation of the Church as the «People of God». Many thought that this name provided a blueprint for changing the Church into a democracy[10]. Democratic «leveling» of distinctions within the Church easily led to a negation of ontological difference and even sacramental character, a line of thought that reduced priesthood to a function among other functions in the Church. The second problem, an ecumenical reading of ordained ministry (influenced by the democratic understanding of Church), involved shifting the language of «priesthood» to that of «ministry». This terminological shift moved almost exclusively in ecclesiological, not christological terms. Finally, the crisis in vocations to the priesthood, through defections and fewer candidates, began in the immediate postconciliar years, continuing today in some parts of the world. The vocational crisis has led to a debate on the right of the community to the Eucharist, including the possible election by the community of its own eucharistic presiders[11]. Additional questions include the ordination of women to the ministerial priesthood and the value of obligatory celibacy.

These historical and contextual considerations are important and deserve more extensive reflection and study, since for our purposes they frame the wider context in which the theological debate took place. The theological perspective gains clarity from the historical context. These problems affect but do not shape the understanding and the exercise of the priesthood. Theology roots the current controversy or crisis surrounding the understanding of the ministerial priesthood.

1.2 Theological Perspective

The controversies surrounding the priesthood during the postconciliar years center on an identity crisis, the roots of which can be traced to the theological disputes centering on the ecclesiological and christological

---

[9] Cf. E. CASTELLUCCI, «L'identità del presbitero», 96.

[10] The Directory on the Ministry and Life of Priests devotes Paragraph 17 to the «temptation of "democratism"» and notes that «[...] the so-called "democratism" becomes a grave temptation because it leads to a denial of the authority and capital grace of Christ and to distort the nature of the Church; it would be almost just a human society. Such a view damages the very hierarchical structure willed by the Divine Founder as the Magisterium has always clearly taught and the Church herself has lived from the start», CC, DMLP, 19-20.

[11] Cf. E. CASTELLUCCI, «L'identità del presbitero», 96.

foundations of the priesthood. To define and frame the nature of this debate, Castellucci offers caricatures, or sketches, of the ecclesiological and christological perspectives[12]. Although exaggerations, they help to delineate the broad lines of contemporary theological approaches to the priesthood and set the context for later exploring priest as leader.

1.2.1 Christocentric Sketch

The first sketch presents an exclusively christocentric understanding of priesthood without any reference to ecclesiology. The formula *sacerdos alter Christus* best exemplifies this approach. In this perspective, the priesthood of Christ, the perfect mediator between God and humanity through his sacrifice on the cross, is directly communicated to the ordained priest. Consequently, the priest is understood as the mediator between Christ and the Church. Thus, the Church passively receives the graces offered by Christ through the mediation of the priest, who unites the sacrifice of the faithful with the sacrifice of Christ. The identity and mission of the priest essentially consists in his celebration of the sacraments, especially the Eucharist which represents Christ's sacrifice on Calvary. In this unnuanced christological perspective the weight of priestly identity falls almost completely on his identification with Christ the priest, present in the ministerial priest in a way that is superior to the laity[13].

1.2.2 Ecclesiocentric Sketch

The second sketch presents an ecclesiocentric understanding of the priesthood, rooted in the democratic claims noted above. Because the entire Church has received Christ's mission to preach the Gospel to the world, and because the Holy Spirit bestows various charisms in the Church, the ecclesiocentric view concludes that Christ did not institute an ordained priesthood: therefore, there is no sacramental priesthood that represents Christ to the Church in a specific way. Ordained ministry is strictly rooted in the community and determined by the need of the community for a ministry of presiding and coordination of charisms. The absence of a sacerdotal or cultic interpretation of ministry in the early centuries of the Church means that today's ministerial priesthood needs to be de-sacerdotalized. Because there is no permanent character,

---

12 Cf. E. CASTELLUCCI, «L'identità del presbitero», 97-101.
13 Cf. E. CASTELLUCCI, «L'identità del presbitero», 98.

no ontological configuration to Christ, and no consecration, ordination is understood as designation by the community, not consecration from on high. Thus priesthood is purely a function determined by the needs of the community[14].

The two perspectives, as presented above, are admittedly caricatures and represent extremes of the two points of view. They do, however, crystallize the nature of the contemporary debate surrounding the priesthood and sketch the arguments found in the christological and ecclesiological perspectives. They indicate the need for further precision and the integration of the two perspectives, since each one, properly understood, contains important elements of truth. Finally, they reveal what is at stake in the debate, namely the future of the ministerial priesthood in the Church. These two foundational perspectives, then, set the context for exploring the conciliar and postconciliar teaching on priesthood. In addition to the ecclesiological and christological perspectives, and flowing from them, a third foundational perspective, the pastoral perspective, or the actual lived experience of the priesthood embodied in the ministry and life of the priest, also frames the approach to the doctrine on the priesthood and must be considered in any exploration of contemporary teaching on ordained priesthood. Approaching the conciliar and postconciliar Church teaching on priesthood from the three perspectives — christological, ecclesiological, and pastoral — will yield a more integrated understanding of the ministerial priesthood, providing the foundation for sketching a portrait of the priest understood from the perspective of leadership.

1.3 *Doctrinal Foundations of Priesthood: Threefold Perspective*

A careful reading of the conciliar and postconciliar documents reveals a rich and complex doctrine of the ministerial priesthood. Within this doctrine some important assertions relative to priestly ministry and life are noticeable: 1) The priesthood is both incarnated in the Church and directed toward the Church (ecclesiological perspective). 2) The priesthood is rooted in a deep identification with Christ (christological perspective). 3) The ecclesiological and christological foundations yield a third perspective: the priesthood is expressed in a set of functions and relationships (pastoral perspective). The remainder of this chapter will explore these three themes as they appear in the conciliar and postconciliar documents mentioned above. This examination leads to conclusions

---

[14] Cf. E. CASTELLUCCI, «L'identità del presbitero», 99-100.

concerning the Council's contribution to an understanding of priest as leader. Although the christological perspective is still primary for an adequate understanding of the ministerial priesthood, we begin with the ecclesiological perspective, because it was both the main preoccupation of the Council and the basis for the Council's teaching on priesthood.

1.4 *Leadership Reading Key*

The notion of «leadership» requires some preliminary consideration. One necessarily approaches the conciliar and post-conciliar texts with a set of implicit and explicit assumptions about the themes contained in them. This is clearly the case with «leadership», which is central to this study. Assumptions about leadership, then, consciously or not, form a kind of key through which specific texts are interpreted. Furthermore, since the notion of leadership is open to a vast array of interpretations from various perspectives, both religious and secular, it is prudent and necessary, at the beginning, to articulate a general description of the notion of leadership, a description flexible and malleable enough to be given clearer definition as the study unfolds.

Bernard Cooke offers such a generalized description of leadership: «[...] leadership is not a specific function, much less an office. It is a broader and more basic reality, a capacity to inspire and direct and support a social group as it moves towards some goal. [...] it is composed of a number of qualities which particularly fit the needs of a given situation»[15]. Cooke notes that the Christian contribution to this understanding of leadership corresponds to the faith, hope, and charity which dwell at the very heart of the Christian community. The leader in such a community must live and operate out of the vision of faith, motivate people through the example of charity, and encourage people by instilling in them his or her own hope in Christ[16]. Although such a generalized description of Christian leadership does not spell out what is specific to the ministerial priesthood, it does offer a broad outline or sketch that can be employed as a key in approaching the texts in order to develop a more precise understanding of how this «basic reality» of leadership, this «capacity to inspire and direct», characterizes the ministerial priesthood. The doctrine on priesthood will be approached using this key.

---

[15] B. COOKE, *Ministry to Word and Sacrament*, 209.
[16] Cf. B. COOKE, *Ministry to Word and Sacrament*, 209.

2. The Priesthood: Rooted in the Church and Directed Toward The Church

2.1 *The Church as Mystery, Communion, Mission*

Before considering specific ecclesial themes that impinge on an interpretation of priest as leader, it is important to consider the broader context in which they developed. As noted above, the Council of Trent approached ordained priesthood from a primarily christological perspective, emphasizing its sacrificial and cultic dimensions, a perspective that dominated the Church's understanding until Vatican II, which, without in any way negating Trent. chose to approach the ordained priesthood from a different, primarily ecclesiological, perspective. The great contribution of Vatican II to the development of the Church's understanding of priesthood was to place it into a wider context, that of the whole Church. A brief consideration of the Church's self-understanding as articulated at the Second Vatican Council, therefore, leads to a better understanding and appreciation of the Church's teaching on the ordained priesthood.

The «Dogmatic Constitution on the Church», *Lumen Gentium*, offers such a self-understanding. It has been described as the document in which the Church seeks to answer a most fundamental question regarding its own existence: «What do you say of yourself?»[17]. In attempting to answer this question the document offers many different scriptural images to describe and convey the meaning of the Church: sheepfold, flock, field, vineyard, temple of God, household of God, holy city, spouse, mother, mystical body[18]. Although these images communicate a sense of the richness and complexity of the Church, there are three concepts or categories that are essential to understanding the Church as portrayed in *LG*. They are mystery, communion, and mission[19].

As a mystery, the Church is understood to be rooted in the Trinity and to spring forth from trinitarian life. It incarnates God's plan of salvation, a plan «[...] which was decreed by the Father, accomplished by

---

[17] Cf. G. PHILIPS, «Dogmatic Constitution on the Church», 107.

[18] Cf. *LG* 6 and 7.

[19] With these three words Pope John Paul II, in his Apostolic Exhortation, *Christifideles Laici*, synthesized the conciliar understanding of the Church. The Church «[...] is *mystery* because the very life and love of the Father, Son and Holy Spirit are the gift gratuitously offered to all those who are born of water and the Holy Spirit (cf. Jn 3,5), and called to relive the very *communion* of God and to manifest it and communicate it in history (*mission*)» (*CL* 8). Cf. *AAS* 81 (1989) 393-521. For a discussion of the impact of conciliar ecclesiology on the understanding of priesthood, see L. GALLO, «Il presbitero nella Chiesa, mistero, comunione e missione», 103-109.

the redemptive Incarnation of the Son, and implemented by the mission of the Spirit in the community of the Church as a visible organ of union with the divine persons»[20]. As a mystery, the Church is rooted in the dynamic love of God, expressed by the Trinity, whose mystery continues to unfold in the life of the Church[21].

The unfolding of this mystery is expressed in the concept of communion[22]. The communion of the Church is structured in the image of the trinitarian life of God which is depicted as a dynamic life of mutual love and union. Each person of the Trinity, while distinct, dwells in union in the one Godhead. As a mirror or icon of God[23] the Church can be understood as the communion, in Christ, of distinct persons in a common life of faith rooted in the life of God. Understood from the perspective of communion the Church can then be called a sacrament, that is, both a sign and an instrument of union with God[24].

---

[20] G. PHILIPS, «Dogmatic Constitution on the Church», 111.

[21] Cf. *LG*, 2-4. In opting for an understanding of ecclesiology as being rooted in the mystery of the Trinity, Vatican II made a distinct shift from the preconciliar ecclesiology which emphasized the socio-juridical nature of the Church, to a profoundly theological understanding of the Church. Cf. L. GALLO, «Il presbitero nella chiesa», 103-104; A. ANTÓN, «Postconciliar Ecclesiology», vol. 1, 412-413.

[22] Cf. *CL* 8. It is precisely in the ecclesiology of communion that the exaggerated claims, noted above, came to be made about the Church; i.e., understanding it in terms of democracy, with ministry merely being a designation by the community in order to have its needs met. For a response to a reductive, exclusively horizontal understanding of the Church as communion, see CDF, «Letter to the Bishops of the Catholic Church on Some Aspects of the Church Understood as Communion», *AAS* 85 (1993) 838-850. The letter makes five essential points: 1) Communion, understood as an ontological reality, entails vertical, horizontal, invisible and visible dimensions whose links constitute the Church as sacrament; 2) The universal Church is not a sum or federation of particular Churches; in reality they take their origin from the universal Church which is prior to them; 3) Communion is rooted in the unity of the Eucharist and in the unity of the episcopate, both of which are intrinsically linked to the mystery of the Church; 4) The unity of the Church fosters a diversity of charisms and ministries which in turn build up the unity of the Church; 5) The Petrine ministry is constitutive of the Church, understood as communion, and has important ecumenical ramifications. Cf. *OR*, «Ultimately There Is One Basic Ecclesiology», 17 June 1992, 1.10.

[23] For descriptions of the Church as the icon of God, see M. A. FAHEY, «Church», vol. 2, 33-34; B. FORTE, *The Trinity as History*, 206-210.

[24] Cf. *LG* 1: «By her relationship with Christ, the Church is a kind of sacrament or sign of intimate union with God, and of the unity of all mankind. She is also an instrument for the achievement of such union and unity». *GS* 24 states: «[...] the Lord Jesus [...] has opened up new horizons closed to human reason by implying that there is a certain parallel between the union existing among the divine persons and the union of the sons of God in truth and love».

This communion finds its origins in the life of Jesus and the Apostles. Consecrated and commissioned by the Father, in the power of the Spirit, Jesus undertook his mission to the world by first gathering a community around himself. From this group of disciples he chose the Twelve to be in a particular relationship with him. This gathering of disciples and Apostles perdured after Jesus' death and resurrection but can only be understood as «Church» in the context of the entire paschal mystery. It is the whole process of the incarnation, crucifixion, resurrection and glorification of Christ, and the outpouring of the Holy Spirit that forms the context for understanding the communion of the Church[25].

As communion, the Church must necessarily include the notion of mission as constitutive of its self-understanding. Rooted in the Paschal Mystery, the communion of the Church is permeated by the Spirit sent by Christ, so that it shares the very life of Christ. As the sacrament of Christ, the communion of the Church cannot be closed in on itself because it shares in his very mission. The concept of mission is thus central to conciliar ecclesiology. LG describes the Church in three places as the universal sacrament of salvation (cf. LG 1, 3, 48). As sacrament, the Church is the place of encounter with Christ — the place of communion — because it is thoroughly permeated by his word and in its work it embodies his mission to the world. The mission of Christ is thus prior to the Church and constitutive of the Church[26]. Jesus Christ is at the center of the Church, understood not only as communion but also as mission, because wherever there is communion there is mission; communion is both the source and the goal of the Church's mission[27].

Since the Council, the concepts of mystery, communion, and mission (to be developed more fully in Chapter Three) frame any consideration of the ministerial priesthood. The ministerial priesthood, considered as a sacrament, expresses in a particular way Christ's faithful presence in and

---

[25] Cf. A. GRILLMEIER, «The Mystery of the Church», CVD, vol. 1, Chap I, 141.

[26] A. Hastings observes, «It is, therefore, somewhat misleading to say that the Church has a mission, as if the existence of the Church comes first. In truth it is because of the mission that there is a Church; the Church is the servant and expression of the mission», A. HASTINGS, «Mission», 968.

[27] R. D. Haight notes that the concept of the Church as mission, like communion, is irreducible to a type, model or paradigm: «It is not a theology or a description of a theology but the basis for a theology. Thus the symbol points to or mediates a fundamental perception or self-understanding that is both inclusive and exclusive. As inclusive, it includes or embraces within itself and does not negate a pluralism of models or images for understanding the Church. But at the same time, all valid models of the Church must meet its demands», R. D. HAIGHT, «The "Established" Church as Mission», 10.

to his body, the Church. The ministerial priesthood is rooted in the communion of the Church and exists for the sake of this communion, which expresses itself in mission. It is ultimately rooted in the very mystery of the Trinity, who in the economy of salvation established the Church and the priesthood to serve the Church.

With this understanding of the Church as mystery, communion, and mission as a foundation, three important ecclesial concepts articulated by the Council and determinative of an understanding of the ministerial priesthood, and especially of the priest as leader, require examination. These concepts are: 1) the common priesthood as context for the ministerial priesthood; 2) the episcopacy as the fullness of Holy Orders; and 3) the presbyterate as a primary category for understanding the ministerial priesthood.

2.2 *The Common Priesthood as Context for the Ministerial Priesthood*

2.2.1 The Common Priesthood

The Council's recovery of the doctrine of the common priesthood of all the baptized was a momentous development, both ecclesiologically and in terms of its impact on the understanding of ordained ministry. First, it recognized and promoted the essential and active role that lay people have in the Church's mission, affirming that they are no longer to be understood as passive bystanders or recipients of the Church's ministry, but as active participants in it. Second, it emphasized that, prior to differences in the Church, there is a profound unity based on the common participation of all the baptized in the one priesthood of Christ. It is the common participation in Christ's one priesthood that marks the Church as a royal priesthood and confers on the baptized a common identity[28].

The Council's emphasis on the common priesthood of the faithful was not without some controversy[29]. Some tried to substitute the adjective «common» with «initial», «certain», or «spiritual». The Theological Commission, however, decided on the term «common priesthood», which is shared by all the baptized and not eliminated in priestly ordination[30]. Because Luther used the rediscovery of the ancient tradition of

---

[28] Cf. P. J. DRILLING, «Common and Ministerial Priesthood», 85.

[29] See P. J. DRILLING, «Common and Ministerial Priesthood», 81-87, for an account of the development of the use of the category «common priesthood» in *LG* 10.

[30] Cf. A. GRILLMEIER, «The People of God», *CDV*, vol. 1, Chap. II, 157; D. DONOVAN, *What Are They Saying About the Ministerial Priesthood?*, 7; P. J. DRILLING, «Common and Ministerial Priesthood», 85.

the common priesthood to denigrate the ministerial priesthood[31], there
were some bishops at the Council who were hesitant to adopt it as a basic
category for understanding the mission of the Church[32], even though
Catholic theology had begun to use the theory in the 1930's and it had
some influence on Pius XII's *Mediator Dei*[33]. Despite these reservations
the concept was used and had profound ramifications for the Church's
understanding of ministry as expressed in the Council and in subsequent
teaching.

Before examining the particular conciliar texts that developed the
doctrine of the common priesthood, it is important to briefly examine
the notion of priesthood, considered generically. In general terms, without a specifically Christian connotation, priesthood can be described as
«[...] the state of one consecrated or set apart to offer sacrifice to
God»[34]. In Old Testament times the purpose of offering sacrifice was
to show reverence, awe, and faithfulness before God. Priesthood and the
sacrifice that it necessarily entailed was revelatory of one's fundamental
stance towards life; that is to say, it was the embodiment of one's
disposition of soul[35]. Priesthood thus implied an intrinsic connection
between the witness of one's life and the worship offered to God. The
continual danger, however, was the breaking of this intrinsic connection
and splitting off one's life from one's worship. Such a division reduced
worship to mere formalism. It was this formalism — compartmentalized,
unintegrated, externalized, and divorced from lived experience — that
the prophets denounced[36]. This background is important for understanding the Christian notion of the common priesthood.

In articulating its doctrinal understanding of the ministerial priesthood
in *PO* the Council began its description by placing the ministerial priesthood in the context of the common priesthood:

> The Lord Jesus, «whom the Father has made holy and sent into the world»
> (Jn 10,36), has made His whole Mystical Body share in the anointing by the
> Spirit with which He Himself has been anointed. For in Him all the faithful
> are made a holy and royal priesthood (*PO* 2).

---

[31] Cf. A. HASTINGS, *A Concise Guide to the Documents of the Second Vatican Council,* vol. 1, 80; D. ORR, «The Giving of the Priesthood to the Faithful», 72.

[32] Cf. D. DONOVAN, *What Are They Saying About the Ministerial Priesthood?*, 7.

[33] Cf. A. HASTINGS, *Concise Guide to the Documents*, vol. 1, 81.

[34] A. HASTINGS, *Concise Guide to the Documents*, vol. 1, 81.

[35] Cf. K. MCNAMARA, *The Church*, 115-116.

[36] Cf. Y. CONGAR, «Le Sacerdoce du nouveau testament», 252.

This both echoes and develops an earlier statement from *LG* which stated that through baptism all «[...] are consecrated into a spiritual house and a holy priesthood» (*LG* 10). Later, the same text specifies some elements of this common priesthood: participation in the Eucharist, reception of the sacraments, prayer and thanksgiving, the witness of a holy life, self-denial, and charity (cf. *LG* 10).

The Council's teaching on the common priesthood relies on 1Pt 2,4-10, and highlights the dignity conferred by the priesthood on all believers. The teaching emphasizes two aspects of the common priesthood: 1) the new life of grace that gives the Christian access to God, according priestly efficacy to his or her good deeds; and 2) «[...] the action of the Holy Spirit in taking possession of the Christian and setting him apart for worship»[37]. The common priesthood is thus expressed not only in ritual worship but in holiness of life.

Following in the tradition of the prophets, the priesthood of Jesus (to be developed below in the christological section) emphasized, not mere ritual sacrifice, but the offering of one's entire life to God[38]. Christian priesthood is rooted in the one priesthood of Jesus Christ whose one sacrifice «[...] was utterly acceptable, and nothing separate from it or adding to its value can ever be offered»[39]. His priesthood is thus the model and pattern for the priesthood of all believers who participate in his priesthood by living holy lives[40]. In baptism they are consecrated and set apart to witness in word and deed to the presence of Christ in their lives, and in doing so, offer themselves as a sacrifice to God. This priesthood reaches its climax and is most fully expressed in the Eucharist which unites the sacrifice of the baptized — that is, the offering of their lives — to the one perfect sacrifice of Jesus[41]. This approach to priesthood leaves no room for mere formalism or compartmentalization, but rather engages the baptized in the totality of their lives. The intrinsic connection between the witness of a holy life and the worship offered to God is crucial for understanding the concept of the common priesthood.

This fundamental priestly identification is intrinsic to the Church's self-definition and is closely related to the sacramentality of the Church emphasized earlier. Because the Church continues the mission of Christ,

---

37 K. MCNAMARA, *The Church*, 114.

38 Cf. Y. CONGAR, «Le Sacerdoce du nouveau testament», 252-253; P. J. DUNN, *Priesthood*, 102.

39 A. HASTINGS, *Concise Guide to the Documents*, vol. 1, 81.

40 Cf. K. MCNAMARA, *The Church*, 116.

41 Cf. P. J. DUNN, *Priesthood*, 102.

it necessarily includes his priestly mission which reached its culmination in his sacrifice on Calvary. The priestly, *kenotic,* dynamism so characteristic of Jesus' own life is at the very core of the Church's identity. The designation of the Church as sacrament means that it is priestly and must bear witness to Christ's presence alive in it. The holiness of life, that is to say the self-sacrificing love which members of the Church exhibit, makes Christ's sacrificial love present to the world[42]. The witness to the power of God is the foundation for corporate Christian worship, which the doctrine of the common priesthood emphasizes. Such corporate emphasis, however, also includes room for individual expression. Just as the entire Church can be characterized as priestly, so each baptized individual is priestly insofar as he or she participates in the life of the Church and embodies its priestly patterns in everyday life[43].

The concept of a universal, or common priesthood, defines Christians and expresses the kind of lives they must lead to identify themselves as belonging to Christ. The common priesthood, then, consists in holy conduct, spiritual sacrifice, witness to God's power, and prayer. «Believers are priests because they express in their everyday lives and relationships the transcendent grace and holiness [...] of God»[44]. Understood in this way, the common priesthood is not a metaphor for official Church ministry[45]: «[...] it is not accompanied by an authority comparable to the authority conferred on the Twelve, nor does it entail a Pastoral mission»[46]. Rather, it expresses the basic identity of all the baptized, ordained and unordained, and the kinds of lives to which they are called: lives patterned on Christ.

2.2.2 The Ministerial Priesthood
in Light of the Common Priesthood

The Council's strong affirmation of the common priesthood of all the baptized caused some questions to be raised about the nature and even the necessity of the ministerial priesthood[47]. Consequently, the Council Fathers needed to articulate and define the ministerial priesthood both in

---

[42] Cf. B. COOKE, *Ministry to Word and Sacrament*, 640-641.

[43] Cf. P. J. DRILLING, «Common and Ministerial Priesthood», 88-89, on the corporate and individual nature of the common priesthood.

[44] N. MITCHELL, *Mission and Ministry*, 284.

[45] Cf. N. MITCHELL, *Mission and Ministry*, 284.

[46] J. GALOT, *Theology of the Priesthood*, 18.

[47] Cf. B. KLOPPENBURG, *Ecclesiology of Vatican II*, 263-265.

its relation to and distinction from the common priesthood. They did so in *LG* 10, *LG* 28, and *PO* 2. In these descriptions of the distinctiveness of the ministerial priesthood, the notion of leadership begins to emerge in a rather general way.

LG 10 offers a crucial beginning in describing, not only the relation ship, but also the distinction between the two modes of priesthood:

Though they differ from one another in essence and not only in degree, the common priesthood of the faithful and the ministerial or hierarchical priesthood are nonetheless interrelated. Each of them in its own special way is a participation in the one priesthood of Christ. The ministerial priest, by the sacred power he enjoys, molds and rules the priestly people. Acting in the person of Christ, he brings about the Eucharistic Sacrifice, and offers it to God in the name of all the people.

This text, then, offers an introduction to what is distinctive about the ministerial priesthood and how it relates to the common priesthood[48]. It is immediately apparent that the priesthood received in the sacrament of ordination is «ministerial or hierarchical», terms to be clarified.

a) *Ministerial and Hierarchical*

Affirming the ordained priesthood as ministerial means that service is at its core. Similarly, affirming its hierarchical character acknowledges that it has some role of sacred authority or leadership[49]. The hierarchical function must be understood in the light of the assertion that the difference between the two modes of priesthood is a matter of essence and not merely degree[50]. In other words, «hierarchical» is used not in the sense

---

[48] *The Catechism of the Catholic Church* describes the relationship in this way: «While the common priesthood of the faithful is exercised by the unfolding of baptismal grace — a life of faith, hope and charity, a life according to the Spirit, the ministerial priesthood is at the service of the common priesthood. It is directed at the unfolding of the baptismal grace of all Christians. The ministerial priesthood is the *means* by which Christ builds up and leads his Church. For this reason it is transmitted by its own sacrament, the sacrament of Holy Orders», *CCC*, par. 1547, 346.

[49] Drilling observes, «"Hierarchical" refers to grades within the holy people and acknowledges that some have the role of *arche* or leadership; they preside over holy people and holy things. "Ministerial" also refers to this role of presiding over the holy, but it refers as well to another aspect of ordained priesthood, one often emphasized in the documents of the Council, namely, its responsibility to be of service to the whole priestly people. "Hierarchical" and "ministerial" are thus not so much synonymous (which might be one reading of *"seu"* as it appears in the text as the conjunctive) as coexistent and complementary», P. J. DRILLING, «Common and Ministerial Priesthood», 89.

[50] *MP* I.4 makes the same distinction between the ministerial and common priesthood. In a discussion of the phrase «[...] they differ from one another in essence and not

of indicating a rank of superiority; the ministerial priest is not «more» of a priest than a non-ordained person nor is he to be understood as a kind of «super-Christian»[51]. The ministerial priesthood is, however, essentially and qualitatively different from the common priesthood and is understood to include dimensions of service and leadership.

In *LG* 10, then, the faint outlines of the leadership associated with the ordained priesthood begin to emerge. «Ministerial» and «hierarchical» modify the nature of such leadership. Service sets the context for a leadership that is dedicated to the Church. Such leadership, in turn, gives definition to the service that is at the heart of the ministerial priesthood. This is not to say that the members of the common priesthood do not exercise leadership in the Church, but rather that the ordained priesthood, in its very essence, is to be understood by the service of leadership that it offers the Church. The remainder of the Council's teaching on the ministerial priesthood fills out what in *LG* 10 is an admittedly vague, undifferentiated notion.

b) *Sacramental Character from an Ecclesiological Perspective*

The faint outlines of *LG* 10 are given clearer definition in *LG* 28 and *PO* 2, which through the principle of sacramentality explain the essential difference between the common and ministerial priesthood and indicate the profound meaning of the leadership associated with ordained

---

only in degree», M. Richards contends that the phrase has often been misinterpreted to mean that the two modes differ in essence *and* in degree, but in reality, the phrase sets «degree» aside completely: «It is saying that if you want to understand what difference ordination makes, you must look for an *essential* difference, a difference *in kind* not a mere difference of degree: degree simply does not enter into it», M. RICHARDS, «Hierarchy and Priesthood», 229. In a more nuanced approach which understands the phrase to mean essence *and* degree, Peter Fink stresses that «degree», as used in *LG* 10, does not connote a quantitative gradation but rather specifies the degree of personal investment that the priest must have in Word, Sacrament and pastoral care. Cf. P. FINK, «The Priesthood of Jesus Christ in the Ministry and Life of the Ordained», 73-77. Similarly, H. Alphonso stresses that the distinction between the hierarchical and common priesthood is a qualitative rather than quantitative difference: «[...] the ministerial priest in the Church is not cut off from the body of the faithful who are all "priests" with that common or universal Christian priesthood in the one priesthood of Jesus Christ: he is rather the *qualitative concentration or intensification* (the operative word [...] is *qualitative*) of that one priesthood of Jesus Christ in a way all peculiarly and qualitatively his own as ministerial priest» [emphasis in original], H. ALPHONSO, «The Spirituality of the Diocesan Priest Today», 3-4. Cf. G. GRESHAKE, *The Meaning of Christian Priesthood*, 69-72.

[51] A comment made by Congar in his critique of a doctoral dissertation; cited by R. BEAUCHESNE, «Worship as Life, Priesthood and Sacrifice in Yves Congar», 96.

priesthood. *LG* 28 affirms that it is through «[...] the power of the sacrament of Orders» that ministerial priests are «[...] consecrated to preach the Gospel, shepherd the faithful, and celebrate divine worship as true priests of the New Testament». Similarly, *PO* 2 connects the ministerial priesthood to «[...] that special sacrament through which priests, by the anointing of the Holy Spirit, are marked with a special character and are so configured to Christ the Priest that they can act in the person of Christ the Head». The sacrament and the character it confers constitute the distinctiveness of the ministerial priesthood and determine its relationship to the common priesthood.

Because those who are baptized and confirmed and those who are ordained participate in the one priesthood of Christ, called «[...] to bring God to the world and to bring the world to encounter God»[52], [...] the difference between the two lies at the level of essence or ontology. Another way to express it is through the traditional teaching on sacramental character. It is of the essence of those who participate in the common priesthood, through the character received in baptism and confirmation, to participate in Christ's threefold ministry of word, sacrament and pastoral witness. It is also of the essence of the ministerial priest to participate in this same threefold ministry. He participates in it, however, in a qualitatively different way because of the character received in the sacrament of Orders. Each modality of priesthood, while rooted in the one priesthood of Christ, enjoys a special ontological relationship with him that both distinguishes them from one another and profoundly orients them towards one another[53]. In light of affirmations of *LG* 28 and *PO* 2 regarding the ministerial priesthood, this distinction from and orientation to can be understood as the service of leadership.

In an important essay which attempted to root the leadership function of the ministerial priest in the sacramental character conferred by the sacrament of Orders, Kasper asserted that «[...] interpersonal relations are the highest ontological reality»[54], which not only determine a person's activities but affect the person on the level of his or her being. From this perspective, the leadership function, which entails a relationship between persons, penetrates to the very core of the priest, determining both his identity and activity. The character conferred by the

---

[52] P. J. DRILLING, «Common and Ministerial Priesthood», 94.

[53] Cf. P. J. ROSATO, «Priesthood of the Baptized and Priesthood of the Ordained», 220.

[54] W. KASPER, «A New Dogmatic Outlook on the Priestly Ministry», 27.

sacrament of orders, then, cannot be understood as a static concept which leads to separateness or notions of clerical superiority[55]. Rather, it is a dynamic concept that points to the fact that the priest, on the level of his being, has been claimed by Christ for a specific relationship of service to the Church, a relationship which is manifest in the activities of his leadership.

Because the doctrine of the relation and distinction between the ministerial and common priesthood is couched in the ontological language of essence and character, it may not be immediately accessible to many people today. Rosato offers a helpful way to understand the dual modes of the one priesthood: the analogy of the nucleus and body of an organic cell. The cell itself is made up of the body (common priesthood) and the nucleus (ministerial priesthood) which, while distinct from each other, are fundamentally ordered to each other in a dynamic way for the life of the cell (the Church). The two modes of priesthood, although ontologically distinct, are fundamentally related to each other for the life of the Church[56]. Again, the articulation of such a relationship implies in its very nature a basic function of leadership as associated with the ministerial priesthood.

The difference, then, between the common and ministerial priesthood is not primarily jurisdictional but sacramental. Categories such as «greater or lesser», «rights or powers», «domination or subordination», do not do justice to the Council's teaching. The difference is «[...] on the level of significant and effective symbol. In his distinctive relation to the rest of the community the priest is an effective sign that Christ is the Lord of the Church and is present in it with his saving work»[57]. This distinction underscores the ministerial priesthood as not merely a *quantitative* intensification of the common priesthood but rather, as *qualitatively* different[58], though rooted in and directed toward the common priesthood. Of their very nature, the common and the ministerial modes of priesthood are ordained to each other, through participation in the priesthood of Christ, although they share in his priesthood in a different

---

[55] P. Fransen claims that in the past «"character" [...] has promoted a mythic theology of the priesthood which places it on a higher level of being than the rest of the faithful, a metaphysical clericalism which is responsible for barring the way to many reforms at the present time», P. FRANSEN, «Orders and Ordination», *SM*, vol. 4, 324.

[56] Cf. P. J. ROSATO, «Priesthood of the Baptized and Priesthood of the Ordained», 222, for further elaboration of the nucleus-body-cell analogy.

[57] G. GRESHAKE, *Meaning of Christian Priesthood*, 71-72.

[58] Cf. H. ALPHONSO, «Spirituality of the Diocesan Priest Today», 3-4.

way[59]. Taken as a whole, the Council, and later the Synod of 1971 (cf. *MP* 1.4), offer a balanced, complementary understanding of the ministerial priesthood in relation to the common priesthood. The ontological language they use to describe the relationship between the two, understood correctly, is not static, but indeed offers a dynamic and holistic understanding of the priesthood as it is embodied in the two modes, providing a basis for beginning to understand leadership as not only a simple function of the ministerial priesthood but as part of its very essence.

In this examination of the relation and distinction of the common and ministerial modes of priesthood, the perspective of priest as leader begins to emerge more clearly. The leadership of the priest is understood at this point to be rooted, not in functions, skills, or personal qualities of the priest himself, but in the sacrament of ordination, which confers on him a sacred character and puts him into a distinct relation to the common priesthood. The nature of such leadership is not clearly defined, except to say that it must be understood in the context of service: ministerial priests «[...] are called to serve the people of God» by gathering them together «[...] as a brotherhood all of one mind» and leading them «[...] in the Spirit, through Christ, to God the Father» (cf. *LG* 28). In examining the rest of the doctrine on the ministerial priesthood, the nature and patterns of this leadership, which is essentially associated with ordination, will be delineated and the portrait of the priest as leader will begin to emerge more clearly.

2.3 *The Ministerial Priesthood in Relation to the Episcopacy*

As noted above, the teaching on the sacramental nature of the episcopacy, as possessing the fullness of Holy Orders, is one of the most important doctrinal contributions of the Council[60] and must be considered in any study of conciliar teaching on the ministerial priesthood. Because this study is limited to the examination of the documents from the perspective of priest as leader, and because of the abundant coverage of the episcopal office in the Vatican II documents, (cf. *LG* 18-27 and all of *Christus Dominus*), the theology of the episcopacy cannot be treated in depth here[61]. Some reference to the salient points about the bishop-priest

---

59 Cf. A. GRILLMEIER, «The People of God», *CVD*, vol. 1, Chap. II, 158.

60 Cf., for example, J. GALOT, *Theology of the Priesthood*, 183.

61 For commentaries on the Council's teaching on the office of bishop, see K. MÖRSDORF, «Decree on the Bishop's Pastoral Office in the Church», vol. 2,

relationship, however, will help to develop and deepen an understanding of the ecclesiological context begun above in the analysis of the relation and distinction between the ministerial and common modes of the priesthood.

2.3.1 Clarification of Doctrine

For centuries the priesthood of the second order, that is the presbyterate, was assumed to be the fundamental priestly order. Because the priest had the power to celebrate the Eucharist and consecrate the Body of Christ, it was thought that he possessed the fullness of priesthood. St. Thomas was thus able to assert, «The whole fullness of this sacrament is to be found in one order, namely priesthood; the other degrees represent participations in the sacrament»[62]. Understood in this way, there was no essential difference between priest and bishop; the bishop was simply a priest with greater jurisdictional powers, which were given to him, not sacramentally, but in a juridical act[63].

In a marked departure from this juridical understanding of episcopal office, the Council emphasized that bishops possess the «fullness» rather than the «highest degree» of orders (cf. *LG* 21) and that priests «[...] are dependent on the bishops in the exercise of their power» (*LG* 28). *PO* 1 acknowledges that priests receive their mission from the bishop[64] but it makes an important clarification in the section describing the apostolic succession: «Their ministerial role has been handed down to them in a limited degree» (*PO* 2). This clarification therefore nuances the assertion in *LG* 28 that the bishops have «[...] handed on to different individuals in the Church various degrees of participation in this ministry». This statement from *LG* 28 appears to imply that priesthood originates it the episcopacy, whereas *PO* 2, although not specifically addressing the historical question of the institution of the priesthood, makes it clear that it originates in Christ. The Synod of 1971 shows awareness of the

---

165-300; K. RAHNER, «Chapter III», *CDV*, vol. 1, 186-218; CB, *Directory on the Pastoral Ministry of Bishops*. For studies on the role of bishop, see R. BROWN, *Priest and Bishop*; A. CUNNINGHAM, *The Bishop in the Church*; K. RAHNER, *Bishops*.

[62] ST. THOMAS AQUINAS, *Summa Theologiae, Supplementum*, q. 37, a. 1, ad. 2, as cited in B. KLOPPENBURG, *The Ecclesiology of Vatican II*, 266.

[63] Cf. B. KLOPPENBURG, *Ecclesiology of Vatican II*, 266; F. WULF, «Commentary on the Decree», 224.

[64] For an analysis of the «missionary chain» described in *LG* 28 and *PO* 2, which places priestly ministry in the context of the bishops' ministry and thus that of the Church, see E. CASTELLUCCI, «L'identità del presbitero», 104-105.

subtlety of the issue by stating, «Bishops and, on a subordinate level, priests by virtue of the sacrament of Orders, which confers an anointing of the Holy Spirit and configures to Christ», share in Christ's priestly ministry (*MP* I.4). Although the bishop ordains the priest, the priest is configured not to the bishop but to Christ, whose consecration and mission he receives.

The Council's teaching on the episcopacy, as embodying the fullness of priesthood, represented a shift in consciousness from an extrinsic, juridical understanding to a more holistic perspective that does justice to the sacramental understanding of the priesthood: «[...] the participation in the sacrament which Christ bestows on priests is granted in full to the bishop»[65]. The teaching on episcopal office as holding the fullness of priesthood ended any speculation which attributed the status of the bishop simply to a matter of jurisdiction: «Episcopal consecration is the primary and comprehensive instance of sacramental ordination»[66]. The bishop is not, therefore, merely a priest with greater jurisdictional powers. Such a shift in the understanding of the episcopacy from a predominantly juridical to a more sacramental perspective is significant. In the past, the bishop was seen primarily as a vicar of the pope, who bestowed jurisdiction, rather than as a vicar of Christ. In the Council, however, the sacramental emphasis on the nature of the episcopacy changes this perspective. The bishop receives the charism of his office from God, which configures him to Christ; as a member of the Apostolic College, then, the bishop is understood as a vicar of Christ[67], not of the pope.

2.3.2 Implications for the Ministerial Priesthood

Grillmeier has noted that this development in the understanding of the episcopacy as possessing the fullness of Orders has significant ramifications for the Church and for the ministerial priesthood:

> It is here that its origin in Christ and its significance for the whole Church are most easily grasped. One must always begin with this original fullness and unity of the office if one is to recognize that the Church has received, along with this very unity and fullness, the authority to introduce a graded

---

[65] G. PHILIPS, «Dogmatic Constitution on the Church», 116. Cf. J. GALOT, *Theology of the Priesthood*, 184.

[66] J. DUNN, *Priesthood*, 104.

[67] Cf. B. KLOPPENBURG, *Ecclesiology of Vatican II*, 222-223. It is to be noted that the power the bishop receives is exercised in the context of hierarchic communion and thus subject to juridical regulation. This does not, however, diminish the full sacramentality of his identity.

participation and distribution of the priestly ministry or to alter this course in time[68].

The significance of the teaching on the episcopacy for priests is that, although their office is dependent upon the bishops, they share in the priesthood in such a way that they are priests in a genuine sense. The sacred character received at ordination configures priests to Christ in such a way that they are able, with the bishop, to officially engage in the threefold ministry (to be examined below) of Christ the Priest.

Within the focus of this study, priest as leader, the teaching on the relation of ministerial priest to bishop is significant in at least three ways. First, it broadens the context of the ministerial priesthood to the entire mission of Christ and the Church, so that it is no longer «[...] exhausted by a role in relation to the Eucharist»[69]. Second, it emphasizes the notion of accountability. The priest does not exercise authority as an independent agent but as a «co-worker of the episcopal order» (*PO* 2), which makes him accountable for his decisions and his actions. In the larger context of his identity and mission, he is responsible to a higher authority, namely the bishop. Third, the connection of priest to bishop emphasizes the notion of collegiality and collaboration. The priest does not exercise his ministry in isolation but in hierarchical communion[70]. The larger context to which he belongs, namely the Church symbolized by the bishop, assures that his ministry is organically connected to the whole Church. Such collaboration cannot be reduced to a function, but is rooted in the communion of the Church and expressed in the structure of the sacrament of Orders which puts the priest in a particular relation to the Church. In summary, the teaching on the relation of the priesthood to the episcopacy broadens the priest's leadership function, revealing it as intrinsically accountable, collegial, and collaborative.

---

[68] A. GRILLMEIER, «The Hierarchical Structure of the Church», *CDV*, vol. 1, 221.

[69] B. KLOPPENBURG, *Ecclesiology of Vatican II*, 273.

[70] The *Directory on the Ministry and Life of Priests* states that such hierarchical communion establishes «[...] some precise ties [between the ministerial priesthood and] the Pope, the College of Bishops and each one's diocesan Bishop». It goes on to say, «Hierarchical communion is vividly expressed in the Eucharistic prayers; when the priest prays for the Pope, the College of Bishops and his own Bishop, he not only expresses a sentiment of devotion, but attests to the authenticity of his celebration as well», CC, *DMLP*, pars. 22 -23, pp. 23-24.

2.4 *Recovery of the Category of Presbyter*

An important ecclesiological development relative to the ministerial priesthood was the Council's recovery of the presbyterate as the proper category in which to locate the priesthood of the second order. This in turn has important implications for understanding the fundamental identity of the priest as leader. Even a brief glance at the evolution of the conciliar decree on the priesthood, along with its various titles, reveals a development in the Council Fathers' understanding, culminating in the recovery of the category of presbyterate. Initially the document was entitled *De Clericis* (1962). After taking account of the feedback of the Council Fathers, the next redaction was entitled *De Sacerdotibus* (1963), and at the third session of the Council the title was changed once again, this time to *De Vita et Ministerio Sacerdotali*. The final text, approved in 1965, was entitled *De Presbyterorum Ministerio et Vita*[71].

2.4.1 «Presbyter» in the Early Church

As the evolution of titles indicates, during the course of the Council's deliberations the topic changed from «clergy» to «priests» (*sacerdotes*) and finally, in order to achieve the precision desired by the Council Fathers, the topic became *presbyters*, «[...] corresponding to the traditional hierarchical ladder of bishops, presbyters, and deacons»[72]. In its very title, therefore, the decree requires close attention because the shift from *sacerdos* to *presbyter* is significant. The Latin word *sacerdos* is the equivalent of the Greek word *hiereus*, referring to priests usually associated with a temple cult — figures who «[...] were well known in the life of Israel. The great temple of Jerusalem, with its extensive and rich sacrificial ritual, was presided over by members of the tribe of Levi»[73]. *Presbyter*, however, has a different meaning[74]. Rooted in Hellenistic Judaism, the word designates the council of elders in Christian congregations. Ignatius of Antioch linked the hierarchical position of the presbyter with that of the Apostle[75]. The growth of a presbyterate, or

---

71 For a review of the chronological elements of the evolution of *PO*, see J. FRISQUE, «Le décret "Presbyterorum Ordinis"», 124-126; F. WULF, «Commentary on the Decree», 210.

72 F. WULF, «Commentary on the Decree», 210.

73 F. WULF, «Commentary on the Decree», 210.

74 For an analysis of *presbyter*, see A. LEMAIRE, *Les ministères aux origines de l'église*, 17-27.184.197; G. BORNKAMM, «*Presbyteros*», *TDNT*, vol. 6, 651-683.

75 Cf. G. BORNKAMM, «*Presbyteros*», 654.

body of elders, is linked to the disappearance of the Twelve and the growth of the Church, which needed people who were older[76] and tested to serve as a *presbyterium*[77]. Thus from a very early time in the Church's life, the title *presbyter* described the office of a leader[78].

2.4.2 Use of «Sacerdos» in Place of «Presbyter»

Initially, the early Christian community avoided the use of the word *sacerdos*, even though their leaders were probably assuming presidential roles at liturgies, especially Eucharist. This is possibly because the early Christian communities were not conscious of being a new religion or that their activities could be considered cultic in the sense of pagan and Jewish temple cults. They had no liturgical accoutrements such as vestments, sacred vessels, etc.; there were no «sacred» persons and no distinguishing cultic activities. Wulf observes, «Quite simply, there was no place to attach the idea that one had to have [...] priests in the cultic sense [...] *sacerdotes* [...] as in Judaism or in the other religions»[79]. Initially, there were leaders, teachers, deacons, and presbyters. Not until Pope Clement (c. 93-97), is «*sacerdos*» employed to designate the leaders at Eucharistic worship[80]. Dunn notes that some «[...] passages in Cyprian and in the *Didascalia* suggest that the presbyters share in the priesthood (*sacerdotium*) with the bishop, but the term priest is not explicitly applied to them»[81]. *Presbyter* was thus initially the basic category for understanding what came to be known as the priesthood of the second order.

---

[76] Lemaire notes that in the Jewish world the title *presbyteros* while signifying an elder, referred more to wisdom than to chronological age: «[...] les oeuvres de Philon supposent que le terme »presbytéros» est un titre qui ne dépend pas de l'âge mais de la sagesse, et ce titre est souvent mis en parallèle avec d'autres fonctions: archontes, docteurs. [...] D'après Philon, le choix et l'installation des soixante-dix par Moïse sont l'origine et l'archétype de l'institution des *présbytéroi*», A. LEMAIRE, *Les ministères aux origines de l'église*, 25.

[77] Cf. G. BORNKAMM, «*Presbyteros*», 663.

[78] For a description of the convergence of patterns in the early Church leading to establishment of the presbyterate as a component of the tripartite structure of ministry, see F. WULF, «Commentary on the Decree», 210; R. BROWN, *Priest and Bishop*, 5-43; J. DUNN, *Priesthood*, 65.

[79] F. WULF, «Commentary on the Decree», 211.

[80] Cf. F. WULF, «Commentary on the Decree», 210: The category of *presbyteros*, however, was primary for Clement, and included within it a pastoral and cultic role. For an analysis of the role of presbyters as a collective leadership body during the time of Clement, see A. LEMAIRE, *Les ministères aux origines de l'église*, 145-151.

[81] J. DUNN, *Priesthood*, 69.

There is a Christological reason for the development of the notion of *sacerdos* in Christian community and worship. Only after Christ's death and resurrection, when the community had reflected on the meaning of his mission, did they become aware that, in the sacrifice of his life as a sin offering for all, he was engaging in priestly activity in an eminent sense, albeit a priestly activity that surpassed and eclipsed all that had gone before it. In reflecting on his life, death and resurrection, and its ongoing meaning and significance for the Church's life, it was thus a natural progression «[...] that Christ should eventually become described explicitly as a priest»[82], as the author of The Letter to the Hebrews does in 80-90 C.E. The Letter to the Hebrews emphasizes the newness, superiority, and finality of Christ's priesthood which put an end to all previous priesthood. Christian priesthood must be seen in this light as entirely different from all priesthood not associated with Christ[83].

Eventually the Eucharist, which commemorated and made present Christ's priestly activity, that is his life-giving sacrifice, came to be seen as a cultic, sacrificial act, and according to Wulf, «It was but one short step further from this understanding of the Eucharist to calling the presidents at the Lord's supper: *sacerdotes*»[84]. Over time, as the notion of *sacerdotium* became more prominent, it became accepted that presbyters were included in the term[85]. Eventually, this sacerdotal component became the definitive element in episcopal and presbyteral offices. Other dimensions, especially the prophetic, became obscured in the priest's identity[86].

2.4.3 Terminology in Vatican II and the Synod of 1971

In *PO*, the Council attempted to bring back a sense of balance by returning to the New Testament word *presbyter* when describing those who are ordained to the second order. Generally, the Council tried to use the word *presbyteros* when referring to ordained priests, and *sacerdos* when referring to Jesus or to the common priesthood[87]. This development, however, labors under certain linguistic difficulties, the most important of which is that the Latin *presbyter*, when translated into

---

[82] F. WULF, «Commentary on the Decree», 211.
[83] Cf. F. WULF, «Commentary on the Decree», 212.
[84] F. WULF, «Commentary on the Decree», 212.
[85] Cf. B. COOKE, *Ministry to Word and Sacrament*, 541.
[86] Cf. J. DUNN, *Priesthood*, 110.
[87] Cf. J. DUNN, *Priesthood*, 110.

modern European languages, does not convey the sense intended by the Council: «[...] the corresponding loan words, while deriving from "presbyter" (priest, prêtre, priester, presbítero), are in fact all imbued with the notion of the cultic priesthood»[88]. Thus even today there is confusion and disagreement about the central, defining understanding of the ministerial priest.

Although the Synod of 1971, unlike the Council, used the terms *sacerdos* and *presbyter* almost interchangeably[89], it did recognize the importance of the *presbyterium*: «Since priests are bound together by an intimate sacramental brotherhood and by their mission, and since they work and plan together for the same task, some community of life or a certain association of life shall be encouraged among them» (*MP* II.2.2). As indicated above, the Synod convened in an atmosphere of crisis surrounding the identity of the priesthood. In this context its use of language is not so much a retreat from the developments of the Council, as maintained by some critics[90], as an attempt to maintain the essential teachings of the Council regarding the priesthood and to offer direction in the midst of the crisis.

From the perspective of this study, the recovery of the notion of *presbyter,* and its use both at the Council and at the Synod, has important implications for an understanding of the ministerial priesthood in terms of leadership. First of all, by definition, with its roots in the earliest days of the Church, the word intrinsically carries a meaning of leadership. The *presbyter* is a leader, an elder in the Christian community. Secondly, the notion of *presbyter* expands the understanding of priesthood without detracting from or downplaying the cultic and prophetic dimensions of the ministry. Thirdly, *presbyter*, by definition, emphasizes collegiality. Priests are co-workers with the bishop — which is the meaning of *presbyterium*: «[...] a college of priests led by their local bishop.»[91]. The notion of *presbyterium* implies that ordination is not a solitary event,

---

[88] F. WULF, «Commentary on the Decree», 213. Dunn observes, «By way of illustration, the word "priest-priestly-priesthood" occurs 14 times in the English version of paragraph 2 of Presbyterorum Ordinis; on 10 of these occasions the Latin original has used the word "presbyteros"; "sacerdos" is used only 4 times — twice referring to Jesus, once to all the baptized, and only once with reference to the ordained priesthood», J. DUNN, *Priesthood*, 110.

[89] Cf. D. DONOVAN, *What Are They Saying About the Ministerial Priesthood?*, 22.

[90] Cf., for example, D. DONOVAN, *What Are They Saying About the Ministerial Priesthood?*, 21-24.

[91] K. B. OSBORNE, *Priesthood*, 331.

but brings the priest into a community of peers, a college of priests, as «[...] prudent cooperators with the episcopal order» (*LG* 28). Their leadership is grounded in a collegial community which demands account-ability, thus ensuring that priests do not operate on their own, but always as part of a network of relationships[92].

2.5 *Conclusions: The Ecclesiological Basis of Priest as Leader*

Having considered the ministerial priesthood in the light of the eccle-siological developments of the Council, especially as it relates to the common priesthood, the episcopacy, and the presbyterate, an initial sketch of the priest as leader begins to emerge. First, the ministerial priest, although a person set apart, is also a person rooted in a people. He shares with all the baptized the one priesthood of Christ even while the ministerial priesthood is different in essence. This means that the priest cannot see himself simply as a leader over and above the people he serves. His leadership and authority has one fundamental purpose: to serve the Church in its mission. Although understood in the context of service, his leadership is nonetheless real, a constitutive dimension of the ministerial priesthood conferred by the sacrament of Orders. Although expressed in ontological terms, such leadership is nevertheless dynamic; the sacred authority which is implicit in the designation «hierarchical» puts the ministerial priesthood into a particular relation of service to the common priesthood (cf. Mt 20,25-28). Second, priestly leadership is not independent, meaning that the priest is not an entity alone and unto himself. Although the ministerial priesthood is rooted in Christ, its rela-tion to the episcopal order implies: a) an expansion beyond, but includ-ing, a cultic role; b) accountability; and c) collaboration. It ensures that his leadership is not directed toward self-service but toward the unity of the Church. Finally, the priest exercises his leadership in the context of a network of relations with other priests; he is part of a presbyterate which by definition implies leadership, albeit a collective leadership, engaged in with peers in service to the Church.

This ecclesiological exploration of the ministerial priesthood from the perspective of leadership gives the barest outlines of what priestly leader-ship looks like, merely establishing the context by showing that the

---

[92] For a description of the presbyterate as a place of sanctification for the priest and the context in which priestly friendships — a valuable help in both the exer-cise of ministry and in the growth of pastoral charity — are formed, see CC, *DMLP*, pars. 27-28, pp. 28-29.

nature of the ministerial priesthood entails leadership and that such is part of the structure of the Church. Although perhaps lacking in detail, this basic affirmation is crucial for constructing an understanding of the priest as leader because it posits leadership as being of the very essence of priesthood, not simply a function. These contours must be filled out in order that the portrait of priest as leader might emerge more clearly. The next section, which approaches an understanding of priestly leadership from a Christological perspective, will build upon what has already been asserted and lead to a more complete portrait of the ministerial priesthood understood from the perspective of leadership.

3. The Priesthood: Rooted in a Deep Identification with Christ

The teaching of the Council, as well as that of the Synod of 1971, is filled with references to the intimate bond that exists between Christ and priests. There are, however, three important aspects that delineate this relationship, suggesting crucial implications for developing an understanding of the priest as leader: 1) the priesthood in relation to Christ the Priest; 2) the priesthood in relation to Christ the Head; and 3) the priesthood in relation to Christ the Shepherd. This section will examine each of these aspects in the light of *Presbyterorum Ordinis, Lumen Gentium,* and *The Ministerial Priesthood.* From the analysis of the Christological underpinnings of priestly identity and mission, the consequent teaching on sacramental character will be revisited, and the implications for priest as leader will then be examined.

3.1 *Christ the Priest*

3.1.1 Consecration and Mission

Both *PO* 2 and *LG* 28 set the context of the Council's doctrinal teaching on the ministerial priesthood by featuring Jn 10,36, a passage that alludes to the priesthood of Christ[93]: «The Lord Jesus, "whom the Father has made holy and sent into the world" (Jn 10,36), has made His whole Mystical Body share in the anointing by the Spirit with which He Himself has been anointed» (*PO* 2). In choosing this passage, Christ's priestly consecration and mission became a central perspective in the articulation of the Council's doctrine on priesthood[94]. The same passage

---

[93] Cf. F. WULF, «Commentary on the Decree», 218.
[94] Cf. G. C. YOUNG, «Priests», 527.

also set the theme for the 1971 Synod's doctrinal teaching on the ministerial priesthood (cf. *MP* I, 1). In all three documents the origin of the priesthood is described, theologically rather than historically, as a participation in Christ's consecration and mission to the world[95].

PO 2 gives greater precision to its reference to Jn 10,36 by appealing to Mt 3,16; Lk 4,18; and Acts 4,27.10,38, all of which refer to «[…] Christ's messianic anointing, signified by the theophany which took place at his baptism in the Jordan»[96]. Echoing the teaching on the universal priesthood found in *LG* 10, *PO* 2 relates this anointing of Christ to the sending of the Holy Spirit to the Church, described as the «whole Mystical Body» and a «royal priesthood»[97]. Jesus' consecration and mission are thus present and active in both the universal priesthood and in the ministerial priesthood.

As demonstrated above, the most basic description of Christian priesthood takes as a given that every baptized person shares in the priesthood of Christ who handed his mission over to the entire Church. A perception of the common priesthood and the ministerial priesthood in relation to each other and to Christ is therefore essential to an adequate and balanced understanding of Christian priesthood. Having examined the relation and distinction between the common and ministerial priesthood above, this section will examine only the ministerial priesthood as it is related to the consecration and mission of Christ. This is not to undervalue the importance of the common priesthood and its particular relation to Christ, but simply reflects the limits of the scope of the topic.

The consecration and mission of Christ referred to in *PO* 2, *LG* 28, and *MP* I.1, is crucial for an understanding of his priesthood. Consecration denotes that Jesus was chosen by the Father and set apart for his service. It also implies that he was equipped «[…] with the corresponding grace, the special gifts of the Spirit, which he received as Messiah»[98]. Because the consecration of Jesus is intimately connected with his incarnation, it is ontological in nature; that is to say that it «[…] is a state that exists prior to the activity in which Jesus engages for the sake of salvation»[99]. It signifies, therefore, nothing less than «[…] the election

---

[95] Cf. A. GRILLMEIER, «The Hierarchical Structure of the Church», *CDV*, vol. 1, 220.

[96] D. N. POWER, *Ministers of Christ and His Church*, 151.

[97] Cf. A. GRILLMEIER, «The Hierarchical Structure of the Church», *CDV*, vol. 1, Chap. III, 220.

[98] A. GRILLMEIER, «The Hierarchical Structure of the Church», *CDV*, vol. 1, 220.

[99] J. GALOT, *Theology of the Priesthood*, 39.

and setting apart of Jesus by God, to fulfill his mandate and mission»[100]. One need only consider the abundance of Gospel passages which feature the healing, forgiving actions of Jesus to realize that his consecration, although described here in ontological terms, is not to be understood as a static reality, but as something dynamic which is expressed in concrete human actions having an existential impact on people's lives.

In the light of Jn 10,36, the mission of Jesus refers to his priestly activity which is both revealing and redemptive. For John the evangelist, «Christ is the "one sent" par excellence, through whom man, living in this world's darkness, receives the light — i.e., faith (cf. Jn 1,4-9)»[101]. MP I.1 stresses that it is the activity and work of Christ which reveal his priestly nature: he «[...] was "sanctified", "sent" and "marked with the seal". He "proclaimed", "preached", "confirmed by signs", "laid down his life", "rose from the dead", "reconciled", "laid the foundation of the people of the new covenant". The priest carries on in this work and therefore expresses the priesthood as Christ's work does»[102]. The Church's understanding of the ministerial priesthood thus arises from the priesthood of Christ.

Galot observes that Christ's consecration «[...] is pervaded by a dynamism that drives it to extend to mankind»[103]. Consecration is thus intrinsically geared to mission. This same dynamism characterizes the ministerial priesthood. MP emphasizes that in ordination the priest receives a gift of the Holy Spirit which «[...] configures the ordained minister to Christ, the Priest, consecrates him (cf. PO 2), and makes him a sharer in Christ's mission under its two aspects of authority and service» (MP I.5). The dynamic nature of Christ's consecration, therefore, has ramifications for priestly spirituality because it signals that a holiness rooted in Christ cannot be understood apart from the mystery of the Incarnation which sets the context of his priestly activity: «It is not a holiness achieved through separation from the world; it is realized instead in the act of entering the world»[104]. An authentic embodiment of the priesthood of Christ in the activities and life of the ministerial priest requires that the priest's actions continue Christ's priestly work. In these activities the identity of the priest shines forth most clearly.

---

[100] F. WULF, «Commentary on the Decree», 219.
[101] F. WULF, «Commentary on the Decree», 219, n. 27.
[102] D. W. WUERL, Catholic Priesthood Today, 59.
[103] J. GALOT, Theology of the Priesthood, 39.
[104] J. GALOT, Theology of the Priesthood, 39. Cf. J. DUNN, Priesthood, 108.

The ministerial priesthood, however, is not to be seen as mere activity or function. Just as consecration is crucial to the mission of Christ, so it is an intrinsic part of the ministerial priesthood: «[...] whatever it was that permitted Christ to complete his priestly work must at the same time permit the priest to carry on the work. Identification with Christ cannot be completed solely in approximating his activities. For those activities depend on a specific spiritual power»[105]. Thus, *MP* stresses the consecration that unites the priest to Christ, a consecration which, like Christ's, is expressed in priestly activity that carries on the mission of Christ.

The manner in which *LG, PO*, and *MP* connect the consecration and mission of Jesus, as well as that of the ministerial priest, achieves a certain balance. The ministerial priesthood is neither isolated by separation, nor dissipated in rootless activity. Both poles are crucial: like Christ, the priest is one set apart, that is, consecrated by God; but the purpose of this consecration is to enable the priest to specifically take part in the mission of Christ, by carrying out the priestly activities of Christ in the midst of the Church. Although «being precedes doing», it is crucial to add that the doing authenticates and gives witness to the being. The two, consecration and mission, are held in balance and so contribute to an integrated understanding of the ministerial priesthood.

The consequences of this for the notion of priest as leader are readily understandable. If the priest is to be described as a leader, it must be a particular kind of leadership that he exercises. Although priestly leadership is anchored in sacramental ordination, it is not enough to say that the priest is a leader in virtue of his consecration and configuration to Christ; mission is always the necessary complement to consecration. Because who he is as a leader and what he does are intimately connected, his configuration must be expressed in his relation to the Church, that is, in mission; the priest comes to be known as a leader through the activities in which he engages. For the ministerial priest's leadership to be authentically Christian and priestly, it must approximate the priestly activities of Christ, broadly delineated in the designations «priest, prophet, and king», which describe his sacramental, preaching, and pastoral activities.

3.1.2 Priest, Prophet, and King

At the very beginning of *PO*, priests are described in terms of the threefold office of Christ, «[...] the Teacher, the Priest, and the King. They share in his ministry of unceasingly building up the Church on

---

[105] D. W. WUERL, *Catholic Priesthood Today*, 63.

earth into the People of God, the Body of Christ, and the Temple of the
Holy Spirit» (*PO* 1). Similarly, *LG* describes priests as being consecrated in the image of Christ the priest in order «[...] to preach the
gospel, shepherd the faithful, and celebrate divine worship as true priests
of the New Testament» (*LG* 28).

The evolution of *PO* during the course of the Council reveals
that many of the Council Fathers wanted to broaden the Church's understanding of the priesthood, treating it from a more theological and
pastoral point of view. Thus several of them suggested the articulation of
Christ's threefold office of teacher, priest, and pastor in the prologue of
the document, a description of Christ that had already been accepted in
describing the hierarchical functions in *LG* 25-28[106]. Although the
synodal document, *MP*, reflects a subtle shift from the Council in the
language it uses to describe the ministerial priesthood[107], it nonetheless
reinforces the Council's emphasis on the priestly, prophetic and pastoral
dimensions of priesthood. For example, in describing the priesthood of
Christ, *MP* stresses that it includes «[...] the prophetic and royal office
of the Incarnate Word of God» (*MP* I.1). Later in the same section, it
describes the Church as participating «[...] in the functions of Christ as
Priest, Prophet, and King, in order to carry out her mission of salvation
in his name and by his power» (*MP* I.4). The ministerial priesthood is
described in a similar manner as making present Christ, the Head of the
community, «[...] by effectively proclaiming the Gospel, by gathering
together and leading the community, by remitting sins, and especially by
celebrating the Eucharist» (*MP* I.4). Describing Christ in terms of the
threefold ministry as the basis for Church ministry, both ordained and
unordained (cf. *LG* 34), marks a development in the official teaching of
the Church regarding priesthood[108], which both the Council and Synod
used in constructing their doctrine of the ministerial priesthood. As noted

---

[106] Cf. J. LÉCUYER, «Decree on the Ministry and Life of Priests», 187.

[107] Cf. above, pp. 82-83. As noted, Donovan observes that, in a departure from their
use in the Council documents, the words *sacerdos* and *presbyter* are used almost
interchangeably. The priestly category becomes the central organizing category for
understanding ordained ministry which «[...] cannot help but lead to a use of sacerdotal
language in which the prophetic and the pastoral dimensions of office fade into the
background. This shift in language from *PO* seems to represent a response to what were
perceived as secularizing trends in the post-conciliar Church. It may also have been
thought that a strong emphasis on the priestly category was required to counterbalance
the importance being given to the common priesthood of the faithful», D. DONOVAN,
What Are They Saying About the Ministerial Priesthood?, 23.

[108] Cf. K. B. OSBORNE, *Priesthood*, 310.

above, in treating ordained ministry from this perspective, the Council and Synod broadened the Church's understanding of priesthood, freeing it from a restricted, centuries-old, almost exclusively cultic under-standing[109].

Although there is a history on the threefold ministry of Jesus, extending back to the Patristic Era, it did not become a popular way to describe his ministry until taken up by Reformed theology[110], «[...] systematized by Calvin»[111]. By the mid-seventeenth century the threefold office of Jesus «[...] had become quite common in theological treatises by Lutheran scholars»[112]. Only in the late eighteenth century was it assimi-lated into Catholic theology, eventually making its way into papal writings[113]. By the late twentieth century, the threefold office became an accepted way of speaking about the ministry of Jesus and about priestly ministry[114], with a measure of its acceptance seen in the fact that the Council chose to make it the very foundation for its theology of priest-hood. In doing so it broadened the concept of a priesthood restricted to cult and placed it in the context of Christ's entire mission[115].

The concept of the threefold mission may have broadened the Church's understanding of priesthood, but it is not without its difficulties. At various times the Scriptures refer to Jesus as prophet or as teacher, and at other times highlight his shepherd-like qualities, but Osborne observes that nowhere in the New Testament are these three ministries mentioned together[116]. In fact, although certain aspects of Jesus' life can be seen as priestly, only the Letter to the Hebrews explicitly calls him a priest[117].

---

[109] Cf. F. WULF, «Commentary on the Decree», 216.

[110] Cf. G. GRESHAKE, *Meaning of Christian Priesthood*, 42.

[111] F. WULF, «Commentary on the Decree», 216. For a brief history of the understanding and use of the threefold ministry and Calvin's influence in applying it to the activities of the faithful, which began the movement to pattern Christian ministry on the threefold ministry of Christ, see P. J. DRILLING, «The Priest, Prophet and King Trilogy», 179-206, especially 186-199. For a brief synopsis of Calvin's understand-ing of the threefold office as presented in his *Institutes of Christian Religion*, see K. B. OSBORNE, *Priesthood*, 311.

[112] K. B. OSBORNE, *Priesthood*, 312.

[113] Cf. F. WULF, «Commentary on the Decree», 216.

[114] Cf. K. B. OSBORNE, *Priesthood*, 312.

[115] Cf. G. GRESHAKE, *Meaning of Christian Priesthood*, 42.

[116] Cf. K. B. OSBORNE, *Priesthood*, 310; F. WULF, «Commentary on the Decree», 216-217.

[117] For studies on the biblical underpinnings of the priesthood of Christ, see J. GALOT, *Theology of the Priesthood*, especially 31-69; A. VANHOYE, *Old Testament*

Because the Scriptures and tradition contain a multitude of expressions and images to express Christ's consecration and mission, it has been claimed that «[...] there is inevitably something arbitrary about focusing on these three terms»[118]. Because the Scriptures do not refer to Christ by the formula «priest, prophet, king», nor sum up his ministry in terms of the priestly, prophetic, and royal functions, the formula is best understood as a theological construct[119]. Additionally, the three offices are only partially distinguishable because the boundaries between them are fluid and at times overlap[120].

The Council nevertheless made the threefold office the organizing principle for its understanding of ministry, stressing that the priest's participation in the mission and ministry of Christ is so profound that in his activities he serves Christ the priest, prophet, and king and in so doing builds up the Church (cf. *PO* 1)[121]. Following the threefold schema adopted by the Council and affirmed by the Synod, the ministry of Christ can be delineated as follows: the prophetic function refers to Jesus' mission to teach and proclaim the Good News; the priestly function refers to the whole of Jesus' life, which was offered in sacrifice for all, so that all in union with him might be made holy; the kingly function of Jesus is also known as the pastoral or shepherd function by which he gathers and leads his people to the Father[122]. The threefold ministry of Jesus is thus bound up with and expressive of the consecration and mission he received from the Father[123]. Because the three offices of priest, prophet, and king express the power of the Gospel and the purpose of the Incarnation, by anchoring the ministerial priesthood in them, the Church situates it at the heart of the mystery of Christ[124].

The designation of the threefold office of Christ as the foundation of the priestly ministry has important implications for understanding the

---

Priests and the New Priest According to the New Testament, especially 61-238; ITC, «The Priestly Ministry», 26-35.

[118] D. DONOVAN, *What Are They Saying About the Ministerial Priesthood?*, 6.

[119] Cf. K. B. OSBORNE, *Priesthood*, 310.

[120] Wulf observes that «[...] one might hand over the teaching office to the pastoral office; likewise, there is a reciprocity between the teaching and the priestly office», F. WULF, «Commentary on the Decree», 217.

[121] F. WULF, «Commentary on the Decree», 217.

[122] Cf. J. GALOT, *Theology of the Priesthood*, 45-48; K. B. OSBORNE, *Priesthood*, 317.

[123] M. SCHMAUS, «Ämter Christi», *LTK*, vol. 1, 457-458, cited in K. B. OSBORNE, *Priesthood*, 317.

[124] Cf. K. B. OSBORNE, *Priesthood*, 318.

ministerial priest as a leader. First, it rules out equating the leadership of the priest with personal qualities or inherent characteristics. Leadership exercised by the ministerial priest, while perhaps enhanced by certain qualities and skills, is rooted in something far deeper, namely, the mystery of Christ. An identification with Christ, in his person and in his work, must therefore be the foundation upon which priestly leadership is built. Christ the priest, prophet, and king is the touchstone by which the priest measures both his attitudes and his behavior. The threefold office of Christ, then, gives content and definition to the kind of leadership the priest is to offer and is expressed in service to word, sacrament, and pastoral care.

3.2 *Christ the Head*

To exercise the priestly ministry of Christ, the ministerial priest must have a certain spiritual authority which enables him to engage in the threefold ministry and so work «[...] simultaneously on three levels: that of carrying the word that gives faith; that of nourishing the faith by the sacraments; and that of leading the community, formed in faith and the sacraments»[125]. Such spiritual authority is conferred in the sacrament of Orders which puts the ministerial priest into a distinct relationship with the common priesthood, a relationship that is described by the Council in terms of the ministerial priest's configuration to Christ the Head. *LG* 28 describes the ministerial priest as exercising «[...] the function of Christ as Shepherd and Head». The «Decree on the Ministry and Life of Priests» develops this and stresses that through the sacrament of Orders priests «[...] are so configured to Christ the Priest that they can act in the person of Christ the Head» (*PO* 2). In other sections it describes priests as exercising «the office of Christ the Head» (*PO* 6) and as «ministers of the Head» (*PO* 12). Similarly, *MP* stresses the connection between the ministerial priest and the headship of Christ by asserting that the ministerial priest «[...] makes Christ, the Head of the community, present in the exercise of his work of redeeming mankind and glorifying God perfectly» (*MP* I.4). The connection of the ministerial priesthood to Christ the Head of his body the Church, in *LG* 28, *PO* 2, 6, and 12, and in *MP* I.4, are indications of the Council and Synod Fathers' desire to distinguish between the ministerial priesthood and the common priesthood. «Headship» is a notion rich in theological significance which gives precision to both the identity and function of the ministerial priesthood

---

[125] D. WUERL, *Catholic Priesthood Today*, 87.

and to the peculiar configuration of the ministerial priest to Christ, traditionally expressed by the term in persona Christi capitis[126].

In his treatment of the priesthood of Christ in the Epistle to the Hebrews, Galot has noted the close association between the notion of «head» and leader: «The term "head" translates hegoumenos, which is the participle of the verb that means "to walk in front of, to guide, to lead, to command", and implies "preeminence, authority, direction"»[127]. Although not referring explicitly to presbyters, Galot asserts that the use of the term attests to the presence of distinct leaders in the early Christian community and the Letter to the Hebrews speaks of them in such a way that implies an association with the priesthood of Christ[128].

3.2.1 Building Up the Body of Christ

PO emphasizes the connection between the ministerial priesthood and the headship of Christ by repeatedly stressing the responsibility of the priest to build up the Body of Christ, the Church[129]. Both *LG* 28 and *PO* 2 make it clear that the priest, along with all the baptized, is a member of this Body as «[...] one of the many parts which make up the united whole»[130]. What then is distinctive about the place of the priest in the Body and how is his responsibility to build up the Body of Christ distinct from that of the rest of the baptized?

This can be explained by the sacramentality discussed above in the ecclesiological section. Because the members of the body rely on the «[...] vital link which results from Christ's headship over his body»[131], Christ must always be present to his body, vivifying it and uniting it to himself. For this reason, it is confided to ministerial priests,

---

[126] For a thorough treatment of the historical development of the terms in persona Christi and in persona Ecclesiae, see B. D. MARLIANGEAS, Clés pour une théologie du ministère.

[127] J. GALOT, Theology of the Priesthood, 63. Cf. C. SPICQ, L'Epître aux Hébreux, vol. 2, 420, as cited by J. GALOT, Theology of the Priesthood, 69, n. 21.

[128] Cf. J. GALOT, Theology of the Priesthood, 65.

[129] Cf. PO 1,6,8,9,12,15,22,25.

[130] M. EVANS, «In Persona Christi», 19.

[131] D. N. POWER, Ministers of Christ and His Church, 153. Klaus Mörsdorf states that the «[...] sacramental significance of the Church is bound to the hierarchical structure proper to the Church, i.e., the Church is only a sacramental sign by reason of the fact that the Lord, who is the invisible head of the Church, is visibly represented in the Church by men: for without a visible head the Church cannot be a visible representation of the Lord's body», K. MÖRSDORF, «Hierarchy», in SM, vol. 3, 27.

members of the Body, to be instruments of Christ's headship[132]. Christ, the Head of the Church, through the instrumentality of the priest, gathers all of the members of the Body under his headship. Based on conciliar and synodal understandings, the relationship of the priest to the Body, the Church, can thus be understood more clearly: all Christians, through baptism, are representatives of Christ, but the priest «[...] represents Christ precisely as Head of the faithful, who are themselves the fullness of Christ (Eph 1,23)»[133]. In this particular configuration to Christ, priests can be understood as instruments and representatives of his headship[134].

3.2.2 Authority in the Body of Christ

Because of this configuration to Christ as representatives of his headship, priests share in Christ's authority over the Church (cf. *PO* 2). This authority, however, is not to be narrowly interpreted as only juridical, for, in the context of *PO* 2 the authority refers to Christ's authority over the Church, an authority through which he «[...] builds up, sanctifies, and rules His Body» (*PO* 2). Power notes that «authority», as it appears in *PO* 2, is used in a similar way to its use in early Christian Latin in that it expresses «[...] any kind of influence which could be said to stand in any way in a causal relation to that over which the influence is exercised»[135]. Connected to the priest's configuration to Christ the Head, such authority is intrinsic and comprehensive, rooted in the very sacramentality of the priestly office.

Because in the Church «[...] it is primarily through sacramental actions, things and persons that he [Christ] makes his presence felt»[136], the priest's authority is situated in his identity as a sacramental sign of Christ the Head. As such, his authority can only be interpreted in the context of service, not as a personal right or power. As a servant of Christ the ministerial priest has only the right or power to be the

---

132 Cf. D. N. POWER, *Ministers of Christ and His Church*, 153.

133 M. EVANS, «*In Persona Christi*», 119. The *Catechism* states: «The whole Body, *caput et membra*, prays and offers itself, and therefore those who in the Body are especially his ministers are called ministers not only of Christ, but also of the Church. It is because the ministerial priesthood represents Christ that it can represent the Church», *CCC*, par. 1553, 348.

134 Cf. D. N. POWER, *Ministers of Christ and His Church*, 153.

135 D. N. POWER, *Ministers of Christ and His Church*, 153. In his description of authority, Power cites A. BLAISE, *Dictionnaire latin-français des auteurs chrétiens*, 103.

136 M. EVANS, «*In Persona Christi*», 120.

instrument of the authority of Christ the Head[137]. As sacramental signs of Christ's headship, priests serve as a reminder that the Church is not the owner of the gift of salvation but rather is completely dependent on Christ[138]. The Church thus needs the ordained priesthood, as sacramentally representing Christ the Head, in order to maintain its sacramental structure[139].

In his commentary on *PO* 2, Wulf takes a rather negative view of the identification of the ministerial priesthood with the headship of Christ. He sees it as too christocentric and isolating because it puts all the emphasis on the association of the ministerial priest with the hierarchy and his distinction from the rest of the Church, while failing to take into consideration the wider context of the common priesthood of all the faithful[140]. But a broader reading of the text, in the light of *PO*, *LG*, and *MP*, shows that the christological perspective, while primary, is to be seen in an ecclesiological context which locates the ministerial priesthood in a network of human relationships. The identification of the ministerial priest with the headship of Christ is not to be understood apart from his membership in the Body of Christ the Church; the two must be held in tension.

Galot notes that as the prototype of the ministerial priesthood, Christ's headship is rooted in his Incarnation, which itself is mirrored in the ministerial priesthood: «Christ wills that priests should participate both in the way in which he, as a man, belongs to God, and in his own nearness to all men»[141]. The identification with Christ's headship, then, does not necessarily distance the priest from the faithful as Wulf implies. On the contrary, it emphasizes that the priest is «[...] the sign and instrument of Christ's direct and immediate leadership of his Church»[142]. Such an understanding is at the heart of the conciliar and synodal doctrine on the priesthood[143].

---

[137] Cf. A. DE BOVIS, «Le Presbytérat», 1033: «Redisons en outre que les détenteurs de l'autorité en vertu du sacrement de l'Ordre ne la possèdent jamais comme un droit et un pouvoir personnel. Ils ne possèdent qu'un droit et qu'un pouvoir: être les signes et les instruments de l'*Auctoritas Christi Capitis*. Ils ne sont que les serviteurs du Christ».

[138] Cf. G. GRESHAKE, *Meaning of Christian Priesthood*, 64.

[139] Cf. M. EVANS, «*In Persona Christi*», 120.

[140] Cf. F. WULF, «Commentary on the Decree», 221-222.

[141] J. GALOT, *Theology of the Priesthood*, 124.

[142] M. EVANS, «*In Persona Christi*», 121.

[143] Cf. M. EVANS, «*In Persona Christi*», 121.

The description of priesthood as participation in the headship of Christ sets the context for the priest's ministry of word, sacrament, and shepherding which are described in *PO* 4, 5, 6. Participating in Christ's headship, these activities can be described as a «diakonia of spiritual leadership»[144]. Such a service of leadership, however, is not merely functional but deeply spiritual, rooted as it is in the Spirit's anointing at ordination, which configures the priest to Christ. Because it is intrinsically a part of a priest's identity, such a spiritual leadership must be embodied in the priest's life so that it permeates his activities[145]. As noted earlier, consecration and mission exist together in a kind of symbiotic relationship and define the priest in his very essence.

Although Wulf's criticism of the identification of the ministerial priesthood with the headship of Christ may be somewhat inaccurate, it does serve as a caution regarding how this configuration is understood. If distorted, the notion can lead to an inflated, grandiose conception of the priesthood. From this perspective, an understanding of priest as leader would also be distorted, representing an isolated, self-serving approach to leadership. In short, it would not be recognizable as Christian, priestly leadership. The context for this configuration, therefore, is all-important and that context is the Body of Christ, the Church. Configuration to the headship of Christ exists for one purpose only: to build up the Body. Because it can only be authentically embodied in a stance of service and solicitude for the Church, it is a leadership and authority which expresses itself as a service[146]. Any other approach would distort the Church's understanding of priesthood's configuration to Christ the Head.

---

[144] D. N. POWER, *Ministers of Christ and His Church*, 167.

[145] Cf. D. N. POWER, *Ministers of Christ and His Church*, 167-168: «This leadership is exercised through an exemplary life and its resultant moral authority, combined with the functions of word, sacrament, and government. It is a leadership because the pastor must help all the individuals within the community, and the community as such, to lead a full Christian life, by the right combination of example, pastoral guidance, word and liturgical worship».

[146] For an exposition and analysis of how the service-awareness of Christ is the consciousness in which the ministerial priest shares, see L. J. CAMELI, *Ministerial Consciousness*, especially 188-202, and 203-236. Cameli notes, «The Church's doctrinal understanding of the priesthood as elaborated in the Council of Trent and Vatican II has viewed the *objective requirement* for the exercise of ministry in consecration and mission which mark the ministry as under and in the power of the Spirit. A person is so situated "objectively" by the sacrament of Orders and communion with the Church. The *subjective requirement* for the exercise of ministry and its exercise as service has received less attention in official teaching. But the results of our exegetical study clearly indicates its importance and its content. According to the Gospels, the

3.3 *Christ the Shepherd*

The designation of priest as shepherd, in the image of Jesus the Good Shepherd, is mentioned nine times in *PO*, making it one of the document's dominant themes[147]. It is also mentioned in *LG* 28 in the same context, as well as in *OT* 4 and 19, and in *MP* I.1. Containing a wealth of meaning, the shepherd image, as applied to priesthood in the image of Christ, can be understood in three basic senses: 1) as the quality of the priest's love and service; 2) as an indication of the authority that the priest exercises; 3) as a sign of the permanence of the priestly vocation — aspects under which the shepherd image will now be examined.

3.3.1 The Quality of the Priest's Love and Service

The shepherd image hints at the inner-quality of the priest himself as it is to be expressed in his love and service. Priests are to live in the midst of people as good shepherds who know their sheep (cf. *PO* 3). Inspired by the love of Christ the Good Shepherd, priests are to guide and nourish God's people, to the point of giving their lives for their sheep (cf. *PO* 13; *MP* I.1). Because part of their duty as shepherds is to be concerned for those who have strayed from the faith, they are to seek out those who have fallen away (cf. *PO* 9; *OT* 19). All of their training and ministerial activity should lead priests to live in the spirit of Christ the Shepherd, gathering and leading their flock to the Father (cf. *PO* 5, 6; *LG* 28; *OT* 4). It is in their role as shepherds that priests discover the principle of unity which connects their inner lives with their activities: the centrality of pastoral charity which is expressed most fully in the Eucharist (cf. *PO* 14; *MP* II.1.3)[148].

The quality of the priest's love and service mirrors the quality of Christ the Good Shepherd, expressed in John's Gospel (cf. Jn 10) to which *PO* makes repeated reference. When Jesus describes himself as the Good Shepherd, he emphasizes that he is not one shepherd among many, but the very prototype for all who would exercise the ministry of

---

subjective requirement for the exercise of ministry as service consists in the experience of Jesus' prior service to the minister and the minister's experience of service to others grounded upon and patterned after Jesus' service. [...] the subjective requirement involves an event in the deep subjectivity of the person affecting and shaping his existence and so creating a consciousness», L. J. CAMELI, *Ministerial Consciousness*, 201-202.

[147] Cf. *PO* 3,5,6,9,11,13,14,18,22.

[148] The concept of «pastoral charity», one of the central features of *Pastores Dabo Vobis*' understanding of the ministerial priesthood, will be examined in the next chapter.

shepherd in his name[149]. He emphasizes the dimensions of care and solicitude over authority, a quality of care revealed by his complete dedication, even to the laying down of his life for his sheep[150]. The shepherd image thus serves as «[...] a window into the redeeming mystery of God, and as a key to understanding the ministry, death and resurrection of Jesus»[151]. As such, it is a paradigm for Christian ministry and has implications for how we understand the quality of that ministry, particularly priestly ministry.

Jn 10 and various passages from the synoptic gospels referring to Christ as Shepherd (cf. Lk 15,4-7; Mk 14,27), offer a description of the attributes or qualities associated with the role of shepherd. They emphasize that there is risk in being a shepherd: it is a life that entails danger, fatigue and pain, possibly even death. Being a shepherd requires a generosity of spirit and a willingness to sacrifice and give one's very self for the life and the safety of the sheep whom the shepherd knows as his own. All of these are qualities which Jesus the Good Shepherd possesses. In describing Jesus as Shepherd, the evangelists emphasize his deep love and concern for his flock, a love and concern which transcend all his activities, but which are illustrated most vividly in his self-giving and self-sacrifice[152]. The shepherd image, with the qualities it implies, transcends, unites, and epitomizes the priestly functions of word, worship, and pastoral leadership[153]. The International Theological Commission similarly describes the image of Christ the Shepherd as the center of unity that best expresses the ministry and life of the priest:

> From a Christological point of view, the «pastor» is he who has received from God the «mandate» and the «power» (Jn 10,18) to give his life for the sheep. [...] All priestly spirituality is governed by the postulate inherent in the ministry and made possible by the grace of the Lord. It is a special spirituality because the pastor, in the exercise of his office, is placed on the side of Christ himself, radically distinct from his flock, though definitely united and associated with them[154].

The ministerial priesthood, then, in both its identity and in its activity, finds its most articulate expression in the self-sacrificing love of Christ

---

149 Cf. J. GALOT, *Theology of the Priesthood*, 41.
150 Cf. M. WINSTANLEY, «The Shepherd Image in the Scriptures», 200.
151 M. WINSTANLEY, «The Shepherd Image in the Scriptures», 205.
152 Cf. M. WINSTANLEY, «The Shepherd Image in the Scriptures», 201-203.
153 Cf. J. GALOT, *Theology of the Priesthood*, 137.
154 ITC, «The Priestly Ministry», 81.

the Good Shepherd, a love that of its very nature seeks only to serve the flock, leading it to the Father (cf. *PO* 6).

3.3.2 An Indication of Priestly Authority

In addition to the quality of self-sacrificing love and service, the image of the shepherd also indicates authority. *LG* 28 states this rather clearly when it speaks of priests «[...] exercising within the limits of their authority the function of Christ as Shepherd and Head». Similarly, *PO* 6, 9, and 13 allude to this authority when speaking of priests as exercising the office of Christ the Head and Shepherd, leading, guiding, and nourishing the People of God.

Although the quality of the shepherd's love emphasizes the relatedness and intimacy between the priest and the people, at the same time the shepherd image signals «[...] an essential distinction which excludes all identification but which signifies a reciprocal relationship»[155]. In addition to expressing union with those being served, therefore, the role of the shepherd expresses the priest's difference from the flock. Such difference, however, does not negate the basic fact that the shepherd's place is always within the flock; like all the baptized, the priest is dependent upon the grace of Christ and upon the help of fellow Christians. Consequently, the ministerial priest invites them to share in the responsibility of his work[156].

The authority that the role of shepherd implies can only be properly understood in the context of the qualities of love and solicitude mentioned above. The shepherd's authority «[...] bespeaks a deeply benevolent attitude on his part. [...] Jesus stands all the way by the principle that authority must be exercised only as love»[157]. The complete commitment of the shepherd to give his life as gift and sacrifice precludes any exercise of power which seeks its own advantage or the

---

[155] G. GRESHAKE, *Meaning of Christian Priesthood*, 67, citing Hans Urs von Balthasar [no reference given].

[156] Greshake observes, «For *firstly*, like every Christian, and together with everyone else, he also needs to be rescued by the grace of Christ, the "chief Shepherd"; *secondly*, both shepherd and flock, in spite of their diversity of function, are absolutely dependent on one another and yoked together in the unity of the people of God, in a multiple and reciprocal spiritual interchange of giving and receiving; and *thirdly*, the shepherd causes his fellow Christians to share in his responsibility. [...] it belongs to the office of shepherd in the Church to be surrounded *by many fellow-workers and helpers*» [emphasis in original], G. GRESHAKE, *Meaning of Christian Priesthood*, 68.

[157] J. GALOT, *Theology of the Priesthood*, 48.

self-aggrandizement of the shepherd[158]. The commissioning of Peter in Jn 21, which emphasizes the necessity of love as a prerequisite for the shepherd role[159], perhaps best illustrates the nature of the shepherd's authority. The love must be, in the first place, love for Christ, for it is only out of devotion to him that one can exercise the role of shepherd in Christ's flock. It is clear in this commissioning that, although Peter shares in the authority of Christ the Shepherd, there is no thought of secular power or prestige associated with his authority: «Jesus looks upon his authority as the practice of service and love, and wills that the Twelve should do likewise»[160]. In order to authentically mirror the pastoral love of Christ, such authority must be characterized by knowledge of the flock, solicitude, care, and generosity[161].

3.3.3 A Sign of the Permanence of the Priestly Vocation

The shepherd image also implies permanence of commitment. In stressing that the priest exercises the office of Christ as Head and Shepherd, *MP* affirms that the priest makes effectively present the self-sacrificing reality of Christ himself (cf. *MP* I.4). The priest does not simply perform pastoral actions but rather «[...] *is* all the time the pastor of the community of the faithful entrusted to his care, made an overseer by the Holy Spirit to shepherd the Church of God» [emphasis in the original][162]. The self-sacrificing nature of the shepherd, even to the giving of his life, is contrasted in Jn 10,12 with the behavior of the hired man who flees in the face of hardship or danger, thereby causing the flock to be scattered. Because the hired man is concerned only with his own well-being and safety, his commitment is fleeting; because the shepherd is concerned for the life and unity of his flock, his commitment is permanent[163].

The identification of the priest with Christ the Shepherd, while implying certain functions such as pastoral care, authority, and leadership, points even more deeply to the being, or essence, of the priest. The identification with Christ and the commitment to his service as a priest is primarily a commitment to live in a certain way: that is, as a shepherd.

---

158 Cf. J. GALOT, *Theology of the Priesthood*, 43.

159 Cf. M. WINSTANLEY, «Shepherd Image in the Scriptures», 203.

160 J. GALOT, *Theology of the Priesthood*, 137.

161 Cf. M. WINSTANLEY, «Shepherd Image in the Scriptures», 203.

162 M. EVANS, «*In Persona Christi*», 122.

163 Cf. M. WINSTANLEY, «Shepherd Image in the Scriptures», 201.

As the analysis of the qualities of Jesus the Shepherd indicates, this way of life is rooted in the complete gift of self, even to the point of the sacrifice of one's life. The conciliar documents treating priesthood, as well as that of the Synod, indicate that in assuming the office of priest in conformity to Christ the Shepherd, there are no half-measures. As with Christ himself, the commitment is to be permanent and total.

3.4 Sacramental Character from a Christological Perspective

Building on *LG* 10, which describes the ministerial priesthood as different in essence from the common priesthood, *PO* 2 speaks of the ministerial priesthood as «[...] marked with a special character» by which priests are configured to Christ the Priest, so that they can act in the person of Christ the Head[164]. *LG* 28 alludes to a special character in speaking of priests as consecrated into the threefold ministry of Christ so they can act in the person of Christ. Although «[...] priests do not possess the highest degree of the priesthood» (*LG* 28), their priesthood is genuine because the sacrament of ordination confers on them the image of Christ, the prototype of the priesthood of the New Testament[165].

Emphasizing priesthood's fundamental identification with Christ, *MP* affirms the traditional notion of character:

> By the laying on of hands there is communicated a gift of the Holy Spirit which cannot be lost (cf. 2Tm 1,6). This reality configures the ordained minister to Christ, the Priest, consecrates him (cf. *PO* 2) and makes him a sharer in Christ's mission. [...] The lifelong permanence of this reality [...] which [...] is referred to in the Church's tradition as the priestly character, expresses the fact that Christ associated the Church with himself in an irrevocable way for the salvation of the world. [...] The minister whose life bears the seal of the gift received through the sacrament of Orders reminds the Church that the gift of God is irrevocable (*MP* I.5).

The conformity to Christ the High Priest, Head, and Shepherd, received at ordination, sets the ministerial priest apart for service, empowering him to engage in Christ's threefold ministry of word, sacrament, and pastoral care. Sacramental character echoes the «consecration and mission» of Jesus emphasized in *PO* 2 and *MP* I.5, and exemplifies the assertion of *PO* 3 that priests are set apart in the midst of God's people

---

[164] For a discussion of Sacramental Character from an ecclesiological perspective, see above, pp. 72-75.

[165] Cf. A. GRILLMEIER, «The Hierarchical Structure of the Church», *CDV*, vol. 1, 221.

so they can be totally dedicated to the work for which the Lord has ordained them.

3.4.1 Traditional Understanding

In traditional Catholic theology the notion of sacramental character refers to the teaching that in the sacraments of Baptism, Confirmation, and Holy Orders «[...] a character is [...] imprinted on the soul, that is, a kind of indelible spiritual sign by reason of which these sacraments cannot be repeated»[166]. The scriptural foundation for the doctrine of sacramental character is located in Rev 7,2-8, which speaks of the «seal» (*sphragis*) of God that marks the elect[167]. Upholding the inviolability of the confession of the Trinity against the Donatist practice of rebaptizing heretics, Augustine gave prominence to the doctrine of character[168]. Augustine stressed that baptism causes «[...] an irreversible and permanent reorientation of our lives towards Christ. [...] once baptized, we are baptized forever and that action is not to be repeated»[169]. Thomas Aquinas understood character to entail a configuration to the priesthood of Christ for the purpose of participating in the Church's worship[170]. Echoing Thomas Aquinas, McGoldrick states, «Christ is the source of this [worship] and its true celebrant, and others can join it only to the extent that he gives them this capacity, through the participation in his priesthood that they receive from him»[171]. This understanding of character applies analogously to Baptism, Confirmation, and Holy Orders, with the character given in Baptism understood by Thomas Aquinas as more of a passive power while that given in Confirmation and Holy Orders understood as more active (relative to worship)[172]. Nichols observes that for Thomas Aquinas sacramental character signifies a new relationship with Christ: the character associated with Baptism and

---

166 COUNCIL OF TRENT, «Decree on the Sacraments», 372.

167 Cf. K. RAHNER – H. VORGRIMLER, *DT*, 64.

168 Cf. P. FRANSEN, «Orders and Ordination», 324. Galot observes that the doctrine of character espoused by Augustine is rooted in earlier patristic tradition, most notably Tertullian and Cyprian. Cf. J. GALOT, *Theology of the Priesthood*, 199.

169 P. BISHOP, «Sacramental Character», 176.

170 Cf. ST. THOMAS AQUINAS, *Summa Theologiae* 3, q. 63, a. 3, 87.

171 P. MCGOLDRICK, «Sacrament of Orders», 903.

172 Cf. D. N. POWER, *Ministers of Christ and His Church*, 121. It should be noted that, although Thomas may have associated a passive quality with the character received at Baptism, Vatican II's emphasis on the laity's active role in the mission of the Church would certainly not interpret their sacramental character as passive.

Confirmation confers prophetic and royal priesthood, whereas the character bestowed in Holy Orders confers ministerial priesthood, with prophetic and royal dimensions[173].

Some have accused the traditional, ontological understanding of character of being too static or too triumphalistic in its representation of ordained ministry, an approach which can lead to an alienating clericalism[174]. These criticisms have more to do with modes of understanding and expression than with sacramental character itself. A correct understanding of sacramental character sees it as «[...] another way of articulating the mysterious relationship of God to the human person. [...] God has chosen to relate to the human person in a permanent way, enabling the person to be sign and minister of salvation»[175]. Thus the ministerial priesthood cannot be reduced to a mere function. Rather, one recognizes in the ministerial priesthood and its sacramental character the enduring fidelity of God, who is present in and to the Church in a very particular way through the person and ministry of the priest[176].

3.4.2 Sign of the Fidelity of Christ

PO 2 emphasizes that in the Sacrament of Holy Orders, through the anointing of the Holy Spirit, priests are «[...] marked with a special character and are so configured to Christ the priest, that they can act in the person of Christ the Head». Priestly activity, therefore, is not simply a matter of personal skills and talents, but rather is linked to the official ministry conferred on him in ordination. The salvific work of Christ is not tied to the subjective ability of particular individuals, «[...] but to a permanent, certain, definitive, institutional entity which transcends the individual office bearer, which of its nature points beyond itself to its original source and foundation — to Jesus Christ himself»[177]. In this perspective, sacramental character is profoundly liberating for the

---

173 Cf. A. NICHOLS, *Holy Order*, 77-78.

174 Cf., for example, P. FRANSEN, «Orders and Ordination», 324.

175 R. SCHWARTZ, «Ordained Ministry», 94.

176 Cf. R. SCHWARTZ, «Ordained Ministry», 94.

177 G. GRESHAKE, *Meaning of Christian Priesthood*, 61-62. W. Kasper observes, «For many priests who feel unequal to the high claims that their ministry imposes on them — and for what priest would this not be the case? — precisely this "ontological" understanding is a help and a consolation, because they can say to themselves that the salvation of their communities and of the people committed to them does not ultimately depend on their own accomplishments and their own success», W. KASPER, «Ministry in the Church», 189.

Church, because it guarantees that the personal quirks and limitations of the ordained priest are not obstructions to contact with God. Although personal qualities of the priest are important, the official, sacramental nature of his office takes priority over his limitations and indeed his gifts and talents. Greshake observes, «Because of its institutional and supra-personal character, the office is no more than a visible and sacramental instrument of immediate contact with God: it does not destroy this contact»[178]. Sacramental character, then, expresses the basic truth that the Church is utterly dependent upon Christ, who alone is Lord and therefore the source of any authority the priest might have: an authority always understood as being directed toward the service of the Church.

3.4.3 Existential Dimensions

Because the ministerial priesthood is a sacramental sign of the presence of Christ, which imprints itself in the very being of the priest, the onto-logical nature inevitably takes on existential dimensions[179]. That the priest is affected on the level of his being will surely have ramifications in all areas of his life, including his activities. Since sacramental charac-ter is intended for the mission of the Church, a mission to be acted on and carried out, then character, of its very nature, has a dynamic core.

In the light of the qualities of Christ the Head and Shepherd, noted above, the character bestowed in ordination inevitably reveals itself in a life of increasingly self-sacrificing love. If this process of transformation does not take place, the problem is not to be located in sacramental character, but rather in the person himself, who has allowed the effects of ordination to remain extrinsic to him, thus preventing his consecration from attaining its full transformational value[180]. Although often criti-cized and misunderstood today, because of the ontological language associated with it, the notion of character is actually a dynamic concept

---

[178] G. GRESHAKE, *Meaning of Christian Priesthood*, 62.

[179] Kasper notes that it is «[...] precisely when one understands function [...] not [as] being an external function quality but [as] something that draws a person completely into service and seizes him, that one can see how it stamps a person in his very nature and how it is an ontological determination of that person, which does not exist *in addition* to that person's essential relations and functions but rather *in* them. As soon as one frees oneself from a purely substantialist and "heavy-handed" ontology, which was certainly not the ontology of the great theologians of the High Middle Ages, alternatives like that between ontological and functional disappear of themselves», W. KASPER, «Ministry in the Church», 189.

[180] Cf. J. GALOT, *Theology of the Priesthood*, 207.

that expresses the configuration of the individual priest to Christ and the enduring faithfulness of God to his people in the Church. The ordained priesthood must be understood in terms of this fidelity of God.

3.5 *Conclusions: The Christological Foundations of Priest as Leader*

To conclude this section on the christological underpinnings of the ministerial priesthood, a number of observations are in order. First, the documents give a portrait of Jesus Christ as the one consecrated and sent by the Father to engage in his mission of preaching, sanctifying, and ruling God's people as the Head and Shepherd of the Church, his Body. The ministerial priesthood thus finds a model for priestly leadership first of all in Christ himself. Second, like Christ, the priest is consecrated and set apart; he represents Christ in his position as Head in the service of unity and, like Christ, engages in the threefold mission. In both his identity and in his activity, then, the reality of leadership is intrinsically present, because it is a leadership rooted in Christ himself, not conferred by a community. The configuration to Christ's headship clearly affirms the priest's leadership role in relation to the body, the Church, with such configuration bestowing upon the priest genuine authority that is rooted in the sacrament and exercised for one purpose only: to build up the Body of Christ. Third, because it is rooted in Christ, priestly leadership must follow the pattern of Christ. Thus, «shepherd», and all it implies, is the controlling image and modifies what was said about the image of headship. Following the pattern of Christ the Good Shepherd, the priest exercises a genuine leadership of self-giving love and service. Immersed in the community, he is nevertheless distinct within it and exercises authority insofar as his life is dedicated to the life of the flock, the Church. Finally, like the Good Shepherd the priest dedicates his entire life to the flock: the sacramental character received in ordination «[...] impresses upon the being of the baptized person an orientation which commits the whole self to the mission of the priest. [...] God engraves that mission in the very person. He makes it inseparable from personal being»[181]. Because this dedication entails the entire life of the priest, it is a permanent commitment.

---

[181] J. GALOT, *Theology of the Priesthood*, 201.

4. The Ministerial Priesthood: Expressed in a Set of Functions and Relationships

Having considered the ministerial priesthood from an ontological perspective, that is from its christological and ecclesiological underpinnings, it will now be examined from the more existential perspective of its activities and relations. Cordes observes, «Both perspectives [ontological and existential] mutually determine one another so that the full form of Holy Orders is neither truncated in actuality nor prejudiced on the ontological level»[182]. The progression follows that of both *LG* 28 and *PO*, which begin by considering the nature or essence of the ministerial priesthood, then move to a description of the actual ministry of priests in terms of their functions and relationships (Cf. *LG* 28 and *PO*, Chapters 1 and 2). *MP* follows the same general structure and order as the conciliar documents, beginning with a doctrinal understanding and then exploring the more practical implications for the ministry and life of the priest. The exploration in this section will naturally touch on themes examined earlier, but whereas before they were approached ontologically, now the more experiential dimensions will be emphasized.

4.1 *The Functional Aspect of Ministerial Priesthood*

Articles 4 through 6 of *PO* describe the prophetic, priestly, and kingly functions of presbyteral office which were examined above in the christological section. Because they constitute the primary categories of ministerial priestly activity, they will now be approached by way of description in order to fill out the portrait of priest as leader.

In the structure of *PO* 2, the prophetic function (preaching) comes first, followed by the priestly function (sanctifying), and finally the kingly function (pastoring or governing)[183], a structure that unfolds in the same order in *LG* 28. Similarly, but with less clarity, *MP* II.1.1 describes the threefold ministry, giving greater emphasis, however, to

---

182 P. J. CORDES, «Commentary on the Decree», 237.

183 Some authors equate priestly leadership with the «kingly» office or function. Cf., for example, K. B. OSBORNE, *Priesthood*, 335: «The office of leader (king) is then discussed [...]»; Also pp. 319.323. This seems to be an excessively narrow understanding of priest as leader which identifies priestly leadership only with one specific role, whereas it has been demonstrated that leadership is rooted in the sacrament of Orders which configures the priest to Christ, Head and Shepherd. Such configuration puts the ministerial priesthood into a stance of leadership towards the Church, a stance which transcends the various functions. The priest acts as a leader in all three dimensions of the threefold office of priest, prophet, and king.

the functions of preaching and sanctifying. The implication seems to be that in exercising the first two functions, the third, or kingly function, is implicitly exercised. The order in which the three offices are listed is significant and follows a certain logic[184]. Ratzinger, however, cautions against understanding the threefold structure as a rigid framework with one of the functions dominating the others: «The unity of priestly ministry, which is constantly at the center of the discussion, emerges so strongly that the classic threefold order of priestly functions decreases considerably in significance»[185]. The framework thus allows for a certain fluidity and flexibility.

4.1.1 Prophetic Function

In listing the prophetic, or preaching function of the priest first, according to Wulf, the Council begins «[...] with a concise but meaty theology of the Word. [...] Thus, in actuality preaching is the start of all priestly activity and its center also»[186]. Similarly, the Synod emphasizes that the priestly mission «[...] must begin with the preaching of God's Word» (*MP* II.1.1). Despite his emphasis on the unity of the threefold ministry, Ratzinger sees preaching as the «construction center» on which the Council builds its understanding of the ministerial priesthood[187].

By asserting in *PO* 4 that priests «[...] have as their primary duty the proclamation of the gospel of God to all», the Council posits the work of evangelization as a basic aspect of priestly activity. Such proclamation is not to be limited to formal liturgical settings, but «[...] they exercise this sacred function of Christ most of all in the Eucharistic liturgy or synaxis» (*LG* 28). The Gospel is to be proclaimed by priests not only in formal preaching, but in their behavior, in their interaction with others, in teaching or explaining the Church's faith, and in helping people to understand the needs and problems of the world through the prism of the Gospel. No matter what the activity, priests are to preach God's Word and summon all people to conversion and holiness (cf. *PO* 4).

---

[184] Cf. F. WULF, «Commentary on the Decree», 228. Castellucci puts the preaching ministry first in the order of logic, the sacramental ministry first ontologically, or in qualitative fulfillment, and the pastoral ministry first in the sphere of quantitative extent. Cf. E. CASTELLUCCI, «L'identità del presbitero», 110.

[185] J. RATZINGER, *Priestly Ministry*, 16.

[186] F. WULF, «Commentary on the Decree», 228.

[187] Cf. J. RATZINGER, *Priestly Ministry*, 17. For a thorough treatment of the preaching office and the ministerial priesthood, see S. R. MIGLIARESE, «The Ministry of the Word as *Primum Officium*».

Such a comprehensive, self-transcending understanding of the function of preaching shows clearly that it cannot be merely an activity to engage in intermittently, but implies a life-stance of allowing oneself to be penetrated to the very core by the Word of God, «[...] even when this proclamation turns against us, even when the sword of God's Word lays bare its necessary two-edged blade»[188]. Acknowledging the centrality of the Word in a priest's ministry, *PO* encourages an accompanying spirituality that exhorts priests to «[...] every day read and listen to that Word which they are required to teach others. [...] Preoccupied with welcoming this message into their hearts [...] priests search for a better way to share with others the fruits of their own contemplation» (*PO* 13).

Imbued with God's Word, priests will be better able to proclaim that Word more fruitfully and apply it to the «[...] concrete circumstances of life» (*PO* 4). Such concern for the Word will also attune priests to the needs of their community so that they will be able to preach more efficaciously and allow God's Word to influence the lives of those who hear them. *PO* 4 and 13 stress that the witness of a priest's life is of primary importance because it is there that the Gospel is most fully proclaimed. Such witness «[...] is particularly important in those situations in which the Gospel cannot be openly preached and men must be brought to God by the lives of others»[189]. Although a priest's talents and skills contribute to the efficacy of his preaching and should be developed, the tenor of *PO* 4 accents the primary importance of the personal, lived faith of the priests, for it is in lived example that his word will both arouse and nourish people's faith[190]. Similarly, Ratzinger says, «The priest has to be a living contemplation of the Word and not simply a cultic technician or manager»[191]. He stresses that, in order to engage in the function of preaching, the Word must penetrate and take hold of the priest's being. Here, interiority and ministry move closer together: «For precisely this permitting oneself to be called upon for the ministry of preaching draws our very selves into this ministry»[192]. The prophetic office of the ordained priesthood, then, is clearly to be understood as more than a function. It is to be grasped at the level of consecration and mission,

---

188 J. RATZINGER, *Priestly Ministry*, 17. For a criticism of PO's failure to acknowledge the modern hermeneutical problems which impinge on the preaching function, see F. WULF, «Commentary on the Decree», 230.

189 D. N. POWER, *Ministers of Christ and His Church*, 156.

190 Cf. F. WULF, «Commentary on the Decree», 229.

191 J. RATZINGER, *Priestly Ministry*, 18.

192 J. RATZINGER, *Priestly Ministry*, 19.

which engages the priest at the level of his being. Thus because of its intrinsically dynamic nature, the prophetic office manifests itself in his activities: the priest is to be immersed in the Word of God and, out of this immersion, engage in prophetic ministry. The implications of this for understanding the priest as a leader seem clear. True priestly leadership, from the perspective of the prophetic office, implies not simply the activity of preaching itself, but the immersion of the priest in the Word of God. Out of such an immersion his prophetic leadership emerges.

4.1.2 Priestly Function

PO 5 examines the sacerdotal function of the ministerial priesthood, concentrating on the liturgical-sacramental role. Relevant to the priest as leader, two aspects of this section of the decree are noteworthy — the emphases on his connection to the bishop and centrality of the Eucharist:

> In administering the sacraments, as St. Ignatius Martyr already bore witness in the days of the primitive Church, priests by various titles are bound together hierarchically with the bishop. Thus, in a certain way, they make him present in every gathering of the faithful (*PO* 5).

Power notes with some irony that this article highlights sacramental celebrations to express the foundational character of the episcopacy for the sacrament of Orders; the irony is, «[...] it was precisely because of sacramental powers communicated through ordination to the presbyterate that scholasticism based its theology of Orders on the presbyterate rather than the episcopate»[193]. As noted earlier, one of the Council's most important doctrinal teachings was to reverse this and affirm that it is the bishop who possesses the fullness of Orders. *PO* 5 stresses the priest's communion with and dependence on the bishop «[...] even in the exercise of his sacramental power, and the relation to the bishop as head of the diocese which must always be present in his liturgical ministry»[194]. This emphasizes the priest's dependence on the bishop, and more importantly, the unity of the ordained ministry which expresses and mirrors the unity of the Church: «This unity must show itself to exist pre-eminently in the manifest realization of the deepest unity of the Church»[195], as expressed in the Eucharist.

Priesthood, in all its functions, is at the service of unity, but most especially so in the Eucharist. Such unity is expressed in the priest's

---

[193] D. N. POWER, *Ministers of Christ and His Church*, 157.
[194] D. N. POWER, *Ministers of Christ and His Church*, 157.
[195] F. WULF, «Commentary on the Decree», 231.

collegial, fraternal, and filial relationship with the bishop, which is a constitutive dimension of the Eucharistic celebration: «The presupposition is, namely, that of brotherhood»[196]. Previously it was shown that priestly leadership was exercised only in the context of his relation to the bishop. Connected with the Eucharist, the goal of such leadership becomes clearer: because its goal is to bring about unity in the midst of diversity, the leadership function of the priest is essentially in the service of the unity which is at the heart of the Eucharist[197].

In unambiguous language *PO* 5 affirms the centrality of the Eucharist in the life of the Church and the sacerdotal function of the priest:

> The other sacraments, as well as every ministry of the Church and every work of the apostolate, are united with the most holy Eucharist and are directed toward it. For the most blessed Eucharist contains the Church's entire spiritual wealth, that is, Christ Himself, our passover and our living bread. [...] Hence the Eucharist shows itself to be the source and the apex of the whole work of preaching the Gospel (*PO* 5).

This passage emphasizes the intrinsic unity of word and sacrament, thus their central place in the Church and in priestly ministry. Similarly, the Synod affirms the unity «[...] between evangelization and sacramental life [which is] [...] always proper to the ministerial priesthood and must be carefully kept in mind by every priest» (*MP* II.1.1). Because the Eucharistic celebration is at the center of the proclamation of the Gospel, is in fact the culmination of the Gospel, it is at the heart of priestly life and ministry[198]. The Eucharist, as «the very heartbeat of the congregation of the faithful» (*PO* 5), places certain exigencies upon the priest, making part of his function to help people understand the profound connection between their own lives and the sacrifice of Christ. *PO* 5 goes on to list ways priests make the Eucharist central in their own lives and the lives of the faithful. To develop a particularly *sacerdotal* spirituality compatible with the priestly function, *PO* 13 encourages priests «[...] to imitate the realities they deal with», and to celebrate Mass each day in order to offer «[...] their whole selves every day to God» in imitation of the sacrifice of Christ celebrated in the Eucharist (*PO* 13). Pastoral love, the bond of priestly perfection and a unifying power in priests' lives, «[...] flows mainly from the Eucharistic sacrifice» which must

---

[196] J. RATZINGER, *Priestly Ministry*, 22.
[197] Cf. J. RATZINGER, *Priestly Ministry*, 22.
[198] Cf. J. RATZINGER, *Priestly Ministry*, 21.

become «[...] the center and root of the whole priestly life» (*PO* 14) if the priest is to properly fulfill all of his priestly functions.

4.1.3 Kingly Function

Exercising the office of Christ the Head and the Shepherd, priests «gather God's family together as a brotherhood of living unity, and lead it through Christ and in the Spirit of God to the Father» (*PO* 6). «They are consecrated to [...] shepherd the faithful» (*LG* 28). Any spiritual authority they receive in ordination is given for the express purpose of building up the Church. In carrying out their ministry of shepherding, therefore, priests are to look to the Lord as their model (cf. *PO* 6).

The assertion of *PO* 6, that the priest represents Christ as Head and Shepherd to the congregation, is a key statement[199]. As noted earlier, a distinctive trait of the shepherd is to have authority over the flock, and it is precisely in this authority that what is unique to the ministerial priesthood stands out[200]. While the bishop's office possesses the fullness of Orders and the priestly office exists in a relationship of dependence to the episcopacy, the authority of the ministerial priesthood is genuine, even if subordinate. «It is a question of a special type of authority, of spiritual authority, which requires and includes the function of ruling [...] but is not that in essence»[201]. The authority of the presbyter is rooted, not in a mere function of governing, but in the sense of «[...] being an instrument, a minister, of him who alone is Head and Shepherd of the congregation»[202]. The authority of the presbyter, while subsidiary to and dependent on the bishop, is no less real; it represents an existential and ontological sharing in Christ's mission, which determines the person of the ordained priest[203]. The purpose of this authority, to build up the Church, is elaborated in the description of the priest's pastoral tasks: education of the members of the Church to Christian maturity and to the formation of a genuine Christian community.

The task of the presbyter, then, is to help individuals and also to form a community «[...] which can take its place as an organ in the mystical body of Christ»[204]. This community is to be both inward looking, foster-

---

199 Cf. F. WULF, «Commentary on the Decree», 234.

200 Cf. J. GALOT, *Theology of the Priesthood*, 138.

201 F. WULF, «Commentary on the Decree», 234.

202 F. WULF, «Commentary on the Decree», 234.

203 Cf. F. WULF, «Commentary on the Decree», 234.

204 D. N. POWER, *Ministers of Christ and His Church*, 157.

ing the development and genuine vocations of its members, and outward looking, with a missionary concern for the local Church and the universal Church, thus placing certain boundaries around the priest's authority:

> The nature of the leadership required of the minister [...] cannot consist only in giving commands and determining lines of conduct. He must educate the faithful in such a way that each one acquires that maturity necessary to determine his own conduct according to Christian principles and show a sense of responsibility for the good of others and for the entire community[205].

Priestly leadership is thus embodied in a twofold context determined by its subsidiarity to the bishop and its service of building up the Church.

As noted above, by itself the emphasis on priestly power and authority, as well as the priest's configuration with the headship of Christ, can lead to a distorted understanding of the «kingly» function of the priesthood. It is crucial, therefore, to approach it from its proper context, which is service to the Church in the image of Christ the Good Shepherd. Power and authority in the Church are associated with the shepherd's office. In this way authority enters a Christian context, thus opening out onto love and service: any authority which the priest may have received in ordination can only be legitimately exercised if it is a reflection of the true Shepherd who «[...] in the Incarnation raises the lost sheep, mankind, onto his shoulders and shows himself to be the true Shepherd»[206]. This understanding of the priest as pastor, a man for others who gives his life for those who are poor, and concerns himself with the Christian edification of his people, reflects the understanding of Shepherd as it is embodied by Christ in his threefold office.

The examination of the prophetic, priestly, and pastoral functions of the priest, as articulated in *PO* 4, 5 and 6, reveals that the three functions are fundamentally interconnected, profoundly integrated, and mutually ordered — not simply juxtaposed to one another[207]. The priest is thus consecrated and given in service for the purpose of building up the Church through the exercise of the threefold ministry. This threefold ministry, as exercised by the ministerial priesthood, finds its clearest expression in the celebration of the Eucharist, «the center of the assembly of the faithful over which the priest presides» (*PO* 5).

---

[205] D. N. POWER, *Ministers of Christ and His Church*, 158. It must also be noted that such authority is regulated and directed by Church law.

[206] J. RATZINGER, *Priestly Ministry*, 23.

[207] Cf. E. CASTELLUCCI, «L'identità del presbitero», 111.

4.2 *The Relational Aspect of Ministerial Priesthood*

Presbyterorum Ordinis explores at length the topic of the relationships that are associated with the ministerial priesthood. Following the order of *Lumen Gentium* 28, *PO* treats of priests as related to bishops (*PO* 7), other priests (*PO* 8), and the faithful or laity (*PO* 9). The Synod also follows this exact order in describing priests' relations (cf. *MP* II.2.1.2.3). The arrangement of these three topics is significant because it indicates the new dimension of life and activity into which the ministerial priest enters[208].

Because the bishop possesses the fullness of Orders and is the primary representative of the priesthood of Christ within his diocese, this relationship is described first. The priest carries out his ministry within the framework of a presbyterate and so his relationship to other priests is explored next. Finally, since his relation to bishops and to fellow priests is directed toward Christ's mission of proclaiming the Gospel to all, his relationship to those served by his ministry is treated[209]. *PO* makes clear that «communion» roots all of ministerial priesthood's relationships:

> the very unity of their consecration and mission requires their hierarchical communion with the order of bishops (*PO* 7); [...] by ordination, all priests are united among themselves in an intimate sacramental brotherhood. [...] by reason of the same communion in the priesthood, priests should realize that they have special obligations toward priests (*PO* 8); [...] priests are brothers among brothers with all those who have been reborn at the baptismal font. They are all members of one and the same body of Christ, whose upbuilding is entrusted to all (*PO* 9).

That the ministerial priesthood is grounded in hierarchical communion and is at the service of the unity of the entire Church has been noted above. In this section the relationships of the ministerial priesthood to the bishop, other priests, and laity will be examined from the perspective of how they impinge on priest as leader, and what they offer for developing a deeper understanding of priestly leadership.

4.2.1 Priests As Related to Bishops

The dependency of the ministerial priesthood upon the episcopacy was examined above. In this section the dynamics of the priest-bishop relationship will be explored. Described in *PO* 7 and *MP* II.2.1, this dynamism is best captured in one word: «collaboration», which seems to be

---

208 Cf. P. J. CORDES, «Commentary on the Decree», 237.
209 Cf. P. J. CORDES, «Commentary on the Decree», 237.

the leitmotif of both paragraphs. The mutual dependency of those who belong to the priestly grade of Holy Orders is emphasized in this section. Such mutual dependency, by definition, implies a relationship of cooperation and collaboration, and is rooted in the one priesthood of Christ in which both priests and bishops share:

> Therefore, by reason of the gift of the Holy Spirit which is given to priests in sacred ordination, bishops should regard them as necessary helpers and counsellors in the ministry and in the task of teaching, sanctifying, and nourishing the people of God (*PO* 7).

Such collaboration is not to be understood simply as a matter of function or expedience but is «[...] at the same time supernatural» (*MP* II.2.1), thus anchored in the Church's faith.

While acknowledging that there is a juridical aspect to the relationship between priest and bishop, and that the exercise of the ministry is dependent upon the canonical mission received from the bishop[210], *PO* 7 emphasizes that the priest-bishop relationship is intrinsically «[...] determined by the fact that the priesthood subsisting in the bishop and in the priest is the one priesthood of Christ»[211]. This communion provides the basis for collaboration between the two orders. *PO* notes that this communion is expressed liturgically in the practice of concelebration and in the mention of the bishop in the Eucharistic prayer (cf. *PO* 7). The same text further notes that the gift of the Holy Spirit conferred on the priest in ordination by the bishop is the basis for participating in the priesthood of Christ and thus, the basis for collaboration: «Through this permanent spiritual endowment the presbyters become genuine, serious, necessary partners of the bishops in the task of leading the people of God»[212]. There was some question about the use of the words «counsellors» and «necessary helpers» in describing the nature of the relationship between priests and bishops: «"Counsellor" had been rejected by the doctrinal commission for the Constitution on the Church (*LG*) as inapplicable to presbyters»[213]. It is, therefore, noteworthy that it is used in the document on the priesthood (*PO* 7). That priests are called «necessary helpers» indicates that their ministry is not an incidental

---

210 Cf. P. J. CORDES, «Commentary on the Decree», 238.

211 P. J. CORDES, «Commentary on the Decree», 238.

212 P. J. CORDES, «Commentary on the Decree», 240. Cordes notes that this collaboration is not simply an expression of good will on the part of the Council Fathers, but a theological proposition.

213 D. N. POWER, *Ministers of Christ and His Church*, 159.

commodity «[...] which the bishops may dispense with at will»[214], but rather an intrinsic aspect of the presbyterate.

The emphasis on priests as collaborators with the bishops in ministry should not simply be interpreted as a sign of the Council and Synod Fathers trying to reach some kind of accomodation with the democratic tendencies of the times. Rather, the mutual dependency of the two priestly orders is rooted in the Church's tradition, to which *PO* 7 appeals in order to strengthen its argument. Such citations of the tradition reveal that the collaborative role of presbyters is not an innovation of the Council, but an ancient part of the Church's tradition[215].

In addition to emphasizing the collaborative nature of the priest-bishop relationship, *PO* goes on to describe the qualities that should characterize their interaction: «[...] on account of this communion in the same priesthood and ministry, the bishop should regard priests as his brothers and friends» (*PO* 7). This description is significant because, whereas in *LG* 28 and *CD* 16 the bishop-priest relationship is described in terms of filial friendship, *PO* 7 adds the notion of fraternity. Consequently, not only is the bishop responsible for the spiritual welfare of his priests and their continual formation, but he is also to «[...] consult them, and have discussions with them about those matters which concern the necessities of pastoral work and the welfare of the diocese» (*PO* 7). Retreating from the language of fraternity, the Synod emphasizes «[...] mutual charity, filial and friendly confidence and constant and patient dialogue» (*MP* II.2.1) as hallmarks of the relationship. Citing St. Ignatius of Antioch and St. Jerome, the Council suggests practical ways in which to make such consultation a reality: by forming a council or a senate of priests for the purpose of assisting the bishop in governing the diocese (cf. *PO* 7)[216].

---

[214] D. N. POWER, *Ministers of Christ and His Church*, 159.

[215] Cf. D. N. POWER, *Ministers of Christ and His Church*, 161. Fransen describes the collegiality of Orders as «the decisive rediscovery of Vatican II». Because «[...] the Church is a fellowship of faith and charity», the collegiality of Orders «[...] is nothing else [...] than sharing in this fellowship on the level of a ministry of authority. Hence the collegiality in question cannot be exercised independently of this fellowship in faith of the people of God. There is a continuous osmosis or interpenetration between the fellowship of faith and the college of those in Orders. This is not the same thing at all as the democratic systems of our age, though the democratic spirit may have favoured the rediscovery of the community dimensions which were already outlined in the NT», P. FRANSEN, «Orders and Ordination», 321.

[216] For patristic evidence of priest councils assisting the bishop in the task of governing see D. N. POWER, *Ministers of Christ and His Church*, 48-52. For

If bishops are to approach priests from a stance of friendship and fraternity, as the Council emphasizes, priests are to relate to the bishop with an attitude of respect, cooperation, and obedience: «This priestly obedience animated with a spirit of cooperation is based on the very sharing in the episcopal ministry which is conferred on priests both through the sacrament of Orders and the canonical mission» (*PO* 7). Such an understanding of obedience reflects a pastoral approach. More than simply an ascetic instrument, obedience is part of and intrinsic to the organic structure of ministry itself: «The official ministry of the Church demands the coordinated action of all those taking part in it»[217]. With the mission of the Church in mind and heart, the natural dynamism that exists at the heart of the bishop-priest relation invites cooperation and obedience for the sake of the life of the Church. While not abjuring the juridical structures that demand such obedience, the text emphasizes the interior qualities of authority and solicitude, which call forth qualities of respect and obedience, and link them with service to the Church.

4.2.2 Priests as Related to Other Priests

Since the topic of the renewal of the notion of *presbyterate* was examined earlier, this section will limit itself to an exploration of the mutual responsibility of priests for one another as it is articulated in *PO* 8. *MP* II.2.2 echoes what the Council has to say on this topic. Such mutual responsibility is rooted in the unity they share as priests: «Each one therefore, is united by special bonds of apostolic charity, ministry, and brotherhood with the other members of his presbyterium» (*PO* 8). After describing the unity in Christ that is the foundation of the presbyterate, the text spells out the practical, human consequences of such unity: hospitality, kindliness, sharing of goods in common, solicitousness for the sick and afflicted among them, care for the over-burdened priests, exiled priests, mutual assistance, companionship, community (cf. *PO* 8). According to Cordes, in this section the Decree departs from its usual starting point for considering all aspects of priestly life, namely, the pastoral task of the priest; instead it emphasizes that the main purpose of priests' obligations to each other is to aid the spiritual life[218]. It should be noted, however, that the text does mention the more effective

---

commentary on the theological precedence of presbyteral councils over pastoral councils in diocesan structures see P. J. CORDES, «Commentary on the Decree», 242.

[217] P. J. CORDES, «Commentary on the Decree», 244.

[218] Cf. P. J. CORDES, «Commentary on the Decree», 253.

cooperation in ministry as one of the primary motivations for their mutual relationships.

Interestingly, the Council was realistic in highlighting the dangers to priestly life arising from loneliness and difficult circumstances. Similarly, it acknowledges the reality of priests who have failed in some way. It is in these situations «[...] that brotherly love must be maintained and provide genuine assistance, tactful admonition, and prayer so that none can be allowed to fall»[219]. *PO* also encourages «[...] some kind or other of community life» (*PO* 8), but is vague as to what form this life might take. What is clear is that such community life is to be determined and governed by personal or pastoral need, and should provide opportunity for «frequent and regular gatherings» (*PO* 8). Such encouragement is important today because of greatly decreased numbers of priests, the complexity of the work, and the common knowledge that priests are human and do «[...] fail in some way» (cf. *PO* 8). In this environment the document is a reminder that priests have obligations to help one another, obligations which are rooted in the very essence and structure of priestly existence.

4.2.3 Priests as Related to the Faithful

PO 9 begins from the premise in *LG* 10 and 28, and in *PO* 2, that all Christians share in the one priesthood of Christ, even though some, through ordination, come to participate in the one priesthood of Christ in an essentially different way: «[...] the text starts from the fact that those enjoying the general priesthood and those bearing the official priesthood are equal in the sight of God»[220]. They are «[...] brothers among brothers with all who have been reborn at the baptismal font» (*PO* 9). Although *MP* II.2.3 appeals to *PO* 9 as its basis, it emphasizes the difference between the two modes of priesthood without putting them into the wider context of first sharing in the one priesthood of Christ, which *PO* differently emphasizes.

What then is distinctive in their relationship? What is its dynamism? This has already been considered from the perspective of the ministerial priest as being configured to Christ the Head and Shepherd. Now it will be considered from the perspective of its existential dynamic.

Ratzinger describes this relationship most cogently in the light of St. Augustine's description of himself in relation to those he was serving

---

[219] P. J. CORDES, «Commentary on the Decree», 255.
[220] P. J. CORDES, «Commentary on the Decree», 255.

as bishop: «Where what I am for you frightens me, what I am with you encourages me. For you I am a bishop, with you I am a Christian. The former refers to the office and its peril, the latter to grace and salvation»[221]. Ratzinger observes that this statement is closely connected to Augustine's understanding of Trinity which emphasizes that the three persons in God are known in their relation to one another: «They are trinitarian persons only in a turning away from self to the other persons, so that the being of person and being-in-relationship are identical»[222]. According to Ratzinger, Augustine approaches Church office as a relational concept because the statement in which he identifies himself both as Christian and bishop follows the same thought pattern as his understanding of the Trinity. Taken in and of itself, the Christian calling is one and indivisible. A Christian is only a Christian, «[...] not some more exalted being. [...] *"Ad se"*, each is a Christian and that is the dignity of each. It is in relation to others, *"pro vobis"*, that one is a bearer of office»[223], in an irrevocable way affecting the person's entire being[224]. This understanding of office elucidates the Council's teaching on the relationship of priests to the faithful. The priest is brother by virtue of baptism, and pastor in his «being for» by virtue of his ordination.

Ministerial authority is «[...] tied to the fact that the priest is an envoy, [...] a being that depends on others and is oriented towards others»[225]. As envoy the priest makes present, in word and action, the one who sends him. It also means that he is completely dedicated to the ones to whom he has been sent. Understood from the perspective of this relational dynamism, the priest's ministry becomes the source of spiritual nourishment and growth because there is a unity between the activity of priestly ministry and the interiority of a life with God. Thus, the concept of office, understood as envoy or ambassador, signifies the «[...] colossal, almost explosive opening up of one's own existence on two sides»[226], because in leading others the priest himself is being formed and led by the Spirit[227].

---

221 ST. AUGUSTINE, Serm. 340, 1 PL 38, 1483, cited in J. RATZINGER, *Priestly Ministry*, 24. Cf. *LG* 32.

222 J. RATZINGER, *Priestly Ministry*, 24-25.

223 J. RATZINGER, *Priestly Ministry*, 25.

224 Cf. J. RATZINGER, *Priestly Ministry*, 24-25.

225 P. J. CORDES, «Commentary on the Decree», 258. For a discussion of presbyter as ambassador, see C. MEYER, «Ambassadors of Christ», 759-766.

226 P. J. CORDES, «Commentary on the Decree», 258.

227 Cf. J. RATZINGER, *Priestly Ministry*, 26.

In terms of priest as leader, the relational dynamism between priests and the laity, as stressed above, can only be understood in relation to service. Terms such as office and authority, as crucial as they are, can only be authentically interpreted and lived out when understood in the larger context of the radical equality which baptism bestows on all Christians. This is the primary identity, and ordained ministry has but one purpose: to serve this identity by building up the Church. As both the ecclesiological and christological perspectives have emphasized, the basic category is service; leadership gives substance and definition to the service and can never be authentically understood apart from the context of service.

5. Conclusions

The exploration of the conciliar and synodal documents on priesthood began with a rather general description of leadership as involving the capacity to inspire, direct, and support a group in its movement towards a goal. Christian leadership corresponds to the faith, hope, and love which are at the heart of the Church. The Christian leader, therefore, must operate out of the Church's vision of faith, motivate by the example of his or her charity, and encourage by instilling in the community his or her own hope in Christ. This is the kind of leadership to which all Christians are called. But what is distinctive about the leadership of priests?

A description or definition of priest as leader, then, will necessarily have ontological and existential, intrinsic and extrinsic aspects. Sharing in the universal priesthood as a member of the Body of Christ, the priest, through ordination, is sacramentally configured to Christ the Head and Shepherd. Although remaining a member of the Body, this configuration essentially changes the quality of his membership. He now stands in relation to the Body from the perspective of Christ's Headship. The configuration to Christ the Head and Shepherd, rooted in the sacrament of Orders, both designates and enables the ministerial priest to serve the Body of Christ in a capacity of leadership. This is a crucial starting point for developing an understanding of priest as leader because it establishes priestly leadership, neither in himself nor in a function, but in his configuration to Christ in the sacrament of Orders. This leadership, moreover, is marked by very specific characteristics, namely those of the Good Shepherd. It is a leadership rooted in love and service, which is to say that it is self-sacrificing, concerned for the life of the community, and permanent. «Sacramental character» best expresses these qualities because it signifies and expresses Christ's presence in and fidelity to his

Church in a very particular way, which leads into some of the external dynamics of priestly leadership.

Although not identified with any one office or function, priestly leadership is naturally and necessarily expressed in a set of functions. The leadership functions of the ministerial priest, however, are not simply external actions he performs but are rooted in certain exigencies associated with his office. In other words, the priest is to personalize his mission as Christ did. The priest's ministry and interiority are not separate compartments, but complementary aspects of his life, mutually nourishing each other. The challenge for the priest is not simply to preach and celebrate the sacraments, but to become himself a living example of the power of the Word and the reality of the Paschal Mystery at work in his own life, so that he will be able to effectively lead after the example of Christ.

Finally, the priest exercises his ministry in the context of a network of relationships: with his bishop, with other priests, and with the faithful. Priestly leadership, rooted in hierarchical communion, is thus accountable, collaborative, and collegial. It is never an end in itself, but always exercised for the sake of the unity of the Church and the Church's mission. This ecclesiological, christological, and pastoral understanding of priestly leadership will be deepened and filled-out even more in the next chapter, which explores Pope John Paul II's 1992 Apostolic Exhortation on the formation of priests, *Pastores Dabo Vobis*.

CHAPTER III

Priest As Leader in *Pastores Dabo Vobis*

1. Development of the Theme

On April 7, 1992, Pope John Paul II's Post-Synodal Apostolic Exhortation, *Pastores Dabo Vobis*: On the Formation of Priests in the Circumstances of the Present Day[1] (*PDV*), was released at a press conference given by the Secretary General of the Synod of Bishops, Archbishop Jan P. Schotte. The Exhortation is the culmination of the work of the Eighth Ordinary General Assembly of the Synod of Bishops, convened in 1990 to consider the theme of priestly formation[2].

The Synod's theme had its origins in the 1987 Synod on the Laity where the intrinsic connection between lay and priestly vocations, and the

---

[1] *AAS* 84 (1992) 657-804. All references to *Pastores Dabo Vobis* (hereafter *PDV*), are taken from the English translation, «*Pastores Dabo Vobis*, Post-Synodal Apostolic Exhortation of His Holiness John Paul II to the Bishops, Clergy and Faithful on the Formation of Priests in the Circumstances of the Present Day, 25 March 1992».

[2] At the April, 1992 Press Conference, Schotte referred to the Synod of Bishops as «[...] one of the first and most direct fruits of the Second Vatican Council [and] one of the most effective means for introducing into the life of the Church the major orientations and total wealth of the Council documents. Every Synod [...] is an event of great importance which contributes continuously to that process of implementing and deepening the Council's intention to ensure the Church's continuous updating. [...] The titles of the various Post Synodal Apostolic Exhortations which have come one after another show how the Church is continually examining herself on the most important aspects of her mission: *Evangelii Nuntiandi* (1974), *Catechesi Tradendae* (1977), *Familiaris Consortio* (1980), *Reconciliatio et Paenitentia* (1983), *Christifideles Laici* (1987), and now *Pastores Dabo Vobis*». Schotte further states, «All these titles, and the Synod Assemblies even more so, constitute *per se* a pastoral programme for constant renewal and a collegial guarantee to the Church's sure progress in fidelity to the mandate received from Jesus Christ», *OR*, «*Pastores Dabo Vobis*», 8 April 1992 [weekly edition in English], 1.4.

important role of the priest as a guide, collaborator, and model of holiness for the laity, was emphasized by a number of participants[3]. In his closing address to the 1990 Synod on priestly formation, Pope John Paul II alluded to the influence of the 1987 Synod by acknowledging that the choice of the topic of priestly formation was a response to a concern expressed at that Synod: «The more the lay apostolate develops, the more strongly is felt the need to have priests — and priests who are formed well»[4]. He also acknowledged the influence of the 1987 Synod in the text of *PDV*:

> This same Synod [1990] also sought to answer a request which was made at the previous Synod on the vocation and mission of the laity in the Church and in the world. Lay people themselves asked that priests commit themselves to their formation so that they, the laity, could be suitably helped to fulfill their role in the ecclesial mission which is shared by all (*PDV 3*).

It was during the deliberations of the Synod on the Laity in 1987, then, that the topic for the 1990 Synod began to emerge[5].

After consulting the Council of the Synod's General Secretariat, subsequent to the 1987 Synod, Pope John Paul II set the topic for the 1990 Synod: «The Formation of Priests in the Circumstances of the Present Day»[6]. Next, a «provisional document» — the *Lineamenta*: The Formation of Priests in the Circumstances of the Present Day (hereafter *Lineamenta*) — was prepared and sent out in order to present the theme and to stimulate suggestions and observations for treating the vari-

---

[3] Cf. J. P. SCHOTTE, «Perché un Sinodo sulla formazione sacerdotale?», 52; *OR*, «Statement by General Secretary», 23 July 1990, 8-10. For a thorough presentation of the Synod of 1990, from its remote preparations to the post-Synodal work of preparing for the ensuing Apostolic Exhortation, see G. CAPRILE, *Il Sinodo dei Vescovi*.

[4] JOHN PAUL II, «Closing Address to the Synod», 378. Cf. *CL* 61: «[...] the Synod Fathers have invited priests and candidates for Orders to be prepared carefully so that they are ready to foster the vocation and mission of the lay faithful».

[5] Archbishop Schotte, the Secretary General of the Synod, noted that in the months following the Synod he officially consulted representatives of the Oriental Churches, Episcopal Conferences, the Roman Curia, and the Union of Superiors General, in order to begin identifying the theme for the Synod of 1990. For a description of this consultation process, see G. CAPRILE, «L'VIII Assemblea generale», 378; J. P. SCHOTTE, «Perché un sinodo?», 52-53; *OR*, «Statement by General Secretary», 23 July 1990, 8-10; SYNOD OF BISHOPS, *Lineamenta*, 3.

[6] Schotte observed that, beginning on the First Sunday of Advent, December 3, 1989, the Holy Father devoted many of his weekly *Angelus* talks to the theme of the forthcoming synod, J. P. SCHOTTE, «Perché un sinodo?», 53.

ous aspects of the topic[7]. The responses to the *Lineamenta* were then gathered and shaped into the Synod «working document» — the *Instrumentum Laboris*: The Formation of Priests in the Circumstances of the Present Day (hereafter *Instrumentum Laboris*) — which became the Synod's agenda[8].

1.1 *The Synod of 1990*

It has been observed that the Synod on priestly formation «[...] probably had a higher proportion of experts than any other Synod because Episcopal Conferences throughout the world tended to elect as their representatives bishops who themselves had been seminary rectors, spiritual directors, professors or vocation directors»[9]. The work of the

---

[7] The *Lineamenta* was a broad outline sent to the Bishops' Conferences, Oriental Churches, Dicasteries of the Roman Curia, and the Union of Superiors General in the hope that these bodies would conduct a widespread consultation in order to produce a comprehensive *Instrumentum Laboris*, or working document, for use at the Synod. Divided into five sections, the *Lineamenta* offered reflections on present day world realities and their impact on priesthood and formation; fundamental presuppositions regarding the doctrine of the ministerial priesthood; the various agents and contexts of formation; the need for integrating the various formational components; and the need for ongoing formation. Responses to the *Lineamenta* revealed ten principal points of convergence. For the purposes of our study, one of the major points of convergence concerns the need for an articulation of a clear and complete statement on the identity and mission of the priest as a central reference point for all formation. As seen in the previous chapter, such an articulation is also a central reference point for an adequate understanding of priest as leader. For an analysis of the *Lineamenta* and the responses to it see SYNOD OF BISHOPS (1989), *Lineamenta*; G. CAPRILE, «L'VIII Assemblea generale», 378-379; ID., *Il Sinodo dei Vescovi*, 3-7; J. P. SCHOTTE, «Perché un sinodo?», 54-64; *OR*, «Statement by General Secretary», 23 July 1990, 8-10.

[8] The *Instrumentum Laboris* was divided into four major sections, generally reflecting the outline of the *Lineamenta*: an exploration of cultural and social environments and their impact on the Church and on priestly formation; a sketch of the doctrinal understanding of the ministerial priesthood and the lines of priestly spirituality; a look at the issues, contexts and agents of formation; and the nature and necessity of ongoing formation for priests. For an analysis of the *Instrumentum Laboris*, see SYNOD OF BISHOPS (1990), *Instrumentum Laboris*; G. CAPRILE, «L'VIII Assemblea generale», 379; ID., *Il Sinodo dei Vescovi*, 7-17; J. P. SCHOTTE, «Perché un sinodo?», 64-66; *OR*, «Statement by General Secretary», 23 July 1990, 8-10.

[9] P. LAGHI, «The Identity and Ministry of the Priest», 22. For a breakdown of Synod membership in terms of places of origin, age, previous synodal or conciliar experience, and seminary formation work experience, see G. CAPRILE, «L'VIII Assemblea generale», 380-381. Archbishop Schotte noted that the Synod was composed of 238 members, 39 of whom were directly appointed by the Holy Father. The other members included the heads of Roman curial offices, patriarchs from Eastern Rite Churches, elected representatives of national episcopal conferences, and regional and

Synod took place in three phases. Phase One, September 30 - October 13, was described as a listening phase during which the Synod Fathers addressed the topic in plenary meetings[10]. Phase Two, October 15-20, was referred to as a period of deeper study of the topic, this time in thirteen small language groups[11] which prepared recommendations that subsequently were submitted to the Synod Special Secretary. With the help of experts, he produced a unified draft list (*Elenchus Unicus*) of *Propositiones* based on those of all the small groups. This preliminary list formed the basis of the work of Phase Three (October 22-27) which was devoted to the final drafting of the *Propositiones* to be given to the Holy Father. From this process a final list (*Elenchus Finalis*) of 41 *Propositiones* (hereafter Propositions) was produced and presented to the Synod Fathers who voted on each one. In keeping with Synod rules, this list of 41 Propositions, overwhelmingly approved by the Synod delegates, was not made public, but was instead given to the Holy Father for use in preparing his post-Synodal Apostolic Exhortation[12].

---

international groups of bishops. Additionally, there were 17 experts assigned to assist the Special Secretary of the Synod, Bishop Henryk Muzynski of Poland, and 43 observers who were able to attend the general sessions and small group discussions. Cf. *OR*, «VIII Synod Opens on Formation Topic». 1 October 1990, 1-2. Schotte later observed that 13 Synod members participated in all sessions of the Second Vatican Council; 9 participated in one or more of them; 131 were attending their first Synod as members; 170 served on seminary staffs; and 74 served on committees related to priestly formation in their respective bishops' conferences. Cf. *OR*, «Major Themes Emerge From Synod Discussions», 15 October 1990, 2. For a complete list of the names of those participating in the 1990 Synod, see D. TETTAMANZI, ed., *La formazione dei sacerdoti*, 19-28; G. CAPRILE, *Il Sinodo dei Vescovi*, 715-729.

[10] See G. CAPRILE, *Il Sinodo dei Vescovi*, 78-324 for a synopsis of each of the interventions at the plenary sessions, 325-382 for the written interventions and 382-426 for the interventions of the auditors. For a synopsis (in Italian) of the *Relatio post disceptationen*, based on the interventions made at the plenary sessions, see pp. 380-381; For the full text (in Latin), see pp. 669-708. The *relatio post disceptationem* was the basis for the small language group discussions.

[11] Cf. G. CAPRILE, «L'VIII Assemblea generale», 386. It was observed that the thirteen small language groups, called *circuli minores*, consisted of three English speaking groups, three French, three Spanish-Portuguese, one German, one Italian, one Latin, one Slav. The Slav group was added because this was the first Synod which Eastern European bishops were able to attend. Cf. *OR*, «Language Groups Elect Moderators», 15 October 1990, 8. For a list of the participants in the small language groups as well as a synopsis of their main points, see G. CAPRILE, *Il Sinodo dei Vescovi*, 427-452.

[12] For a description of the process leading to the final list of recommendations, see *OR*, «VIII Synod Opens on Formation Topic», 1 October 1990, 1-2; G. CAPRILE, «L'VIII Assemblea generale», 385-386; ID., *Il Sinodo dei Vescovi*, 453-454; *OR*,

At a press conference on October 27, 1990, Bishop Muszynski, the Synod Special Secretary, released a Synod-prepared overview of the proposals. This overview emphasized three salient points emerging from the 41 Propositions. First, the overview cited the ambiguity of the modern world, with its negative and positive aspects, which forms the context for the Church and for vocations. Second, the overview stressed the necessity of keeping a theological concept of priesthood which affirms the divine origin of the priestly vocation, its Christological foundation, and its specific destination for service to the Church and to the world. Such an understanding is the source of authentic priestly ministry and spirituality. Finally, having taken account of the present-day circumstances of the world and the theological nature of priestly identity and mission, the overview moved on to the topic of formation itself, describing its various environments, contents, and agents[13].

In his closing address to the Synod, 27 October 1990, Pope John Paul II spoke of the Synod of Bishops as «[...] a realization and an illustration of the collegial nature of the order of bishops»[14]. Although by its very nature the Synod of Bishops is consultative, it indirectly has a deliberative role because the «[...] post-synodal document takes its inspiration from and [...] contains what was planned out in common»[15]. Because in the Apostolic Exhortation the Pope expresses the «[...] reflections and discussion which led up to the synodal Propositions», it can be said that the Propositions «[...] indirectly assume the importance of decisions»[16].

1.2 *Pastores Dabo Vobis*: *Culmination of the Synod*

Over a year after John Paul II's final address to the Synod, *PDV* was released and, indeed, was revealed to be post-synodal in every sense. That is to say that «[...] it reflects the entire sense and content of the Synod Assembly. [...] it is based on the total results of the Synod's activity»[17]. Inherently «synodal» in both its spirit and in its content, the

---

«English Groups Report», 29 October 1990, 3; H. MUSZYNSKI, «Overview of Synod Proposals», 353-355; D. TETTAMANZI, *La formazione dei sacerdoti*, 288.317.

13 Cf. H. MUSZYNSKI, «Overview of Synod Proposals», 353-355. Giovanni Caprile offers a review of the themes treated, but with more in-depth commentary than Bishop Muszynski's «Overview». Cf. G. CAPRILE, «L'VIII Assemblea generale», 486-495; ID., *Il Sinodo dei Vescovi*, 485-487.

14 JOHN PAUL II, «Closing Address to the Synod», 378.

15 JOHN PAUL II, «Closing Address to the Synod», 378.

16 JOHN PAUL II, «Closing Address to the Synod», 378.

17 OR, «Pastores Dabo Vobiss», 8 April 1992, 1.

document contains eighty-two citations directly based on the Synod's Propositions, along with others containing implicit reference to them; it also draws on «[...] the consensus shown in the course of the preparations, in the *"Lineamenta"*, in the *"Instrumentum laboris"*, and in the interventions of the Synod Fathers»[18]. Although much lengthier[19], *PDV* structurally resembles both the *Lineamenta* and the *Instrumentum Laboris*, in that it follows the basic order of the themes treated. Chapter One puts the topic of priestly formation into the larger context of present day realities, along with the challenges and opportunities they pose. Chapter Two focuses on the identity and mission of the priest, establishing the doctrinal foundation for the remainder of the document. Chapter Three examines the spiritual life of the priest and develops the theme of «pastoral charity» as the heart of priestly ministry and spirituality. Chapter Four looks at the nature of priestly vocations and the Church's responsibility in promoting and supporting vocations. Chapter Five analyzes the process, content, places, and agents of the formation of candidates to the priesthood. Chapter Six explores the topic of permanent, or ongoing, formation as an essential aspect of priestly life. The Exhortation concludes with a prayer to the Virgin Mary as a guide and model for priestly formation[20]. As the Holy Father indicated in his Closing Address to the Synod, the post-Synodal document truly does take its inspiration from the Synod, thus enabling Archbishop Schotte to declare at the April 7, 1992 press conference releasing *PDV*, «The whole Synod is contained in the pages of the post-synodal document»[21].

1.2.1 Conciliar and Post-Conciliar Teaching on Priesthood

In addition to its reliance on the Synod process, particularly the Propositions, the Exhortation also makes abundant reference to the texts of the Second Vatican Council (sixty-four citations), the 1967 Synod on the renewal of seminaries, the 1971 synodal document on priesthood,

---

[18] *OR*, «*Pastores Dabo Vobis*:», 8 April 1992, 1. Caprile notes that it is truly synodal not only because it reflects what was said at the Synod but also because of the fact that the Holy Father collaborated with cardinals and bishops from the Council of the General Secretariat of the Synod whose work he wished to make use of in all redactional phases of the text. G. CAPRILE, «Un dono del Papa», 285.

[19] Caprile observes that at the time of its writing, *Pastores Dabo Vobis* was the lengthiest of the papal documents of John Paul II's pontificate. Cf. G. CAPRILE, «Un dono del Papa», 284.

[20] For a synopsis of the entire document see G. CAPRILE, «Un dono del Papa», especially 286-291.

[21] *OR*, «*Pastores Dabo Vobis*:», 8 April 1992, 4.

and documents of the various dicasteries of the Roman Curia[22]. Because it represents the culmination of a rather long and arduous process of thinking and reflecting about the ministerial priesthood and priestly formation in the light of the Church's tradition, it can be said that *PDV* is truly a *summa*, that is, «[...] a theological, spiritual and pastoral synthesis — destined to long remain a faithful companion of all priests, not only those involved in the educational journey to priesthood»[23].

Although the Synod of 1990 and the subsequent Apostolic Exhortation had as its central theme the topic of priestly formation, a review of the planning stages — the *Lineamenta* and the *Instrumentum Laboris*, the interventions at the Synod[24], and the final document, *PDV* — reveals an abiding concern for the doctrinal foundations of priestly identity and spirituality; it can even be described as a preoccupation of the Synod fathers[25]. Both in his closing address to the Synod and in *PDV* the Holy Father addressed the topic of the postconciliar priestly identity crisis:

> This crisis arose in the years immediately following the Council. It was based on an erroneous understanding of — and sometimes even a conscious bias against — the doctrine of the Conciliar Magisterium. Undoubtedly, herein lies one of the reasons for the great number of defections experienced then by the Church, losses which did serious harm to pastoral ministry and priestly vocations, especially missionary vocations. It is as though the 1990 Synod, rediscovering by means of the many statements which we heard in this hall, the full depth of priestly identity, has striven to instil hope in the wake of these sad losses. These statements showed an awareness of the specific ontological bond which unites the priesthood to Christ the High Priest and Good Shepherd (*PDV* 11)[26].

In this statement John Paul II situates the roots of the postconciliar crisis in a distorted theological understanding of the ministerial priesthood[27],

---

[22] Cf. G. CAPRILE, «Un dono del Papa», 285, citing Schotte's statistics.

[23] G. CAPRILE, «Un dono del Papa», 285, citing Archbishop Schotte at the press conference releasing *Pastores Dabo Vobis*, on 7 April 1992.

[24] For summaries of interventions see *OR*: (8 October 1990) 8-12, (15 October 1990) 3-12, (22 October 1990) 3-12, (29 October 1990) 3-10; *Origins* 20: (11 October 1990) 281.283-284, (18 October 1990) 299-316, (25 October 1990) 317-332, (1 November 1990) 333-348, (8 November 1990) 349-380; G. CAPRILE, *Il Sinodo dei Vescovi*, 78-426; D. TETTAMANZI, *Formazione dei sacerdoti*, 33-288.

[25] Cf. F. RYPAR, «*Pastores dabo vobis* alla luce del pensiero conciliare sul sacerdozio e sulla formazione sacerdotale», 534.

[26] Cf. JOHN PAUL II, «Closing Address to the Synod», 379.

[27] For a discussion of the postconciliar misunderstandings of the ministerial priesthood, see above, pp. 57-62; E. CASTELLUCCI, «L'identità del presbitero in prospettiva cristologica ed ecclesiologica», 92-139.

and indicates that the way out of the crisis is a clear articulation of the nature and mission of the priesthood «[...] as the Church's faith has acknowledged them down the centuries of its history and as the Second Vatican Council has presented them anew to the people of our day» (*PDV* 11). In Chapter Two of *PDV* the Pope presents such an articulation and, based on this, describes a corresponding priestly spirituality in Chapter Three.

Because they articulate the doctrinal foundations of priestly ministry and spirituality, an analysis of Chapters Two and Three will serve as the focus for continuing our exploration of priest as leader which the examination of *PO* and *MP* and related documents revealed to be rooted in the very nature of priesthood itself, that is in its sacramental structure, and expressed existentially in the functions and relationships of the priest. The portrait that emerged from these documents revealed that the leadership dimension is intrinsically part of the ministerial priesthood conferred in the sacrament of Orders, irrevocably rooted in service, and transcending the various functions and relationships that characterize priestly ministry and life. *PDV* will be approached to determine how this understanding is developed and strengthened.

1.2.2 Doctrine and Spirituality of the Ministerial Priesthood: Ecclesiological, Christological, and Pastoral Perspectives

Chapter Two of *PDV*, «The Nature and Mission of the Ministerial Priesthood», provides the doctrinal basis for understanding the ministerial priesthood[28]. Because it is imbued with the teaching of the Second Vatican Council, the 1971 Synod of Bishops, and subsequent Church reflection on the ordained ministry, Chapter Two provides a synthesis of the Church's understanding of the ministerial priesthood[29] and can

---

[28] Unlike *PO*, which referred to the priesthood of the second order almost exclusively in terms of *presbyter* or *presbyterium*, the preferred mode of expression in *PDV* is the term «ministerial priesthood», although it often simply refers to the «priesthood», the «priest», or the «ordained ministry». Although its terminology regarding the priesthood of the second order is not as precise as that of the conciliar documents, *PDV*, like the conciliar teaching, is careful to distinguish between the common and ministerial priesthood. For a discussion of the postconciliar evolution in terminology relative to the ministerial priesthood, see G. GOZZELINO, «Il presbitero continuazione di Cristo», 84-85.

[29] In stating the necessity for summarizing «[...] the nature and mission of the ministerial priesthood as the Church's faith has acknowledged them down the centuries of its history and as the Second Vatican Council has presented them anew to the people of our day» (*PDV* 11), the Exhortation cites, in footnote 19, the following sources: *Lumen*

be described as the hinge and pivot of the entire Exhortation[30]: it is integrally connected to priestly spirituality as articulated in Chapter Three of the Exhortation; it provides the context for a proper under-standing of the priestly vocation as described in Chapter Four; and it is the foundation for the various components of priestly formation, both initial and ongoing, which Chapters Five and Six delineate. In fact, the Exhortation asserts that the surest way to develop activities and programs for the support of the ministerial priesthood is, in the first place, to articulate the goal of such activities and programs (cf. *PDV* 11). Hence, a clear knowledge and understanding of the nature and mission of the ministerial priesthood is the *sine qua non* for sketching the components of an appropriate priestly spirituality, for creating a proper understanding of the meaning of priestly vocations, and for establishing a suitable initial formation to the priesthood as well as an ongoing formation in the priesthood. For the purposes of this study, as the previous chapter demonstrated, such doctrine is also the foundation for constructing a proper understanding of priest as leader.

In its description of the nature and mission of the priesthood *PDV* employs three distinct yet profoundly interconnected perspectives that serve to bring the picture of the ministerial priesthood into clearer focus. They are the pillars upon which the document's balanced, coherent, and comprehensive understanding of contemporary priesthood is established. The three perspectives are ecclesial, christological, and pastoral[31]. Although it has been shown that these themes also permeate the Church's conciliar and postconciliar teaching on the ministerial priesthood, they are much more clearly articulated in *PDV* which uses them to organize the major sections of the doctrinal exposition and then reiterates them in each subsequent chapter of the document[32]. As presented in *PDV* Chapter Two, the perspectives are described as follows: «In the Church as Mystery, Communion and Mission» (*PDV* 12: ecclesiological perspective); «The Fundamental Relationship With Christ the Head

---

Gentium; Presbyterorum Ordinis; Optatam Totius; Ratio Fundamentalis Institutionis Sacerdotalis; Synod of Bishops, Second Ordinary General Assembly, 1971.

   [30] Cf. G. GOZZELINO, «Il presbitero continuazione di Cristo», 83.

   [31] P. Laghi cites only two basic perspectives in *PDV* for articulating the identity and mission of the ministerial priest. Cf. P. LAGHI,«*Pastores dabo vobis*. Presentazione», 506-509. A reading of the text of *PDV*, however, reveals that three perspectives are present within the structure itself of Chapter Two.

   [32] C. Dumont has noted that John Paul II uses a «spiral style» (*en spirale*) of always coming back to basic themes around which the various components of the document converge. Cf. C. DUMONT, «La "charité pastorale" et la vocation au presbytérat», 211.

and Shepherd» (*PDV* 13-15: christological perspective); «Serving the Church and the World» (*PDV* 16-18: pastoral perspective). These three perspectives or approaches to understanding the ministerial priesthood provide a kind of reading key for penetrating and unfolding the meaning of the entire Exhortation[33], in the sense that the perspectives recapitulate, clarify, and deepen the Church's conciliar and postconciliar understanding of priesthood which was described in the previous chapter. Although each perspective must be examined individually, the individual perspective is inadequate, taken alone, for the task of articulating a full definition and description of the priesthood. Each perspective is part of a larger whole to which it refers and in which it must be located in order to be properly understood; they are thus interconnected and have a reciprocal relation to each other. Reflecting what has been called John Paul II's «spiral style», there is a kind of circular pattern to the perspectives, each leading into and deepening the understanding of the next[34]. Taken separately they yield only a partial understanding, but taken as a whole they offer a rich picture of the Church's contemporary understanding of the nature and role of the ministerial priesthood. Hence, although the perspectives will be examined individually, their interrelatedness will also be demonstrated.

Because the three perspectives are so deeply intertwined, there is perhaps a certain artificiality in separating them for analysis. The benefit of such analysis, however, is not only a clearer picture of each perspective, but more importantly, a clearer understanding of how they coalesce, leading to a comprehensive portrait of the ministerial priesthood, a portrait that is essential for an adequate understanding of priest as leader. The remainder of this chapter, then, will examine the three perspectives as they appear in Chapters Two and Three of *PDV*, concluding with the notion of «pastoral charity», an important contribution of the Exhortation to a deeper understanding of the ministerial priesthood. This concept will be particularly examined and its implications explored, for it is within the context of «pastoral charity» that the three perspectives merge most completely and comprehensively, yielding an understanding of the ministerial priest today, as one who «[...] by virtue of the consecration which he receives in the sacrament of Orders, is sent forth by the Father through the mediatorship of Jesus Christ, to whom he is

---

[33] In a two-part article, P. Vanzan describes how the threefold perspective spirals throughout the entire document, thus setting the context for each section. Cf. P. VANZAN, «*Pastores dabo vobis*», part one, 233-243, part two, 353-361.

[34] P. VANZAN, «*Pastores dabo vobis*», part one, 233.

configured in a special way as Head and Shepherd of his people, in order
to live and work by the power of the Holy Spirit in service of the Church
and for the salvation of the world» (*PDV* 12). Using Cooke's description
of leadership as a reading key[35], an analysis of the doctrine and
spirituality of the ministerial priesthood as articulated in *PDV*, and
epitomized in the notion of «pastoral charity», will yield a more
complete understanding and portrait of priest as leader.

2. Ecclesiological Perspective and Doctrine of Priesthood

2.1 *Trinitarian Ecclesiology*

Chapter Two pointed out that an ecclesiological perspective was the
context for developing the Council's teaching on the ministerial priesthood. This perspective emphasized that the Church is rooted in the
Trinity and carries out God's plan of salvation «[...] which was decreed
by the Father, accomplished by the redemptive incarnation of the Son,
and implemented by the mission of the Holy Spirit in the community of
the Church as a visible organ of union with the divine persons»[36]. The
Church is thus «[...] a people brought into unity from the unity of
the Father, the Son and the Holy Spirit» (*LG* 4). As noted in the previous
chapter, Pope John Paul II's Apostolic Exhortation, *Christifideles Laici*,
synthesized conciliar ecclesiology by describing the Church as mystery,
communion, and mission:

> She is *mystery* because the very life and love of the Father, Son and Holy
> Spirit are the gift gratuitously offered to all those who are born of water and
> the Holy Spirit (cf. Jn 3,5), and called to relive the very *communion* of God
> and to manifest it and communicate it in history (*mission*) (*CL* 8).

This trinitarian ecclesiology, as articulated by *CL*, is quoted in *PDV* 12
and grounds *PDV*'s articulation of the doctrine and spirituality of the
ministerial priesthood. Although the Council's ecclesiology was briefly
described in Chapter Two, because it is so explicitly invoked as the
context of *PDV*'s understanding of the ministerial priesthood, further
elaboration is required.

Before exploring this ecclesiology in more detail, however, *PDV*'s
teaching on the Trinity as the source of priestly identity requires some

---

[35] For Cooke's description of leadership, see above, p. 63; B. COOKE, *Ministry to
Word and Sacrament*, 209.

[36] G. PHILIPS, «Dogmatic Constitution on the Church», vol. 1, 111. See *CCC*,
especially secs. 758-769, pp. 174-177, on the Church's origin in the Trinity.

clarification. *PDV* begins its doctrinal exposition by quoting Proposition 7 of the Synod: «"The priest's identity, [...] like every Christian identity, has its source in the Blessed Trinity". [...] It is within the Church's mystery, as a mystery of Trinitarian communion in missionary tension, that every Christian identity is revealed, and likewise the specific identity of the priest and his ministry» (*PDV* 12). Although this assertion has been described as one of the most significant theological contributions of *PDV*[37], it is not without its difficulties.

It is pointed out in Chapter Two that although a conciliar understanding of the Church as mystery, communion, and mission grounds any adequate understanding of the priesthood — both common and ministerial — the *specific* identity of the ministerial priest can only be fully understood in Christological terms. The conciliar teaching on the priesthood, as well as that of the 1971 Synod, are filled with such references: «[...] in the image of Christ the eternal High Priest [...] they [priests] are consecrated to preach the Gospel, shepherd the faithful, and celebrate divine worship» (*LG* 28); «[...] priests, by the anointing of the Holy Spirit, are marked with a special character and are so configured to Christ the Priest that they can act in the person of Christ the Head» (*PO* 2); «By the laying on of hands there is communicated a gift of the Holy Spirit which [...] configures the ordained minister to Christ the Priest, consecrates him and makes him a sharer in Christ's mission» (*MP* I.5). John Paul II reinforces this teaching on ministerial priesthood's fundamental identity with Christ: «The priest finds the full truth of his identity in being a derivation, a specific participation in and continuation of Christ himself» (*PDV* 12). To say, then, that the priest's *specific* identity has its source in the Trinity and is revealed in the Church, understood «[...] as a mystery of Trinitarian communion in missionary tension» (*PDV* 12), is confusing and requires clarification.

PDV 12 itself offers such clarification and nuance. Immediately after quoting Proposition 7, which roots the source of priestly identity in the Trinity, the text adds that the Trinity «[...] is communicated to people in Christ, establishing in him and through the Spirit, the Church» (*PDV* 12). Later in the same section it describes the Church as the «[...] sign and instrument of Christ» and «[...] *essentially related to Jesus Christ*» [emphasis in original]. Christ, then, is the revelation of the Father through the power of the Holy Spirit, and it is in Christ, through

---

[37] Cf. L. TERRIEN, «Theology and Spirituality of the Priesthood in *PDV* and *CCC*», 11.

the Spirit, that the Church — both the common and ministerial priest-hood — experiences Trinitarian life. Thus the «[...] multiple, rich inter-connection of relationships which arise from the Blessed Trinity [...] are prolonged in the communion of the Church, as a sign and instrument of Christ» (*PDV* 12). It is in this relation with Christ, in the Church, that the Trinity can be understood as the source of Christian and priestly identity. Offering further clarification, Gallo, commenting on *PDV* 12, has pointed out that the configuration of the ministerial priesthood to Christ calls to mind the supreme relation to the Trinity, who is the ulti-mate source of all reality, both in the order of creation and in the order of salvation, hence the source of the mission of Christ which is prolonged in the Church[38]. Although the Trinity grounds all reality and is the ultimate source of every identity, including the priesthood, it would thus seem more accurate to say that the *specific* identity of the ministerial priest-hood is rooted in its particular configuration to Christ. Indeed, this has clearly been the emphasis in both conciliar and postconciliar teaching on the ministerial priesthood. It is in «[...] Jesus Christ, to whom he is configured in a special way as Head and Shepherd of his people» (*PDV* 12), that the specific identity of the ministerial priesthood is found. Although a Trinitarian ecclesiology *grounds* an adequate under-standing of priesthood, «[...] reference to Christ is [...] the absolutely necessary key for understanding the reality of priesthood» (*PDV* 12).

As noted above, *PDV* 12 quotes from the previous Apostolic Exhor-tation, *Christifideles Laici* 8, which in turn offered a synthesis of concil-iar ecclesiology: the Church is mystery because «[...] the very life and love of the Father, Son and Holy Spirit» are given to the baptized; it is communion because these same baptized are «[...] called to relive the very communion of God»; it is mission because in reliving the communion of God, all are called «[...] to manifest it and communicate it» in the concrete circumstances of life   (cf. *PDV* 12 and *CL* 8)[39]. As a sign and instrument of Christ, the Church is therefore patterned on the

---

[38] Cf. L. GALLO, «Il presbitero nella Chiesa, mistero, comunione e missione», 100: «[...] a monte ancora del rapporto con Cristo, viene rammentato anche quello definitivamente supremo, ossia quello che il presbiterato ha con il Dio Uno e Trino ([*PDV*] n. 12a), fonte ultima di tutto, tanto nell'ordine della creazione quanto in quello della salvezza, e quindi anche della stessa missione di Cristo».

[39] C. M. LaCugna notes, «The nature of the Church should manifest the nature of God. Just as the doctrine of the Trinity is not an abstract teaching about God apart from us but a teaching about God's life with us and our life with each other, ecclesiology is not the study of an abstract Church but a study of the actual gathering of persons in a common faith and a common mission», C. M. LACUGNA, *God for Us*, 403.

dynamic interrelationship of the Trinity. In offering a trinitarian ecclesiology as a context for understanding the priesthood's particular configuration to Christ, *PDV* confirms the Council's insight about the Church
and affirms the essentially relational, mission-focused dynamic of the
ministerial priesthood.

2.1.1 Church as Mystery

The description of the Church as mystery is rooted in conciliar ecclesiology as articulated in Chapter One of *LG*, and it «[...] "points to a
transcendent, divine reality that has to do with salvation and that is in
some sensible way revealed and manifested"»[40]. In this way Vatican II
shifted from an exclusively extrinsic, institutional understanding of the
Church to a more balanced, intrinsic understanding (without negating
the institutional aspect)[41]. To describe the Church as mystery, then,
«[...] means that *the Church is a divine, transcendent, and salvific reality
which is visibly present among men*»[42]. Understood as mystery, the
Church cannot be seen only as a human reality, but as a theological,
supernatural reality. In its deepest sense the Church is rooted in the
Mystery of the triune God and is the instrument of his eternal designs for
the salvation of humanity[43]. God's eternal plan for humanity's salvation
is most explicitly and fully expressed in the life, death, and resurrection
of Jesus Christ who established the Church; thus, «[...] as a mystery, the
Church is essentially related to Jesus Christ» (*PDV* 12).

2.1.2 Church as Communion

Although *PDV* affirms a trinitarian ecclesiology (the Church as
mystery, communion, and mission) as foundational for understanding the
nature and mission of the ministerial priesthood, it stresses that a particular dimension of this ecclesiology, «communion», is «[...] decisive for
understanding the identity of the priest» (*PDV* 12). This is a natural
progression from the articulation of the Church as mystery. Although the

---

[40] B. KLOPPENBURG, *The Ecclesiology of Vatican II*, 14, citing the official
explanation of «mystery» given to the bishops in 1964 by the Theological Commission
of Vatican II. Cf. *Acta Synodalia* II/1, 455, as cited by Kloppenburg, *op. cit.*, 77, n. 2.

[41] Cf. L. GALLO, «Il presbitero nella Chiesa, 104.

[42] B. KLOPPENBURG, *The Ecclesiology of Vatican II*, 14 [emphasis in the original];
Cf. PAUL VI, «*Salvete Fratres*: Address to the Council Fathers at the Opening of the
Second Session», 131, as cited by Kloppenburg, *op. cit.*, 77, n. 3.

[43] Cf. L. GALLO, «Il presbitero nella Chiesa, 104.

term «mystery» may be ambiguous and difficult to grasp, it refers to the God of Christian revelation who is not some generic divinity, but the triune God, an infinite communion of love among three equal yet distinct persons[44]. This same God has communicated his life to the Church, and to describe the Church as communion is to give it a clearer definition and focus, allowing the dimension of mystery to unfold in an intelligible way. The concept of communion thus specifies that of mystery.

There is a certain dynamism or logic in the nature of the Trinity that is reflected in the communion of the Church. The characteristics of the Trinity, mirrored in the Church, were affirmed by the Councils of Nicea (325 C.E.) and First Constantinople (381 C.E.) as equality of persons, in that each person is truly, fully God; distinction of persons, which bespeaks a relationship or order among equals; and mutuality of persons, which describes the complete indwelling and exchange of divine life and love shared among the three persons[45]. The triune God has chosen, not only to create the world, but to enter into relationship with it, establishing the Church as «[...] the community of persons who self-consciously live out the new interpersonal relationships established by the divine missions in human history»[46]. This trinitarian dynamism of communion is at the heart of the Church's self-understanding. Just as in the Trinity there is a radical equality among persons by which each person of the Trinity can be said to be fully divine, so analogously, because of baptism, members of the Church are initiated into the People of God (cf. *LG*, ch.2) and are thus radically equal in dignity, fully sharing the benefits of Christ's redemptive Paschal Mystery. In the same way, just as each person of the Trinity has a distinct identity, constituted by relationship to the other two persons, so in the Church each member has a distinct and unique identity. The radical equality shared by all of the baptized does not eliminate the distinctiveness, individuality and freedom of the person to whom God relates as a subject. Similarly, just as the life of the Trinity is characterized by a kind of absolute mutuality and self-giving[47], so «[...] the church exists as a *koinonia*, a fellowship in

---

[44] Cf. L. GALLO, «Il presbitero nella Chiesa», 105.

[45] For a description of the trinitarian structure and dynamism as the basis of the Church and of its ministry, see P. J. DRILLING, *Trinity and Ministry*, especially 33-42.

[46] P. J. DRILLING, *Trinity and Ministry*, 35.

[47] Drilling recalls that the ancient Greek designation, *perichoresis*, best describes the mutual interpenetration of the divine persons of the Trinity. Cf. P. J. DRILLING, *Trinity and Ministry*, 34. LaCugna observes that «[...] the doctrine of the Trinity is not

which each member stands ready to offer the gifts [...] with which he or she has been blessed, in service to the other and to receive from the other the gifts lacking in herself or himself»[48]. The Church, then, can be said to mirror the Trinity in its equality, distinction, and mutuality.

These same characteristics of equality, distinction, and mutuality which distinguish the Trinity and analogously the Church as communion, are also characteristic of the Church's ministries. That is, the radical equality that marks the trinitarian life of the Church characterizes the Church's ministries as well. Appearances notwithstanding, insofar as ministers and ministries contribute to the life of the Church, they are equal — radically so. Similarly, just as in the Trinity and thus the Church, persons are distinct in their identity and relationships, so in the Church's ministries a minister exercises different gifts and charisms which determine how he or she will relate to the Church. These ministries and ministers receive their distinctiveness not from any innate superiority or inferiority, but from the way in which they extend the Trinity's mission into the Church[49]. Finally, the mutuality and self-giving characteristic of the Trinity and of the Church is also a hallmark of the Church's ministers, who are called to give their lives in loving service to God and to their fellow human beings through their ministry in the Church[50].

The trinitarian dynamism, which characterizes the Church and its ministries, has profound implications for an adequate understanding of the ministerial priesthood and for priest as leader. This dynamism is at the heart of an ecclesiology of communion and makes it possible to understand «[...] the fundamentally "relational" dimension of priestly identity» (*PDV* 12). In the Church as a communion, «[...] the priest sacramentally enters into communion with the bishop and with other priests», as well as the People of God; «[...] consequently, the nature and mission of the ministerial priesthood cannot be defined except through this multiple and rich interconnection of relationships which arise from

---

ultimately a teaching about "God" but a teaching about *God's life with us and our life with each other*» [emphasis in the original], C. M. LACUGNA, *God For Us*, 228.

[48] P. J. DRILLING, *Trinity and Ministry*, 35-36.

[49] Drilling observes: «The Word entered into history by assuming a full human nature, and the Spirit entered into history as animator. Their missions in history are extensions of what the Word and the Spirit are within divine community. [...] The Church is the community of persons who self-consciously live out the new interpersonal relationships established by the divine missions in human history», P. J. DRILLING, *Trinity and Ministry*, 35.

[50] Cf. P. J. DRILLING, *Trinity and Ministry*, 37-38; L. GALLO, «Il presbitero nella Chiesa», 105-106; G. GOZZELINO, «Il presbitero continuazione di Cristo», 94-95.

the Blessed Trinity and are prolonged in the communion of the Church» (*PDV* 12)[51]. The relational dimension of the identity of the priest is not simply accidental nor extrinsic to the priesthood, as if it were something «added» to his identity. Rather, rooted in a trinitarian Church, relationality is intrinsic to the priesthood itself, indeed part of its very essence[52]. As such, it has profound ramifications for the the pastoral role of the priest.

2.1.3 Church as Mission

Although the concept of the Church as communion expresses the richness of the complex of relationships that exist in the Church, thus mirroring the communion of the Trinity, this communion is not simply an intraecclesial, self-referred reality. Such an understanding of communion would portray the Church as turned in on itself. Rather, as demonstrated in the previous chapter, intrinsically connected to the understanding of the Church as commmunion is the Church as mission: «Called to relive the very communion of God», the Church is also called «[...] to manifest it and communicate it in history» (cf. *PDV* 12). In this way the Church's very self-definition includes its mission of manifesting and extending its communion to all the world[53]. From this it is obvious that what concerns and preoccupies the Church should be, not primarily its own internal concerns, but the life and the problems of the world, always with the goal of extending to the world the salvation of Christ.

From the perspective of mission, the priest's purpose and role within the communion of the Church is «[...] to serve the People of God who are the Church and to draw all mankind to Christ» (*PDV* 12). The place of the priest in this ecclesiology of mission must be seen in the wider context of the ecclesiology of communion. In other words, the mission is the mission of Christ which has been entrusted to the entire Church. Although an important instrument in the work of this mission, the priest is not the only one. Rooted in the Church as communion and thus essentially characterized as a relational entity, the priest serves the mission of the Church, not as the «[...] absolute indisputable pivot of the work of

---

[51] *PDV* 12 does not emphasize the equality priests enjoy with the People of God as much as the essential difference between them which is characterized as service on the part of the priest. Such service, however, only takes place within the context of communion. *PDV* 17 emphasizes that ministerial priests relate to the people of God as brothers and friends. Cf. P. VANZAN, «*Pastores dabo vobis*», part one, 235, n. 2.

[52] Cf. L. GALLO, «Il presbitero nella Chiesa», 100.

[53] Cf. L. GALLO, «Il presbitero nella Chiesa», 108.

salvation entrusted to him, but — simultaneously — [as] one who receives and gives, who is "connected to" and effects "links with" all the People of God»[54]. It is not, therefore, a one-way relationship. Rather, rooted in the trinitarian principle of mutuality, the priest serves collegially, particularly with his bishop and other priests, but also with all the people of God, both giving to them and receiving from them. His work, although crucial to the Church's mission, must be seen in its wider, more proper context which serves as a safeguard against any tendency to identify the mission of the Church solely with the work of the priest.

By rooting the doctrine of the ministerial priesthood in a trinitarian ecclesiology as articulated in *PDV* 12, the Exhortation is faithful to the Second Vatican Council's articulation of its understanding of the Church. The three terms are not simply juxtaposed, but instead they express and interpret each other: «communion» expresses and specifies «mystery», and «mission» specifies «communion» as a service to the world[55]. Although most clearly articulated in the early part of *PDV* 12, the ecclesiological perspective also emerges, in a more muted way, in the other sections of *PDV* Chapter Two, which focus primarily on the Christological and pastoral aspects of the ministerial priesthood[56].

2.1.4 Ecclesiological, Christological, and Pastoral Perspectives

The christological section (*PDV* 13-15) shifts from an explicitly trinitarian ecclesiology and puts the accent on a description of the Church as «[...] the new priestly people which [...] not only has its authentic image in Christ, but also receives from him a real ontological share in his [...] priesthood» (*PDV* 13). The description of the Church as a priestly people in the image of Christ, however, is firmly rooted in a trinitarian ecclesiology, which emphasizes that all the baptized relive the very communion of God, which of its very nature is expressed in mission. The description of the Church as a «priestly people» is significant because in the very next section the Exhortation declares that the apostolic ministry, which is continued in the ministerial priesthood[57],

---

[54] P. VANZAN, «*Pastores dabo vobis*», part one, 235: «[...] non il perno assoluto e insindacabile dell opera salvifica affidatagli, ma — contemporaneamente — uno che riceve e dà, che è "collegato a" e opera "collegamenti con" tutto il popolo di Dio».

[55] L. GALLO, «Il presbitero nella Chiesa», 111.

[56] Cf. P. VANZAN, «*Pastores dabo vobis*», part one, 236.

[57] *PDV* 15 states that «[...] the Apostles, appointed by the Lord, progressively carried out their mission by calling, in various but complementary ways, other men as Bishops, as priests and as deacons, in order to fulfil the command of the Risen Jesus

exists «[...] for the sake of this universal priesthood of the New Covenant» (*PDV* 14). As noted earlier, the teaching on the relationship between the ministerial and common priesthood was one of the great contributions of the Council[58]. *PDV* reinforces this teaching, highlighting the intrinsically relational nature of the ministerial priesthood. The priest does not exist in and of himself, or in a position above the Church, but only in the communion of and service to the Church.

The pastoral section of Chapter Two (*PDV* 16-18), which highlights the relations and duties of the priest, also makes explicit reference to the ecclesiological perspective as a basis for the pastoral work of the priest. The priest's insertion *in* the Church and his relation *to* the Church is part of his very being as a priest. The Exhortation affirms that the priest's configuration to Christ (christological perspective) puts him into a particular relation to the Church as mystery, communion, and mission: his participation in the Church as mystery is most fully expressed when he «[...] actuates the Church's sacramental signs of the presence of the risen Christ» (*PDV* 16); his participation in the Church as communion is most fully expressed when, in collaboration with bishops and other priests, he is involved in the work of building up the unity of the Church; his participation in the Church as mission is most fully expressed in his service to the Church community's witness to the Gospel (cf. *PDV* 16)[59]. In this section the intrinsic relation of the ecclesiological and pastoral perspectives can be clearly seen. The importance of *PDV* 16 in terms of the ecclesiological perspective is that it strongly reaffirms the priest's essentially relational character and roots the activities of the ministerial priest in an explicitly trinitarian ecclesiology. This affirmation is immediately reinforced in the next section: «[...] the ordained ministry can be carried out only to the extent that the priest is united to Christ through sacramental participation in the priestly order, and thus to the extent that he is in hierarchical communion with his own bishop» (*PDV* 17)[60]. To add further strength to this affirmation,

---

who sent them forth to all people in every age». *PDV* 16 states: «Through the priesthood of the Bishop, the priesthood of the second order is incorporated in the apostolic structure of the Church».

[58] For an examination of conciliar teaching on the relationship of the common to the ministerial priesthood, see above, pp. 67-75.

[59] For a discussion of the seeming artificiality in associating specific aspects of the threefold ministry with specific dimensions of the Church, see below, pp. 161-162.

[60] For an examination of the Council's teaching on the ministerial priesthood in relationship to the episcopacy, see above, pp. 75-78.

the Exhortation asserts that, rooted in the communion of the Church, the priesthood has a «radical "communitarian form"», and thus can only be carried out collectively (*PDV* 17)[61]. The ecclesiology of communion is stressed again in dealing with the priest's ministry in a particular Church, for whose service each priest, whether diocesan or religious, forms with the bishop a single presbyterate[62]. Priestly ministry is thus carried out in the context of communion with the bishop, fellow priests, and the laity (cf. *PDV* 17). The characteristics of such communion are spelled out: precisely because the priest is a man of communion, «[...] in his relations with all people he must be a man of mission and dialogue» (*PDV* 18).

Chapter 2 closes by rearticulating all three aspects of the ecclesial perspective:

> Today in particular, the pressing pastoral task of the new evangelization calls for the involvement of the entire People of God, and requires a new fervour, new methods and a new expression for the announcing and witnessing of the Gospel. The task demands priests who are deeply and fully immersed in the mystery of Christ and capable of embodying a new style of pastoral life, marked by a profound communion with the pope, the bishops and other priests, and a fruitful cooperation with the lay faithful, always respecting and fostering the different roles, charisms and ministries present within the ecclesial community (*PDV* 18).

The ecclesial perspective of the ministerial priesthood, which firmly situates the identity of the priest in the Church as mystery, communion, and mission, is thus woven into the very fabric of *PDV*'s doctrinal understanding of the ministerial priesthood and is an essential component of an adequate understanding of the priesthood and for priest as leader.

2.2 *The Ecclesiological Perspective and Priestly Spirituality*

In the opening section of Chapter Three, «The Spiritual Life of the Priest», *PDV* affirms that through baptism into the Church all share a common vocation to holiness[63]. Citing the same passage from the Gospel of Luke (Lk 4,18) that opened *PDV* Chapter Two, it emphasizes that the Spirit of the Lord who was upon Jesus at the beginning of his ministry is the same Spirit who penetrates the lives of all members of the Church. The Spirit reveals the Father's universal call to holiness and configures all members of the Church to Jesus Christ, thus making all the

---

[61] Cf. JOHN PAUL II, «Angelus Talk, 25 February 1990», *OR* (5 March 1990) 5.

[62] For a discussion of the Council's teaching on presbyterate, see above, pp. 79-83.

[63] Cf. *LG* 40: «[...] all Christians in any state or walk of life are called to the fullness of Christian life and to the perfection of charity».

baptized «[...] sharers in his life as Son, that is, sharers in his life of love for the Father and for our brothers and sisters» (*PDV* 19). The trinitarian ecclesiological perspective, with a specific accent on the ecclesiology of communion, thus sets the context for what unfolds in Chapter Three.

Baptized into the Church, Christians are initiated into the trinitarian life of God; in this new life the Holy Spirit reveals God's call to holiness and is also «[...] the principle and wellspring of its fulfillment» (*PDV* 19). The Christian life is, therefore, a «[...] "spiritual life", that is, a life enlivened and led by the Spirit toward holiness or the perfection of charity» (*PDV* 19). If, because of the radical equality that Christians share through their life in the Trinity, all have a common vocation to holiness, then it is also within the trinitarian context that a distinctive or specific call to holiness can be understood. It is here that the distinctiveness of the spiritual life of the ministerial priest can begin to be grasped. Sharing the call to holiness that pertains to all the baptized, the priest's call to holiness receives further precision and specificity. This specificity derives precisely from ordination to the ministerial priesthood, «[...] that is, under a new title and in new and different ways deriving from the sacrament of Holy Orders» (*PDV* 19).

Thus far, the trinitarian foundation of priestly spirituality has been looked at in terms of radical equality (all are called to holiness) and distinction (the specific call to holiness of the ministerial priest derives from the sacrament of Orders). The third dimension of a trinitarian ecclesiology of communion includes mutuality: imitation of the *perichoresis* of the Trinity. The persons of the Trinity find their distinction in relation to one another and this relationship is understood as the mutual indwelling of love, or the radical gift of self to one another. This dimension of trinitarian life has important implications for the life of every Christian in that it is in the gift of themselves to one another that their identity is discovered. In this way the Christian becomes assimilated to the Trinity and mirrors the Trinitarian image in his or her own life[64]. For the priest, this gift of self takes on particular dimensions deriving from his specific call to holiness in the sacrament of Orders.

The spirituality of the ministerial priest, then, is distinctive insofar as it is connected to the sacrament of Holy Orders. In living out the exigencies of this sacrament the priest's specific sanctity unfolds. Since in the remainder of Chapter Three these demands and implications are

---

[64] Cf. J. RATZINGER, «Biblical Foundations of Priesthood», 312.

described primarily in christological and pastoral terms, the ecclesiological perspective recedes into the background. It does not, however, entirely disappear because the priest's life and activity, that is, his consecration and mission, understood from the christological and pastoral perspectives, are «[...] under the seal of the Spirit and the influence of his sanctifying power» (*PDV* 24), and can only be understood as being lived out in the context of the Church as mystery, communion, and mission. Thus in the priest's spiritual life the christological perspective gives definition to the ecclesiological and both are expressed in the pastoral perspective.

2.3 *Conclusions*

In Chapter Two, the examination of the ecclesiological foundation of the ministerial priesthood, as articulated in conciliar and postconciliar documents, demonstrated that leadership is one of its intrinsic components. Rooted in the sacrament of Orders, the priesthood is described as ministerial and hierarchical (*LG* 10), and directed to the common priesthood. Service is thus specified as leadership which, in turn, can only be understood in the broader context of service. Dependent on the office of bishop, the ministerial priesthood shares in Christ's threefold ministry of word, worship, and pastoral guidance. Priestly leadership, then, is not confined to any single one of these ministries but rather transcends all three. Because of the bishop-priest relationship, however, such leadership is not exercized independently but rather collegially and accountably. Similarly, as a member of a presbyterate, priestly leadership is necessarily collaborative; it is not simply an individual's prerogative. Rooted in a priestly people, the ministerial priest serves this people as a leader through the ministry of word, sacrament and pastoral guidance. He does this in collaboration with his bishop, to whom he is accountable, with his brother priests, with whom he exercises his ministry, and with the baptized whom he is ordained to serve.

The Council's teaching on the priesthood, particularly the ecclesial context articulated during Vatican II, is foundational for *PDV*'s teaching on the ministerial priesthood. This trinitarian-ecclesiology, articulated during the Council, systematized in *Christifideles Laici*, and reiterated in *PDV*, is very important for understanding the priest as leader, because in the context of such an ecclesiology priestly leadership is authentic to the extent that the priest is 1) immersed in the mystery of the Church: that is, insofar as he continues «[...] Christ's prayer, word, sacrifice, and salvific action in the Church», thus celebrating the «[...] sacramental signs of the presence of the Risen Christ»[65]; 2) situated in the communion of the Church: that is, insofar as he builds up the unity of the Church in union with his bishop, in cooperation with his presbyterate, and in collaboration with the laity; 3) directed towards the mission of the Church: that is, insofar as he is at the service of the common priesthood, dedicated to making «[...] the community a herald and witness of the Gospel» (*PDV* 16).

As noted above in Chapter Two, such an ecclesiological foundation is important because it serves to contextualize a proper understanding of priestly leadership. Prior to the Second Vatican Council, because the understanding of the priesthood was so exclusively connected to cult, the theological understanding (and often enough the experience) of the priest was of a leader over and above the community. Remote and removed from the ordinary experience of life, the separateness of the priest and passivity of the people were emphasized. The conciliar understanding of the priesthood, strengthened by *PDV*'s explicit articulation of a trinitarian ecclesiology as a foundation of the ministerial priesthood, emphasizes the priest's participation in the communion of the Church and conditions any understanding of priest as leader. John Paul II stresses the «[...] fundamentally "relational" dimension of priestly identity» (*PDV* 12), stating, «The ordained ministry has a radical "*communitarian form*" and can only be carried out as a collective work» (*PDV* 17). Constitutively a leader in virtue of the sacrament of Orders, such leadership is understood as service and is embodied, not apart from people, but in the midst of a complex web of relationships. Rooted in a trinitarian Church, the priest's distinctiveness as a leader is thus tempered by the radical equality he shares with all of the baptized and conditioned, too, by the self-giving love with which it must be authentically exercized.

3. Christological Perspective and Doctrine of Priesthood

Although *PDV* 12 asserts that reference to the Church is necessary for an adequate understanding of the ministerial priesthood, reference to Christ is even more fundamental: it is «[...] the absolutely necessary key for understanding the reality of the priesthood» (*PDV* 12). The christological perspective is so fundamental that, according to John Paul II, «The priest finds the full truth of his identity in being a derivation, a specific participation in and continuation of Christ himself» (*PDV* 12). Specifically, the ministerial priesthood is «[...] a participation, in the

---

[65] *Instrumentum Laboris* 16, p. 18.

Church, in the very priesthood of Christ himself» through «[...] a specific ontological bond which unites the priesthood to Christ the High Priest and Good Shepherd» (*PDV* 11). These assertions, made even before the central christological teaching of *PDV* 13-15, «The Fundamental Relationship With Christ the Head and Shepherd», are indications of the central role that the christological perspective plays in *PDV*'s teaching on the identity and mission of the ministerial priest.

3.1 *Sacramental Representation of Christ*

In a key statement *PDV* declares that «[...] priests are a sacramental representation of Jesus Christ the Head and Shepherd» (*PDV* 15). Through ordination they are called to exercise the same ministry as the Apostles who, in turn, exercised «[...] the same mission as Jesus» (*PDV* 14). In stating this the Exhortation adopts a fundamentally sacramental hermeneutic for understanding the ministerial priesthood[66]. As a sacrament the ministerial priesthood is understood as a visible representation of the salvific presence of Christ[67], actuating in time and space the plan of God for humanity, a plan that has begun to be realized in the person of the risen Christ[68]. Because of their sacramental configuration to Christ, priests are to live out their ordination in three inter-related ways: 1) by prolonging Christ's presence; 2) by embodying his way of life; and 3) by making him visible in the midst of the people they serve (cf. *PDV 15*). They do this by proclaiming his word, repeating his acts of forgiveness, and showing his loving concern for the flock (cf. *PDV* 15). The ministerial priesthood as the sacramental representation of Jesus Christ, Head and Shepherd, then, is the central focus of *PDV* 13-15.

---

[66] Gozzelino states that *PDV* «[...] opta senza esitazioni per la prospettiva fatta propria dal Vaticano II: quella chiamata del segno, o detta sacramentale, secondo la quale lo specifico di tale ministero consiste nell'essere la visibilizzazione (o rappresentazione) efficace, a livello di persone, della presenza salvifica del Signore [...]», G. GOZZELINO, «Il presbitero continuazione di Cristo», 85.

[67] Cf. G. GOZZELINO, «Il presbitero continuazione di Cristo», 85. A. Dulles offers a «representational» model for understanding the ministerial priesthood: «In designating priestly ordination as a sacrament the Church tells us that Christ is himself involved in making certain individuals his qualified representatives. The essential characteristics of priestly existence flow from the call of Christ and from the abiding structures of the Church as such», A. DULLES, «Models for Ministerial Priesthood», 289.

[68] Cf. G. GOZZELINO, «Il presbitero continuazione di Cristo», 85.

3.1.1 The Priesthood of Jesus Christ

Citing Proposition 7, *PDV* roots the features of the priesthood of the New Covenant in the person of Jesus Christ himself, in whom they were perfectly and definitively revealed (cf. *PDV* 13). The essential features of the priesthood of Christ are revealed in his role as mediator, a role in which Jesus, fully human and yet Son of God, «[...] gives us immediate access to God» (*PDV* 13). Alphonso has described the nature of Jesus' role as mediator:

> In his Person or his very self, Jesus Christ is at once and indissolubly God-for-us-human beings *and* we-human beings-for-God. That is, he is in person the Father's truth, love, merciful forgiveness, and life for us human beings (a sort of descending movement) *and* at the same time he is in person, in his very self, the perfect expression of human beings in their obedience, worship, and self-gift to God (a sort of ascending motion). Now, because Jesus Christ is this double movement in his very self or person, his Mission is the expression or unfolding, the epiphany or manifestation of this same double movement: namely, his Mission of Revelation — Jesus revealing to us the Father's truth, love, merciful forgiveness, and life — and his Mission of Redemption — Jesus taking us back to the Father in his great sacrifice of obedience and perfect worship[69].

The priesthood of Jesus is thus characterized by his redemptive self-giving and self-sacrifice, which are at the same time revelatory of the Father's love for all human beings.

The Exhortation describes the features of the priesthood of Jesus Christ by citing scriptural references to the shepherd image: he is the «[...] promised Good Shepherd [...] who offers his life. [...] who has come "not to be served but to serve" [...] who in the paschal action of the washing of the feet leaves to his disciples a model of service» (*PDV* 13)[70]. Very clearly, *PDV* stresses that the priesthood of Jesus Christ, the one priesthood in which all in the Church share, is characterized by selfless service[71]. Any actualization of this one priesthood, whether ministerial or common, is measured by this standard of service. Although the notion of service must be given fuller articulation and precision, *PDV*, in the tradition of the teaching of Vatican II, clearly affirms that the priesthood cannot be understood apart from service.

---

[69] H. ALPHONSO, «The Spirituality of the Diocesan Priest Today», 1.

[70] Cf. Ez 34; Jn 10,11-16; Mt 20,28; Jn 13,1-20; Jn 1,36; Rev 5,6.12.

[71] For a systematic presentation of service in the Gospel, see L. J. CAMELI, *Ministerial Consciousness*, 191-198.

3.1.2 The Common Priesthood

The culmination of Jesus' life of service and sacrifice is, of course, «[...] the one definitive sacrifice of the cross» through which «[...] Jesus communicated to all his disciples the dignity and mission of priests of the new and eternal covenant» (*PDV* 13). The communication of the priesthood to his disciples established the Church as a priestly people which not only exists in the image of Christ, but has a «[...] real ontological share in his one eternal priesthood» (*PDV* 13). In this crucial passage the Exhortation delineates the character of Christ's priesthood which can be summed up by the words «sacrificial love», and thus identifies the characteristics of the priesthood of the Church which must conform to Christ «[...] in every aspect of her life» (*PDV* 13). Having affirmed the common priesthood of the new covenant as being rooted in and expressive of the very priesthood of Jesus Christ, characterized by his *kenosis*, the Exhortation then goes on to explain the evolution of the specifically ministerial priesthood and how it relates to and is distinct from this universal, or common, priesthood[72].

3.1.3 The Ministerial Priesthood

Ultimately, the roots of the ministerial priesthood can be traced to the Twelve whom Jesus gathered «[...] for the sake of this universal priesthood of the new covenant» (*PDV* 14). This echoes the Council's teaching that the ministerial and common priesthood are ordered to each other. The Exhortation emphasizes the Apostles' irreplaceable unity with the person of Jesus and «the close relationship between the ministry entrusted to the Apostles and his own mission» (*PDV* 14). Any power or authority the Apostles received from Jesus was given to them for the sake of his mission: «Their mission is not theirs but is the same mission of Jesus» (*PDV* 14). The Apostles are to continue in history Jesus' saving mission on behalf of humanity, but the key to their efficacy and authenticity in this mission is «unity with Jesus and in him with one another and the Father»(*PDV* 14). «In their turn, the Apostles [...] progressively carried out their mission by calling, in various complementary ways, other men as Bishops, as priests and as deacons» (*PDV* 15).

---

[72] For a discussion of the relationship between the common and ministerial modes of priesthood, see above, pp. 67-75. For a systemization of four different theological approaches (ontological, existential, practico-social and eschatological) to the relation and distinction of the two modes of priesthood, see P. ROSATO, «Priesthood of the Baptized and Priesthood of the Ordained», 215-266.

Citing various scriptural passages, *PDV* asserts that through the laying on of hands priests receive the gift of the Spirit and can thus continue Christ's «ministry of reconciliation, of shepherding the flock of God and of teaching» (*PDV* 15). Through ordination priests «prolong the presence of Christ» in a particular way and can be described as sacramental representations of Jesus Christ, who exist for the sake of the common priesthood and who «act in order to proclaim the Gospel to the world and to build up the Church in the name and person of Jesus Christ the Head and Shepherd» (*PDV* 15).

3.1.4 «*In Persona Christi Capitis et Pastoris*»

A traditional understanding of the ministerial priesthood stresses that the priest acts *in persona Christi*. In the Church's theological tradition, this term is exclusively associated with the ministerial priesthood. Removed from its technical, sacramental context, however, this description, while accurate, is rather generic and even problematic in the light of the Council's teaching on the common priesthood. To say, generally, that the priest is called to act in the person of Christ can be said about any Church member[73]. The problem with this term today is that it is inadequate to describe what is distinct about the identity and meaning of the ministerial priesthood. All Christians, in virtue of baptism, are called to «act in the person of Christ» and to become «other Christs». The term is thus in need of further precision if it is to describe what is unique to the ministerial priesthood.

Following the lead of the Second Vatican Council, *PDV* specifies the formula, *in persona Christi*, by adding the words *capitis et pastoris*: «In a word, priests exist and act in order to proclaim the Gospel to the world and to build up the Church in the name and person of Christ the Head

---

[73] This is not to contradict the Church's teaching that only the ministerial priest acts *in persona Christi* in a unique way. M. M. Schaefer and J. F. Henderson observe, «*In persona Christi* refers to the priest's real representation of Christ. It functions as a code phrase for the understanding that Christ really acts through the minister, both in the celebration of sacraments and in other activities of pastoral office which are his by office. The priest's mode of representation of Christ is therefore to be distinguished from that of the laity externally by its public institutional character. It is distinguished from that of the laity internally by the bestowal of the Spirit who is publicly invoked for this individual's ministry in the ordination rite, an action of the diocesan Church. *Therefore the priest's leadership role is not simply functional or determined by Church tradition. Rather, it is personal and sacramental*» (emphasis added), M. M. SCHAEFER – J. F. HENDERSON, *The Catholic Priesthood*, 62. Cf. C. MEYER, «Ambassadors of Christ», especially 762-763; B. MARLIANGEAS, *Clés pour une théologie du ministère*, especially 231-244.

and Shepherd» (*PDV* 15)[74]. This formula plays like a refrain throughout the entire document, emphasizing not only the priest's configuration to Christ, but exactly how his configuration to Christ is distinctive, namely through the appositional phrase «Head and Shepherd». At
times the priest is also described as representing Christ the Spouse of the
Church (cf. *PDV* 16). The meaning of Head, Shepherd, and Spouse, as
well as their implications for understanding the ministerial priesthood,
will be explored ahead in more detail. The affirmation of the priest's
configuration to Christ the Head and Shepherd is significant because it
clarifies the ministerial priesthood's relation to the common priesthood,
and it emphasizes that the ministerial priesthood is not simply a
functional reality. Rather, a «[...] specific ontological bond [...] unites
the priesthood to Christ the High Priest and Good Shepherd» (*PDV* 11),
which leads to the conclusion that the ministerial priest's particular
relation to Christ «[...] is found in the very being of the priest by virtue
of his sacramental consecration/anointing» (*PDV* 16).

Since this consecration is for the sake of mission[75], the ontological
nature of the priesthood is emphasized by *PDV* and cannot be miscon-
strued as a static reality. For the sake of emphasis and to avoid an overly
functionalistic approach to the ministerial priesthood, however, the
Exhortation makes it clear that sacramental ordination allows the priest
to share in Christ's consecration and mission «[...] in a specific and
authoritative way [...] by virtue of which he is configured *in his being* to
Jesus Christ, Head and Shepherd» (*PDV* 18; emphasis added). In this
specific emphasis on both the being and the doing of the priest, the priest
can be understood to be a sacramental representation of Christ, prolonging his presence and embodying his way of life (cf. *PDV* 15). Although
PDV does not explicitly refer to the traditional notion of priestly «character», its repeated emphasis on the ontological configuration of the
priest to Christ the Head and Shepherd puts it solidly in this traditional
understanding of the ministerial priesthood, moving it away from the
primarily functional understanding that has dominated so much of the
postconciliar discussion on priesthood[76].

---

[74] Cf. *AAS* 84 (1992) 680: «Uno verbo, existunt et operantur pro Evangelio mundo
nuntiando, *et nomine et persona Christi Capitis et Pastoris*, ad Ecclesiam ipsius
aedificandam» [emphasis added].

[75] For a discussion of consecration and mission in the ministerial priesthood, see
above, pp. 84-87.

[76] For a discussion of *PDV*'s ontological approach to priesthood as being expressive
of the traditional notion of character, see C. DUMONT,«La "charité pastorale"»,

3.2 *The Christological Perspective and Priestly Spirituality*

In describing the christological foundations of the spiritual life of the priest, *PDV* quotes extensively from *PO* 12 which affirms that through the sacrament of Orders the priest is consecrated in a «new way» that configures him to Christ in a particular way, a configuration that makes him both an instrument and a representative of Christ. This representation endows the priest with a «special grace» by which «[...] through his service of the people committed to his care and all the people of God» he «[...] is better able to pursue the perfection of Christ, whose place he takes» (*PDV 19*). The spiritual life of the priest is thus rooted in his sacramental consecration to Christ and expressed in his ministry through which he acts as Christ's instrument and representative. The consecration is the foundation for the ministry and the ministry gives expression to the consecration. Both dimensions are intrinsically constitutive of the priest's spiritual life. There is thus no dualism between priestly consecration and its associated apostolic mission: consecration is the stimulus for pastoral dedication, and pastoral activity embodies the priest's radical configuration to Christ and deepens priestly holiness[77]. The spiritual life of the priest, therefore, is not rooted in a vague generic relationship with God but in his specific configuration to Christ the Head, Shepherd, and Spouse. This sacramental representation of Christ, concretely expressed in priestly ministry, shapes the spiritual life of the ministerial priest[78].

218-219. Rypar notes that *PDV*'s difference from *PO* 2 is not in doctrinal content but in the various accents and particular aspects which *PDV* emphasizes, thus making it a guide for priests today: «La differenza dalle formulazioni del Concilio (il quale, nel *PO* 2, usa il termine di "carattere speciale" sancito dal Concilio Tridentino) consiste ovviamente non nel contenuto dottrinale, ma piuttosto nei vari accenti ed aspetti particolari i quali, considerati con riferimento alle circostanze attuali, costituiscono per i sacerdoti e per la formazione sacerdotale luce e guida. Il riferimento a Cristo inteso come configurazione ontologica illuminerà la loro vita», F. RYPAR, «*Pastores dabo vobis* alla luce del pensiero conciliare», 536.

[77] V. Gambino states: «La "consacrazione" è stimolo per la dedicazione apostolica e pastorale e l'azione pastorale è configurazione radicale a Cristo e incremento della santità sacerdotale», V. GAMBINO, «Formazione spirituale», 175. Pio Laghi observes that the priest's spirituality is not generic but derives from his specific configuration to Christ the Head, Shepherd, and Spouse: «[...] la sua spiritualità è nutrita non genericamente dal rapporto con Dio, ma specificamente dal rapporto "ministeriale" con Cristo Capo, Pastore, Servo e Sposo della Chiesa», P. LAGHI, «Le principali chiavi di lettura», 197. For a description of the interplay between priestly ministry and spirituality, see E. E. LARKIN – G. T. BROCCOLO, eds., *Spiritual Renewal of the American Priesthood*, 11-24.

[78] Cf. P. LAGHI, «Le principali chiavi di lettura», 197.

PDV's sacramental understanding that the identity and mission of the priest represented Christ the Head, Shepherd, and Spouse of the Church (cf. *PDV* 16) is thus the foundation for the fruitfulness of the priest's spiritual life[79]: «By virtue of this consecration brought about by the outpouring of the Spirit in the sacrament of Holy Orders, the spiritual life of the priest is marked, molded and characterized by the way of thinking and acting proper to Jesus Christ» (*PDV* 21). *PDV* 21-23 describes the spiritual life of the priest under the three images of Head, Shepherd, and Spouse.

3.2.1 Christ the Head of the Church

The Exhortation repeatedly refers to Christ as Head of his Body, the Church. This is a clear reference to the leadership and authority that Jesus has vis-à-vis the Church, an authority whose purpose is to give life to the Church. It was noted above that the purpose of emphasizing Christ's headship was to accent the truth that it is Christ who gives life to his body, the Church, and that he must always be present to his body, vivifying it, building it up, and uniting it to himself (cf. Eph 4,11-16). It has already been shown that the priest's distinction is rooted in being a sacrament of this headship[80]. It is precisely in this that his relationship to the common priesthood can be understood (cf. *LG* 10). In keeping with the teaching of the Council, *PDV* makes clear that this is not an authority as it is conventionally understood outside of the context of faith. Rather, it is an authority that can only be expressed as service because Jesus is «[...] the "Head" in the new and unique sense of being a "servant"» (*PDV* 21)[81].

---

[79] Rypar observes that *PDV* develops the doctrinal aspects of the ministerial priesthood, not only for a further deepening of priestly identity, but «[...] anche per la sua vita spirituale e pastorale», F. RYPAR, «*Pastores dabo vobis* alla luce del pensiero conciliare», 538.

[80] For a discussion of Christ's headship over the Church, and priests as sacramental representations of Christ the Head, see above, pp. 91-95. T. Lane observes, «[...] the headship of the ordained person is the sacramental assurance of the saving presence of Christ to all the members of his body. This is why the fuller description of priesthood in the teaching of the Second Vatican Council is in terms of acting in the person of Christ "the Head" (*PO* 2). This headship and leadership is not confined to sacramental activity. It overflows into every expression of pastoral care, by those called to be "examples to the flock" (1 Pt 5:3). Those ordained to priesthood act in the person of Christ who is at the same time Head and Shepherd», T. LANE, *A Priesthood in Tune*, 103.

[81] The Exhortation refers to Mk 10,45 to illustrate the meaning of service associated with Christ's Headship: «The Son of Man came not to be served but to serve, and to

PDV uses the pauline notion of *kenosis* to give fuller resonance to the meaning of Christ's service and to demonstrate its radical nature as an obedient service which «[...] attains its fullest expression in his death on the cross» (*PDV* 21)[82]. Obedience and service, then, are the salient characteristics of Christ's authority which is expressed in the notion of headship. The authority of Jesus coincides with his obedience to the Father, his service, and his *kenotic* gift of self. It is only in this context that his headship and authority over the Church can be properly understood. This understanding of the authority of Christ as Head of the Church, conditioned as it is by a radical understanding of obedience and service, has profound implications for the spiritual life of the priest. Through ordination the priest becomes a sacramental representative of Christ the Head. It must be emphasized that Christ, not the priest, is the Head of the Church. But through sacramental ordination, the priest represents Christ in his headship. If this representation is to be accurate and effective, it must approximate the attitudes and dynamics of Christ's own headship. Any authority and leadership that the priest has, therefore, is only in virtue of his imitation of Christ as servant of the Church. To reinforce this understanding the Exhortation cites St. Augustine who stressed that «[...] because the Lord of Lords did not disdain to make himself our servant», then neither should one who is placed in a position of leadership in the Church (cf. *PDV* 21)[83]. A «[...] fundamental attitude of service to the People of God» is thus a primary characteristic of priestly spirituality (cf. *PDV* 21). Such an attitude has important ramifications for the type of leadership the ministerial priest practices, because it prevents a self-aggrandizing understanding of authority from taking root and establishes the priest as an elder of the community, or «model of the flock», thus accurately expressing the configuration he has with Christ the Head (cf. *PDV* 21)[84].

---

give his life as a ransom for many». For an analysis of Mk 10,35-45, see L. J. CAMELI, *Ministerial Consciousness*, 37-94, particularly 63-86, for a discussion on the significance of v. 45.

[82] To illustrate Christ's *kenosis*, the Exhortation quotes Phil 2,7-8: «He emptied himself, taking the form of a servant, being born in the likeness of men. And being found in human form, he humbled himself and became obedient unto death, even death on a cross».

[83] Cf. ST. AUGUSTINE, *Sermo Morin Guelferbytanus*, 32, 1: PLS 2, 637, as cited in *PDV*, footnote 47.

[84] Lane observes, «The headship of Christ is never a headship of domination or mastery since Christian power is the exact opposite of worldly power. The only headship which Christ recognises as exercised in his name is a headship of love, a headship

3.2.2 Christ the Shepherd of the Church

The central image of *PDV* is that of Christ as Shepherd of the Church[85], an image closely associated with that of «Head». The common reference is to «Christ, Head and Shepherd of the Church». The Shepherd image thus expresses «[...] the same content as that of Jesus Christ Head and Servant», but in a more evocative, biblical manner (cf. *PDV* 22). Citing numerous biblical references as well as a liturgical text, the Exhortation resumes the theme it developed at length earlier in the document where it encouraged priests to prolong the presence of Christ by «[...] embodying his way of life and making him visible in the midst of the flock entrusted to their care» (*PDV* 15)[86]. In the context of the spiritual life of the priest, the Exhortation emphasizes the interior dispositions and external activities of the shepherd: compassion and empathy, intimate knowledge and careful protection of the flock, a willingness to go to any length for the sake of the flock. In short, because the activities of Jesus the Shepherd manifest and express his love, his entire life can be described as «[...] a continual manifestation of his "pastoral charity"» (*PDV* 22)[87].

Significantly, *PDV,* in an allusion to apostolic succession, quotes 1Pt 5,4 which refers to Jesus as the «Chief Shepherd». The mission of the «Chief Shepherd» is carried on in the Church first through the ministry

---

of self-giving, a headship of self-sacrifice, a headship of service, a headship in which the head is in continual life-giving organic interaction with all the members of the body, all of whom share his kingly, priestly and prophetic mission. [...] Any day on which ministerial priesthood is perceived as domination or monopoly is a day on which what should be light has been turned into darkness», T. LANE, *A Priesthood in Tune*, 103.

[85] For a discussion of Christ the Shepherd in the Conciliar and 1971 Synodal documents on priesthood, see above, pp. 96-100.

[86] *PDV* refers to the following passages in developing the «Shepherd» theme: Ps 22,23; Ez 34,1ff; Jn 10,11.14; Mt 9,35-36; Mt 18,12-14; Jn 10,3; also see *PDV*, n. 48 which cites the Roman Missal, communion antiphon from the Mass of the Fourth Sunday of Easter.

[87] N. Cachia did an in-depth textual analysis of the shepherd image in Chapter Ten of the Gospel of John, and concluded, «The unifying criterion of the shepherd image as it emerges from this Johannine chapter is, what may be called, the pastoral love or charity of the shepherd. He is presented as the shepherd essentially *for others*. There is no action which he does which does not have a relation to the sheep entrusted to him. His life is projected towards the safety, the well-being and growth of the sheep. His life is one of complete service, dedication, and constant reaching out towards the sheep, notwithstanding the consequences this might have on him. All this springs from his love. A love which he receives from the Father and which he transmits to all those who were given to him» [emphasis in the original], N. CACHIA, «"I Am the Good Shepherd. The Good Shepherd Lays Down His Life for the Sheep"», 136-214.

of the Apostles, then through their successors, then through priests who through ordination have a share in this apostolic ministry (cf. *PDV* 22). Because they share in the apostolic ministry which has its source in Christ, priests are called to imitate him, making his interior attitudes and dispositions their own and putting them into practice.

3.2.3 Christ the Spouse of the Church

Although used infrequently in the Exhortation, the spousal image adds an important christological clarification to the understanding of the ministerial priesthood. First used in the Introduction (*PDV* 3) and again in Chapter Two (*PDV* 16), the image of Christ the Spouse of the Church gives further definition to the meaning of Christ's relation to the Church, and thus to the priest's «being towards» the Church. In a controversial phrase the English translation of *PDV* states, «"Inasmuch as he represents Christ the Head, Shepherd and Spouse of the Church, the priest is placed not only in the Church but also *in the forefront of the Church*"» (*PDV* 16, quoting Proposition 7) [emphasis added]. Cardinal Laghi has pointed out that this is an error of translation and can give the wrong impression that the priest enjoys a position of superiority or privilege in the Church. The original Latin text reads *erga ecclesiam*[88] which has been rendered «in the forefront of the Church». A more accurate translation reads «towards the Church»[89]. Hence, the text should read that «the priest is placed not only *in the Church*, but also *towards the Church*»[90], a reading that has a decidedly different connotation than «in the forefront of»[91].

The priest is both in the Church (through baptism) and towards the Church (through ordination). This latter relationship is explained in terms of his configuration to Christ the Head and Shepherd, but now it is also understood in terms of his configuration to Christ the Spouse of the

---

[88] Cf. *AAS* 84 (1992) 681.

[89] Cf. P. LAGHI, «The Identity and Ministry of the Priest», 27.

[90] P. LAGHI, «The Identity and Ministry of the Priest», 27. The Italian translation of *Pastores Dabo Vobis* renders *erga ecclesiam* as *di fronte alla Chiesa* which captures the intended meaning of «towards the Church» or «facing the Church».

[91] It is interesting to note that the English language edition of the *Directory on the Ministry and Life of Priests*, contains a similar translation of *erga ecclesiam*: «Through the mystery of Christ, the priest lives his multiple ministries and is inserted also into the mystery of the Church which "becomes aware in faith that her being comes not from herself but from the grace of Christ in the Holy Spirit" (*PDV* 16). In this sense, while the priest is in the Church, he is also set *in front of* it», CC, *DMLP*, sec. 12, p. 14.

Church. Through the sacrament of ordination the priest is «towards the Church» in that same manner as Christ, that is, spousally; he thus represents Christ the Bridegroom[92]. The gift of himself that Christ makes to the Church is analogous to the gift of self that a bridegroom offers to a bride. If the Church, then, is the body, of which Christ is the Head, or the flock of which he is the Shepherd, to express the intimacy of this relationship even more clearly, the Church is also the bride for whom he is the Bridegroom. As a bride the Church «[...] proceeds like a new Eve from the open side of the Redeemer on the Cross» (PDV 22). As a bridegroom Christ stands before (towards) the Church and gives his life to her.

The implications for the priest's spiritual life of his configuration to Christ the Spouse are evident. Through the sacrament of Orders the priest becomes a representative of Christ. As such he is called to relate to the Church in a way analogous to Christ, which means that his relation to the Church must have a spousal quality, which, as described by PDV, demands that the priest «[...] be capable of loving people with a heart which is new, generous and pure, with genuine self-detachment, with full, constant and faithful dedication and at the same time with a kind of "divine jealousy"» (PDV 22).

The three images of Christ, and by extension of the ministerial priest described in PDV 21-22, show a progression and amplification in understanding both the identity and the spiritual life of the priest. In the movement from Head to Shepherd to Spouse, the external image and the associated interior life of the priest are given fuller clarity. Although three separate images, they seek to describe one type of priesthood. They should not simply be understood as three separate, disassociated figures but rather as deeply interconnected images that interpret one another and give texture, nuance, and shading to the understanding of the identity, mission, and spiritual life of the priest.

The priest exercises a leadership or authority role because of his configuration to Christ the Head. Such authority or leadership can only be properly understood in its larger sacramental context: Christ the Head is the source of life for his body, the Church (cf. Eph 4,15-16). The

---

[92] S. Butler observes: «What can be understood according to the analogy of head-body is now placed within the analogy of bridegroom-bride. Both analogies convey the idea of communion, but bridegroom-bride symbolizes communion as the "unity of the two", whereas head-body could be read — apart from this new situation *within* the nuptial symbol — as the somatic unity of a single organism», S. BUTLER, «The Priest as Sacrament of Christ the Bridegroom», 516.

authority of the priest, rooted in sacramental ordination, must mirror and express the headship of Christ; it thus must be at the service of the life of the Body. It is not a dominating leadership, but rather sustaining and life-giving[93]. But this description is inadequate, taken alone, to fully express the ministry and spiritual life of the priest. The figure of Christ the Shepherd brings the picture into clearer focus, expressing as it does the solicitude and care-unto-death that the priest is to have for the Church, Christ's flock. But even this needs to be nuanced and shaded in order bring the image of the priest into full relief. Hence, the image of Spouse is added in order to give the accent and depth needed to express the spousal relationship which the priest, through ordination, has with the Church. Taken together, these three images express clearly and rather forcefully the centrality of the christological perspective in defining the identity and spiritual life of the ministerial priest, thus its centrality in developing an understanding of priest as leader. Although all three perspectives (ecclesial, christological, and pastoral) are needed to construct an adequate understanding of the priesthood, the christological clearly takes precedence over the ecclesiological and the pastoral. It is the configuration to Christ the Head, Shepherd, and Spouse which gives expression to the ecclesiological perspective and direction and motivation to the pastoral. Indeed, it is «[...] only in loving and serving Christ the Head and Spouse» that the the priest's pastoral ministry will be properly lived out (*PDV* 23).

3.2.4 Consecration: Foundation for Mission

The christological perspective is also present in *PDV* 24-26, «The Spiritual Life in the Exercise of the Ministry», which focuses on the pastoral dimension of priestly spirituality. The principle of «consecration-for-mission» establishes the context for understanding how the spiritual life of the priest is both expressed in and nourished by his pastoral activities. Just as the priest's consecration, which configures him to Christ the Head and Shepherd, is under the seal of the Holy Spirit, so is the mission of the priest: «The priest's mission is not extraneous to his consecration or juxtaposed to it, but represents its intrinsic and vital purpose: consecration is for mission» (*PDV* 24). Thus the Spirit is active in both the consecration and in the mission of the priest.

. *PDV* stresses that it is crucial for the priest to cultivate a consciousness or awareness of being consecrated for mission: «It is essential that the

---

[93] Cf. G. GOZZELINO, «Il presbitero continuazione di Cristo», 86.

priest should continually renew and deepen his awareness of being a minister of Christ by virtue of sacramental consecration» (*PDV* 25). «Awareness» is critical for understanding the connection between the christological and pastoral dimensions as they are lived out in the life of a priest, who is to be aware that he is a «living instrument of Christ» (*PDV 25)*, a steward of the mystery of Christ which seeks to be expressed in the priest's own life. As a steward of the mystery of Christ and as his living instrument, «[...] there is need for great vigilance and lively awareness» (*PDV* 24).

Awareness or consciousness of being a living instrument of Christ, then, is «a focus for the spiritual life of the priest» (*PDV* 25). It causes the priest to realize that he is chosen by Christ, not as a passive object, but as a «[...] conscious, free and responsible person» who precisely out of the deep relationship with Christ, established by ordination, is able to carry out the mission of Christ, acting as his steward and living instrument (cf. *PDV* 25). This consciousness of being intimately united with Christ is necessary in order to create the interior aptitude to carry out the mission of Christ in accordance with the Church's intentions (cf. *PDV* 25). Furthermore, this bond with Christ «[...] tends by its very nature to become as extensive and profound as possible, affecting one's way of thinking, feeling and life itself; in other words, creating a series of moral and spiritual "dispositions" which correspond to the ministerial actions performed by the priest» (*PDV* 25).

The pastoral activities can thus be adequately expressed and understood only in the light of the foundational christological perspective that «consecration-for-mission» expresses. This illustrates the twofold bond that exists in the priest's life: 1) configuration to Christ, Head and Shepherd, and flowing from this, 2) dedication to the Church's mission expressed in the priest's ministry[94]. The consciousness of being chosen to be a living instrument of the Lord provides the impetus for engaging in the Church's ministry, which in turn «[...] provides an incentive to grow in ever greater love and service of Jesus Christ the Head, Shepherd, and Spouse of the Church, a love which is always a response to the free and unsolicited love of God in Christ. Growth in the love of Jesus Christ

---

[94] Gozzelino describes the priest's twofold relationship to Christ and the Church and notes that the relation to Christ is primary: «In conformità con quanto suggerisce la qualifica di relazione "fondamentale" attribuita al dato cristologico, insegna piuttosto che il rapporto del presbiterato alla Chiesa consegue (come e perchè la Chiesa deriva dal Cristo e non viceversa) dal suo riferimento al Cristo e non viceversa», G. GOZZELINO, «Il presbitero continuazione di Cristo», 88-89.

determines in turn the growth of love for the Church» (*PDV* 25). The influence of the christological-pastoral interplay on the spiritual life of the priest, which is very apparent in this section, can be described as a circular relationship, with the christological both feeding into the pastoral and being nourished by it[95].

3.2.5 Configuration to Christ and Personal Witness: The Evangelical Counsels

The fourth section of Chapter Three, «Priestly Life and the Radicalism of the Gospel» (*PDV* 27-30), focuses on the place of the Evangelical Counsels in the life of priest[96]. Although they are approached primarily from a pastoral perspective by the Exhortation, they can be viewed from a christological vantage point as well. From the christological perspective, the Evangelical Counsels are expressive of the spiritual life of the priest, insofar as they express his configuration to Christ, Head, Shepherd, and Spouse — that is, insofar as they mirror and express Christ's total gift of himself.

Jesus, who was an example of «[...] complete exterior and interior emptying of self, is both the model and source of the virtues of obedience, chastity and poverty which the priest is called to live out» (*PDV* 30). Significantly, the Evangelical Counsels are not to be seen by priests as absolutes, or as ends in themselves. Rather, the priest is to live them «[...] in accordance with those ways and, more specifically, those goals and that basic meaning which derive from and express his own priestly identity» (*PDV* 27). As noted above, the basic meaning of priestly identity «[...] is to live and work by the power of the Holy Spirit in service of the Church and for the salvation of the world» (*PDV* 12). Priests are configured to Christ in order that «[...] they may build up and establish his whole Body which is the Church» (*PDV* 20). The pastoral

---

95 *PDV* 24-26 reinforces the conciliar and postconciliar teaching on priestly spirituality. *MP* II.1.3, for example, states, «Every priest will find in his very vocation and ministry the deep motivation for living his entire life in oneness and strength of spirit. Called like the rest of those who have been baptized to become a true image of Christ (cf. Rom 8,29), the priest, like the Apostles, shares besides in a special way companionship with Christ and his mission as the Supreme Pastor. [...] Therefore in the priestly life there can be no dichotomy between love for Christ and zeal for souls». Cf. *PO* 4-6, 13; E. E. LARKIN – G. T. BROCCOLO, eds., *Spiritual Renewal of the American Priesthood*, 11-24.

96 For discussions of the Evangelical Counsels and ministerial priesthood, see C. POZO, «Sacerdocio ministerial y radicalismo de los consejos evangélicos», 550-560; J. ESQUERDA BIFET, *Teologia de la espiritualidad sacerdotal*, 226-230 and 264-275.

horizon is thus the background against which the Evangelical Counsels are approached by the Exhortation.

But, because the Evangelical Counsels are expressive of the self-emptying of Christ, the priest who embraces them will be better able to discover and appropriate the consciousness of Christ and so «[...] discover, in a charity which is obedient, chaste and poor, the royal road of union with God and unity with his brothers and sisters» (*PDV* 30)[97]. From the christological perspective, obedience refers to that «[...] disposition of soul by which priests are always ready to seek not their own will, but the will of him who sent them» (*PDV* 28); priestly celibacy takes on spousal connotations and is undertood as representing the «[...] total and exclusive manner in which Jesus Christ her Head and Spouse» loved the Church (*PDV* 29); and priestly poverty follows «[...] the example of Christ who rich though he was became poor for love of us» (*PDV 30*). Again, the circular perspective is evident: the christological and pastoral perspectives feed into one another, but always in the larger context of the ecclesiological perspective. The witness of the ministerial priest to his configuration to Christ takes place within the Church, mystery, communion, and mission, through the Holy Spirit who is both the «source of holiness and a call to sanctification» (*PDV* 27).

3.3 *Conclusions*

The examination of the christological foundations of the ministerial priesthood, in the teachings of the Second Vatican Council and the Synod of 1971, emphasized that the ministerial priest, through ordination, is configured to Christ the Head and Shepherd, shares in his consecration and mission, and is thus able to engage in the threefold ministry of Christ. The model for priestly leadership is Christ himself. Christ is the Head of his Body, the Church, and through ordination the ministerial priest becomes a representative of the headship of Christ. Following the pattern of Christ the Good Shepherd's leadership, the ministerial priest is called to give his life in love and service to the Church. Immersed in the community, the priest is distinct within it, and his permanent commitment to Christ and to the Church is a sign of Christ's fidelity and presence in and to the Church.

PDV's understanding of the christological basis of the ministerial priesthood is built on the foundation and permeated by the flavor of the

---

[97] Cf. Phil 2,5 for a description of the consciousness or mind of Christ, which is expressed in his *kenosis* or self emptying.

teachings of Vatican II and the Synod of 1971, thus reinforcing the christological dimension of an understanding of priest as leader. *PDV* emphasizes that the Christological perspective is «absolutely necessary» for understanding the ministerial priesthood (cf. *PDV* 12), and thus for an adequate understanding of priestly leadership. As sacramental representations of Christ himself, priests are to prolong, embody, and make visible the presence of Christ. Such an understanding sets the context for an interpretation of priest as leader: it is not simply a functional reality but rather engages the priest both on the level of his being and on the level of activity. Configured to Christ the Head, Shepherd, and Spouse, the priest becomes his instrument and so his life and ministry are to be characterized by obedient service (Christ the Head), pastoral solicitude (Christ the Shepherd), and spousal love (Christ the Spouse). Such configuration to Christ carries with it certain exigencies, the foremost of which is the cultivation of a deep consciousness of consecration, of being Christ's instrument. Love for Christ is the basis of love for the Church; priestly ministry is inscribed in this prior relation to Christ. Such awareness of configuration to Christ, which can only come from a deep relationship with him, extends into all areas of the priest's life, touching his will, intellect, and affect. Awareness, then, has existential ramifications: it will lead the priest to want to take on certain characteristics of Christ himself, the most salient of which are self-emptying, obedient service, radical availability for God's mission, and complete gift of self in love to God and the Church. These Christlike characteristics are expressed in the Evangelical Counsels of obedience, poverty, and chastity. The Christological perspective, as articulated in *PDV*, points to a ministerial priest who acts as a leader, not simply through his activities, but through the example of his own life, lived in the conscious awareness of his sacramental configuration to Christ. Removed from its christological moorings the ministry of the priest would degenerate into mere activism. It is out of this prior relationship with Christ, and the existential impact it has on his life, that the priest moves into the pastoral activities that are the visible expressions of his leadership.

4. Pastoral Perspective and Doctrine of Priesthood

The final section of *PDV* Chapter Two, «Serving the Church and the World» (*PDV* 16-18), focuses on the pastoral perspective of priesthood, that is, the mission of the priest and the goals, methods, and recipients of his ministry. As with the previous two sections, all three perspectives intermingle, but since the pastoral predominates here, it will be the focus of examination. Before approaching this section, however, it is to be noted that the pastoral perspective has surfaced earlier in *PDV* Chapter Two, in connection with the ecclesiological and christological perspectives. The pastoral perspective first appeared in the discussion of the trinitarian ecclesiology that grounds both the common and the ministerial priesthood. Because the ministerial priesthood is rooted in an ecclesiology of communion and thus essentially relational, the Exhortation can affirm that it exists «[...] in order to serve the People of God who are the Church and to draw all mankind to Christ» (*PDV* 12). That the ministerial priesthood exists in order to serve the Church is given further emphasis in the christological section. Configured to Christ, Head and Shepherd, the purpose or mission of priests can be summed up succinctly: «[...] priests exist and act in order to proclaim the Gospel to the world and to build up the Church» (*PDV* 15).

4.1 *The Relation of the Ministerial Priesthood «Towards» the Church*

PDV 15 describes the sacramental relationship with Christ that enables the ministerial priest to be and act *in persona Christi capitis et pastoris*. Before all others, this is the priest's fundamental relationship; but intimately linked with his relationship to Christ is his relationship to the Church. His relationship to the Church finds its source and inspiration in his relationship to Christ. In fact the two are so closely and intrinsically related that the priest's relationship to the Church is inscribed in his relationship to Christ (cf. *PDV* 16). Once again, *PDV* stresses that the christological perspective takes priority over both the ecclesiological and pastoral perspectives[98].

PDV 16 highlights the nature of the relationship between the ministerial priesthood and the common priesthood, and in doing so gives a clearer image of the priest as leader. As noted above, the ministerial priest is not only *in* the Church but also *towards* the Church[99]. This relationship towards the Church emphasizes two points: first, it reflects the christological affirmation that the ministerial priest is configured to Christ the Head, Shepherd, and Spouse, thus analogously enjoys the same relationship to the Church that Christ himself enjoys; and second, «towards the Church» emphasizes the relationship of service. It is

---

[98] Cf. above, p. 156, n. 94.

[99] Regarding the controversy over the English translation of *erga ecclesiam,* it was pointed out that the present English version, «in the forefront of the Church», would be more appropriately translated as «towards the Church». See above, p. 153.

towards the Church that the priest directs his energies, solicitude, and ministry.

The emphasis on the priest's relationship *towards* the Church explains *PDV*'s affirmation that the priest's relationship to the Church is inscribed in his relationship to Christ. The priesthood, sacramentally representative of Christ, Head, Shepherd, and Spouse, is a constitutive element of the Church; the priest's ministry is thus «[...] entirely on behalf of the Church; it aims at promoting the exercise of the common priesthood of the entire people of God» (*PDV* 16, quoting Proposition 7). The priest therefore relates to the Church from the perspective of his configuration to Christ, Head and Shepherd[100].

PDV's treatment of the relationship of the ministerial priesthood to the common priesthood, despite the disputed English translation, helps to clarify *LG* 10, one of the Council's foundational teachings on the priesthood. The «difference in essence and not merely degree» can be explained by the sacramental configuration of the priest to Christ the Head, Shepherd, and Spouse, which not only affirms the priest's place in the Church, but more importantly his relationship towards the Church. In this position the priest is «[...] a visible continuation and sacramental sign of Christ in his own position before the Church and the world» (*PDV* 16). Giving further precision to this «towards the Church» of the ministerial priesthood, the Exhortation states that «[...] the ordained priesthood ought not to be thought of as existing prior to the Church, because it is totally at the service of the Church» (*PDV* 16). Nor should it be thought of as ancillary to the Church since it is a constitutive element of the Church. The priest is thus in the Church, but with a particular relation towards the Church, which shapes both the content and style of his ministry.

4.2 *Pastoral Functions*

Having established that the relationship of the priest to the Church is rooted in his sacramental relationship to Christ, the Exhortation delineates the nature of the priest's ministry. In doing so the ecclesiological perspective emerges once again, but this time in order to set the context

---

100 Cf. G. GOZZELINO, «Il presbitero continuazione di Cristo», 88-89; P. LAGHI, «The Identity and Ministry of the Priest», 27. Michael Evans points out, «... precisely in order to maintain its sacramental structure, the Church needs the active presence of its Head, leading and uniting, and it is primarily through the ordained priesthood that this particular aspect of Christ's involvement with his Church is made manifest», M. EVANS, «*In Persona Christi*» 120.

for the pastoral perspective and point to the goal of the priest's ministry: he is the «[...] "servant of Christ present in the Church as mystery, communion and mission"» (*PDV* 16)[101]. As noted previously, the ministry of the priest, delineated at Vatican II, follows the threefold structure of Christ's ministry of word, sacrament, and pastoral care and guidance. The Exhortation, however, rather artificially applies these categories to specific aspects of the Church understood as mystery, communion, and mission: the priest's service to the Church as mystery emphasizes the cultic dimension of his ministry, particularly presiding at the sacraments; his service to the Church as communion emphasizes the pastoral dimension — harmonizing the various charisms for the purpose of building up the Church; his service to the Church as mission empha-sizes the prophetic dimension by which he enables the community to become the herald of the Gospel (cf. PDV 16). As noted above, Vatican II and *Christifideles Laici* articulated an understanding of the Church as mystery, communion, and mission, three intrinsically related dimen-sions. Every aspect of priestly ministry — whether it be preaching, presiding at the sacraments, or pastoral care — is at the service of the *entire* Church, understood as mystery, communion, and mission. It therefore seems «forced» to associate particular aspects of priestly minis-try with particular dimensions of the Church; in such a description priestly ministry seems too compartmentalized[102]. All of priestly minis-try, in reality, takes place within the context of the Church and is at the service of the Church understood as mystery, communion, and mission. In all of this the priest, through his particular configuration to Christ, continues «[...] Christ's prayer, word, sacrifice and salvific action in the Church» (*PDV* 16). Despite the artificiality of associating specific aspects of the threefold ministry with specific dimensions of the Church, the value of this section is that *PDV* reiterates the teaching of Vatican II in affirming that the threefold ministry of word, sacrament, and pastoral guidance is constitutive of the priest's ministerial activities.

---

[101] Cf. *Instrumentum Laboris* 16, p. 18.

[102] Ratzinger, in discussing the evolution of *PO* at the Council, says this about a rigid interpretation of the schema of the threefold ministry: «It is important to realize, however, that the framework of this schema loses its rigidity quite thoroughly, becomes fluid and flexible, as the decree progresses through its discussion of this question. The unity of priestly ministry, which is constantly at the center of the discussion, emerges so strongly that the classical threefold order of priestly functions decreases considerably in significance», J. RATZINGER, *Priestly Minsistry*, 16.

4.3 *Pastoral Relations*

The exposition of the pastoral perspective strongly emphasizes the collegial structure of the ministerial priesthood[103]. Once again, the inter-mingling of perspectives can clearly be seen in this treatment. The collegial nature is rooted in the ecclesiology described previously. The pastoral perspective, however, shifts the emphasis and articulates what the radically communitarian, «collective work» of ordained ministry means for the pastoral work of the ministerial priest[104] (cf. *PDV* 17).

First it means that the priest must cooperate with the bishop's ministry, showing concern for both the universal Church and for the particular Church he was ordained to serve, and second that the priest is inserted into a presbyterate and carries out his pastoral ministry as part of a larger body. The priest works, not alone, but with his brother priests in «building up the Body of Christ», a work which calls for differentiation of functions as well as the ability to adapt to new realities. This demands that the priest show a spirit of openness to gifts and charisms that may be present in other members of the presbyterate. Finally, the pastoral perspective emphasizes that the priest, because he exists for the purpose of promoting the common priesthood, must «[...] have a positive and helping relationship to the laity» (*PDV* 17), relating to them in a fraternal context of friendship.

In addition to the collegial nature of priestly ministry vis-à-vis bishops, priests, and laity, the Exhortation stresses that the priest «[...] should be animated by a profound missionary spirit» which both motivates and prepares him «[...] to preach the Gospel everywhere» (*PDV* 18). This missionary spirit is directed not only towards the Church, but towards other Christian denominations, to other religions, and to all people of good will (cf. *PDV* 18). Significantly, this missionary spirit is not only revealed in the actual preaching ministry, but even more importantly, in the example of life that the priest sets before others: «Deeply rooted in the truth and charity of Christ [...] the priest is called to witness in all his relationships to fraternity, service and a common quest for the truth, as well as a concern for the promotion of justice and peace» (*PDV* 18).

---

[103] Cf. L. TERRIEN, «Theology and Spirituality of the Priesthood», 14.
[104] Cf. JOHN PAUL II, «*Angelus* Talk, 25 February 1990», *OR* (5 March 1990) 5.

4.4 *The «New Evangelization»*

The section on the pastoral perspective concludes by reflecting on the «new evangelization»[105] as being both a motive and an expression of the priest's pastoral mission. The «new evangelization», a key theme of John Paul II's pontificate, indicates what is to be the Church's response to the challenges of the present age at the threshold of the third millennium of Christianity[106]. The «new evangelization» should not be confused with a re-evangelization which «[...] presumes that little or no memory is left of the original evangelization. A new evangelization [...] seeks to arrest and reverse any trend to dechristianization or alienation from the Word while the Church is still able to strike a responsive chord»[107]. Such takes into consideration the needs and reality of the world today, its difficulties, problems, and challenges, in order to respond with the age old message of Christianity, albeit using new language and methods fitted to the needs of the modern world[108]. Given the nature of the quickly changing world, the complexity of contexts and situations in which a priest is called to minister, and the need for the Gospel to be proclaimed anew in every time, place, and culture, the pressing pastoral task of the new evangelization places special demands on the priest's ministry[109].

These demands, as articulated in *PDV*, recapitulate the ecclesiological, christological, and pastoral perspectives, presenting a compact, compre-

---

[105] The first time that Pope John Paul used the formula new evangelization» was at Nowa Huta, Poland, in 1979. He used it again at the 19th Assembly of CELAM in Haiti in 1983 when he spoke of the need for a new evangelization — new in its ardor, methods and expressions. A year later he touched on the same theme in Santo Domingo. In Europe, at the 5th and 6th symposia of the European Council of Episcopal Conferences in 1982 and 1985, he spoke of the need for a new evangelization in order to respond to the challenges of secularization. The theme is touched on in two of his Post-Synodal Apostolic Exhortations, *Christifideles Laici* and *Pastores Dabo Vobis*, as well as his encylicals *Centesimus Annus* and *Veritatis Splendor*. The «new evangelization» is thus a theme that has concerned John Paul II throughout his entire pontificate, and that, as he indicates in *PDV*, requires that ministerial priests be in the forefront in promoting such an evangelization. For a brief description of the evolution of the «new evangelization» in the thought and writings of John Paul II, see «La nuova evangelizzazione», no author given, 351-363.

[106] The principal coordinates of the «new evangelization» have been described as fervor, structure, expressions, methods, and purpose. For a description of these principal coordinates see «La nuova evangelizzazione», 354-363.

[107] R. CHRISTIAN, «Priestly Formation for a New Evangelization», 119.

[108] Cf. I. GONDA, «La nouvelle évangélisation d'après», 357-358.

[109] Cf. D. COLETTI, «Il ruolo delle istituzioni (seminari, università, scuole) per la "nuova evangelizzazione"», 148-149.

hensive understanding of priesthood today. The new evangelization has need of priests «[...] who are deeply and fully immersed in the mystery of Christ and capable of embodying a new style of pastoral life, marked by a profound communion with the Pope, the Bishops and other priests, and a fruitful cooperation with the lay faithful, always respecting and fostering the different roles, charisms and ministries present within the ecclesial community» (*PDV* 18). As mentioned earlier in the Exhortation, there is an «[...] absolute necessity that the new evangelization have priests as its initial "new evangelizers"» (*PDV* 2)[110]. This is not to imply, however, that priests are the only evangelizers. Rather, the leadership role of priests in the new evangelization is tempered by what was said in another section of the Exhortation, namely that the priest, in his ministry to the Church, «[...] makes the *community* a herald and witness of the Gospel» (*PDV* 16; emphasis added).

4.5 *The Pastoral Perspective and Priestly Spirituality*

4.5.1 Mission: Rooted in Consecration

The pastoral dimension of the spiritual life of the ministerial priest is treated in the third section of Chapter Three, «The Spiritual Life in the Exercise of the Ministry» (*PDV* 24-26). Reinforcing what has been noted before, the text states that consecration is for mission: «The priest's mission is not extraneous to his consecration or juxtaposed to it, but represents its intrinsic and vital purpose» (*PDV* 24). There is, therefore, an «[...] intimate bond [...] between the priest's spiritual life and the exercise of his ministry» (*PDV* 24). Because both are under the Spirit's influence, as has been emphasized, there is a connection of reciprocal influence and immanence, so that the one favors the growth and better expression of the other[111].

Because the pastoral perspective constitutes one of the pillars upon which priestly identity is built, the spirituality of the priest necessarily grows as he exercises his ministry[112]. Thus, his spirituality is not

---

110 The *Directory for the Ministry and Life of Priests* states that «[...] the priest, conscious that each person is, in diverse ways, looking for a love that is capable of bringing them beyond the anguishes concomitant with human weakness and egoism, and above all with death itself, must proclaim that Jesus Christ is the answer to all these anxieties. In the new evangelization, the priest is called to be the *herald of hope*» [emphasis in original], CC, *DMLP*, sec. 35, p. 37.

111 Cf. P. VANZAN, *Pastores dabo vobis*, part two, 358.

112 Commenting on the influence of Vatican II and The Synod of 1971 on priestly spirituality, Larkin and Broccolo observe: «According to one venerable theory, the priest

constituted by a flight from the world, but rather, under the Spirit's guidance, it is an engagement in the world. To emphasize this particular dynamic of priestly spirituality the Exhortation makes reference to *PO*, which asserts that priests are grounded in the life of the Spirit in the actual exercise of their ministry, as long as they allow the Spirit to guide them. It is in these «everyday actions» of ministry that «[...] they are being directed toward perfection of life» (*PDV* 24; cf. *PO* 12).

The reciprocity between priestly spirituality and ministry has already been examined from the christological perspective, but the pastoral perspective is also important. The deepening of the priest's awareness that he is a minister of Christ, in virtue of his consecration to him, is not simply a matter of private spirituality. Rather, this consciousness has public ramifications: it ensures that the priest is actually engaging in Christ's, not his own, mission. Again, the double bonding is essential: bonded to Christ, Head and Shepherd, the priest is also bonded to the mission of Christ as the Church articulates that mission[113]. The strict correspondence between consecration and mission is highlighted here, and the reciprocity between the two is characteristic of the spiritual life

---

stores up spiritual energy in his spiritual exercises and expends that energy in the apostolate, so that he has to return to his prie-dieu to refurbish his depleted reserves. Vatican II and the Synodal document [1971] have enlarged this theory. They have emphasized that the ministry itself is the prime source of the priest's spirituality. Our question [...] is *how*? How is the ministry inserting the priest more deeply into the paschal mystery? How is the ministry contributing to that personal enrichment of spiritual qualities that make him a man of God? The answer basically is through people. People mediate the saving presence of Christ: they are his opportunity for dying with Christ and rising with him in a life of unbounded outgoing love. The law of Christ's life, operative in ministry, is sanctifying for minister and ministered alike», E. E. LARKIN – G. T. BROCCOLO, eds., *Spiritual Renewal of the American Priesthood*, 11. Although Larkin and Broccolo correctly negate the dichotomy between priestly spirituality and ministry, their explanation is not completely satisfactory. Herbert Alphonso has identified the centrality of inner-freedom for the spiritual life of a priest actively involved in apostolic ministry: «The true secret of union with God at the heart of absorbing activity — as at the heart of the exercise of prayer — is to be found in the incessant denial and dispossession of self, with true interior freedom, in the very thing in hand at every moment — a self-dispossession which makes one free and open to the God who comes perpetually and ceaselessly [...] into our lives to redeem and transform them», H. ALPHONSO, «Discernment and Careful Nurturing of the First Seeds of Priestly Vocation», 329; For further discussion of the topic see pp. 329-332, in which Alphonso identifies the principal means for cultivating and deepening inner-freedom: these are deemed to be frequent participation in the Eucharist, personal prayer, and the consciousness examen.

[113] Cf. G. GOZZELINO, «Il presbitero continuazione di Cristo», 88-89; L. GALLO, «Il presbitero nella Chiesa», 100.

of the priest. Consecration without mission, for the ministerial priest-hood, is unthinkable; similarly, mission without consecration is a contra-diction in terms. For the priest, consecration is for mission, and the carrying out of the mission in his ministry leads to a deeper conscious-ness of being consecrated, being chosen by Christ to be his living instrument. Consciousness of this double bond creates within the priest «[...] a series of moral and spiritual dispositions» (*PDV* 24), which reflect the integrity and interior resonance of priestly activity (mission) as being expressive of his very being (consecration).

4.5.2 The Threefold Ministry

The intimate connection between the spiritual life and the ministry of the priest is concretized in the exercise of the triple office of preaching (word), sanctifying (sacraments), and shepherding (pastoral ministry)[114]. While acknowledging that «[...] the priest is first of all a minister of the Word of God», who is «[...] consecrated and sent forth to proclaim the Good News of the Kingdom to all», the Exhortation emphasizes that the priest is the servant of the Word, and is himself «[...] continually in need of being evangelized»; in order to be faithful to his ministry, he needs to «abide» in the Word, approaching it with a «[...] docile and prayerful heart». He also «[...] is called to develop a special sensitivity, love and docility to the living tradition of the Church and to her magisterium» (*PDV* 26), so that he can more faithfully fulfill the mission which flows from his consecration and thus deepen his consciousness of being Christ's minister.

Regarding the worship or cultic dimension of priestly ministry, it is stated in *PDV* 26 that in the celebration of the sacraments «[...] the priest's spiritual life receives certain features»: that is, although he may be the presider at sacramental celebrations such as the Eucharist, he is also the recipient of the graces of those sacraments. This hints at the deli-cate balance, described earlier, between being a member of the Church through baptism and being in a particular relationship with the Church in virtue of ordination. Even while being «towards» the Church through ordination, which configures the priest to Christ the Head, thus putting him into a position of leadership vis-à-vis the Church, the priest is always

---

[114] For an exploration of the implications of the threefold ministry in the spiritual life of the priest as expressed in *PDV*, see H. MUSZYNSKI, «Il sacerdozio e i "tria munera"», especially 220-224. For an examination of the relationship of the threefold ministry to priestly spirituality, see CC, *DMLP*, secs. 45-55, pp. 45-59.

a member of the Church who stands in need of salvation and thus
the graces received through the sacraments. While giving, he must also
be able to receive. In this regard, particular emphasis is placed on the
priest's regular reception of the sacrament of Penance, which will have
a tonic effect both on the priest's ministry and in his spiritual life
(cf. *PDV* 26).

Regarding the third of the threefold ministry, that of shepherding,
or the «*munus regendi*», particular emphasis is placed on an «intense
spiritual life» that will enable the priest to act as a leader who helps to
coordinate the many charisms of the community in order to build up the
Church, gathering it as the family of God and leading it «[...] in Christ
through the Spirit to God the Father» (*PDV* 26, quoting *PO* 6). The
qualities and virtues associated with such an intense spiritual life are
enumerated and said to be «[...] typical of a person who "presides over"
and "leads" a community»[115].

In describing these ministries and their connection to the spiritual life
of the priest, the Exhortation demonstrates that the ministry, in all its
forms, cannot be separated from his spiritual life; thus priestly spirituality is not limited to the cultic dimension of his ministry, as has sometimes been the understanding. Consecration is for mission, whether it
takes the form of the ministry of word, worship, or pastoral leadership.
Each of these ministries, in turn, fills out and deepens the meaning of
the priest's consecration, giving it depth, texture, and resonance, leading
to a deeper union with Christ and a more effective ministry on Christ's
behalf. Thus no aspect of the priest's ministry is outside the orbit of his
spiritual life and no aspect of his spiritual life is outside the orbit of
his ministry. The mutual reciprocity is complete[116].

---

[115] Referring to Tit 1,7-8, *PDV* 26 lists the qualities and virtues necessary for
priestly leadership: «faithfulness, integrity, consistency, wisdom, a welcoming spirit,
friendliness, goodness of heart, decisive firmness in essentials, freedom from overly
subjective viewpoints, personal disinterestedness, patience, an enthusiasm for daily
tasks, confidence in the hidden workings of grace as manifested in the simple and the
poor».

[116] Larkin and Broccolo observe, «The ministry of the priest is sanctifying
[...] because Christ comes to both minister and recipient in priestly ministrations». They
describe four distinct perspectives from which the ministry of the priest deepens the
mystery of Christ in himself: «[...] (1) from the perspective of the people to whom he
ministers; (2) from the perspective of the presence and power of Christ in his ministry;
(3) from the perspective of what is demanded within himself in order to minister
effectively; and (4) from the perspective of the ritual celebration of these previous
dimensions of his ministry when he presides in liturgical prayer, especially in the

4.5.3 The Evangelical Counsels

From the pastoral perspective, section four of Chapter Three, «Priestly Life and the Radicalism of the Gospels» (*PDV* 27-30), presents the Evangelical Counsels as helping the priest to deepen his identification with Christ and with the Church, thus having a positive impact on the exercise of his ministry[117]. Although all Christians are confronted by the radicalism of the Gospel, priests are confronted in a particular way in virtue of their stance «towards» the Church. This basic configuration to Christ and to the Church shapes the way in which the Evangelical Counsels are to be understood and lived by the priest, who must incorporate them into his spirituality and ministry.

Obedience, for example, «[...] helps the priest to exercise in accordance with the Gospel the authority entrusted to him for his work with the people of God» and disposes him to be «[...] "consumed" by the needs and demands of the flock» (*PDV* 28)[118]. Celibacy is seen from the pastoral perspective as «[...] a sign of God's love for this world and of the undivided love of the priest for God and for God's people» (*PDV* 29). As such, it «[...] expresses the priest's service to the Church in and with the Lord» (*PDV* 29). Poverty, in the pastoral perspective, is seen as availability for mission. It «[...] ensures that the priest remains available to be sent wherever his work will be most useful and needed, even at the cost of personal sacrifice» (*PDV* 30). It also creates within priests a disposition whereby they stand in solidarity with the underprivileged and those on the margins of society. In this way they «[...] consider the poor and the weakest as people entrusted in a special way to them» (*PDV* 30)[119]. In the Exhortation's treatment of the Evangelical Counsels, the reciprocity between consecration and mission, between

---

Eucharistic liturgy», E. E. LARKIN – G. T. BROCCOLO, eds. *Spiritual Renewal of the American Priesthood*, 13.

[117] For a description of various aspects of the Evangelical Counsels and their impact on the priest's ministry and spirituality, see CC, *DMLP*, secs. 57-67, pp. 59-73.

[118] *PDV* 28 emphasizes that because obedience has apostolic and community dimensions, it can also be approached from the ecclesiological perspective: accepting «[...] the demands of an organized and organic ecclesial life», the priest practices an obedience that «[...] recognizes, loves and serves the Church in her hierarchical structure». This obedience is not individualistic but «[...] is deeply a part of the unity of the presbyterate».

[119] In describing the poverty associated with the ministerial priesthood, *PDV* 30 quotes Proposition 10, which, citing *OT* 9 and *CIC*, Canon 282, highlights a «simple and austere lifestyle» and a «renunciation of superfluous things» as ways for priests to witness to poverty.

spirituality and ministry, can be seen. They point to the need for integration of the interior life and the activities and lifestyle of the priest, emphasizing that there is no dichotomy between the two, but rather a mutual enhancement and expression.

4.5.4 The Particular Church

The particular Church figures prominently in the Exhortation's articulation of the spiritual life of the priest[120]. Although implicitly rooted in a trinitarian ecclesiology of mystery, communion, and mission, this particular aspect of the priest's spiritual life is approached mainly from the pastoral perspective. Incardination in a specific diocese concretizes and contextualizes the spiritual life of the priest[121]. The particular

---

[120] PDV 31 and 32 refer numerous times to the «particular» Church and not once to the «local» Church. M. A. Fahey points out that some ambiguity surrounds the use of the term «local Church»: at times it refers to a diocese, sometimes a parish, and at times the Catholic Church in a particular nation. Cf. M. A. FAHEY, «Church», vol. 2, 39. A. Wolanin points out that the terms «local Church» and «particular Church» are often used interchangeably, both by individual authors and in official Church documents. For example, *Christus Dominus* 11 speaks of a «particular Church» while *Presbyterorum Ordinis* 6 and 11 refer to the «local Church». Cf. A. WOLANIN, *Teologia della missione*, 148-156. In *PDV* 31, John Paul II seems to use the term «particular Church» as it is defined by Canon 368 in the 1983 Code of Canon Law. Commenting on Canon 368, T. J. Green states, «In the fullest and proper canonical sense the term "particular Church" means the diocese, that portion of the People of God entrusted to the bishop to be nurtured in faith along with the presbyterate (c. 369)», T. J. GREEN, «Particular Churches and Their Groupings», 316. Reflecting this understanding, PDV 31 states that «[...] the priest's relationship with his bishop in the one presbyterate, his sharing in the bishop's ecclesial concern, and his devotion to the evangelical care of the People of God in the specific historical and contextual conditions of a particular Church are elements which must be taken into account in sketching the proper configuration of the priest and his spiritual life». The *Catechism of the Catholic Church*, sec. 833, p. 193 states: «The phrase "particular Church", which is the diocese (or eparchy), refers to a community of the Christian faithful in communion of faith and sacraments with their bishop ordained in apostolic succession».

[121] Castellucci has pointed out that the conciliar articulation of the ministerial priesthood has benefitted from the Council's deep reflection on the nature of the universal Church. As noted, this understanding has highlighted the Church as the whole People of God to whom the mission of Christ has been entrusted. The Council's reflection on the universal Church, Castellucci maintains, would have benefitted from a deeper reflection on the particular Church in that it would have examined the concrete place in which the People of God live and act as a sacrament of the Trinity, and thus led to a clearer illumination of various aspects of the theology of priesthood, specifically the connections between priests and bishops, priests and the faithful, priests and the world.
Because of this lack of emphasis, *PDV*'s teaching on the priesthood and the particular Church is an important contribution. While emphasizing the intrinsic connection to the

Church is not to be understood simply as a juridical reality, but rather as a «[...] significant element in his living a Christian spirituality» (*PDV* 31). Belonging to a particular presbyterate, working in union with a particular bishop, having solicitude and care for a particular people in concrete historical circumstances — all give to the priest «[...] a wealth of meaning, criteria for discernment and action which shape both his pastoral mission and spiritual life» (*PDV* 31)[122].

Emphasis on the particular Church, without limiting the scope of priestly concern and activity to that particular Church, is a significant contribution of the Exhortation to the spirituality and ministry of the priest, providing the basis for a peculiarly diocesan priestly spirituality. All of the priest's charisms and talents are aimed at strengthening his dedication to the building up of the particular Church. With other Christians, part of the priest's spiritual life consists in the ability to discern his own charisms and to have a knowledge of the charisms of others in order to build up the Church which every charism is meant to serve (cf. *PDV* 31). Focus on the importance of the particular Church for priestly spirituality, as articulated in *PDV* 31, is balanced and put into a larger context by stressing the universal mission of the Church and thus of the ministerial priesthood (cf. *PDV* 32). Understanding priestly ministry as sharing in the universal mission which Christ entrusted to the Apostles precludes any narrow restrictions on the scope of priestly ministry. Therefore, although dedicated to serving a particular Church, the «[...] spiritual life of the priest should be profoundly marked by a missionary zeal and dynamism», which ensures that in the work of ministry priests will seek «[...] to form the community entrusted to them as a truly missionary community» (*PDV* 32)[123]. This missionary spirit

---

larger context of the universal Church, it allows for greater specificity in articulating the connection between priestly spirituality and ministry because it focuses on the particular Church where the universal Church is realized and concretized. To say that the priest enjoys a particular relation with the bishop, or fellow priests, or lay people, which the Council did articulate, is to say that the ministerial priest is tied to concrete persons and a concrete environment which is the particular Church. *PDV* thus makes an important contribution in attempting to integrate the universal, «vertical» aspect with the particular, «horizontal» aspect of ministerial priesthood. Cf. E. CASTELLUCCI, «L'identità del presbitero», 133-138.

122 The *Directory on the Ministry and Life of Priests* emphasizes that priests, both secular and religious, who are not incardinated in the particular diocese in which they are living and ministering, «belong by full or a diverse title» to the clergy of that diocese. CC, *DMLP*, sec. 26, pp. 27-28.

123 M. Zago observes that the papal documents preceding *PDV* were marked by a deep sensitivity to the theme of the missionary nature of the Church: «Gli ultimi

gives the ministry of the priest in a particular Church a global accent and prevents a narrow, restricted approach to ministry and spirituality[124].

4.6 *Conclusions*

The examination of the pastoral perspective in *PDV*'s doctrine and spirituality of the priesthood reveals important implications for understanding the priest as leader. First, it recalls the emphasis on service that is basic to both the Council's and *PDV*'s understanding of the ministerial priesthood: it exists «[...] in order to serve the People of God [...] and to draw all mankind to Christ» *(PDV* 12). Second, the relationship of the priest to the Church is inscribed in his relationship to Christ, meaning that since he is configured to Christ the Head and Shepherd, the priest relates to the Church from this perspective: he is not only in the Church, but he is «towards» the Church. Out of this relationship in Christ to the Church, the priest leads through the ministries of word, sacrament, and pastoral guidance, but with the understanding that he too is in need of evangelization, the grace of the sacraments, and the spiritual qualities that will help him to offer a shepherd's care to his people. As emphasized earlier, the priest offers his particular leadership in the context of communion with his bishop, fellow priests, and lay people, thus marking his leadership as profoundly collegial. Although the priest is to be characterized by a profound missionary attitude, his leadership is exercized in a concrete, particular context. It is in a particular Church that he carries on the work of the «new evangelization», thus making the community itself an important instrument in the work of evangelization. Finally, the priest leads most convincingly through his own personal example and witness to his relationship with Christ. The Evangelical Counsels of poverty, celibacy, and obedience are concrete examples of such personal witness, and create the interior dispositions and freedom which allow the priest to put himself completely at the service of the

---

documenti pontifici sono profondamente marcati dalla missionarietà. Sono cioè caratterizzati da una apertura evangelica all'umanità e da un richiamo al mandato fondamentale di Cristo che è carità e invio», M. ZAGO, «Sacerdoti per la missione», 225.

[124] B. McGregor states, «The episcopacy is pivotal for understanding the missionary identity of the priest. It is the college of bishops in union with the pope that is primarily responsible for the mission of the Church both *ad intra* and *ad extra*. There remains in the episcopal consecration — and in like manner, in presbyteral or diaconal consecrations — a double order of mission: to the particular community to whose service one is assigned, and to the universal community of men», B. MCGREGOR, «The Missionary Identity of the Priest», 204. Cf. Y. CONGAR, «The Missions in the Theology of the Church», 9.

Church. The priest leads, therefore, not merely through words, directives, and management, but through an official, threefold ministry which is informed and enriched by his own personal, living witness to the power of his relationship with Christ. Here the ontological and the existential dimensions come together in the person of the priest, making his leadership not only official, but profoundly personal.

5. «Pastoral Charity»: Integrating Dynamism of Priesthood

As the examination of Chapters Two and Three of *Pastores Dabo Vobis* has revealed, the identity, mission, and spiritual life of the ministerial priest is articulated from three distinct yet profoundly related perspectives: ecclesiological, christological, and pastoral. The ministerial priesthood is grounded in a Church that is mystery, communion, and mission, which mirrors the essentially relational nature of the Trinity; the Church is essentially related to Jesus Christ — Head, Shepherd, and Spouse — to whom the priest is configured through the anointing of the Holy Spirit received in ordination. This consecration to Christ, Head and Shepherd, puts the priest in a particular position «towards» the Church, while remaining in it, which enables and equips him to carry out Christ's mission of service to the Church and to the world.

It has been emphasized that these three perspectives, although distinct, are deeply interconnected. They lead into one another and interpret one another in a kind of symbiotic relationship. They are the essential elements that together create the foundation upon which to construct an adequate, coherent understanding of the identity, mission, and spirituality of the ministerial priest. Separately, they are insufficient, but together they allow an accurate sketch of the ministerial priest to come into focus.

5.1 *Pastoral Charity: Integrating Core of the Ministerial Priesthood*

Until this point the identity, mission, and spiritual life of the ministerial priest have been explored from the three separate perspectives as they appear in Chapters Two and Three of *PDV*. But because it is together that the three perspectives offer a clear understanding of the ministerial priesthood, their integration is essential. *PDV* provides such an integration point in its repeated reference to «pastoral charity», one of the key concepts of the entire Exhortation. «Pastoral charity» draws the ecclesiological, christological, and pastoral perspectives together in a dynamic way to yield a rich and comprehensive picture of the identity, mission, and spiritual life of the ministerial priesthood. The concept of «pastoral charity» as the integrating core of priestly life will now be examined[125].

The term «pastoral charity» appears approximately thirty times in the Exhortation and is found in each of its chapters[126]. Because of its prominence and repeated, formula-like use throughout the Exhortation, it cannot be interpreted simply as a generic description or as a rhetorical device. Its intentional and systematic usage in describing the ministerial priesthood seems to indicate that it is a device or formula that has a new and global significance. In fact, an analysis of its usage in the Exhortation reveals that it is a synthesizing concept for describing the identity, activity, and spirituality of the ministerial priesthood[127]. As such, it is laden with meaning and significance, and is used in key passages to bring into a coherent whole the various components of priestly life and spirituality:

> The internal principle, the force which animates and guides the spiritual life of the priest inasmuch as he is configured to Christ the Head and Shepherd, is *pastoral charity*, as a participation in Jesus Christ's own pastoral charity, a gift freely bestowed by the Holy Spirit and likewise a task and a call which demands a free and committed response on the part of the priest. The essential content of this pastoral charity is *the gift of self*, the total gift of *self to the Church*, following the example of Christ. [...] Within the Church community the priest's pastoral charity impels and demands in a particular and specific way his personal relationship with the presbyterate, united in and with the bishop. [...] Pastoral charity, which has its specific source in the sacrament of Holy Orders [...] is the dynamic inner principle capable of unifying the many different activities of the priest (*PDV* 23).

This passage illustrates not only the central place of «pastoral charity» in the ministry and life of the priest, but also the way in which it integrates the three perspectives. The ecclesiological, christological, and pastoral perspectives come together in the concept of «pastoral charity», which so fully expresses the meaning of the priesthood that it can be called «the soul of the priestly ministry» (*PDV* 48): «The relation between a priest's spiritual life and the exercise of his ministry can also be explained on the basis of the pastoral charity bestowed by the sacrament of Holy Orders»

---

125 R. Gerardi states: «La carità pastorale è il principio che unifica vitalmente le diverse articolazioni e i più svariati impegni, l'esercizio del ministero e la ricerca della perfezione», R. GERARDI, «La "Caritas Pastoralis" nella formazione e nella vita del presbitero», 557.

126 Cf. C. DUMONT, «La "charité pastorale"», 212.

127 Cf. C. DUMONT, «La "charité pastorale"», 212.

(*PDV* 24). The novel and repeated usage of the term, as well as its density of meaning, make it one of the key contributions of *PDV* to the Church's understanding of the ministerial priesthood.

5.2 *Pastoral Charity and Traditional Teaching on Priesthood*

Dumont observes that one aspect which points to the novel importance of «pastoral charity» for a contemporary understanding of the ministerial priesthood, is its paucity of usage, indeed its absence, in earlier papal documents on the priesthood. Although charity in the exercise of priestly ministry has often been addressed in papal documents related to the priesthood, the specific formula «pastoral charity», especially in the light of its position as a leitmotif of *PDV*, is notably absent[128]. Dumont points out that the formula, «pastoral charity», was not present in the moral theology current before the Second Vatican Council. The emphasis was on the obligations associated with office, which certainly included the idea of pastoral love, or putting the needs of the flock before one's own, even to the point of giving one's life. Thus the idea was present, but the specific designation, «pastoral charity», was not employed[129]. Similarly, in the area of virtues, «pastoral charity» was not named because the theological virtue of charity is one and indivisible. Even though there are two commandments of charity — love for God and love for one's neighbor — there is still only one charity and the one who is loved in one's neighbor is God himself[130].

---

[128] Cf. C. DUMONT, «La "charité pastorale"», 213-217. Dumont traces the evolution of language in papal documents regarding the charity of priests for the people entrusted to their care. The idea conveyed is that of «the greater love» — to the point of giving his life — that the priest must have for his people. More often the notion of «zeal» was used in traditional spirituality to describe the apostolic impulse in priests. Dumont cites Leo XIII's encyclical *Depuis le jour* which speaks of the need for discretion to accompany the zeal associated with the exercise of charity. Pius X's rescript establishing Jean-Marie Vianney as the patron of French parish priests, refers to his zealous pastoral ministry as a true ministry of love. Pius XI's encyclical *Ad catholici sacerdotii fastigium* describes priestly zeal as a «heavenly light [...] for the glory of God and the salvation of souls». However, it is Pius XII's *Menti nostrae* which articulated the formula that comes closest to that of «pastoral charity». There he speaks of the «bond of perfection» as the unifying source of a priest's life. This same «bond of perfection» appears in *PO* 14: «[...] assuming the role of the Good Shepherd, they [priests] will find in the very exercise of pastoral love the bond of priestly perfection which will unify their lives and activities». Thus can be seen an evolution from greater love to apostolic zeal to bond of perfection — all of which are expressed in the lapidary formula «pastoral charity».

[129] Cf. C. DUMONT, «La "charité pastorale"», 215.

[130] Cf. C. DUMONT, «La "charité pastorale"», 215.

Within the one virtue of charity, however, there is room for nuance and coloration without an interior division; the virtue of charity remains one despite these shadings[131]. For instance, the love one has for a spouse is different in color, tone, and intensity from that which one has for a friend or neighbor. In this nuance and coloration «pastoral charity» can be understood[132]. The love that a priest has for his people can be seen as analogous to the love that a shepherd has for his flock. It has long been a part of the Church's tradition, all the way back to the interchange between Jesus and Peter, that love has been connected to leadership of Christ's flock, the Church (cf. Jn 21,15-17). In fact, it is in this sense that the Second Vatican Council used the term «pastoral charity». It is mentioned seven times, once in *LG* 41 in reference to bishops; three times in *PO* 14; and once each in *PO*, 15, 16 and 17[133]. Thus, while *PDV*'s use of the term pastoral charity in a formula-like manner to express the deepest meaning of the ministerial priesthood is new, it does not present a radical departure from tradition. Instead, it gathers and synthesizes the tradition, giving it new expression and focus. In this sense it represents a real flowering or development in the traditional understanding of the ministerial priesthood.

5.3 *Pastoral Charity in the Ecclesiological Perspective*

As has been emphasized, the communion of the Church establishes all of the baptized as radically equal members, who are nonetheless distinct and have specific roles to play in this communion, based on the charisms given to them by the Spirit. In the Church, led by the Spirit, these charisms are put at the service of the community, thus expressing the relational dynamics of self-giving and mutuality.

---

[131] Cf. C. DUMONT, «La "charité pastorale"», 215. Dumont cites St. Thomas Aquinas, *Summa Theologiae*, 2a 2ae, q. 23, a. 5, to describe the various shadings within the one virtue of charity.

[132] Esquerda Bifet distinguishes between Christian charity and the charity associated with the priest: «La perfección cristiana consiste en la caridad: reaccionar amando como Cristo. Tal es el sermón de la montaña, el precepto del amor y la actitud para rezar el padrenuestro (*LG* cap.5). La perfección sacerdotal consiste en la caridad pastoral. Su espiritualidad o ascesis es la "ascesis propia del pastor de almas" (*PO* 13) La caridad pastoral hace que el ministerio sea fuente de sanctificación, y no de desgaste. El ministerio es santificante para el mismo ministro cuando éste "ejerce sincera e incansablemente sus ministerios en el espíritu de Cristo" (*PO* 13)», J. ESQUERDA BIFET, *Teología de la espiritualidad sacerdotal*, 261.

[133] For an examination of the use of the term at the Council, see R. GERARDI, «La "Caritas Pastoralis"» 553-556.

The ministerial priest, of course, «[...] will always remain a member of the community as a believer alongside his brothers and sisters who have been called by the Spirit» (*PDV* 22). But because of his consecration in the sacrament of Orders, the priest stands in a relation to the Church that represents the pastoral, spousal relation of Christ towards the Church. At the heart of Christ's spousal love is pastoral charity. Analogously, pastoral charity is at the heart of the priest's relation to the Church: «[...] the total gift of self to the Church [...] is the source and synthesis of pastoral charity» (*PDV* 23).

Pastoral charity, then, is what is distinctive of the ministerial priest as he stands in and towards the Church. It «[...] distinguishes the exercise of priestly ministry as an *amoris officium*» and positions the priest «[...] to make this [pastoral charity] a loving choice, as a result of which the Church and souls become his first interest» (*PDV* 23)[134]. This same pastoral charity which shapes the relationship of communion between the ministerial priest and the faithful also determines the priest's relationship to the bishop and other priests, ensuring that he remain in a bond of communion with them (cf. *PDV* 23).

5.4 *Pastoral Charity in the Christological Perspective*

Reference to Christ is the indispensable key for understanding pastoral charity as the «dynamic inner principle» at the heart of the life of the ministerial priest: «[...] the spiritual life of the priest is marked, molded and characterized by the way of thinking and acting proper to Jesus Christ, Head and Shepherd of the Church, and which are summed up in his pastoral charity» (*PDV* 21). As noted above, the characteristics of Christ's relationship to the Church are understood from the perspective of his being Head, Shepherd, and Spouse of the Church, images that represent the total gift of himself to the Church. They express his servanthood, his willingness to give his life for the flock, his compassion, and his generous, faithful love. These interior attitudes of Christ expressed the core convictions and values that shaped his way of acting and relating to people. In short, these qualities of Christ, expressed in the head, shepherd, and spousal imagery, reveal his complete gift of himself, which is «[...] the essential content of this pastoral charity» (*PDV* 23). In other words, «His whole life is a continual manifestation of his "pastoral charity", or rather, a daily enactment of it» (*PDV* 22). Because of their

---

134 For a description of the authority as *amoris officium*, see CC, *DMLP*, sec. 16, pp. 18-19.

ordination, by which they are configured to Jesus Christ, Head and
Shepherd, priests «[...] are called to imitate and live out his own pastoral
charity» (*PDV* 22). This is no mere external imitation, disconnected
from the interior sources of a priest's life. Rather it is an intrinsic part of
his being a priest. It is thus not an addition but part of the essential
structure of the ministerial priesthood[135].

Earlier it was noted that the entire People of God, the Church,
«[...] not only has its authentic image in Christ, but also receives from
him a real ontological share in his one eternal priesthood» (*PDV* 13).
This emphasis on «ontological share» alludes to the baptismal character
of all members of the Church. Regarding the ministerial priesthood,
however, the Exhortation refers to the «[...] specific ontological bond
which unites the priesthood to Christ the High Priest and Good
Shepherd» (*PDV* 11)[136]. This is different from that which gives all
members of the Church a share in Christ's priesthood, in other words,
the common priesthood.

The way in which the Exhortation expresses the ministerial priesthood's specific ontological bond to Christ the Head and Shepherd of the
Church is by declaring that «[...] priests are a sacramental representation of Jesus Christ, the Head and Shepherd» and as such «[...] exist and
act in order to proclaim the Gospel to the world and to build up the
Church in the name and person of Christ the Head and Shepherd»
(*PDV* 15). In this distinctive relation that priests have to Christ in
virtue of the sacramental anointing received in Orders, the Holy Spirit
«[...] forms and strengthens them with his pastoral charity» giving them
an «[...] authoritative role in the Church as servants of the proclamation
of the Gospel» (*PDV* 15). In this sacramental representation of the
servant leadership of Christ the Good Shepherd, pastoral charity is an

---

[135] Approaching priestly spirituality from the perspective of Canon Law, V. Fagiolo
stresses that priesty obligations, as spelled-out in Canon law, are not extrinsic
impositions, but flow out of the exigencies of pastoral charity: «Il Codice non impone
mai ai pastori compiti e doveri puramente formali, burocratici o adempimenti semplice-
mente esteriori. Ogni compito, dovere e missione da compiere sono visti, presentati,
raccomandati o prescritti sempre come esigenza dell'amore di Cristo per il bene della
Chiesa, come sollecitudine materna della Chiesa per il bene delle anime, come strumento
di crescita spirituale. La carità è il movente, la causa determinante sia del legislatore che
codifa la norma sia del pastore che la deve applicare», V. FAGIOLO, *La spiritualità del
prete diocesano*, 98-99.

[136] Dumont has noted that nowhere in the document is reference explicitly made
to the notion of sacramental character. However, the reality is certainly present with
the pointed assertions about the ontological nature of both Baptism and Orders.
Cf. C. DUMONT, «La "charité pastorale"», 218.

intrinsic part of the structure and dynamic of the ministerial priest-hood[137].

Through sacramental ordination, because it configures the priest to Christ the Head and Shepherd, with all that such configuration entails[138], the priest, of his very nature as a priest, participates «[...] in Jesus Christ's own pastoral charity, a gift freely bestowed by the Holy Spirit and likewise a task and a call which demand a free and committed response on the part of the priest» (*PDV* 23). It is thus that pastoral charity can be understood as «[...] the internal principle, the force which animates and guides the spiritual life of the priest» (*PDV* 23).

To describe pastoral charity in terms of the priest's ontological connection to Christ, Head and Shepherd, is not to reduce it to a static reality. As noted, the consecration received in ordination which config-ures the priest to Christ in his specificity as Head and Shepherd of the Church (ontological dimension) is always to be undertood in terms of mission. The priest's «being» is expressed in his activity. Pastoral charity is thus an intrinsically dynamic concept as is demonstrated by the Exhor-tation's reference to it as «the force» which drives the priest's spiritual life, which of course is intrinsically related to his ministerial life (cf. *PDV* 23)[139]. Pastoral charity, then, is at one and the same time both gift bestowed and call to be answered.

5.5 *Pastoral Charity in the Pastoral Perspective*

«Consecration-for-Mission» expresses how pastoral charity is the core dynamism of the ministerial priesthood. The priest's relationship with Christ is primary, «[...] but intimately linked to this relationship is the priest's relationship with the Church» (*PDV* 16), and the pastoral activi-ties that arise from this relationship. As noted earlier, the priest's dual relationship to Christ and to the Church is not simply a matter of juxtaposition, but rather of interior union «[...] in a kind of mutual immanence» (*PDV* 16). In this sense, «[...] the primary point of refer-ence of the priest's charity is Jesus Christ himself. Only in loving and

---

137 Cf. V. GAMBINO, «Formazione spirituale», especially section 3.2, «La carità pastorale, fisionomia spirituale del sacerdote», 179-181.

138 For a discussion on the Christological perpective and the spiritual life of the priest, see above, pp. 149-158.

139 Cf. V. GAMBINO, *Dimensioni della formazione presbiterale*», 194: «La spiritualità presbiterale si sviluppa a partire da questa "unzione" e si manifesta operante come "carità pastorale", in un'esistenza in cui l'essere, lo stile di vita e la missione del presbitero prolungano quelli di Cristo».

serving Christ the Head and Spouse will charity become a source, [...] for the priest's love and service to the Church» (*PDV* 23)[140]. Moreover, «[...] the priest's mission is not extraneous to his consecration», but «[...] represents its intrinsic and vital purpose» (*PDV* 24).

Because, according to *PDV*, pastoral charity is the internal, driving principle at the heart of the priest's spiritual life, then this same pastoral charity is the fuel that energizes and shapes his pastoral ministry. The connection between the spiritual life of the priest and the exercise of his ministry is thus «[...] explained on the basis of the pastoral charity bestowed by the sacrament of Holy Orders» (*PDV* 24). Because the priest sacramentally represents Christ, the Head, Shepherd, and Spouse in his relationship to the Church, and because the essence of Christ's relation to the Church is expressed by pastoral charity, meaning the total gift of himself in love, then the priest, in his ministerial activity, will necessarily express the pastoral charity of Christ, which is the source and spirit of the priest's own gift of self. The pastoral charity which is expressed in the priest's ministry, then, is not simply something that he «does», as though it were a specific, concrete activity[141]. Rather it is the «force» or energy, flowing from Christ himself through the gift of the Spirit received in ordination, which permeates all of the priest's ministerial activities. In this sense, pastoral charity is concrete, because it is enacted and experienced in specific actions and relationships. It is not, however, limited to any one action but is intrinsic to and transcends all priestly ministerial activity.

---

[140] O'Donnell and Rendina stress that the priesthood and priestly ministry can only be properly and sensibly understood as expressive of the love that the priest has for Christ: «Il sacerdozio ministeriale non ha senso se non è vissuto come espressione personale dell'amore del sacerdote per Cristo. La spiritualità del prete consiste nel fatto che il suo amore per Cristo lo conduce ad un amore per il popolo di Cristo. [...] Per il sacerdote l'amore di Cristo diventa incarnato e sacramentale nell'amore per il popolo di Cristo. Questi due amori formano un'unità inscindibile in cui la preghiera e il ministero sono integrati in modo tale che lo stesso volto di Cristo viene rispecchiato in ambedue», J. O'DONNELL – S. RENDINA, *Sacerdozio e spiritualità ignaziana*, 49-50.

[141] The *Directory on the Ministry and Life of Priests* states, «Pastoral charity faces the danger, today especially, of being emptied of its meaning through so-called "functionalism". It is not rare, in fact, to perceive, even in some priests, the influence of an erroneous mentality which reduces the ministerial priesthood to strictly functional aspects. To merely play the role of the priest, carrying out a few services and ensuring completion of various tasks would make up the entire priestly existence. Such a reductive conception of the identity of the ministry of the priest risks pushing their lives towards an emptiness, an emptiness which often comes to be filled by lifestyles not consonant with their very ministry», CC, *DMLP*, sec. 44, pp. 44-45.

In this spirit, the Exhortation can assert, «It is not just what we do, but our gift of self, which manifests Christ's love for his flock. Pastoral charity determines our way of thinking and acting, our way of relating to people» (*PDV* 23). The inner dynamism of pastoral charity, consciously lived out in the priest's life, allows him to exercise his ministry in the awareness that he is a «living instrument» of Christ; in his ministry of word, sacrament, and pastoral leadership, he is continuing the ministry of Christ himself[142]. This same pastoral charity synthesizes the values and demands contained in the Gospel, and inspires and enables the priest to respond to the radical call of the Gospel by embracing obedience, chastity, and poverty (cf. *PDV* 27), thus empowering him to lead through the example of his own life.

5.6 *Conclusions*

It was pointed out that the *PDV* adopted a fundamentally sacramental hermeneutic for understanding the priesthood. The sacrament of Orders determines the priest's particular configuration to Christ, his distinctiveness within the Church, and his ensuing activities and relationships. The sacrament of Orders is also the source of the pastoral charity that is to be the animating force in a priest's life. Pastoral charity, then, is at the heart of priestly identity, ministry, and spirituality. The centrality of pastoral charity in *PDV*'s articulation of the ministerial priesthood has profound implications for understanding the priest as leader and comprehensively expresses everything that has been said about the priesthood from the various perspectives. *PDV*'s emphasis on pastoral charity leads to the inevitable conclusion that love is at the heart of the ministerial priesthood in all its dimensions, including leadership. The love is, in the first place, rooted in and expressive of the love of Christ the Head, Shepherd, and Spouse. Second, the communion of the Church is the «arena», or milieu, in which this love — pastoral charity — is lived out, although it aims even beyond the Church and is to embrace all of

---

[142] For a description of the importance of ministerial awareness or consciousness, which is an incentive to greater love for Christ and in turn for the Church, see above, pp. 155-157, and *PDV* 25. Lane observes, «The man of pastoral charity keeps breaking the bread of the word in every situation in which human beings need to be fed, by the preached word, by the sacraments which are special highpoints of the word, and by every form of pastoral care and service. [...] The heart is the meeting point of his ministry of word, sacrament, and pastoral care. In the daily life of the man of pastoral charity, the word of God keeps going out to people wherever they are, and gathering them for sacramental worship. That going out and that gathering authenticate each other», T. LANE, *A Priesthood in Tune*, 306.

humanity. The priest is distinguished by this pastoral love which, as the Exhortation emphasizes, can only be adequately expressed by the complete gift of himself. The gift of himself, rooted in his particular configuration to Christ through Ordination, is expressed in a ministry of word, sacrament, and pastoral care, as well as in relationships motivated by pastoral solicitude and at the service of unity. Pastoral charity is thus at the heart of each of the perspectives — ecclesiological, christological, and pastoral — and it integrates them in a comprehensive way so that all of the various aspects of the ministerial priesthood are unified in a love that receives its particular accent and color from Christ, the Head, Shepherd, and Spouse of the Church. Pastoral charity, the integrating core and dynamic inner-principle of the ministerial priesthood, is thus at the heart of a proper understanding of priest as leader.

6. Summary and Synthesis of Priest as Leader: Church's Teaching on the Ministerial Priesthood

In establishing a methodology for our study of priest as leader in a United States context, it was pointed out that such a study brings together two epistemologically distinct categories: the transcultural reality of the ministerial priesthood of the Catholic Church, and leadership as it is understood in the culture of the United States. The topic of priest as a leader in a U.S. context, then, brings us into the realm of the theology of inculturation: a proper understanding of the priest as leader in a U.S. context must be faithful to the tradition of the Catholic teaching on the priesthood, and at the same time it must be adequate to the reality of leadership as it is understood in the culture of the U.S. To understand the priest as leader in a U.S. context, therefore, demands a close reading of the Church's teaching on the ministerial priesthood in order to draw from that teaching the Church's perspective on priestly leadership; it also demands an articulation of leadership as it is understood in a U.S. context. Finally, it demands a profound, critical dialogue and inter-action between the two perspectives in order to lead to a synthesis that is faithful to the Church and adequate to the culture, in other words, in order to lead to a moment of inculturation.

Chapters Two and Three have examined the Church's teaching on the ministerial priesthood as it is presented in *Presbyterorum Ordinis* and related documents of the Second Vatican Council: the 1971 Synodal document, *The Ministerial Priesthood*; and John Paul II's Post-Synodal Apostolic Exhortation *Pastores Dabo Vobis*, published in 1992. The documents have been analyzed in order to articulate an understanding of priestly leadership that is faithful to the Church's teaching and not an extrinsic projection onto the doctrine. As the examination of the various documents has revealed, the Church's teaching on the ministerial priesthood is built on a foundation that has ecclesiological, christological, and pastoral components. Since the documents have been approached from these perspectives, our conclusions follow the same format, with a summary and synthesis of this teaching, from the perspective of leadership, to be offered in order to set the stage for an examination of leadership as it is understood in the culture of the United States.

6.1 *Ecclesiological Perspective*

Chapter Two briefly considered the Church as mystery, communion, and mission, and in the context of this understanding, explored the following aspects of priesthood from an ecclesiological perspective: the ministerial priesthood in the context of its relation to the common priesthood, the teaching on the ministerial priesthood and its relation to episcopal office, and the category of «presbyter». Three important conclusions follow for understanding priest as leader. First, «leadership» is not an extrinsic addition, but rather a constitutive dimension of the ministerial priesthood conferred by the sacrament of Holy Orders. Although ontologically distinct from the common priesthood, the ministerial priesthood is ordered to the common priesthood and is to be at the service of promoting it. The adjectives «ministerial» and «hierarchical» signify that the ministerial priesthood possesses a sacred authority to be exercised only as a service. Thus the leadership associated with the ministerial priesthood is understood fundamentally as a service. Second, because of priesthood's dependent relationship to the bishop, the leadership associated with priesthood is exercised collegially and with accountability, and is at the service of the unity of the Church. Finally, because through ordination the priest becomes part of a presbyterate, the leadership of the ministerial priesthood is collective; it is part of the structure of the particular Church; and it is exercised within the context of a network of relationships with other priests, the bishop, and the laity.

As the study of the ecclesiological perspective of *PDV*'s teaching on the priesthood illustrated, John Paul II took the ecclesiology of the Second Vatican Council, which he had systematized in *Christifideles Laici*, and made it part of the foundation of *PDV*'s teaching on the ministerial priesthood. Rypar has commented that *PDV*'s articulation of conciliar ecclesiology contributes to the identity, spirituality, and pastoral life of the ministerial priesthood because it draws out the practical

consequences of the doctrine and emphasizes that, «[...] like the Church,
the priest must live his mission animated by a supernatural sense of
mystery, of communion, and of missionary tension»[143]. Rooted in a
trinitarian ecclesiology the priest must exercise a leadership that is
expressive of the specific call to holiness he received in ordination, and
that reveals him to be a man of communion, dialogue, and mission
(cf. *PDV* 18). *PDV*'s ecclesiology is firmly rooted in that of the Council
and is important because it highlights the implications of such an ecclesiological grounding of the ministerial priesthood and offers some
indications for developing an understanding of priestly leadership: it is
inherently and fundamentally relational; it is radically communitarian;
and it can only be carried out as a collective work.

6.2 *Christological Perspective*

Chapter Two approached the christological underpinnings of the
ministerial priesthood by examining the priesthood of Christ, the consecration and mission of Christ, the threefold ministry, the image of Christ
the Head, the image of Christ the Shepherd, and the teaching on sacramental character. The image that emerged from the analysis of the documents revealed a portrait of Jesus as Head and Shepherd of the Church;
the one consecrated and sent by the Father to preach, to sanctify, and to
guide God's people. This image of Christ is the model for priestly
leadership. In the sacrament of Holy Orders the priest, like Christ, is
consecrated and set apart for ministry of word, worship, and pastoral
care. He is configured to Christ the Head and, therefore, becomes his
instrument, sacramentally representing Christ's headship in the Church.
Configured to Christ the Shepherd, the priest is to live out in his own life
Christ's solicitude, authority, and permanent commitment to the Church.
The configuration to Christ through ordination bestows a sacramental
character that marks the priest's entire life and is symbolic of Christ's
commitment to the Church. The leadership of the priest is thus rooted in
Christ himself and follows the pattern of Christ's self-giving love on
behalf of the Church. It is not simply associated with the functions of the
priest, but through ordination is rooted in his very being as priest.

At the beginning of Chapter Two it was pointed out that the Council's
teaching on the ministerial priesthood was carried out in an atmosphere

---

143 F. RYPAR, «La *Pastores Dabo Vobis* alla luce del pensiero conciliare», 538:
«Come la Chiesa anche il presbitero deve vivere la sua missione animato dal senso
soprannaturale di mistero, di comunione e di tensione missionaria».

of relative calm and serenity, while that of the Synod of 1971 unfolded in an atmosphere characterized by crisis. *PDV* 11 alludes to the crisis of priestly identity and indicates that the only way out of such a crisis is a correct and in-depth awareness of the nature and mission of the ministerial priest. At the heart of the understanding of the ministerial priesthood in *PDV* is a christological perspective. Rypar observed that *PDV* does not add any new doctrinal content to the Council's articulation of the christological dimension of the priesthood, but rather accents certain aspects of it[144], particularly the «[...] specific ontological bond that unites the priesthood to Christ the High Priest and Good Shepherd» (*PDV* 11).

PDV emphasizes that priests are sacramental representations of Christ himself, who are to prolong, embody, and make visible the presence of Christ. Sacramental representation, then, is the context for understanding the priest as leader. *PDV* reinforces the teaching of Vatican II that such priestly leadership it is not simply a functional reality but rooted in the sacrament itself. Through ordination the priest becomes an instrument of Christ the Head, Shepherd, and Spouse. The relationship to Christ is foundational for every aspect of the priest's life; his ministry is inscribed in this prior relationship to Christ. It is precisely in his configuration to Christ the Head, Shepherd, and Spouse, that the priest can stand in a relationship of service and solicitude «towards» the Church. Sacramental representation of Christ has direct implications for priestly spirituality and places existential demands on the priest to embrace and mirror, to the greatest extent possible, the characteristics of Christ: self-emptying, obedient service, radical availability for God's mission, and complete gift of self in love to God and the Church.

In gathering and synthesizing previous Church teaching on priesthood, particularly its emphasis on the christological underpinnings of the priesthood, *PDV* offers a foundation for articulating an understanding of priest as leader. As emphasized above, *PDV* encourages a harmony between interiority and pastoral activity. Conscious awareness of

---

144 Cf. F. RYPAR, «La *Pastores Dabo Vobis* alla luce del pensiero conciliare», 536. M. Thurian cites three principal aspects of the Church's doctrine on priesthood that *PDV* highlights: «Il sacramento dell'ordinazione *configura* il sacerdote alla persona di Cristo Profeta, Sacerdote e Pastore. [...] Il sacerdote *partecipa* alla funzione profetica, sacerdote e pastorale del Cristo e agisce così *in persona Christi*, in nome di Cristo, come ambasciatore per Cristo, come se Dio parlasse e agisse per mezzo di lui (cf. 2 Cor 5,20). [...] Il sacerdote *rappresenta* il Cristo, Capo e Pastore della Chiesa, egli si situa sia *nella* Chiesa sia *davanti* alla Chiesa», M. THURIAN, *L'Identità del sacerdote*, 69-71.

sacramental configuration to Christ becomes the foundation for priestly activities, and it is only in the context of sacramental representation of Christ that a proper understanding of priest as leader can be described. The christological foundations of the priesthood prevent it from deteriorating into mere activism. The prior relation to Christ, rooted in and defined by the sacrament of Holy Orders, and the existential impact it has on the priest's life, is the springboard from which the priest moves into the pastoral activities which are the visible expressions of his leadership[145]

6.3 *Pastoral Perspective*

In examining the pastoral perspective of the conciliar teaching on priesthood as well as that of the Synod of 1971, Chapter Two emphasized the functions and relationships that are intrinsic to the ministerial priesthood. Rooted in the sacrament of Orders, the priest is configured to Christ so that he can perform Christ's threefold ministry of preaching, worship, and pastoral care: priestly leadership is concretely expressed in these activities. It was noted, however, that in order to be a leader after the example of Christ, the priest is to personalize the threefold mission by becoming an example of the power of the Word and the reality of the Paschal Mystery at work in his own life. It was also noted that because the ministerial priesthood is necessarily lived out in the context of a set of relationships — with the bishop, other priests, and the laity — priestly leadership, therefore, will always be marked by accountability, collegiality, and collaboration, always with the goal of building up the unity of the Church.

The treatment of the pastoral perspective in *PDV* follows the same lines as those of the Council and the Synod of 1971, emphasizing the functions and relationships that are intrinsically connected with the priest's pastoral life. It added a number of important clarifications, however, which help to fill out the understanding of priest as leader. First, as noted above, *PDV* emphasizes the priest's relationship *towards* the Church, which is rooted in his configuration to Christ the Spouse and which grounds his pastoral activities; such activities are expressive of his spousal relationship to the Church. Second, the pastoral perspective of *PDV* emphasizes the importance of the priest as a leader in the new evangelization. Third, *PDV* emphasizes the Evangelical Counsels as means for the priest, not only to express and deepen his configuration to

---

[145] Cf. above, pp. 158-159.

Christ, but to create the interior dispositions and freedom to put himself completely at the service of the Church, offering a leadership that gives personal witness to his relationship with Christ. Finally, *PDV* stresses the particular Church as a significant element in the life of the priest: communion with a particular bishop, belonging to a particular presbyterate, and dedication to a particular people are elements that contextualize the priest's ministry and shape the exercise of his leadership.

6.4 *Conclusions*

The investigation of the documents on priesthood was undertaken using a reading key based on Cooke's broad description of leadership. He described leadership as «[...] a capacity to inspire and direct and support a social group as it moves towards some goal. [...] it is composed of a number of qualities which particularly fit the needs of a given situation»[146]. He further noted that the Christian slant on such an understanding corresponds to the faith, hope, and charity which dwell at the heart of the community[147]. Using this key, a portrait of priest as leader, based on the documents on the ministerial priesthood, can now be more completely filled-out and articulated.

1. First, Cooke asserts that leadership is a capacity. But from where does such a capacity come? In what is it rooted? Normally, in a secular context, such a capacity is almost exclusively associated with personal qualities, skills, or talents. But although personal qualities are critically important in the exercise of leadership, they are not, in the first place, the source of the priest's ability to lead[148]. Rather, the priest's capacity to lead is anchored in the sacrament of Ordination. Initially and foundationally, the capacity comes from outside of himself; it comes from God through the sacrament of Ordination.

Such a bold assertion must immediately be put into its proper context. As *PO* and *MP*, and even more so *PDV* have taken pains to emphasize, the Church is the context for the exercise of priestly leadership. The trinitarian ecclesiology that was implicit in *PO* and is quite explicit in *PDV*, emphasizes that as a baptized person the priest is radically equal to all other Christians: it is the entire Church to which Christ has entrusted

---

[146] B. COOKE, *Ministry to Word and Sacrament*, 209.

[147] Cf. B. COOKE, *Ministry to Word and Sacrament*, 209.

[148] Galot stresses that the leadership or authority associated with priesthood is rooted in the sacrament of Holy Orders and stems «[...] from the fact that Christ instituted it and shared his pastoral responsibility», J. GALOT, *The Theology of the Priesthood*, 138.

his mission. What makes the priest distinctive is the sacrament of Holy Orders which configures him to Christ in a very particular way. The documents pointedly emphasize that the difference between the ministerial priesthood and the common priesthood is essential, or qualitative. Thus there can be no association of superiority or higher degree of holiness with the ministerial priesthood.

To highlight this difference in essence, *PO, MP*, and again especially *PDV*, emphasize that in ordination the priest is configured to Christ the Head and Shepherd of the Church. Such a configuration to Christ sets the terms for the priest's relationship to the Church: it is fundamentally a relationship of service. To assert such service, however, requires more precision and definition. In what does the service consist? Both images, head and shepherd, imply that the service consists in leadership. The description of the priesthood in *LG* 10 as ministerial and hierarchical also implies such an understanding. The conciliar documents and *MP* assert that the priest has a character conferred on him through the sacrament of Orders. *PDV* does not use the term «character», but its repeated insistence on the priest's ontological configuration to Christ the Head and Shepherd indicates the same reality as that connoted by «character», and emphasizes the dynamic nature of the priesthood which exists for the service of leadership in the Church and is a sign of Christ's abiding presence, authority, and permanent love for the Church. Rooted in the sacrament of Orders, the priest's leadership must primarily be understood as love — a sign of Christ the Head's permanent fidelity to his Body, the Church. «Pastoral charity», described as the internal dynamism of the ministerial priesthood, is thus also at the heart of an understanding of priestly leadership. All of the ontological assertions about the ministerial priesthood, which must be understood in the wider context of the lived reality of the Church, stress that the capacity to be a priest and thus to lead as a priest, comes from the Sacrament itself and is therefore not dependent on the talents of the priest.

2. Second, Cooke describes leadership as a capacity to inspire and to direct and support a social group as it moves towards some goal. This assertion points to a concretization of the priest's ministry of leadership. The documents emphasize that the support, inspiration, and direction that priests provide for Church communities is mediated through their participation in Christ's threefold ministry of word, sacrament, and pastoral guidance. Leadership is thus not limited to the last of the threefold *munera* which some writers seem to indicate, but transcends all three. The priest exercises leadership in his preaching, in presiding at the sacraments, especially the Eucharist, and in offering pastoral guidance to the

community and to individuals within the community. It is to be emphasized however, that such leadership is not a one way reality: the priest
himself always stands in need of evangelization, the grace of the sacraments, and pastoral guidance. This points to another important dimension
of priestly leadership. Not only is it carried out in certain functions, but
through a web of relationships including the bishop, fellow priests, and
lay people. It has been noted that membership in a presbyterate emphasizes that the priest is an elder or leader, and that the nature of this
leadership is collegial. His leadership is thus accountable, collegial, and
collaborative. It is here that the importance of personal qualities begin to
emerge. The priest needs skills that will enable him to be an effective
leader in his particular Church. Preaching, presiding at the sacraments,
collaborating with people in the various ministerial activities as he seeks
to offer pastoral guidance to the Church — all require a certain measure
of leadership qualities and skills. Such qualities and skills will certainly
enhance a priest's ability to lead and make his ministry more effective,
and it is incumbent upon the priest to develop these qualities to the best
of his ability, especially in the light of his crucial role in the «new
evangelization». It must be emphasized, however, that important as such
qualities and skills are, the primary capacity to lead comes from the
sacrament and not from the priest's skills. It is Christ whom the priest
represents and it is Christ's ministry in which he engages.

3. Third, Cooke emphasizes that in the Christian context the leader
lives in a specific community, operates out of a vision of the Church's
faith, motivates through the example of charity, and encourages by instilling in people his or her own hope in Christ. Here the more personal,
existential dimensions of priestly leadership can be understood. While
emphasizing the universal scope of the Church's mission, hence of the
mission of the priest, *PDV* locates the priest's ministry in the particular
Church. The priest lives in a particular time and place, and he serves a
particular people. This is his arena of ministry and leadership. But such
leadership cannot be fully grasped if only approached in terms of ontology or function; the existential reality of the priest's life is thus crucial to
fill out the portrait of priest as leader.

The priest's configuration to Christ the Head and Shepherd, creates
certain exigencies in his life. In other words, his consecration seeks to
extend itself as fully as possible into all aspects of his life. Consecrated
and configured to Christ Head and Shepherd, the priest is called to
become like Christ in his own life in order to be a more effective
minister of Christ. The tradition of the Evangelical Counsels is meant
to enable the priest to take on the characteristics of Christ's life. *PDV*,

therefore, encourages priests to embrace those dispositions of soul, namely poverty, chastity, and obedience, in order to imitate the complete self-emptying love of Christ. Such dispositions will help him to cultivate a consciousness of being Christ's instrument and also dispose him to give himself more completely in his ministry — with a love that is at once spousal and pastoral. In terms of priest as leader, such a way of life, dedicated to being Christ's instrument, personalizes his ministry and enables him to lead, not only in his formal ministry, but with the example of his own life.

To say that the priest is a leader is to say that he has the «[...] capacity to inspire and direct a social group» — the local Church — «[...] as it moves towards some goal» — fullness of life in Christ — and that he does this most effectively when he lives out of the Church's vision of faith, motivates people through the example of charity, and encourages people by instilling in them his own hope in Christ. In other words, to say that a priest is a leader is to say that he is a pastor, one who patterns his life on the Good Shepherd, one who himself is motivated by the Shepherd's love, that is to say, by pastoral charity. Here the full meaning of priest as leader begins to open up. Rooted in the Trinity, the priest patterns his life on the *perichoresis* of the Trinity and gives himself to the Church in love. Configured to Christ the Head, Shepherd, and Spouse of the Church, the priest seeks to make Christ's way of thinking, feeling, and acting his own. The priest's consecration thus drives him into action and in his relationship towards the Church he makes a total gift of himself, not only in the specific ministerial functions he performs, but in the pattern of his life which seeks to mirror the radicalism of the Gospel and thus his complete dedication to Christ. Pastoral charity, then, the integrating core or nucleus of the ministerial priesthood, is also at the heart of priestly leadership. Perhaps the best way to express priest as leader is with the image of shepherd or pastor. This is the preferred image in both *PO* and *PDV*, and it is perhaps the most accurate and evocative way of expressing the notion of priest as leader.

Cooke's broad description of leadership has been used as a key to approach *Presbyterorum Ordinis* and other pertinent Vatican II documents, *The Ministerial Priesthood* and *Pastores Dabo Vobis*. The study of these documents has sought to fill out an understanding of leadership, specifically as it applies to the ministerial priesthood, in other words, to sketch a portrait of priest as leader. The study has indicated that such a portrait is fairly nuanced and complex because leadership is not something extrinsic to the priesthood, but is rooted in its theological and spiritual foundations. To arrive at an adequate understanding of priest as leader requires an examination of the identity, mission, and spirituality of the ministerial priesthood, which in turn requires an exploration of its ecclesiological, christological, and pastoral foundations. No description of priest as leader can hope to be accurate or adequate without the theological and spiritual foundation that the documents studied provide. With this foundation we can turn in the next chapter to a more secular or cultural understanding of leadership in order to continue our examination of priest as leader, the inculturation of a spiritual-theological theme of priesthood in a U.S. context.

CHAPTER IV

Leadership in a U.S. Cultural Context

1. Introduction

In his Pulitzer Prize-winning book on leadership, James MacGregor Burns states, «Leadership is one of the most observed and least understood phenomena on earth»[1]. Bernard Bass, in his magisterial *Bass and Stogdill's Handbook of Leadership:* Theory, Research, and Management Applications [hereafter *Handbook of Leadership*], describes leadership as «[...] one of the world's oldest preoccupations»[2], and attempts both to catalogue what is known about leadership and to suggest further paths for study[3]. Robert Hogan, et al., claim that in the field of applied psychology the sheer number of printed pages devoted to the study of leadership affirm that it is a central preoccupation[4]. They assert that the reason leadership is not understood on a scale commensurate with the amount of study devoted to it is because psychological research on the topic tends to focus on narrowly defined issues and is read primarily by other psychologists; thus little impact is made on the wider public, especially those people who make decisions about leadership[5]. Burns has noted that, although no central concept of leadership has emerged because scholars in various disciplines have been approaching the topic from

---

1 J. M. BURNS, *Leadership*, 2.

2 B. M. BASS, *Bass & Stogdill's Handbook of Leadership*, 3rd edition, 11.

3 J. R. Love observes that Bass' *Handbook of Leadership*, an 1182-page study based on 7500 sources, deals with both classic and modern issues of leadership theory and practice. It is probably the most comprehensive and complete treatment of the topic, prompting Love to call it the «bible» of leadership research. Cf. J. R. LOVE, *Liberating Leaders from the Superman Syndrome*, 1.

4 Cf. R. HOGAN et al., «What We Know about Leadership», 493.

5 Cf. R. HOGAN et al., «What We Know about Leadership», 493.

different perspectives, there is a large reservoir of data and theories which makes it possible to generalize about leadership and its development[6]. The problem with such generalization is that it has generated a vast array of descriptions, definitions, and understandings. Bass contends, «There are almost as many different definitions of leadership as there are persons who have attempted to define the concept. Moreover [...] many of the definitions are ambiguous»[7]. Warren Bennis and Burt Nanus cite the existence of 350 definitions of leadership but claim that «[...] no clear and unequivocal understanding exists as to what distinguishes leaders from non-leaders»[8]. Similarly, Kenneth E. Clark and Miriam B. Clark say, «Studying leadership is like viewing a great work of art: there is still much to see after the first glance»[9].

Despite the great number and variety of understandings of leadership, Bass contends that there is adequate similarity among the many definitions to allow for broad classification:

> Leadership has been conceived as the focus of group processes, as a matter of personality, as a matter of inducing compliance, as the exercise of influence, as particular behaviors, as a form of persuasion, as a power relation, as an instrument to achieve goals, as an effect of interaction, as a differentiated role, as initiation of structure, and as many combinations of these definitions[10].

As these categories suggest, leadership can be approached from a variety of perspectives that both shape and determine understandings. No single definition is able to offer a universal understanding of leadership that is applicable in every instance. Although no single definition is universally adequate, Bass does note, «The hope is that the [various] definitions will provide critical new insights into the nature of leadership»[11].

Despite the «gap» noted above, between scientific research and the general public's understanding of leadership, certain authors whose works are widely popular have attempted to describe leadership and suggest ways to identify and develop it. Although the study of leadership

---

6 Cf. J. M. BURNS, *Leadership*, 3.

7 B. M. BASS, *Handbook of Leadership*, 11.

8 W. BENNIS – B. NANUS, *Leaders*, 4.

9 K. E. CLARK – M. B. CLARK, eds., *Measures of Leadership*, 41.

10 B. M. BASS, *Handbook of Leadership*, 11. For a description of each of these twelve categories, see pp. 11-18.

11 B. M. BASS, *Handbook of Leadership*, 19.

has become an international phenomenon, national and cultural contexts give rise to various accents on the concept and its meaning[12]. In his overview of leadership in various countries and cultures, Bass points out that the preponderance of research in the area of leadership has been carried out in a United States context[13]. Because our work is considering priest as leader in a U.S. context, this chapter will study some popular works by U.S. authors writing in the leadership field, in order to arrive at a description of leadership as it is understood in the U.S. culture today. Some of the writers to be examined are Peter F. Drucker, Warren Bennis and Burt Nanus, James M. Kouzes and Barry Z. Posner. The criteria for choosing these authors include their expertise in the field and their popularity: most of these writers are acknowledged experts in the field of leadership, frequently cited by other authors, and most have written books that have been widely disseminated among the general public, making them very influential in how «non-experts» understand leadership. In addition, they represent a cross-section of those popular authors currently writing in the leadership field. Because some of these are prolific authors, a review of their entire corpus of work cannot be attempted here. Rather, a synthetic analysis of a representative sample of their work will be presented in order to highlight general themes about leadership that are current in U.S. culture today. Before approaching their works, however, a brief examination of the evolution of leadership theory will help to establish a context for understanding their teaching.

2. Leadership Theory

J. Richard Love has noted that most writers in the field of leadership theory delineate three general approaches to leadership which follow an historical development: trait theory, behavioral theory, and situational

---

[12] Bass points out: «The differences in socialization in the various nations of the world give rise to different conceptions of leadership. What is good leadership will vary. Even the English word *leader* may not be directly translatable! For instance, it does not easily translate into French, Spanish, or German, so *le leader, el lider, and der leiter* may be used instead of the available French, Spanish, or German words, *le meneur, el jefe,* or *der Führer* that tend to connote only leadership that is directive», B. M. BASS, *Handbook of Leadership*, 760.

[13] Bass adds, «To a large degree, the preceding chapters were a review of what is known about the antecedents and effects of leadership in the United States, buttressed, to some extent, by relevant work elsewhere», B. M. BASS, *Handbook of Leadership*, 769.

theory[14]. Bass identifies five general theoretical categories — personal and situational, interaction and social learning, interactive processes, perceptual and cognitive, hybrid explanations — which, in turn, he subdivides into a total of twenty-two theories[15]. For the sake of clarity and simplicity, our presentation will follow the delineation of leadership theory described by Michael Z. Hackman and Craig E. Johnson: 1) traits approach; 2) functional approach; 3) situational approach; and 4) transformational approach[16].

2.1 *The Traits Approach to Leadership*

The «traits» perspective is the earliest theoretical approach to leadership and it rests on this assumption: «If the leader is endowed with superior qualities that differentiate him from his followers, it should be possible to identify these qualities»[17]. As Love points out, one can only assume that the motive behind distinguishing leadership qualities was to identify those people who possessed such traits in order to mark them for future positions of leadership[18]. Popular until the late 1940's, the traits approach favored the «nature» side of the nature vs. nurture debate: «Either individuals were born with the traits needed to be a leader or they would always lack the physiological and psychological characteristics necessary for successful leadership»[19]. In other words, leaders pos-

---

[14] Cf. J. R. LOVE, *Liberating Leaders from the Superman Syndrome*, 34. In his presentation of leadership theory, Love uses five categories: trait, behavior, situational, contingency, and transformational.

[15] For a description of each theory, see B. M. BASS, *Handbook of Leadership*, 37-55. Love provides an outline of Bass' leadership theories. Cf. J. R. LOVE, *Liberating Leaders from the Superman Syndrome*, 166.

[16] Cf. M. Z. HACKMAN – C. E. JOHNSON, *Leadership*, 41-68. Hackman and Johnson's approach is being followed because it is both simple enough to serve as the basis for an overview of leadership theory, and comprehensive enough to present the salient features of the historical development of the major theories. Although Hackman and Johnson's categories will be used here, the order in which they will be presented is altered in order to reflect the historical progression of the evolution of leadership studies. Love points out that the historical progression moves from trait-based to behavior to situational. We will follow Love's order, but, with Hackman and Johnson, the transformational theory will be treated as a category unto itself; it is the most recent general category in the evolution of leadership theory. Cf. J. R. LOVE, *Liberating Leaders from the Superman Syndrome*, 34-35.

[17] B. M. BASS, *Handbook of Leadership*, 38.

[18] Cf. J. R. LOVE, *Liberating Leaders from the Superman Syndrome*, 35.

[19] M. Z. HACKMAN – C. E. JOHNSON, *Leadership*, 42.

sessed fixed, inborn characteristics which caused them to be leaders; such characteristics were universal and applicable across diverse situations[20]. Hackman and Johnson note that, based on the traits approach, numerous studies were devised which focused on physical characteristics, intelligence, personality, temperament, and other social traits in order to determine which of these characteristics were most clearly correlative with leadership: «Researchers wanted to know, for example, were leaders: Tall or short? Bright or dull? Outgoing or shy?»[21].

Over the course of time, for various reasons, the traits approach to leadership fell into disrepute among researchers. First, the findings of the various studies and surveys were inconsistent: there was not a direct correlation between a given personal trait and leadership capability[22]. In an analysis of 124 «traits» studies conducted between the years 1904 and 1947, Ralph Stogdill concluded, «A person does not become a leader by virtue of the possession of some combination of traits»[23]. Corroborating Stogdill's conclusions, Estela M. Bensimon asserted that no particular trait has proven essential to be a successful leader[24]. Second, the traits approach to leadership failed to consider the situation faced by the leader, the followers within the given context, and the quality of the leader's performance[25]. Finally, as Bass notes, «pure trait theory» was seen to be inadequate because both person and situation had to be considered in order to explain the phenomenon of leadership. The trait theory alone was insufficient to explain the process of leadership because it concentrated on only one aspect of the leadership equation[26].

---

[20] Cf. E. P. HOLLANDER – L. R. OFFERMAN, «Relational Features of Organizational Leadership and Followership», 84.

[21] M. Z. HACKMAN – C. E. JOHNSON, *Leadership*, 43.

[22] Cf. M. Z. HACKMAN – C. E. JOHNSON, *Leadership*, 44.

[23] R. M. STOGDILL, «Personal Factors Associated with Leadership», 35-71, cited in M. Z. HACKMAN – C. E. JOHNSON, *Leadership*, 44. Stogdill added, however, that although traits were not predictive of leadership, «[...] the pattern of personal characteristics of the leader must bear some relevant relationship to the characteristics, activities and goals of the followers». For a revision of Stogdill's article, see Chapter Four, «Traits of Leadership: 1904-47», B. M. BASS, *Handbook of Leadership*, 59-77.

[24] Cf. E. M. BENSIMON et al., *Making Sense of Administration*, 7, cited in J. R. LOVE, *Liberating Leaders from the Superman Syndrome*, 36.

[25] Cf. E. P. HOLLANDER – L. R. OFFERMAN, «Relational Features of Organizational Leadership and Followership», 84.

[26] Cf. B. M. BASS, *Handbook of Leadership*, 38; J. R. LOVE, *Liberating Leaders from the Superman Syndrome*, 36.

Although the traits approach alone proved insufficient to explain the complex reality of leadership, it cannot simply be dismissed out of hand. In a later study Stogdill emphasized that certain traits of the leader are important to the extent that they are relevant to the goals and activities of the followers:

> Strong evidence indicates that different leadership skills and traits are required in different situations. The behaviors and traits enabling a mobster to gain and maintain control over a criminal gang are not the same as those enabling a religious leader to gain and maintain a large following. Yet certain general qualities — such as courage, fortitude, and conviction — appear to characterize both[27].

Based on his 1948 research, Stogdill recognized six factors associated with leadership and classified them under the following general headings as 1) *capacity*: intelligence, judgment, verbal skills; 2) *achievement*: scholarly and athletic training and accomplishments; 3) *responsibility*: dependability, persistence, desire to excel; 4) *participation*: willingness to get involved, adaptability, humor and sociability; 5) *status*: popularity, socio-economic position; 6) *situation*: mental level, skills, status, needs and goals of the followers[28]. As these categories indicate, leadership is not guaranteed by personal traits alone but is shaped by situational components as well. The categories also indicate that many «traits» are not simply inborn, but can be acquired through education, training, and practice[29]. By itself, the traits approach has proven insufficient to explain the process of leadership, but it does suggest that certain patterns of traits (whether learned or inborn) can be advantageous to the exercise of leadership in certain situations[30].

2.2 *The Functional Approach to Leadership*

Unlike the traits approach which focused on the inborn personality characteristics of leaders, the functional approach studied individuals' behaviors while acting as leaders of groups[31]. Functional approach

---

[27] R. M. STOGDILL, *Handbook of Leadership*, 72, quoted in M. Z. HACKMAN – C. E. JOHNSON, *Leadership*, 45. Cf. B. M. BASS, *Handbook of Leadership*, 78.

[28] Cf. B. M. BASS, *Handbook of Leadership*, 76.

[29] Cf. M. Z. HACKMAN – C. E. JOHNSON, *Leadership*, 44-45.

[30] Cf. M. Z. HACKMAN – C. E. JOHNSON, *Leadership*, 46; B. M. BASS, *Handbook of Leadership*, 86-87.

[31] For descriptions of the functional, or behavioral, approach, see B. M. BASS, *Handbook of Leadership*, 472-543; M. Z. HACKMAN – C. E. JOHNSON, *Leader-*

studies identified two major types of leader behavior: task-oriented behavior, and relations-oriented (socio-emotional) behavior[32]. Although these two orientations alone are insufficient for identifying effective leadership[33], they provide a helpful framework for recognizing basic communication behaviors or orientations that affect the exercise of leadership[34].

2.2.1 Task Orientation

Those leaders who most strongly focus on the goals of the group, and the methods and means to achieve those goals, are considered to be primarily task-oriented: work, production, and achievement are the primary concerns of this type of leader. The set of behaviors associated with a predominantly task-oriented leader has been described as «structuring» or «initiation of structures», which consists of task-assignment, standard-setting, evaluation, and the direction of the work[35]. The focus is on the task to be done and the leader acts in a directive manner. The following leadership roles have been associated with task-oriented leaders: the *initiator* defines problems, proposes procedures, strategies, and solutions; the *information/opinion seeker* solicits ideas and evaluations of information and procedure; the *information/opinion giver* offers information and evaluates strategies and procedures; the *elaborator* helps to clarify ideas and draws out the implications of proposed strategies; the *orienter/coordinator* synthesizes disparate information and keeps the group focused on the task at hand; the *energizer* acts as a stimulus by encouraging the group to achieve excellence[36]. Each of these roles contributes to the planning and completion of the group's tasks.

---

ship, 56-60; J. R. LOVE, *Liberating Leaders from the Superman Syndrome*, 36-43; F. E. FIEDLER – J. E. GARCIA, *New Approaches to Effective Leadership*, 15-16.

[32] For an analysis of the research conducted on these two leader behavior orientations, see Chapter 23, «Task- versus Relations-Oriented Leadership» in B. M. BASS, *Handbook of Leadership*, 472-510.

[33] Cf. F. E. FIEDLER – J. E. GARCIA, *New Approaches to Effective Leadership*, 15.

[34] Cf. M. Z. HACKMAN – C. E. JOHNSON, *Leadership*, 60.

[35] Cf. B. M. BASS, *Handbook of Leadership*, 511-512; F. E. FIEDLER – J. E. GARCIA, *New Approaches to Effective Leadership*, 15.

[36] Cf. K. D. BENNE – P. SHEATS, «Functional Roles of Group Members», 41-49, in M. Z. HACKMAN – C. E. JOHNSON, *Leadership*, 57-58; B. M. BASS, *Handbook of Leadership*, 29-30.472-473.

2.2.2 Relations Orientation

Those leaders who are more people-centered and concerned with establishing and maintaining relations within the group are primarily relations-oriented; they facilitate and support group interaction, trying to maintain friendly relations with their followers. The set of behaviors that are associated with the relations-oriented leader has been described as «consideration» or «considerate behavior», and consists of such things as demonstrating appreciation for good work, approachability, strengthening the self-esteem of followers, and consultation in decision-making[37]. The following set of leadership roles have been associated with relations-oriented leaders: the *encourager* promotes solidarity among the group members by supporting individuals' contributions and accepting divergent points of view; the *harmonizer/compromiser* mediates conflicting viewpoints and tries to reduce group tensions; the *gatekeeper* tries to involve all in the group process by creating an environment amenable to everyone's participation; the *standard-setter* articulates the values of the group and holds them up as an ideal to be followed. Each of these roles is aimed at promoting healthy relations among group members[38].

In addition to the leadership roles described above, Benne and Sheats described roles which were neither task- nor relations-oriented: the *aggressor*, the *blocker*, the *recognition-seeker*, the *player*, and the *dominator* roles. Because these roles center on individual satisfaction, to the detriment of the group and the task, they are not normally associated with leadership[39]. Love has delineated three leadership styles that relate to the leader's use of authority[40]. The *Authoritarian Style*[41], often called the efficient style of leadership, emphasizes the authority of the leader;

---

[37] Cf. B. M. BASS, *Handbook of Leadership*, 511-512; F. E. FIEDLER –J. E. GARCIA, *New Approaches to Effective Leadership*, 15; J. R. LOVE, *Liberating Leaders from the Superman Syndrome*, 38.

[38] Cf. K. D. BENNE – P. SHEATS, «Functional Roles of Group Members», cited in M. Z. HACKMAN – C. E. JOHNSON, *Leadership*, 58-59; B. M. BASS, *Handbook of Leadership*, 29-30.473-474.

[39] Cf. K. D. BENNE – P. SHEATS, «Functional Roles of Group Members», cited in M. Z. HACKMAN – C. E. JOHNSON, *Leadership*, 59-60.

[40] Cf. J. R. LOVE, *Liberating Leaders from the Superman Syndrome*, 40-41.

[41] For an analysis of the Authoritarian Style of leadership, see Chapter 21, «Autocratic and Authoritarian versus Democratic and Egalitarian Leadership» in B. M. BASS, *Handbook of Leadership*, 415-435.

there is very little consultation because the leader simply makes all the decisions. The *Laissez-faire Style* is the exact opposite of the authoritarian style because the so-called leader takes no initiative and offers nothing to the group; such «leadership» is really a contradiction in terms[42]. The *Participative Style*, often considered inefficient, while allowing for consultation and group participation in the decision-making process, also allows for more directive leadership depending upon the circumstances[43]. The participative style can include both task- and relations-oriented behaviors.

Although the functional approach does not give a prescription for leader behavior, it is beneficial in developing leadership theory because it provides guidelines and suggests certain behaviors that leaders should have in their repertories in order to be able to function in various circumstances. The functional approach is also important because it stresses that the leader must be aware that the way he or she behaves, both in actions and in styles of acting, has an influence, for good or bad, on the followers and their ability to achieve the task before them.

2.3 *The Situational Approach to Leadership*

Because of the inadequacy of an exclusive traits and/or behavioral approach, researchers began to widen their scope and pursue situational explanations for leadership[44]. In its pure form, the situational approach, which is the direct opposite of a pure traits approach, holds that leadership is totally dependent upon the situation: «[...] situational factors determine who will emerge as leader»[45]. Most situational theory, however, is more nuanced than this extreme view. Love points out that in situational research, personal styles or traits are still important[46]. The context, or situation, however, is also a crucial factor in determining

---

[42] For an analysis of the Laissez-faire Style, see Chapter 25, «Laissez-faire Leadership versus Motivation to Manage», B. M. BASS, *Handbook of Leadership*, 544-559.

[43] For an analysis of the Participative Style, see Chapter 22, «Directive versus Participative Leadership», B. M. BASS, *Handbook of Leadership*, 436-471.

[44] Cf. B. M. BASS, *Handbook of Leadership*, 38-39; M. Z. HACKMAN – C. E. JOHNSON, *Leadership*, 46-56; E. P. HOLLANDER – L. R. OFFERMAN, «Relational Features of Organizational Leadership and Followership», 84-86; J. R. LOVE, *Liberating Leaders from the Superman Syndrome*, 43-48.

[45] B. M. BASS, *Handbook of Leadership*, 38.

[46] Cf. J. R. LOVE, *Liberating Leaders from the Superman Syndrome*, 34.

leadership: variations in the situation influence the emergence and process of leadership. In addition to the traits or characteristics of the leader, situational elements — such as the task or activity itself, available human and material resources, the quality of leader-follower interaction, the history of the situation and the persons involved — also affect the process of leadership[47].

In the situational approach, the leader must assess the situation and decide to use whatever style or set of personal traits is appropriate to the circumstances:

> For example, the strategy for effectively leading a high tech research and development team is much different from the strategy for most effectively leading a military combat unit. The differences in leadership style might be attributed to task and relational structure, superior-subordinate interactions, the motivation of followers, or any one of a number of situational structures[48].

The situational approach recognizes the complexity of the process of leadership; it is not simply the traits or characteristics of an isolated individual, but a complex process of interaction influenced by a variety of factors. Three influential theories falling under the umbrella of the situational approach are Contingency Theory, Path-Goal Theory, and Hersey and Blanchard's Situational Leadership Theory.

2.3.1 Contingency Theory

A refinement of the situational approach, Contingency Theory was developed by Fred E. Fiedler in the 1960's and attempted to sketch the conditions in an organization in which leaders with a certain personality were effective; it addressed the question of «[...] why certain individuals perform better than others in identical leadership situations. [...] the contingency model was the first to spell out how personality and situational variables interacted, and the first to provide substantial empirical support for this position»[49]. Fiedler's model distinguished between task-oriented and relationship-oriented leadership styles and his research

---

[47] Cf. E. P. HOLLANDER – L. R. OFFERMAN, «Relational Features of Organizational Leadership and Followership», 84.

[48] M. Z. HACKMAN – C. E. JOHNSON, *Leadership*, 46.

[49] F. E. FIEDLER – J. E. GARCIA, *New Approaches to Effective Leadership*, 18. For an analysis and critique of Fiedler's Contingency Theory, see B. M. BASS, *Handbook of Leadership*, 494-510.

discovered that a leader's effectiveness in a given situation was contingent upon three factors that control the extent of the leader's influence over the followers: leader-position power, task structure, and leader-member relations[50]. Love observes that Fiedler's discovery that some followers were more productive under certain leadership styles led to the conclusion that leaders had to be capable of practicing varied styles of leadership in order to be effective. This reinforced the conviction that the leader's traits were no longer the only criterion to be considered; the traits of the followers and the nature of the task also had to be taken into consideration[51]. Garry Wills wryly acknowledges the necessity of taking followers and context into account when describing leadership:

> A Leader whose qualities do not match those of potential followers is simply irrelevant. The world is not playing his or her game. My favorite example of this is the leadership of Syrian holy men in the fifth century of the Common Era. Those men, who made policy for whole communities, were revered for their self-ravaging austerity. The man who had starved himself most spectacularly was thought the best equipped to advise pious consultants. So delegations went to consult Simeon the "Stylite" (Pillar Man), perched in his mid-air hermitage. Leadership was entirely conditioned by the attitudes of contemporary followership. Who would now write a manual called *The Leadership Secrets of Simeon Stylites*, telling people to starve and whip and torture themselves into command positions?[52]

Contingent Theory emphasizes the importance of followers, and that the leader should be placed into a situation suitable to his leadership style or, barring that, the leader must be capable of adapting his or her style to suit the situation of his or her followers[53].

2.3.2 Path-Goal Theory

Simply put, this theory, developed by R.J. House and T.R. Mitchell, refers to «[...] the leader's effectiveness in increasing followers' motivation along a path leading to a goal»[54]. In this model the contingencies

---

[50] Cf. E. P. HOLLANDER – L. R. OFFERMAN, «Relational Features of Organizational Leadership and Followership», 86; M.Z. HACKMAN – C. E. JOHNSON, *Leadership*, 47-51; J. R. LOVE, *Liberating Leaders from the Superman Syndrome*, 45.

[51] Cf. J. R. LOVE, *Liberating Leaders from the Superman Syndrome*, 45.

[52] G. WILLS, *Certain Trumpets*, 15.

[53] Cf. B. M. BASS, *Handbook of Leadership*, 47.

[54] E. P. HOLLANDER – L. R. OFFERMAN, «Relational Features of Organizational Leadership and Followership», 86. Cf. R. J. HOUSE, «A Path-Goal Theory of Leader

faced by the leader are the nature of the followers' group, the characteristics of the followers, and the task itself. House and Mitchell identify four leader communication styles that enhance the leader's ability to motivate a group, depending upon the operative contingencies: 1) *directive leadership*, to be used with inexperienced, uncertain followers and/or unstructured tasks; 2) *supportive leadership*, to be used with competent followers in the face of a structured but difficult or stressful task; 3) *participative leadership*, to be used when followers are uncertain and the task is unstructured; and 4) *achievement-oriented leadership*, to be used when the followers are competent and the task is unstructured[55]. The Path-Goal Theory neglects certain contingencies that might have an impact on leader performance, but is important because it recognizes the complexity of leadership and takes seriously its various components, including tasks, followers, and leaders[56].

2.3.3 Hersey and Blanchard's Situational Leadership Theory[57]

Both Fiedler and Bass acknowledge the popularity of this approach but claim that, because it has no empirical or logical justification, its appeal is more intuitive[58]. According to this theory, leadership style should be contingent upon the maturity level of followers, with maturity, in this model, having two components: job maturity and psychological maturity. Four maturity levels are delineated, along with four corresponding leadership styles — level 1) *follower lacks both skills and willingness*: requires a leadership style of «directing» or «telling»; level 2) *follower lacks skills but is willing*: requires a leadership style of coaching or supportive guidance; level 3) *follower is skilled but lacks willingness*: requires an encouraging style of leadership which draws the follower into the decision-making process; level 4) *follower is skilled and willing*: requires a delegating style of leadership which turns over responsibility

---

Effectiveness», 321-338; R. J. HOUSE – G. DESSLER, «The Path-Goal Theory of Leadership; R. J. HOUSE – T. R. MITCHELL, «Path-Goal Theory of Leadership», 81-97.

[55] Cf. M. Z. HACKMAN – C. E. JOHNSON, *Leadership*, 51-53; F. E. FIEDLER – J. E. GARCIA, *New Approaches to Effective Leadership*, 18-19;

[56] Cf. M. Z. HACKMAN – C. E. JOHNSON, *Leadership*, 53.

[57] Cf. P. HERSEY – K. BLANCHARD, «Life-Cycle Theory of Leadership», 26-34; ID., *Management of Organizational Behavior*, 5th edition.

[58] Cf. B. M. BASS, *Handbook of Leadership*, 492; F. E. FIEDLER – J. E. GARCIA, *New Approaches to Effective Leadership*, 19.

to the follower[59]. Bass points out that, despite the theoretical inadequacies and the paucity of supportive empirical evidence for this theory, it is popular because of its intuitive appeal and its simplicity, which may give leaders a sense of mastery over complex problems[60].

Love asserts that the various approaches constituting situational theory have a «common thread» which emphasizes the leader's style, the situation itself, and the leader-follower interaction[61]. No theory of leadership is adequate that does not take into consideration the attributes or traits of the leader, the various components of the situation, and the complex interaction of all the factors involved in the process.

2.4 *Transactional and Transformational Approaches to Leadership*

As this general review of various broad approaches to leadership indicates, there have been major paradigm shifts over the years: the traits approach gave way to a more functional or behavioral approach, which in turn evolved into the situational approach described above. The evolution of theory has led to a more dynamic understanding of leadership. No longer simply a matter of traits alone, or of behaviors alone, or of situational components alone, the process of leadership has come to be seen as a combination of all three: it is contingent on traits, behaviors, and situations, involving a transaction between the leader and the followers[62]. In the transactional model the leader gives rewards and benefits to the follower, such as direction and clarity, and the followers reciprocate with more responsiveness to the leader and fulfillment of agreements made with the leader. The transactional approach emphasizes the significance of the followers' expectations and perception of the leader[63], and appeals to the self-interest of the follower[64]:

---

[59] For a graph which schematizes Hersey and Blanchard's situational theory, see P. HERSEY – K. BLANCHARD, *Management of Organizational Behavior*, 171. Cf. B. M. BASS, *Handbook of Leadership*, 488-494; M. Z. HACKMAN – C. E. JOHNSON, *Leadership*, 54-56; R. J. LOVE, *Liberating Leaders from the Superman Syndrome*, 46.

[60] Cf. B. M. BASS, *Handbook of Leadership*, 495.

[61] Cf. R. J. LOVE, *Liberating Leaders from the Superman Syndrome*, 46.

[62] Cf. E. P. HOLLANDER, «On the Central Role of Leadership Processes», 39-52, cited in B. M. BASS, *Handbook of Leadership*, 53.

[63] Cf. E. P. HOLLANDER – L. R. OFFERMAN, «Relational Features of Organizational Leadership and Followership», 86-87.

[64] Cf. J. R. LOVE, *Liberating Leaders from the Superman Syndrome*, 47.

The leader provides a benefit in directing the group, hopefully toward desirable results. Therefore, a person who fulfills the role of leader well is normally valued. In return the group members provide the leader with status and the privileges of authority that go with it. [...] However, influence is not all one way. As part of the exchange, the followers may assert influence and make demands on the leader. The soundness of the relationship depends upon some yielding to influence on both sides[65].

The transactional approach, briefly described here, set the stage for the emergence of the transformational approach to leadership, first outlined by Burns in contrast to the transactional:

The relations of most leaders and followers are *transactional* — leaders approach followers with an eye to exchanging one thing for another: jobs for votes, or subsidies for campaign contributions. [...] *Transforming* leadership, while more complex, is more potent. The transforming leader recognizes and exploits an existing need or demand of a potential follower. But, beyond that, the transforming leader looks for potential motives in followers, seeks to satisfy higher needs, and engages the full person of the follower. The result of transforming leadership is a relationship of mutual stimulation and elevation that converts followers into leaders and may convert leaders into moral agents[66].

Hollander and Offerman observe that transformational leadership is an extension of transactional leadership, but with greater leadership intensity and follower stimulation[67].

In explaining the difference between transactional and transformational approaches to leadership, Hackman and Johnson relate both models to Maslow's hierarchy of human needs[68]. The transactional leader is concerned with satisfying the three lowest needs: physiological, safety, and social. Although transformational leaders are also concerned with satisfying these basic needs of followers, they go beyond the mere transactional exchange by engaging the whole person to try to meet the higher human needs of esteem and self-actualization[69]. According to Burns,

---

65 E. P. HOLLANDER, *Leadership Dynamics*, 7, quoted in J. R. LOVE, *Liberating Leaders from the Superman Syndrome*, 47.

66 J. M. BURNS, *Leadership*, 4.

67 Cf. E. P. HOLLANDER – L. R. OFFERMAN, «Relational Features of Organizational Leadership and Followership», 88.

68 For the articulation of this theory, see A. MASLOW, *Motivation and Personality*, 146-154.

69 Cf. M. Z. HACKMAN – C. E. JOHNSON, *Leadership*, 61-63. W. H. Clover reports the results of a study of transformational leadership he conducted at the United

transformational leadership engages both leaders and followers in such a way that all are raised to higher levels of motivation and morality[70].

Subsequent research has affirmed Burns' articulation of transformational leadership. Bernard Bass found four factors at play in a leader described as transformational: charismatic leadership[71], inspirational leadership, intellectual stimulation, and individualized consideration[72]. According to Bass, «The transformational leader sharply arouses or alters the strength of needs which may have lain dormant. [...] It is leadership that is transformational that can bring about the big differences and big changes in groups, organizations, and societies»[73]. In their analysis of works by researchers on transformational leadership, Hackman and Johnson identified five primary characteristics of transformational leaders: they are 1) *creative*, willing to experiment and innovate, even at the risk of failure; 2) *interactive*, closely involved with followers and able to communicate well and organize meaning for them; 3) *visionary*, not only able to communicate the overarching vision, goal and direction to followers, but also able to reinforce the stated vision; 4) *empowering*, encouraging the initiative, achievement, participation and involvement of followers; and 5) *passionate*, motivating through the communication of a genuine love for both the task and for the people they work with[74].

The transformational approach to leadership is still relatively young and more research needs to be done. However, it already shows promise

---

States Air Force Academy during the 1987-88 academic year. In his summary he observed, «To be sure, we are not convinced that transformational leadership rules out the need for good transactional leadership. In fact, we are convinced of just the opposite: good transformational leadership is balanced and aided by good transactional leadership», W. H. CLOVER, «Transformational Leaders», 183.

[70] Cf. J. M. BURNS, *Leadership*, 20.

[71] Hollander and Offerman observe, «The potential for damage from a leader with charismatic appeal is evident. [...] such a leader has narcissistic needs for continual approval from others. Coupled with personalized power needs, the outcome of a charismatic appeal can be destructive. [...] Although not all charismatic leaders provide trouble in these ways, their potential for affecting many others adversely requires attention, if only to rectify the balance of views», E. P. HOLLANDER – L. R. OFFERMAN, «Relational Features of Organizational Leadership and Followership», 88.

[72] Cf. B. M. BASS, *Leadership and Performance Beyond Expectations*, cited in ID., *Handbook of Leadership*, 218.

[73] B. M. BASS, *Leadership and Performance Beyond Expectations*, 17, quoted in M. Z. HACKMAN – C. E. JOHNSON, *Leadership*, 63.

[74] Cf. M. Z. HACKMAN – C. E. JOHNSON, *Leadership*, 63-65.

as a paradigm for understanding leadership[75]. Reflecting an evolution in leadership theory, it builds upon the traits, functional, and situational approaches. Its appeal lies in its emphasis on the leader's going beyond the ordinary, and engaging the followers' higher needs and motivations in order to bring about a change in thinking that will translate into a change of behavior as both leader and followers pursue the articulated goal[76]. The transformational model has become the most popular approach to understanding leadership and the authors to be considered below represent, in varying degrees, this understanding of leadership.

3. A Review And Synthesis of Selected American Literature on Leadership

In *Liberating Leaders from the Superman Syndrome*, J. Richard Love attempted a synthetic analysis and evaluation of both secular and religious writing on leadership[77]. His perspective in approaching the literature was rooted in an undertaking called the «Project Cathedral Leadership Hypothesis»[78], which offers a description of a Christian leader: «An effective Christian leader 1) maximizes strengths, 2) minimizes limita-

---

[75] Clover points out, «It is this author's belief, shared by many, that transformational leadership is changing the focus of leadership research in two ways. First, we are moving away from the issue of solely rational models of supervisory behavior. Such models as the Hersey and Blanchard model, Fiedler's contingency theory, House's path-goal theory [...] were generally rational approaches and prescriptions as to how a supervisor should deal with a subordinate. Transformational models, starting with the work of Burns [...] are pursuing the issue of using and dealing with emotion in the leadership process. For many the issue is equated to the distinction between leadership and management», W. H. CLOVER, «Transformational Leaders», 171.

[76] Cf. E. P. HOLLANDER – L. R. OFFERMAN, «Relational Features of Organizational Leadership and Followership», 88.

[77] Love points out that his synthesis «[...] represents the "high points" of the 239 books, 138 theological journal articles, and 26 unpublished materials» that were used in his research. J. R. LOVE, *Liberating Leaders from the Superman Syndrome*, 67.

[78] «Project Cathedral» involves faculty members and students of Dallas Theological Seminary who are attempting to create a tool for senior pastors to use for analyzing their leadership ability and for making adjustments that will increase leadership effectiveness. Phase One of «Project Cathedral» consisted of a series of meetings over a year and one-half period for the purpose of developing a leadership hypothesis. As part of Phase Two, J. Richard Love, a student participant in «Project Cathedral», has analyzed leadership literature using this hypothesis as a grid. The five parts of the hypothesis guided his analysis of the literature. For a description of «Project Cathedral» and the development of its leadership hypothesis, see J. R. LOVE, *Liberating Leaders from the Superman Syndrome*, 6-17.

tions, and 3) develops in character 4) in order to attract others 5) to accomplish a common vision»[79]. The purpose of his analysis of the literature was to test the «Project Cathedral» hypothesis, determining how the literature both validated and contradicted its definition of Christian leadership.

Unlike Love's project, the purpose of this chapter is not to test a leadership hypothesis, Christian or otherwise. The purpose, rather, is to review some popular works on leadership by selected U.S. authors in order to arrive at some general conclusions about how leadership is generally understood in U.S. culture today. In order to do this in a systematic way, Love's methodology is very helpful and will be followed here. Because his use of the «Project Cathedral Leadership Hypothesis», however, is not germane to the purpose of this chapter, another «key» will have to be used; such a key is already implicit in the survey of leadership theories articulated above.

Commenting on the process of leadership, Garry Wills observes, «Most literature on leadership is unitarian. But life is trinitarian. One-legged and two-legged chairs do not, of themselves, stand. A third leg is necessary. Leaders, followers and goals make up the three equally necessary supports for leadership»[80]. Wills emphasizes that the goal is not an addition to the leadership equation but an intrinsic part of it. The leader and follower join together because they share in common the same goal. They may have little else in common, but the goal brings them together in relationship to one another[81].

Although Wills' assertion that leadership literature is mostly unitarian is questionable, especially in the light of the leadership theory survey above, his point that leadership entails three intrinsically connected components is accurate. The leadership theory survey revealed an evolution in the understanding of leadership. From a narrow focus on leadership traits and behaviors, to the situational perspective which recognizes the importance of followers and the broader context, to the transformational perspective which acknowledges the interaction between leader and followers as they pursue a common goal, the understanding of leadership has expanded and now must include all three aspects — leader, followers, and goals — to be adequate.

---

[79] J. R. LOVE, *Liberating Leaders from the Superman Syndrome*, 9.
[80] G. WILLS, *Certain Trumpets*, 17.
[81] Cf. G. WILLS, *Certain Trumpets*, 17.

Wills' tripartite understanding of the process of leadership, then, will be the reading key for approaching selected literature on leadership in the remainder of this chapter. Three basic questions will be asked of the literature: 1) what does it say about the person of the leader? 2) what does it say about followers? 3) what does it say about the goals or vision shared by leader and followers? In approaching the literature from this threefold perspective, the general outlines of a popular understanding of leadership in the culture of the United States will emerge more clearly.

3.1 *Peter F. Drucker*

3.1.1 Review of the Works

Peter F. Drucker is recognized as both a seminal writer and prolific contributor to the field of leadership studies[82] — even though he prefers to speak of «management» rather than «leadership». In *The Practice of Management*, first published in 1954, Drucker asserted:

> We have defined the purpose of an organization as "making common men do uncommon things". We have not talked, however, about making common men into uncommon men. We have not, in other words, talked about leadership. This was intentional. Leadership is of utmost importance. Indeed there is no substitute for it. But *leadership cannot be created or promoted. It cannot be taught or learned.* [...] Leadership requires aptitude — and men who are good chief engineers or general managers are rare enough even without aptitude for leadership. Leadership also requires basic attitudes. And nothing is as difficult to define, nothing as difficult to change as basic attitudes [emphasis added][83].

He nuances this position in a later book titled *Managing the Non-Profit Organization: Principles and Practices*:

> There are simply no such things as «leadership traits» or «leadership charac-teristics». Of course, some people are better leaders than others. By and large, though, we are talking about skills that perhaps cannot be taught *but they*

---

[82] For example, in reviewing Drucker's *The Effective Executive*, Love states: «If there is a "Bible" in the leadership library, this book is it. Nobody lists books on leadership without listing this one. It is quite remarkable that this book first appeared in 1966 and — after 25 years of voluminous writing in the area of leadership — still makes everybody's "chart" of the classics in leadership books», J. R. LOVE, *Liberating Leaders from the Superman Syndrome*, 181. Love's comment may seem confusing since, as noted above (p. 193, n. 3), he has already called Bass' *Handbook of Leadership*, the «bible» of leadership theory.

[83] P. F. DRUCKER, *The Practice of Management*, 158-159.

can be learned by most of us. True, some people genuinely cannot learn the skills. They may not be important to them; or they'd rather be followers. But *most of us can learn them* [emphasis added][84].

In his writings, Drucker emphasizes the skills that a manager or leader needs to be effective. In order to identify some of his more important and salient themes, the following books will be examined: *The Effective Executive*; *The New Realities*: In Government and Politics, In Economics and Business, In Society and World View [hereafter *The New Realities*]; *Managing the Non-Profit Organization*: Principles and Practices [hereafter *Managing the Non-Profit Organization*]; and *Managing for the Future*: The 1990's and Beyond [hereafter *Managing for the Future*].

In *The Effective Executive* Drucker defines an executive as a «knowledge worker», manager, or professional who, by virtue of position or knowledge, «[...] is responsible for a contribution that materially affects the capacity of the organization to perform and to obtain results»[85]. These knowledge workers and managers are expected to make decisions that have an effect on both the performance and results of the organization. The aim of *The Effective Executive* is to help knowledge workers and managers — leaders — to learn five practices in order to overcome the built-in organizational conditions that would otherwise render them ineffective[86]. Drucker dismisses a traits approach to managerial leadership[87], concentrating on learnable skills and five practices: 1) *time*

---

84 P. F. DRUCKER, *Managing the Non-Profit Organization*, 18. In a subsequent book Drucker recounts a phone conversation in which he described «leadership» to a bank vice-president. At the end of Drucker's description the banker replied, «But that's no different at all from what we have known for years are the requirements of being an effective manager». Drucker's closing comment: «Precisely». From this conversation one can infer that Drucker equates effective management with leadership. Cf. ID., *Managing for the Future*, 119-123.

85 P. F. DRUCKER, *The Effective Executive*, 5; See also p. 3, in which Drucker describes the knowledge worker as the one «[...] who puts to work what he has between his ears rather than the brawn of his muscles or the skill of his hands. Increasingly, the majority of people who have been schooled to use knowledge, theory, and concept rather than physical force or manual skill work in an organization and are effective insofar as they can make a contribution to the organization».

86 See P. F. DRUCKER, *The Effective Executive*, 9-18, for Drucker's description of the organizational realities which, if unchecked, render the executive ineffective.

87 Cf., for example, P. F. DRUCKER, *The Effective Executive*, 18: «The books on manager development [...] envisage a "man for all seasons" in their picture of the "manager of tomorrow". A senior executive, we are told, should have extraordinary abilities as an analyst and as a decision-maker. He should be good at working with people

management, 2) *focus on contribution to achieve results*, 3) *build on strengths*, 4) *concentrate on a few major areas*, and 5) *make effective decisions*[88]. These, according to Drucker, are the elements of executive leadership effectiveness, forming the nucleus of the book.

In *The New Realities*, Drucker establishes a four-part framework in order to examine the forces that are changing U.S. society in the 1990's: political realities, government and the political process, economic and ecological concerns, and the «new knowledge society». In Chapter Thirteen, «Management as Social Function and Liberal Art», Drucker sketches the history and evolution of management, and observes that its meaning has been profoundly altered as a result of the above-mentioned forces and the changes they are bringing about:

> To be sure, the fundamental task of management remains the same: to make people capable of joint performance through common goals, common values, the right structure, and the training and development they need to perform and to respond to change. But the very meaning of this task has changed, if only because the performance of management has converted the workforce from one composed largely of unskilled laborers to one of highly educated knowledge workers[89].

The advent of the highly-educated knowledge worker has had a deep impact on the way managers [leaders] must perform their functions.

Drucker offers what he calls essential principles to guide leaders and managers of today: 1) because management is about human beings, its task is to make people capable of joint performance; 2) because it is embedded in culture, management must identify and use cultural elements as management tools in order to unite people in a common effort; 3) commitment to common goals and shared values are essential for any enterprise; 4) management must enable its members to grow and develop; 5) every enterprise must be built on communication and individual responsibility; 6) an organization needs a diversity of measures, not just a «bottom line», to assess its performance; 7) results exist on the outside of the enterprise. According to Drucker, these principles are crucial for exercising effective leadership[90].

---

and at understanding organization and power relations, be good at mathematics, and have artistic insights and creative imagination. What seems to be wanted is a universal genius, and universal genius has always been in scarce supply».

[88] Cf. P. F. DRUCKER, *The Effective Executive*, 23-24.

[89] P. F. DRUCKER, *The New Realities*, 222.

[90] Cf. P. F. DRUCKER, *The New Realities*, 228-231.

In *Managing the Non-Profit Organization*, Drucker uses a combination of management principles, anecdotes, and interviews to delineate the role and function of non-profit organization leaders. The book is centered on five chapters, each of which focuses on an aspect of the non-profit organization and its implications for the manager or leader of the enterprise: 1) the primacy of the mission of the organization; 2) strategies that enable the organization to perform effectively; 3) management practices that enhance performance; 4) how to cultivate relationships with the various constituencies connected to the organization; 5) the importance of self-development for the leader. Each chapter closes with a set of «action implications» which draw the various strands of teaching together and offer the reader a coherent summary.

One of the striking aspects of *Managing the Non-Profit Organization*, in comparison to Drucker's other books, is his interchangeable use of the terms «leader» and «manager». In his other books he seldom uses «leader» to describe the managerial role, but here the role of leader is explicitly described:

> Leadership is accountable for results. And leadership always asks, Are we really faithful stewards of the talents entrusted to us? The talents, the gifts of people — the talents, the gifts of money. Leadership is *doing*. It isn't just thinking great thoughts; it isn't just charisma; it isn't play-acting. It is doing [emphasis in the original][91].

In addition to emphasizing the leader's actions, *Managing the Non-Profit Organization* also stresses that the leader is a visible example who represents the organization and its aspirations, ethos and goals. This representative role requires a certain consonance between the public persona and private life of the leader. Because of the visibility that comes with the role, the leader is expected to live up to the expectations and standards regarding his or her behavior[92].

Managing for the Future is comprised of forty-one essays written between 1986 and 1991. Like *The New Realities*, it attempts to identify and describe the historical and cultural forces at work in the world today that are changing the world's economy, having an impact on people, management practices, and organizations. In Chapter Fifteen, «Leadership: More Doing Than Dash», Drucker offers some reflections on a proper understanding of leadership in a world that is drastically

---

[91] P. F. DRUCKER, *Managing the Non-Profit Organization*, 47.
[92] Cf. P. F. DRUCKER, *Managing the Non-Profit Organization*, 47-49.

changing[93]. As noted above, Drucker dismisses the notion of leadership qualities, traits, or charisma, seeing it as essentially a matter of performance. According to Drucker, leadership «[...] is mundane, unromantic and boring»[94]. It is work that is rooted in both the vision and goals of the organization, as well as the leader's understanding of his or her role as a responsibility, rather than rank and privilege. Such work cannot be effectively carried out unless the leader shows himself or herself to be a person of integrity and earns the trust of the followers[95].

At the close of the book, Drucker offers suggestions about skills that a leader [he uses the term executive] will need in view of the transformations taking place on all levels of society. First, he recommends «management by going outside», emphasizing the importance of an external perspective on one's organization. As noted in the discussion of *The New Realities*, the results of an organization take place outside of it, so it is crucial to have an «outside» perspective on the organization's effectiveness. Second is taking responsibility for the information needed to do the job properly, enabling the leader to identify a) what he or she is doing now, b) should be doing, and c) how to move from a to b. Similarly, the leader should focus on what specific contribution he or she can make to the organization and how to do it more effectively; in other words, prioritizing is crucial for effectiveness. Third, a leader must make ongoing learning a priority, which includes receiving feed-back that identifies strengths and weaknesses, in order to improve on strengths and minimize weaknesses. It also means development of skills and exposure to new ideas that challenge established and accepted ways of doing things[96]. The salient features of Drucker's books will now be examined through the lens of the «leader-follower-goal» grid.

---

[93] Drucker states that «[...] at some point between 1965-1973, we passed a "great divide" into the next century, leaving behind the creeds, commitments and alignments that had shaped politics for a century or two. At the most profound level, the Enlightenment faith in progress through collective action — "salvation by society", which had been the dominant force in politics since the eighteenth century — was thoroughly dashed. [...] The last such divide was crossed a century earlier, in 1873. [...] The period 1968-73 is a divide fully comparable to 1873. Whereas 1873 marked the end of *laissez-faire*, 1973 marked the end of the era in which government was the "progressive" cause, the instrument embodying the principles of the Enlightenment», P. F. DRUCKER, *Managing for the Future*, 1-3.

[94] P. F. DRUCKER, *Managing for the Future*, 119.

[95] Cf. P. F. DRUCKER, *Managing for the Future*, 120-123.

[96] Cf. P. F. DRUCKER, *Managing for the Future*, 345-351.

3.1.2 Synthesis

a) *Leader*

For Drucker, it is only in view of the mission and goals of an organization that the role and function of the leader can be adequately discussed[97]. Once these are fairly clear, the leader must focus on what he or she can contribute to the goals of the whole organization, becoming aware of the need for ongoing self-development and asking:

> What is the most important contribution I can make to the performance of this organization? [...] What self development do I need? What knowledge and skill do I have to acquire to make the contribution I should be making? What strengths do I have to put to work? What standards do I have to set myself?[98].

He emphasizes that these kinds of questions should lead to accountability and high standards on the part of the leader. Developing oneself and building on one's strengths in this way reveals a fundamental attitude of respect, not only for the individual, but for other members of the organization; it reveals the value system of the leader and integrates the leader's purpose, capacity, and achievement with the organization's needs, results, and opportunities[99]. Drucker similarly stresses that the self-development of a leader proceeds along two parallel tracks, which he identifies as improvement and change:

> One works constantly on doing a little better, identifying the little step that will make the next step possible. But it is [...] foolish to focus only on improvement and forget that the time will inevitably come to do something new and quite different. Listening for the signal that it is time to change is an essential skill for self-development[100].

The tools for achieving such improvement and change are teaching opportunities — opportunities both to act as a mentor and to receive the support and feedback of a mentor — and «keeping score» on oneself, that is, closely monitoring one's behavior «[...] to see how great the gap is between what I should have done and what I did do»[101]. Such practices

---

[97] Cf. P. F. DRUCKER, *Managing the Non-Profit Organization*, 3-49.

[98] P. F. DRUCKER, *The Effective Executive*, 68.

[99] Cf. P. F. DRUCKER, *The Effective Executive*, 168.

[100] P. F. DRUCKER, *Managing the Non-Profit Organization*, 223.

[101] P. F. DRUCKER, *Managing the Non-Profit Organization*, 224; See also pp. 200-201, in which Drucker identifies teaching, going outside the organization, and serving down in the ranks as tools for self-renewal.

help the leader to stay focused on his or her contribution to the whole and to either improve or let go of those practices that are ineffective.

Drucker also stresses that «character» is important in a leader. A fundamental question that reveals one's perception of the leader's character is, «If I had a son or a daughter, would I be willing to have him or her work under this person?»[102]. Because subordinates tend to model themselves on a strong superior, nothing is more destructive to an organization than a leader who is fundamentally corrupt:

> By themselves, character and integrity do not accomplish anything. But their absence faults everything else. Here, therefore, is the one area where weakness is a disqualification by itself rather than a limitation on performance capacity and strength[103].

Elsewhere, Drucker reinforces the emphasis on character by insisting on congruence between a leader's actions and his or her professed beliefs. Such consistency is necessary if the leader is to engender trust among the members of the organization[104]. Ultimately, to be effective, a leader must see his or her role as a responsibility rather than as a privilege. Because he or she represents the organization in a very visible way, a leader is not a private person. The leader must, therefore, set an example and live up to the expectations regarding his or her behavior[105].

b) *Followers*

In *Managing for the Future*, Drucker tersely describes the leader-follower relationship:

> The final requirement of effective leadership is to earn trust. Otherwise there won't be any followers — and the only definition of a leader is someone who has followers. [...] Trust is the conviction that the leader means what he

---

102 P. F. DRUCKER, *The Effective Executive*, 86.

103 P. F. DRUCKER, *The Effective Executive*, 87.

104 Cf. P. F. DRUCKER, *Managing for the Future*, 121-123.

105 Drucker is very strong on this point: «[...] it is a very good rule when you do anything as a leader, to ask yourself, Is that what I want to see tomorrow morning when I look into the mirror? Is that the kind of person I want to see as my leader? And if you follow that rule, you will avoid the mistakes that again and again destroy leaders: sexual looseness in an organization that preaches sexual rectitude, petty cheating, all the stupid things we do. Maybe the individual does them; well, that's his or her business. But a leader is not a private person; *a leader represents*» [emphasis added], P. F. DRUCKER, *Managing the Non-Profit Organization*, 48.

says. [...] Effective leadership [...] is not based on being clever; it is based primarily on being consistent[106].

With trust and integrity as the bedrock upon which leadership is built, Drucker, in numerous places, describes the leader-follower interaction.

In *The Effective Executive* followers are approached from the perspective of what the leader can do to capitalize on their strengths and make them more productive. Drucker repeatedly stresses that a leader must focus on the strengths of followers and not on their weaknesses. When the avoidance of weakness rather than the development of strength is emphasized, the organization ends up with mediocrity:

> The executive who is concerned with what a man cannot do rather than with what he can do, and who therefore tries to avoid weakness rather than make strength effective is a weak man himself. He probably sees strength in others as a threat to himself[107].

This is not to say that a leader should ignore a follower's weaknesses or limitations, but rather that he or she should focus on the strengths and gifts of a person and put him or her into a position where those strengths can contribute to the organization. For Drucker the focus must be on the person's performance: «Achievement must be measured against objective criteria of contribution and performance»[108].

In other works Drucker also emphasizes the importance of focusing on followers' strengths and appraising them on their performance and contribution to the goals of the organization. In discussing how to develop people he stresses, «Look always at performance, not at promise. [...] The lesson is to focus on strengths. [...] Performance is what counts»[109]. In another place he states, «Management is about human beings. Its task is to make people capable of joint performance, to make their strengths effective and their weaknesses irrelevant»[110]. In order to capitalize on the strength of followers, Drucker stresses the need for the leader to provide opportunities for followers to grow and develop, which means that training and education must be a built-in feature of an organization[111]. Similarly, because of the diversity of members in

---

106 P. F. DRUCKER, *Managing for the Future*, 122.

107 P. F. DRUCKER, *The Effective Executive*, 73.

108 P. F. DRUCKER, *The Effective Executive*, 77.

109 P. F. DRUCKER, *Managing the Non-Profit Organization*, 148-149.

110 P. F. DRUCKER, *The New Realities*, 229.

111 Cf. P. F. DRUCKER, *The New Realities*, 230.

an organization, an effective enterprise must have clear lines of communication which enable followers to clearly understand their individual responsibilities and how they interact with one another in pursuing the goals of the organization[112]. Drucker clearly emphasizes that the mission and goals of the organization determine the way in which leaders interact with and treat followers. By focusing on their strengths and performance, the organization's mission and goals are put first, and criteria for both appraisal and development are established.

c) *Goals*

In all of the writings considered here, Drucker gives goals (also called vision and mission) a central focus. In fact, it is so central that Part One of *Managing the Non-Profit Organization* is entitled, «The Mission Comes First»:

> The most common question asked me by non-profit executives is: What are the qualities of a leader? The question seems to assume that leadership is something you can learn in a charm school. [...] *the first job of the leader is to think through and define the mission of the institution* [emphasis added][113].

He identifies three essential components of a successful mission: 1) it must reflect the basic value of the institution and be built upon its strengths; 2) it must respond to an external need or opportunity; 3) it must be something believed in so that people can commit themselves to it[114].

In *Managing for the Future* he uses the image of a conductor and an orchestra to emphasize the importance of vision:

> what distinguishes a competent conductor from a great one, is to get the orchestra to hear and play that Haydn symphony in exactly the way the conductor hears it. In other words, there must be a clear vision at the top. This orchestra focus is the model for the leader of any knowledge-based organization[115].

---

112 Cf. P. F. DRUCKER, *The New Realities*, 230

113 P. F. DRUCKER, *Managing the Non-Profit Organization*, 3.

114 P. F. DRUCKER, *Managing the Non-Profit Organization*, 7.

115 P. F. DRUCKER, *Managing for the Future*, 337. In an article on leadership, Craig Lambert quotes Ronald Heifetz, a lecturer in leadership education at Harvard, who describes the problems of the conductor-orchestra analogy for leadership: «In that situation you have the written score. [...] There are conflicts over interpretation but not over direction. There's a clear line of authority: the conductor gets great authority with

In another section of the same book, he states that effective leadership is built on the ability to think through, define, and establish clearly the organization's mission[116].

In *The Effective Executive* Drucker devotes an entire chapter to the importance of focusing on what one can contribute to the organization. Instead of focusing on work, the leader focuses on the goals, or purpose, of the group and how he or she can contribute to accomplishing those goals:

> He is likely to have to think through what relationships his skills, his special-ty, his function, or his department have to the entire organization and its purpose. [...] As a result, what he does and how he does it will be materially different[117].

Such attentiveness to the larger goals of the organization is a key aspect of effective leadership and makes the leader accountable for the organization's performance.

Finally, *The New Realities* also highlights the importance of a clear mission and common vision:

> Every enterprise requires commitment to common goals and shared values. [...] The enterprise must have simple, clear, and unifying objectives. The mission of the organization has to be clear enough and big enough to provide a common vision[118].

It is the leader's task to think through, articulate, and uphold the vision so that the mission of the organization is clear and can be carried out by all the members.

d) *Conclusions*

In Chapter Fifteen of *The New Realities*, Drucker describes management as a «technology» and a «humanity», and claims that it «[...] is deeply involved in spiritual concerns — the nature of man, good and

---

regard to decisions and interpretation. It's a different situation in organizations that have to *construct* new directions and authority structures — where they have to invent the score as the music is being played. A better model would be an improvisational jazz group. [...] The musicians listen carefully to each other. Within stretches certain soloists stand out. There's latitude for surprises, and the interplay can generate inspiring moments of creativity», C. LAMBERT, «Leadership in a New Key», 32-33.

[116] Cf. P. F. DRUCKER, *Managing for the Future*, 121.

[117] P. F. DRUCKER, *The Effective Executive*, 53.

[118] P. F. DRUCKER, *The New Realities*, 229.

evil»[119]. He describes it as a liberal art because it involves the practice and application of self-knowledge, wisdom, and leadership. Thus, a leader must be able to draw upon the wisdom of the social sciences and humanities, focusing this knowledge so that it serves the vision and goals of an organization. He predicts that management, as both an academic and practical discipline, will revive and renew the «humanities»[120].

Drucker does not describe himself as such, but this review of four of his recent works on leadership places him in the transformational school of leadership theory, with his emphasis on innovation, self-development, character, integrity, communication, follower-development, mission, and vision indicating a concern not only for doing a task but for calling forth the best out of people in the process. Although he gives attention to the roles of followers and goals, his primary emphasis is on the person of the leader. Despite his positive portrayal of the process of leadership and management, however, Drucker acknowledges the hard work, drudgery, and failure that are also part of the leadership process.

3.2 Warren Bennis and Burt Nanus

3.2.1 Review of the Works

Bennis and Nanus' 1985 book, *Leaders*: The Strategies for Taking Charge [hereafter *Leaders*] is based on ninety interviews conducted with leaders of corporations and with public sector leaders. The three guiding questions for each of the interviews were: «"What are your strengths and weaknesses?" "Was there any particular experience or event in your life that influenced your management philosophy or style?" [...] "What were the major decision points in your career and how do you feel about your choices now?"»[121]. After two years of sifting through the interviews, looking for patterns, uniformities, and kernels of truth about leadership, Bennis and Nanus delineated four major themes, or behavior competencies, embodied by the ninety leaders. They then translated these four major themes into four strategies for effective leadership. The book is structured around these four strategies: 1) attention through vision; 2) meaning through communication; 3) trust through positioning; 4) deployment of self[122].

---

[119] P. F. DRUCKER, *The New Realities*, 231.

[120] Cf. P. F. DRUCKER, *The New Realities*, 231.

[121] W. BENNIS – B. NANUS, *Leaders*, 24.

[122] Cf. W. BENNIS – B. NANUS, *Leaders*, 26-27.

In 1989 Bennis published two more books on leadership, *On Becoming a Leader* and *Why Leaders Can't Lead*: The Unconscious Conspiracy Continues [hereafter *Why Leaders Can't Lead*]. *On Becoming a Leader* follows the same methodology as the book he co-authored with Nanus in 1985. Bennis describes his paradigm as leaders themselves, not theories about leaders[123]. Like the earlier book, *On Becoming a Leader* is based on a series of interviews with leaders from the world of business as well as the public sector[124]. The interviews were based on questions dealing with the following themes: qualities of leadership, life-experiences influencing development as leaders, turning points in life, the role of failure, methods for learning, influential people, and organizations as both stiflers and encouragers of leaders[125]. Among the points of convergence based on his analysis of the interviews were the conviction that leaders are made and not born; the belief that no one sets out to be a leader *per se,* but rather to fully express him- or herself; the observation that all those interviewed have been committed to a life-long process of growth and development; and the possession of a clear overarching vision or guiding purpose as characteristic of each of the persons interviewed[126]. The book is structured around a number of themes that Bennis sees as crucial for the development of leadership: the need for education; the need to «unlearn» in order to learn; the need to reflect on learning; the need to take risks; the need to make mistakes; the need for competence; and the need for mastery of the task[127].

Bennis also published *Why Leaders Can't Lead* in 1989. In this book he attempts to analyze the hidden forces in organizations and elements in

---

[123] Bennis does not identify leadership with management; in fact, he contrasts the two: «The manager administers; the leader innovates. The manager is a copy; the leader is an original. The manager maintains; the leader develops. The manager focuses on systems and structure; the leader focuses on people. The manager relies on control; the leader inspires trust. The manager has a short-range view; the leader has a long-range perspective. The manager asks how and when; the leader asks what and why. The manager has his eye always on the bottom line; the leader has his eye on the horizon. The manager imitates; the leader originates. The manager accepts the status quo; the leader challenges it. The manager is the classic good soldier; the leader is his own person. The manager does things right; the leader does the right thing», W. BENNIS, *On Becoming a Leader*, 45.

[124] For a list of the twenty-eight interviewees, see W. BENNIS, *On Becoming a Leader*, 9-11.

[125] Cf. W. BENNIS, *On Becoming a Leader*, 7.

[126] Cf. W. BENNIS, *On Becoming a Leader*, 5-6.

[127] Cf. W. BENNIS, *On Becoming a Leader*, 9.

U.S. culture that conspire against the exercise of leadership; he also describes some of the solutions to the problem. In a significant section he cites «virtues» as basic ingredients of leadership and notes that «[...] our unwillingness to tap these qualities in ourselves explains, to a large extent, the leadership shortage»[128]. The virtues he sees as crucial for effective leadership to happen are *integrity*, conduct based on standards of moral and intellectual honesty; *dedication*, the passionate belief in and commitment to something; *magnanimity*, nobility of mind and heart, closely related to humility; *openness*, willingness to try new things and to tolerate ambiguity; and *creativity*, an almost childlike willingness to move beyond the conventional, to see things afresh, from the perspective of wonder[129]. Many other themes are variations on those expressed in *Leaders* and *On Becoming a Leader*, but the emphasis is more on practical advice. For example he suggests strategies that will enable the leader to overcome both routine which saps time, energy, and creativity, and organizational inertia which threatens the best ideas and plans[130].

Nanus also published two books subsequent to his collaboration with Bennis, *The Leader's Edge*: The Seven Keys to Leadership in a Turbulent World [hereafter *The Leader's Edge*], and *Visionary Leadership*. Like Drucker's *New Realities* and *Managing for the Future*, as well as Bennis' *Why Leaders Can't Lead*, Nanus' *The Leader's Edge* identifies the forces at work in the world and the accomodations in leadership that must be made to these forces. The book is built around «seven keys», or «megaskills», that stress the competencies a leader must master to be effective in today's world: farsightedness, mastery of change, organizational design, anticipatory learning, initiative, interdependence, and integrity. In addition to these «megaskills», Nanus describes four roles that are critical for effective leadership: 1) the *direction setter* establishes a compelling vision that all in the organization will want to invest in; 2) the *change agent* is attuned to developments and able to promote necessary changes in response to them; 3) the *spokesperson* acts as both the medium and the message in communicating the ethos of an organization to those outside of it; 4) the *coach* is a team builder who is committed to the success of each person in the organization[131]. Nanus

---

[128] W. BENNIS, *Why Leaders Can't Lead*, 117.

[129] Cf. W. BENNIS, *Why Leaders Can't Lead*, 116-120.

[130] Cf. W. BENNIS, *Why Leaders Can't Lead*, xiii.

[131] Cf. B. NANUS, *The Leader's Edge*, 73-79; ID., *Visionary Leadership*, 10-15.

stresses that the ability to develop and implement a guiding vision for the organization is crucial for a leader, and he devotes his next book to an examination of vision — what it is, how it is developed, and how it is implemented.

Nanus structures *Visionary Leadership* around three aspects of vision: naming the vision, developing the vision, and finally, implementing the vision. He states his thesis in the first sentence of Chapter One: «There is no more powerful engine driving an organization toward excellence and long-range success than an attractive, worthwhile, and achievable vision of the future, widely shared»[132]. Nanus' goal is to convince readers of the crucial importance of vision for effective leadership, and to assist them in developing and articulating their own group vision.

The five books will now be examined from the perspective of what they have to say about each component of the leadership equation: leader, followers, and goal.

3.2.2 Synthesis

a) *Leader*

A central theme of *Leaders*, as well as of the two subsequent books by Bennis, is «the creative deployment of self», the fourth major behavior competency, or strategy, noted above[133]. The creative deployment of self, or the management of self, is approached from two perspectives: 1) positive self-regard and, 2) the «Wallenda Factor». According to Bennis and Nanus, positive self-regard consists of a) the recognition of one's strengths and compensation for one's weaknesses; b) the nurturing of one's skills with discipline, or systematically and continually working on and developing one's talents; and c) the capacity to discern the fit between one's skills and the job's requirements[134]. The possession of positive self-regard, according to Bennis and Nanus, is related to maturity or «emotional wisdom», and is reflected in five skills that the ninety interviewees demonstrated: 1) the ability to accept people as they are, on their own terms; 2) the capacity to approach relationships in terms of the present; 3) the consistent treatment of close associates with the same courteous attention shown to strangers; 4) the ability to trust others; and

---

132 B. NANUS, *Visionary Leadership*, 3.

133 Cf. W. BENNIS – B. NANUS, *Leaders*, 55-79, 187-214; W. BENNIS, *Why Leaders Can't Lead*, 21-22; ID., *On Becoming a Leader*, 113-142.

134 Cf. W. BENNIS – B. NANUS, *Leaders*, 58-62.

5) the ability to do without constant recognition and approval from others. Bennis and Nanus acknowledge that positive self-regard is crucial for effective leadership, but it is not clear how this is acquired[135].

Closely related to the deployment of self through positive self-regard is the deployment of self through the «Wallenda Factor», named after the famous aerialist Karl Wallenda who was known for always putting his complete energy and attention into his task. Wallenda plunged to his death in 1978 while traversing a high wire in Puerto Rico. The walk was among the most dangerous he had ever attempted, and uncharacteristically, in the months prior to this particular walk, Wallenda worried about falling and focused his energies on not falling rather than on successfully walking the high wire. For Bennis and Nanus, the lesson to be drawn from Wallenda is clear: focusing on what can go wrong almost guarantees failure. Concentrating on successfully completing the task at hand was the secret to Wallenda's success and «[...] it became increasingly clear that when Karl Wallenda poured his energies into *not falling* rather than walking the tightrope, he was virtually destined to fail»[136]. Bennis and Nanus note that the leaders interviewed were not overly concerned about potential failures, but instead spoke of learning from mistakes: «[...] for the successful leader, failure is a beginning, the springboard of hope»[137]. Positive self-regard concerns judgment about one's competence and the Wallenda Factor is focused on the positive outcome of the task. According to Bennis and Nanus, successful leadership includes a fusion of these two components of the deployment of self: positive self-regard and optimism about the desired outcome of the task must come together for successful leadership to occur[138].

In addition to self-development and the «deployment of self», both authors stress the importance of the leader's character. As noted above, Bennis cites four basic virtues — integrity, dedication, magnanimity, and open ess — as being essential for leadership[139]. Nanus also emphasizes

---

[135] Cf. W. BENNIS – B. NANUS, *Leaders*, 66-68.

[136] Bennis describes the dynamic at work when Karl Wallenda fell to his death. His wife reported that before his death, for the first time since she had known him, he had been concentrating on not falling rather than on walking the tightrope. His focus had shifted from concern for the task to fear of failure. Cf. W. BENNIS, *Why Leaders Can't Lead*, 22; W. BENNIS – B. NANUS, *Leaders*, 70.

[137] W. BENNIS – B. NANUS, *Leaders*, 71.

[138] CF. W. BENNIS – B. NANUS, *Leaders*, 79.

[139] CF. W. BENNIS, *Why Leaders Can't Lead*, 116-120.

the importance of the leader's character: «Nothing is noticed more quickly — and considered more significant — than a discrepancy between what executives preach and what they expect their associates to practice»[140]. Perhaps Bennis and Nanus' collaborative effort, *Leadership*, best expresses the importance of the leader's character and its impact on an organization:

> The leader is responsible for the set of ethics or norms that govern the behavior of people in the organization. Leaders can establish a set of ethics in several ways. One is to demonstrate by their own behavior their commitment to the set of ethics they are trying to institutionalize. [...] Leaders set the moral tone by choosing carefully the people with whom they surround themselves, by communicating a sense of purpose for the organization, by reinforcing appropriate behaviors, and by articulating these moral positions to external and internal constituencies[141].

The issue of character figures prominently in all of the authors' works. For Bennis, «Character is vital in the leader, the basis for everything else»[142]; and for Nanus, it is the basis for trust that enables leader and followers to work together effectively in pursuit of a common goal[143]. The theme of the leader's character will emerge again below in the discussion of followers.

b) *Followers*

In terms of followers, the most significant theme is that of «trust through positioning», the third of Bennis and Nanus' major themes or strategies noted above. They state, «Trust is the lubrication that makes it possible for organizations to work»[144]. This trust is established when the leader clearly, constantly, and reliably holds up the collective vision before the followers, establishing a permanent niche or position for the vision: «Through establishing the position — and, more important, staying the course — leadership establishes trust»[145]. This establishment and maintenance of trust through positioning is important for two reasons: it helps to establish and maintain organizational integrity, that

---

140 B. NANUS, *The Leader's Edge*, 102.
141 W. BENNIS – B. NANUS, *Leaders*, 186.
142 W. BENNIS, *On Becoming a Leader*, 140-141.
143 Cf. B. NANUS, *The Leader's Edge*, 101-105.
144 W. BENNIS – B. NANUS, *Leaders*, 43.
145 W. BENNIS – B. NANUS, *Leaders*, 46.

is, the identity of the group; and it provides the context and incentive for the perserverance and successful development of the organization[146]. Without the establishment of trust through positioning of the core vision, the group will lack integrity and will not be able to successfully develop as an organism. Bennis describes the basic ingredients that leaders must possess in order to generate trust as *constancy*: they are able to «stay the course»; *congruity*: they practice what they preach; *reliability*: they are ready to offer support whenever it is needed; and *integrity*: they honor their commitments and promises[147]. These four qualities in a leader, according to Bennis, engender loyalty within followers and draw them to the leader's side.

Both *Leaders* and *Why Leaders Can't Lead* discuss the effects of good leadership on followers. The key effect is identified as empowerment: effective leaders, that is, leaders who display the four basic competencies described above, «[...] empower others to translate intention into reality and sustain it»[148]. Bennis describes empowerment as the collective effect of leadership which is reflected in four basic attitudes of the followers: significance, competence, community, and enjoyment[149]. 1) Effective leadership enables people to feel that they make a difference, are vital to the goals of their organization, and are at the center of its efforts: «The difference may be small — prompt delivery of potato chips to a mom-and-pop grocery store or developing a tiny but essential part for an airplane»[150]. Effective leadership leads to empowerment which leads to feelings of meaning and significance in followers. 2) Effective leadership empowers followers to increase their levels of competence and mastery in their given areas. As noted above, the Wallenda Factor emphasizes that leaders do not focus on failures, but rather see their mistakes as opportunities for growth and improvement. This attitude is communicated to followers who are then able to learn from their mistakes, increase their competency, and better serve the organization's goals[151]. 3) Effective leadership empowers followers to feel a sense of common purpose, a

---

[146] Cf. W. BENNIS – B. NANUS, *Leaders*, 48-53.

[147] Cf. W. BENNIS, *On Becoming a Leader*, 160.

[148] W. BENNIS, *On Becoming a Leader*, 80.

[149] Cf. W. BENNIS, *On Becoming a Leader*, 80-84; ID., *Why Leaders Can't Lead*, 22-23.

[150] W. BENNIS, *Why Leaders Can't Lead*, 23.

[151] Cf. W. BENNIS – B. NANUS, *Leaders*, 83; W. BENNIS, *Why Leaders Can't Lead*, 23.

sense of belonging to a team or community. This is not to imply the existence of forced or artificial friendships, but rather that they can rely on each other in service to their common cause[152]. 4) A fourth result of the empowerment of effective leadership is the stimulation that followers feel in their work. It is seen as something challenging and even enjoyable. According to Bennis, this is a direct result of a «pull» style of leadership: «An essential ingredient in organizational leadership is pulling rather than pushing people toward a goal»[153]. A «pull» style of leadership seeks to attract and energize people to invest themselves in the organization's goal. Such investment leads to stimulation and enjoyment in their tasks.

c) *Goals*

The first two of Bennis and Nanus' strategies, attention through vision and meaning through communication, are most germane to understanding goals, or vision, as an integral aspect of the leadership equation. Attention through vision refers to leaders' ability to draw others to themselves. «[...] not just because they have a vision but because they communicate an extraordinary focus of commitment»[154]. Nanus gives a succinct description of vision: «Quite simply, *a vision is a realistic, credible, attractive future for your organization*»[155]. He observes that transforming visions have the following properties: they are appropriate for the organization and the times; they set high standards and reflect high ideals; they clarify purpose and direction; they inspire enthusiasm and commitment; they are clearly articulated and easily understood; they reflect the uniqueness of the organization; and they are ambitious[156]. The leader's commitment to a vision must be such that it captures the attention of followers and

---

[152] Cf. W. BENNIS – B. NANUS, *Leaders*, 83; W. BENNIS, *Why Leaders Can't Lead*, 23.

[153] W. BENNIS, *Why Leaders Can't Lead*, 23.

[154] W. BENNIS, *Why Leaders Can't Lead*, 19.

[155] B. NANUS, *Visionary Leadership*, 8. More than the other authors, Nanus is concerned with establishing a clear understanding of what vision is and what it is not: «While a vision is about the future, it is not a prophecy. [...] A vision is not a mission. To state that an organization has a mission is to state its purpose, not its direction. [...] A vision is not factual. It doesn't exist and may never be realized as originally imagined. [...] A vision cannot be true or false. It can be evaluated only relative to other possible directions for the organization. [...] A vision is not — or at least should not be — static, enunciated once for all time. [...] A vision is not constraint on actions, except for those inconsistent with the vision», ID., *Visionary Leadership*, 31-32.

[156] Cf. B. NANUS, *Visionary Leadership*, 28-30.

draws them into a commitment to the same vision. Bennis and Nanus observed that all of the ninety people interviewed had a vision, or agenda, and in their commitment to their vision, each showed «[...] an unparalleled concern with outcome»[157].

All five books stress that vision is crucially important for an organization because only a clear, shared sense of purpose and direction will enable the members to have a sense of their own roles in the organization and to work effectively for the overriding vision. This is especially true during times of great change and in a complex environment[158]. Although the leader of a group is the person who must articulate and uphold the vision, Bennis and Nanus point out that the vision does not necessarily originate with the leader. It is important, therefore, that the leader be a listener and pay close attention to other sources that will enable him to develop and articulate the vision. Leaders must take into consideration data from the past and present, as well as well-founded speculation about the future, and then be able to interpret the information received during this consideration[159]. An important aspect of this «taking-into-consideration» process is collaboration with other people and ideas.

Bennis and Nanus claim that all the leaders they interviewed were expert in «[...] selecting, synthesizing, and articulating an appropriate vision for the future»[160]. But they emphasize that such a skill is of little value if the vision is not communicated and institutionalized as the group's guiding principle. This can only be done by the leader's effective communication of the vision and personification of it. The articulated vision is not a once and for all proposition, but must be repeated again and again so that it forms the very ethos of the group. This points to an important principle: although the leader may be the one to articulate and legitimize the vision, it must be «owned» by the followers in order for the group to move forward toward its goal[161].

The second strategy, meaning through communication, is also important in terms of the goal or vision of the group. Bennis refers to «meaning through communication» as the «management of meaning»[162].

[157] W. BENNIS – B. NANUS, Leaders, 28.
[158] Cf. W. BENNIS – B. NANUS, Leaders, 89-94.
[159] Cf. W. BENNIS – B. NANUS, Leaders, 95-101.
[160] W. BENNIS – B. NANUS, Leaders, 101.
[161] Cf. W. BENNIS – B. NANUS, Leaders, 106-109.
[162] Cf. W. BENNIS, Why Leaders Can't Lead, 20.

He stresses three important points relative to the management of meaning: shared meanings or interpretations of reality are essential for all organizations and it is the leader's role to organize this meaning; there is no one style by which leaders shape meaning; and «meaning» is more than a matter of facts or knowledge and is more closely related to the process of creative thinking[163].

«Meaning» is closely related to what Bennis and Nanus refer to as the «social architecture» of a group or organization; the social architecture «[...] presents a shared interpretation of organizational events, so that members know how they are expected to behave. It also generates a commitment to the primary organizational values and philosophy»[164]. If such an organization is to change, then the social architecture also must be altered and it is up to the leader to articulate the new vision, develop commitment to it, and institutionalize the new meaning and direction of the group[165]. In this way the leader can be described as a «social architect» whose most important tool is his ability to manage meaning, thus ensuring that his vision not only guides the organization but that it forms the ethos of the group, fueling it in the accomplishment of its tasks and goals[166]. As noted above, Nanus considers vision to be the most powerful force in driving an organization towards success, and he devotes his latest book to exploring the nature of an organization's vision, how to develop it, and how to implement it.

d) *Conclusions*

In all of the works examined in this section, the transformational theory is foundational for the authors' approach to leadership. They state this explicitly at the close of their collaborative work, *Leaders*:

> [Leadership] is collective, there is a symbiotic relationship between leaders and followers, and what makes it collective is the subtle interplay between the followers' needs and wants and the leader's capacity to understand, one way or another, these collective aspirations. Leadership is "causative", meaning that leadership can invent and create institutions that can empower employees to satisfy their needs. Leadership is morally purposeful and elevating, which means [...] that leaders can, through deploying their talents,

---

163 Cf. W. BENNIS – B. NANUS, *Leaders*, 38-41.

164 W. BENNIS – B. NANUS, *Leaders*, 112. For a description of types of social architecture, or distinct organizational types, see *Leaders*, 118-130.

165 Cf. W. BENNIS – B. NANUS, *Leaders*, 139-145.

166 Cf. W. BENNIS, *Why Leaders Can't Lead*, 155.

choose purposes and visions that are based on the key values of the work force and create the social architecture that supports them. Finally, leadership can move followers to higher degrees of consciousness, such as liberty, freedom, justice, and self-actualization[167].

Bennis and Nanus thus express an understanding of leadership that seeks to move followers and leader beyond a *quid pro quo* approach by engaging one another in such a way that they not only share in the same vision and goals, but are transformed in the process of pursuing them.

3.3 *James M. Kouzes and Barry Z. Posner*

3.3.1 Review of the Works

Kouzes and Posner have written two popular books on leadership, *The Leadership Challenge*: How to Get Extraordinary Things Done in Organizations [hereafter *The Leadership Challenge*] and *Credibility*: How Leaders Gain and Lose It, Why People Demand It [hereafter *Credibility*]. Their first book, *The Leadership Challenge*, is based on research into the experiences of more than five-hundred middle- and senior-level managers in both private and public-sector organizations. Their goal was to discover what leaders did when they did their «personal best» at leading others. From their analysis of «personal best» cases, they were able to develop a model of concrete leadership practices which they then tested by asking more than 3,000 managers and subordinates to assess the extent to which the above-mentioned middle and senior-level managers actually employed these practices[168].

Kouzes and Posner uncovered five leadership practices in their analysis[169]. They found that, at their «personal best», leaders 1) *challenged the process*: recognized and supported good ideas even to the extent of challenging established systems and procedures in order to implement the ideas; 2) *inspired a shared vision*: saw a clear mission, goal or purpose which drew them forward and invited/inspired others to want to share in the same mission or vision; 3) *enabled others to act*: involved others in

---

167 W. BENNIS – B. NANUS, *Leaders*, 217-218.

168 Cf. W. BENNIS – B. NANUS, *The Leadership Challenge*, xx-xxi. For a list of the survey questions, see Appendix A; and for the model of leadership practices («Leadership Practices Inventory») see Appendix B, J. M. KOUZES – B. Z. POSNER, *The Leadership Challenge*, 303-308.309-322.

169 For a brief description of the five leadership practices, see J. M. KOUZES – B. Z. POSNER, *The Leadership Challenge*, 7-13.

the project by encouraging collaboration and team-work[170]; 4) *modeled the way*: were clear about their business beliefs and tried to show by their behavior that they lived these values; in other words, they practiced what they preached; 5) *encouraged the heart*: through genuine acts of caring, leaders gave people the needed encouragement to carry on their work.

Kouzes and Posner also discovered ten behavioral commitments[171] that went along with the leadership practices: 1) in challenging the process, leaders a) *search for opportunities*, and b) *experiment and take risks*; 2) in inspiring a shared vision, leaders a) *envision the future*, and b) *enlist others in the vision*; 3) in enabling others to act, leaders a) *foster collaboration*, and b) *strengthen others for the task*; 4) in modeling the way, leaders a) *set an example*, and b) *plan small wins;* 5) in encouraging the heart, leaders a) *recognize contributions*, and b) *celebrate accomplishments*. Most of the book explores and elaborates upon each of these behavioral commitments through examples from their research and anecdotes from their interviews.

In their survey of three-thousand managers and subordinates, Kouzes and Posner found that followers most admired leaders who are honest, competent, forward-looking, and inspiring. Taken together, Kouzes and Posner claim that these four characteristics «[...] comprise what communications experts refer to as "credibility"»[172]. Credibility, according to the authors, is such an important dimension of leadership that they devoted their entire next book to the subject[173]. *Credibility* is the result

---

170 Cf. J. M. KOUZES – B. Z. POSNER, *The Leadership Challenge*, 10-11; Kouzes and Pozner observe that in 91% of the cases they analyzed, leaders were enthusiastic about the importance of collaboration; in addition, their data on others' perceptions of leaders revealed that this is the most significant of all the five practices. Cf. ID., *The Leadership Challenge*, 10.

171 For a brief description of the ten behavioral commitments, see J. M. KOUZES – B. Z. POSNER, *The Leadership Challenge*, 14.279-280. The book is actually structured around the five leadership practices and ten behavioral commitments: each leadership practice forms a section which is then subdivided into two behavioral commitments. As illustrated in pp. 29-78, for example, the first practice, Challenging the Process, forms Part Two, and is subdivided into two chapters, Chapter Three, «Search for Opportunities», and Chapter Four, «Experiment and Take Risks».

172 J. M. KOUZES – B. Z. POSNER, *The Leadership Challenge*, 21.

173 Kouzes and Posner claim, «It is this credibility that establishes the foundation upon which dreams for the future can be built». They also see credibility as an important factor in distinguishing leaders from managers: «If there is a clear distinction between the process of managing and the process of leading, it is in the distinction between getting others to do and getting others to want to do. Managers, we believe, get other people to

of a study of leadership from the constituent's perspective[174]. Based on a
survey of more than fifteen-thousand people, more than four-hundred
written case studies, and forty in-depth interviews with managers, *Credibility* seeks to identify and describe the specific actions that give leaders
credibility[175]. From the data collected, Kouzes and Posner developed a
framework to describe the actions that effective leaders take in order to
build a productive leader-constituent relationship. The results of their
survey were strikingly similar to the results of the survey of three thousand managers and subordinates reported in *The Leadership Challenge*:
constituents apparently admire and look for leaders who are honest,
forward-looking, inspiring, and competent. In other words, constituents
admire credible leaders. Although there have been slight fluctuations in
emphasis, for over a decade these four characteristics have remained
remarkably stable in the responses to Kouzes and Posner's surveys[176].

The authors observe that although credibility is mostly a matter of
consistency between words and deeds, such congruence must be understood in a wider, collective context when applied to leadership:

> When you do what you say, it may make you credible, but it may not make
> you a credible leader. Your constituents also have needs and interests,
> values and visions. To earn and strengthen leadership credibility, leaders

---

do, but leaders get other people to want to do. Leaders do this by first of all being
credible. That is the foundation of their leadership. They establish this credibility by their
actions — by challenging, inspiring, enabling, modeling, and encouraging»,
J. M. KOUZES – B. Z. POSNER, *The Leadership Challenge*, 26-27.

174 Kouzes and Posner observe that the term *follower* seems much too passive for
the times in which we live. Instead, they opt for the term *constituent*: «We use the word
constituent throughout this book because in this age of empowerment and self-direction
we believe it provides a much more accurate description than either *follower* or
employee. A constituent is someone who has an active part in the process of running an
organization and who authorizes another to act on his or her behalf. A constituent confers
authority on the leader, not the other way around. Constituents can be employees, but
they can also be customers, shareholders, suppliers, other business partners, and
citizens», J. M. KOUZES – B. Z. POSNER, *Credibility*, xix.

175 For a description of the methodology they employed, see J. M. KOUZES –
B. Z. POSNER, *Credibility*, xxi, 11-13; See also, «Appendix; Studies on the Impact of
Credibility and What Constitutes Credible Behavior», pp. 275-287.

176 Kouzes and Posner point out that both the quality of being forward-looking and
of being inspiring have increased in importance while competence has been given less
value than in the past. They stress that this deemphasizing of competence is troublesome
because the increasing complexity of organizations demands competent leaders. For a
comparison of the 1987 and 1993 surveys on the characteristics of admired leaders, see
J. M. KOUZES – B. Z. POSNER, *Credibility*, 13-21.

must do what *we* say *we* will do. [...] That *We* is crucial to leadership credibility. Certainly leaders are expected to do what they say. They are expected to keep their promises and follow through on their commitments. But what they say must also be what we, the constituents, believe. To take people to places they have never been before, leaders and constituents must be on the same path [emphasis in the original][177].

In this wider, collective context Kouzes and Posner describe a process of strengthening credibility through three phases which they describe as clarity, unity, and intensity. Clarification of the needs, interests, values, visions, aims, and aspirations of the leader and constituents is the beginning of strengthening credibility. To create a strong organization people must be united in their purpose, motives, and principles. The leader and constituents build a community of shared vision and values, the sharing and support of which lead to unity. The authors describe intensity as almost a moral dimension which includes taking the principles of the organization seriously and making them the basis of organizational resource allocation. In other words, «[...] people who feel strongly about the worth of values will act on them»[178].

In the analysis of common themes in their research on credibility, Kouzes and Posner identified six practices that they call the disciplines of credibility, described as 1) *discovering yourself*: the leader must have a clear sense of his or her guiding values and principles, a realistic assessment of his or her competence, and the self-confidence to meet the challenges; 2) *appreciating constituents*: the leader must know the collective values and desires of his or her constituents which can only come about as the result of engaging with them in a dialogical relationship; 3) *affirming shared values*: the leader must find the common ground, a core of shared values, upon which the diversity of constituents can stand together in a community; 4) *developing capacity*: the leader must be an educator who is concerned with providing resources and opportunities for constituents to build their knowledge and skills; 5) *serving a purpose*: leaders must set an example by investing the bulk of their time and energy on core values, holding themselves accountable to the same standards as everyone else; 6) *sustaining hope*: by supporting, understanding, and rewarding constituents, leaders help to engender enthusiasm

---

177 J. M. KOUZES – B. Z. POSNER, *Credibility*, 47-48.
178 J. M. KOUZES – B. Z. POSNER, *Credibility*, 49; For a more complete description of «clarity, unity, and intensity», see pp. 48-49.

and commitment to the shared goals of the group[179]. Based on the authors' data and illustrative anecdotes from their interviews, the six disciplines of credibility are explored in detail, each one the subject of a chapter of the book. As with the previous authors, Kouzes and Posner's works will be explored using the leader-followers-goals framework, in order to identify salient themes regarding the process of leadership.

3.3.2 Synthesis

a) *Leader*

Kouzes and Posner place strong emphasis on the person of the leader, emphasizing the qualities and practices necessary for effective leadership. For example, in *The Leadership Challenge*, the five leadership practices and ten behavioral commitments stress the initiative of the leader: the leader *challenges* by experimenting and taking risks, *inspires* by envisioning the future and enlisting the help of others, *enables* by fostering collaboration and strengthening the competency of others, *models* by setting the example and planning small wins, and *encourages* by recognizing individual contributions and celebrating accomplishments. Similarly, *Credibility* puts great stress on the person of the leader. In order to maintain credibility, which the authors see as foundational for effective leadership, the leader must engage in the six disciplines described above. Again, the stress is on the leader's initiative: the discovery of self, appreciation of constituents, affirmation of shared values, development of capacity, service of a purpose, and sustenance of hope are all activities which begin with the leader.

Central to Kouzes and Posner's understanding of leadership is that it is something that can be learned[180]:

> Myth has it that leadership is a function of position. Nonsense. Leadership is a set of skills and practices that can be learned regardless of whether or not one is in a formal management position. Leadership is to be found in those in the boiler room and those in the board room. It is not conferred by title or degree. In fact, often those responsible for the smooth and successful operation of organizations [...] have neither[181].

---

[179] For a more detailed description of the six disciplines, see J. M. KOUZES – B. Z. POSNER, *Credibility*, 51-57.

[180] For a discussion of the merits of the theory that leaders are born versus the theory that leaders are made, see J. M. KOUZES – B. Z. POSNER, *The Leadership Challenge*, 290-298.

[181] J. M. KOUZES – B. Z. POSNER, *Credibility*, 156.

Although acknowledging that because of certain psychological and physiological characteristics, as well as familial or sociological circumstances, some people have greater aptitude for leadership than others, the authors cite psychological research to assert that «[...] there is no perfect predictor of leadership»[182]. Because leadership is a complex set of traits and behaviors that are not reducible to one psychological measure, reducing leadership to a non-learnable set of character traits creates a self-fulfilling prophecy that impedes the development of leadership[183].

Rather than approaching leadership as a nonlearnable set of traits, Kouzes and Posner see it as a learnable art whose point of departure is the self:

> Leadership is an art, a performing art. And in the art of leadership, the artist's instrument is the self. The mastery of the art of leadership comes with the mastery of the self. Ultimately, leadership development is the art of self-development[184].

Both books stress the development of the self in order to become a leader. The five practices, the ten commitments, the six disciplines — all are attempts to strengthen and develop various facets of the individual so that he or she can be a more effective leader. This emphasis on the person of the leader, however, is not the only aspect of leadership development. As the next section will show, Kouzes and Posner also put great emphasis on the perspective of the follower, or constituent, in their articulation of the process of leadership.

b) *Followers*

In *The Leadership Challenge* Kouzes and Posner attempt to give a balanced portrait of leadership, not only by studying leaders themselves, but by investigating the expectations that followers have of leaders. As noted above, followers most admired leaders who were honest, competent, forward-looking, and inspiring. It was further noted that these characteristics, taken together, comprise credibility[185]. *Credibility* builds on the previous book, but is different in that it approaches leadership

---

182 J. M. KOUZES – B. Z. POSNER, *The Leadership Challenge*, 293.

183 Cf. J. M. KOUZES – B. Z. POSNER, *The Leadership Challenge*, 297.

184 J. M. KOUZES – B. Z. POSNER, *The Leadership Challenge*, 298.

185 For a discussion of what followers expect of their leaders, see J. M. KOUZES – B. Z. POSNER, *The Leadership Challenge*, 15-27.

completely from the perspective of the follower, or to use the authors' preferred term, the constituent[186].

Kouzes and Posner's research led them to the conclusion, «Leadership is a reciprocal relationship between those who choose to lead and those who decide to follow»[187], and that the concrete behaviors of leaders has a profound impact on the trust and loyalty of constituents to both the leader and the organization:

> Leadership acts [...] and the reception of those acts are inseparable. Constituents most often experience their needs being met or not met at the moment of the encounter. They are not engineered into a tangible good and delivered in a package whole to the constituent. What the constituent experiences is an interaction. [...] Leadership is a relationship, one between constituent and leader that is based on mutual needs and interests[188].

In analyzing over four-hundred case studies, the authors discovered ten words that were commonly used by people to describe how they felt when working with leaders they admired: valued, motivated, enthusiastic, challenged, inspired, capable, supported, powerful, respected, and proud. They point out that this evidence is supported by other organizational research, leading to significant conclusions: admired leaders are not self-centered but place others in the center; give attention to others rather than seek it for themselves; try to respond to the needs and desires of constituents instead of seeking to satisfy their own desires; concentrate on their constituents, not on themselves[189]. When asked to give specific examples of what admired leaders actually did to gain constituents' trust and respect, the constituents' responses closely corresponded with how they felt when working with leaders they admired.

Kouzes and Posner concluded that credibility, respect, and loyalty are earned by leaders through actions that display leaders' belief in the intrinsic self-worth of others: by showing appreciation; by affirming and developing others; and by acting in ways that show trust in others. Credibility, respect, and loyalty are also earned by behavior that corresponds with declared values; by persistence in the face of adversity; by admitting

---

[186] For a discussion of the evolution of Kouzes' and Posner's interest in credibility as growing out of their realization that leadership is reciprocal in nature, and that it depends in a large part on how it is perceived by the beholder, or constituent, see J. M. KOUZES – B. Z. POSNER, *Credibility*, 275-277.

[187] J. M. KOUZES – B. Z. POSNER, *Credibility*, 1.

[188] J. M. KOUZES – B. Z. POSNER, *Credibility*, 11.

[189] Cf. J. M. KOUZES – B. Z. POSNER, *Credibility*, 30-31.275-287.

mistakes when wrong; and by optimism and enthusiasm. From the followers', or constituents', perspectives the authors developed their six disciplines of credibility[190], emphasizing the relational nature of leadership and the importance of the follower in influencing the nature of the relationship and the concrete practice of leadership.

c) Goals

The Leadership Challenge identifies one of the five basic leadership practices as inspiring a shared vision. Associated with this practice are two behavioral commitments: envisioning the future and enlisting others. Kouzes and Posner define vision as «[...] an ideal and unique image of the future»[191]. According to the authors, a vision has four attributes described as 1) *future orientation*: leaders must be concerned with the future and have the imagination to be able to project themselves forward in time; 2) *image*: visions are conceptualizations, mental pictures, that become real as they are expressed more concretely; 3) *ideal*: visions are concerned about possibilities and represent the choice of an ideal that practical actions will attempt to attain; 4) *uniqueness*: visions set a person or group apart and proclaim what is different and unique about them[192].

The Leadership Challenge describes the process of developing a common vision: in order to enlist others to share in a vision, leaders must appeal to a common purpose, communicate expressively, and sincerely believe what they are saying[193]. In order for this process to unfold successfully, the authors stress that leaders must have a deep knowledge of their constituents; they must know what motivates them, in order to show them how their values will be served by the vision[194].

In *Credibility*, the authors devote a chapter to the discipline of serving a purpose. In the words of Robert Greenleaf, «The great leader is seen as servant first, and that simple fact is the key to [the leader's] greatness»[195]. In order to be credible the leader is to become the servant of both his or her constituents and the vision they share in common. The

---

190 Cf. J. M. KOUZES – B. Z. POSNER, *Credibility*, 51

191 J. M. KOUZES – B. Z. POSNER, *The Leadership Challenge*, 85.

192 Cf. J. M. KOUZES – B. Z. POSNER, *The Leadership Challenge*, 83-92.

193 Cf. J. M. KOUZES – B. Z. POSNER, *The Leadership Challenge*, 113-125.

194 Cf. J. M. KOUZES – B. Z. POSNER, *The Leadership Challenge*, 125.

195 R. GREENLEAF, *Servant Leadership*, 7, quoted in J. M. KOUZES – B. Z. POSNER, *Credibility*, 185.

emphasis here is not so much on the vision but on the leader as a servant of the common vision:

> They put the guiding principles of the organization ahead of all else and then strive to live by them. They are the first to do what has been agreed upon. In serving a purpose, leaders strengthen credibility by demonstrating that they are not in it for themselves; [...] Being a servant may not be what many leaders had in mind when they chose to take responsibility for the vision and direction of their organization or team, but serving others is the most glorious and rewarding of all leadership tasks[196].

In affirming the vision of the group, leaders are essentially promising that their behavior will be consistent with the shared values of the group and at the service of the vision they share in common.

d) *Conclusions*

Kouzes and Posner are clearly in the Transformational Theory school of leadership[197]. Their stress on relationships, close personal attention, shared values, shared vision, and the importance of constituents as partners rather than subordinates, move them away from the traditional understanding of leadership which stresses a boss-follower relationship. Their conviction is that, in the complex process of pursuing their common vision, leaders and constituents will be transformed and grow in their humanity.

4. Synthesis, Critique, and Conclusion

In the previous section three different sets of authors were examined from the perspective of «leader-followers-goal» in order to identify and synthesize their understandings of leadership. In this section a final synthesis will yield a general picture of how leadership is popularly understood in the U.S. today. This will be followed by a brief critique and some general conclusions.

---

[196] J. M. KOUZES – B. Z. POSNER, *Credibility*, 185.

[197] Cf. J. M. KOUZES – B. Z. POSNER, *The Leadership Challenge*, 281: «Bernard M. Bass of the State University of New York investigated the nature and effect of two types of leaders: *transactional* and *transformational*. In terms of practices, his transformational leader closely resembles the leader we describe in this book, inspiring others to excel, giving individual consideration to others, and stimulating people to think in new ways».

4.1 *Synthesis*

4.1.1 Leader

All of the authors put heavy emphasis on the person of the leader and suggest ways to make the leader more effective: Drucker describes five practices; Bennis and Nanus offer four strategies; and Kouzes and Posner outline five practices, ten commitments, and six disciplines. The self-development of the leader is a central theme in all the works. Drucker stresses the importance of building on one's strengths and developing one's skills for maximum effectiveness. For Drucker, the leader must confront the key question of what he or she needs to do in order to best contribute to the goals of the organization. How the leader answers that question will determine what he or she needs to do in order to improve or change. Bennis and Nanus nuance the concept of self-development and call it effective self-deployment. They point out that such self-deployment includes positive self-regard and optimism about the successful outcome of tasks and undertakings. Effective self-deployment requires maximizing one's strengths and compensating for one's weaknesses, disciplined development of skills, and the capacity to match one's skills with a potential task. Similarly, Kouzes and Posner stress the importance of self-development. They liken leadership to an art and say that the instrument for this art is the self: «The mastery of the art of leadership comes with the mastery of the self»[198]. Their five practices, ten commitments, and six disciplines are all tools to foster the leader's self development.

All of the works considered also stress the importance of the leader's character. Bennis and Nanus name four virtues — integrity, dedication, magnanimity, and openness — as essential for the practice of leadership. Bennis stresses that character is the *sine qua non* for effective leadership, the foundation for everything else. Similarly, Kouzes and Posner list the four qualities that followers most admire in leaders: honesty, competence, the ability to look forward, and the ability to inspire. Taken together, these qualities comprise credibility. In other words, followers expect the leader to display consistency between words and deeds, between behavior and declared values; he or she is to be a model and example for followers. Kouzes and Posner's six disciplines express qualities that are expected in a leader: he or she is to be a person who practices the discipline of self-knowledge, appreciates followers, affirms

---

[198] J. M. KOUZES – B. Z. POSNER, *The Leadership Challenge*, 298.

shared values, develops in capacity, serves the larger purpose, and sustains hope. Drucker, too, insists on the importance of the leader's character and stresses that leadership is not a rank or privilege, but a responsibility that holds the leader accountable to his or her organization. Such accountability shows not only self-respect, but respect for followers. For Drucker, the character of the leader is of utmost importance because of the impact that he or she has on subordinates.

4.1.2 Followers

All of the authors stressed that leadership consists in a relationship between leaders and followers and that for this relationship to be effective it must be characterized by trust. Bennis and Nanus suggest that trust can be established only when the leader clearly, constantly, and reliably holds up the collective vision before the followers, establishing a permanent niche or position for the vision. This trust through positioning helps to establish and maintain organizational integrity, and provides the context and incentive for the successful development of the organization.

For Drucker the performance of followers must be a central concern of leaders. He stresses that leaders are to focus on the strengths of followers, not on weaknesses, in order to help followers improve their performance. Drucker suggests objective criteria for judging the performance of followers as well as for promotions, etc. It is the duty of the leader to create opportunities and encourage followers to grow and develop their skills. It is also up to the leader, in the face of followers' diversity, to establish clear lines of communication so that all have clarity about the goals of the organization and their own role within the larger whole. Bennis and Nanus describe the effects of good leadership on followers as empowerment. Empowerment, in turn, leads to feelings of significance, competence, community, and enjoyment on the part of the followers. Bennis and Nanus also suggest that a «pull» style of leadership is much more effective than a «push» style. This means that the leader stands as an example and attracts followers to invest themselves in the goals and mission of the organization.

Kouzes and Posner most specifically emphasized the role of followers in the leadership process: «Followers determine whether someone possesses leadership qualities. [...] Leadership is in the eye of the follower»[199]. As noted above, they devoted a chapter of one book and then an entire

---

[199] J. M. KOUZES – B. Z. POSNER, *The Leadership Challenge*, 15.

volume to approaching leadership from the perspective of the followers. Perhaps more than the other authors, Kouzes and Posner stressed the reciprocity of the leader-follower relationship, stating that leadership is an interaction, a relationship between leader and followers, and describing qualities that followers admired in leaders: other-centeredness, attentiveness to others, responsiveness to others' needs, ability to look beyond themselves, and focus on their followers (constituents). In this way, leaders earn credibility and the loyalty of their constituents, thus deepening their commitment to the goals of the organization.

4.1.3 Goals

All of the authors place a heavy emphasis on the importance of vision for the life of any organization and stress that the leader has a unique role to play in developing and articulating the vision. Sometimes the terms «vision», «mission», and «goals» are used interchangeably to express the same reality, although, as noted above, Nanus is more precise in his use of the term. For Drucker, the vision, or mission, is primary and must reflect the values of an organization, express its strengths, respond to a real need, and be communicated clearly so that people can commit to it. He stresses that the larger vision is the key to the relationship between leader and followers which he likens to the relationship between a conductor and an orchestra. Just as it is the conductor's role to get the orchestra to play the score as the conductor hears it, so it is the leader's role to get an organization to perform according to its guiding vision, as the leader interprets and articulates it. Similarly, Bennis and Nanus stress the importance of attention through vision but they make it clear that, although the leader must uphold the vision for all to see and communicate its meaning, the vision itself does not necessarily originate in the leader. It may, rather, be rooted in many sources, including the followers, but the leader must make it his own in order to be able to communicate it effectively. Kouzes and Posner include vision in one of their five basic practices: a leader inspires a shared vision by envisioning the future and enlisting others to take ownership of it. In fact, their research found that this was seen by leaders as the most difficult of their five practices[200]. For Kouzes and Posner, vision is a future-oriented, concrete image that expresses both the ideals and the uniqueness of an organization. For Bennis, the vision shapes what he calls the social

---

[200] Cf. J. M. KOUZES – B. Z. POSNER, *The Leadership Challenge*, 109.

architecture of an organization; it is the role of the leader to express this vision or «meaning» and to generate commitment to it. Both Drucker and Bennis observe that vision must govern the behavior and relationships of members of an organization if the organization is to effectively accomplish its goals. This conviction is also the basis of Nanus' book, *Visionary Leadership*.

All of the authors also stressed that the vision must be held in common, despite its particular origin. Kouzes and Posner see one of the leader's tasks as enlisting others to invest in the larger vision, which they do by appealing to a common purpose, communicating expressively, and sincerely believing what they are saying. The leader's credibility is thus important in both the effective communication of the vision and enlisting others to share in the vision. For Drucker, the vision, or mission, is the key to the relationships among members of the organization. Bennis and Nanus also stress the necessity of common ownership of the vision if the organization is to successfully achieve its goals. But Nanus offers a detailed description of the various roles a leader must play in order to mobilize followers to invest themselves in a vision and take ownership of it[201]; for Nanus, vision is the key to leadership.

4.2 *Critique*

In his analysis of secular and religious literature on leadership, Love correctly contends that the various writers tend to construct a kind of «phantom» leader to whom it is impossible to relate[202]. The emphasis is always on positive traits or strengths — and the importance of developing and building on one's strengths. Drucker's five habits, Bennis' and Nanus' four strategies, or leadership competencies, Kouzes and Posner's five practices, ten commitments, and six disciplines — all focus on the leader and the bewildering array of qualities or skills he or she should have. One can easily become lost in the jungle of prescriptive qualities, practices, and strategies that are offered. Love observes that in focusing on these qualities that a leader should have, the authors are implicitly taking a «traits» approach to leadership[203]:

---

[201] For a description of the four basic roles a visionary leader must play — direction-setter, change agent, spokesperson, and coach — see B. NANUS, *Visionary Leadership*, 10-15.

[202] Cf. J. R. LOVE, *Liberating Leaders from the Superman Syndrome*, 138.

[203] Cf. J. R. LOVE, *Liberating Leaders from the Superman Syndrome*, 138.

There is far too much material concerning what "a leader *should do* [...] " in their books. The leader who is reading such material is forced into either the role of: 1) "superman", and actually *can* do everything the writers suggest for leaders, or he is 2) "ego-man", and cannot do it, but really believes he can or is doing it all, or 3) he is "mediocre-man", feeling himself slowly submerging, deeper and deeper under the "billowing sea" of his own inadequacy. The first individual simply does not exist[204] [emphasis in original].

Although the practices, habits, commitments, and disciplines that the authors describe can be very helpful in the exercise of leadership, a more realistic approach would have balanced the positive traits-emphasis with a clearer acknowledgement of the reality of the leader's personal limitations, and ways of dealing with them.

Related to this over-emphasis on positive traits, is the motivational flavor of the literature and the somewhat glib manner in which the authors describe leadership development. This is not to fault their research but rather to suggest that it is applied in a rather prescriptive manner. It is almost as if the authors are saying, «If you have these five habits, or if you implement these four strategies, or if you engage in these five practices with their ten commitments, or if you learn these six disciplines — you will be an effective leader». A representative example of this tendency is found in Bennis and Nanus' *Leaders:*

Leadership seems to be a marshalling of skills possessed by a majority but used by a minority. But it's something that can be learned by anyone, taught to everyone, denied to no one[205].

Similarly, the authors are sometimes given to facile explanations and distinctions, such as Bennis' list contrasting leaders and managers, noted above. After reading through the list, one is still uncertain as to what is the difference between a leader and a manager. Nanus also contrasts leaders and managers: «If managers are known for their skills in solving problems, then leaders are known for being masters in designing and building institutions; they are the architects of the organization's future»[206]. Again, such a statement does little to shed light on the difference between leaders and managers.

In another criticism of the literature on leadership, Love observes that very seldom are the leader's limitations or weaknesses addressed in more

---

204 J. R. LOVE, *Liberating Leaders from the Superman Syndrome*, 139.
205 W. BENNIS – B. NANUS, *Leadership*, 27.
206 B. NANUS, *The Leader's Edge*, 7.

than an oblique way[207]. This has certainly been the case with the literature reviewed in this chapter. In most cases, limitations are only mentioned in passing, but very little effort is made to examine what a leader must do in order to confront, acknowledge, and grow beyond or compensate for his or her limitations. In many ways the leaders they describe seem «larger than life», or «supermen», and when limitations are mentioned they usually refer to subordinates or followers, and how the leader can minimize weaknesses by capitalizing on the followers' strengths. But little attention is given to the weaknesses or potential limitations of leaders.

In addition to the overemphasis on the positive qualities of the leader, the authors studied in this chapter approach the topic of leadership primarily from the perspective of business and management. (This approach certainly seems to reflect a U.S. bias; the majority of books on leadership are to be found in the business section of most bookstores.) For example, Bennis and Nanus' *Leaders* is centered on «[...] a series of ninety interviews, [...] sixty with successful CEO's, all corporate presidents or chairmen of boards, and thirty with outstanding leaders from the public sector»[208]. In *On Becoming a Leader*, Bennis claims that U.S. culture is dominated and shaped by business; thus almost a third of the interviewees in the book are business leaders[209]. Similarly, Drucker's books are focused on business management, with the exception of *Managing the Non-Profit Organization*, which still approaches the question of leadership from a business management perspective[210]. Both of the books by Kouzes and Posner also take a management approach to leadership[211].

---

[207] Cf. J. R. LOVE, *Liberating Leaders from the Superman Syndrome*, 143.

[208] W. BENNIS – B. NANUS, *Leaders*, 20. The public sector leaders included university presidents, heads of government agencies, coaches, orchestra conductors, and public-interest leaders. Cf. ID., *Leaders*, 24-25.

[209] Cf. W. BENNIS, *On Becoming a Leader*, 4-11. He also includes figures from the arts, the media, nonprofit enterprises, government, and the academy.

[210] For example, Drucker states, «In this part [Part Two] we talk about the strategies that convert the plan into results. How do we get our service to the "customer" that is, to the community we exist to serve? How do we market it? And how do we get the money we need to provide the service?», P. F. DRUCKER, *Managing the Non-Profit Organization*, 53.

[211] Kouzes and Posner state, «Since aspiring or working managers are the professionals with whom we interact most often, and since they are the ones who have supported us most in our research and professional practices, the majority of examples cited in this book are from managerial leadership cases», J. M. KOUZES – B. Z. POSNER, *Credibility*, xxi-xxii. Cf. ID., *The Leadership Challenge*, 16.

Most of the anecdotes and examples in the books come from the business world, with a sprinkling of stories from other areas such as governmental and public service organizations.

Finally, because of the focus on characteristics and behaviors of the leader, very little was said about the followers. Kouzes and Posner's works notwithstanding. When followers are featured, it is primarily to obtain their impressions of leaders; the focus is on the qualities of the leaders, not the followers. Perhaps this is the nature of leadership studies. But it would be valuable to focus on the followers as followers: do they have peculiar characteristics or sets of behaviors? How do they influence leaders? What is it that makes them followers and/or prevents them from becoming leaders? Such a focus would help to balance current leadership studies and begin to compensate for the dearth of attention paid to followers.

4.3 *Conclusion*

This chapter began with a review of leadership theory and demonstrated that there has been an evolution in the understanding of leadership: researchers have progressed from a traits approach, to a functional, or behavioral approach, to a situational approach, and finally to what has come to be identified as the transformational approach. As noted in the review, the transformational approach is not a radical departure from what went before it, but rather a natural outgrowth of the previous approaches. The process of leadership has come to be seen as a combination of personal traits, behaviors, situations, and transactions between leader and followers. But whereas the previous approaches emphasized one or another aspect of the leadership process, the tranformational approach includes all aspects of the process: transformational leadership seeks to engage both leaders and followers in common pursuit of a goal, in such a way that they are transformed in the process, that is, in such a way that their higher human needs for esteem and self-actualization are addressed. As noted above, Hackman and Johnson have identified the characteristics of transformational leaders as creative, interactive, visionary, empowering, and passionate[212]. The appeal of transformational theory lies in its emphasis on the leader's going beyond the ordinary, and engaging the followers' higher needs and motivations in order to bring about a change in thinking that will translate into a change

---

212 Cf. M. Z. HACKMAN – C. E. JOHNSON, *Leadership*, 63-65.

of behavior as both leader and followers pursue the articulated goal. Transformational theory is currently the popular leadership theory in the U.S., and the authors examined in this chapter represent the transformational school of thought.

As stated above, the goal of this chapter is not to arrive at a definition of leadership, but rather to review some popular works on leadership by selected U.S. authors in order to arrive at some general conclusions about how leadership is generally understood in U.S. culture today. To this end, selected works of five authors, Peter Drucker, Warren Bennis and Burt Nanus, and James M. Kouzes and Barry Z. Posner, were reviewed and analyzed, using a grid suggested by Garry Wills' comment on the tripartite nature of leadership[213]. Three questions were asked of the literature: What does it say about the person of the leader? What does it say about followers? and What does it say about goals? The goal was to synthesize their writings according to the three-part grid. Finally, after separately synthesizing the works of the three sets of authors, a general synthesis of their works was attempted above. From this, some conclusions can now be made about leadership as it is popularly understood in the culture of the United States.

First, as the research of this chapter indicates, leadership is a complex process composed of certain variables, including the leader, followers, goal or vision, and the situation in which this relationship unfolds. The literature examined suggests that the leader must be a person of high character, or integrity, whose public persona and demonstrated behavior are congruent and who can act as an example for the followers. Additionally, the literature suggests that the leader, to be truly effective, must be committed to self-development in order to hone his or her intellect and skills for better service to the larger whole or organization. The literature also makes clear that the relationship between leader and followers is not so much one of being «over against», as «along with». In other words, the leader serves the well-being of the followers and acts to encourage them in their own self-development; it clearly is not merely a *quid pro quo* relationship. As described by the authors examined in this chapter, the relationship of the leader to followers can be expressed as one of service. The leader serves the needs of the followers, and the

---

[213] Although the three-part structure was suggested by Wills' comment on leadership, as noted above, the attempt at a synthetic analysis of various works was suggested by the methodology used in the work of J. R. LOVE, *Liberating Leaders from the Superman Syndrome*.

larger common vision, by encouraging and empowering followers in their self development and skills. Such a relationship entails the building of trust, which is contingent on the credibility of the leader. All of this is contingent upon the vision that guides and shapes the relationship and activities of leader and followers. The vision must be held in common and it must be articulated and re-articulated with great regularity so that the organization stays on track and headed in the desired direction.

«Leader-followers-goal» has been the framework for trying to understand the process of leadership. In some ways, delineating them as three separate categories is misleading, because, as is clear from the analysis, the three aspects of the leadership process are intrinsically connected to each other and exist in a rather circular relationship. The value of approaching them as separate categories has been to allow a synthetic analysis of the readings and thus the emergence of a clearer picture of leadership as it is understood in contemporary U.S. culture.

Having already explored the Church's understanding of priestly leadership in the previous two chapters, the examination in this chapter of an understanding of leadership in a United States cultural context makes it possible to proceed to the next chapter, which will explore the concern for leadership relative to priesthood, as this concern emerges in the United States Bishops' *Program of Priestly Formation.*

The Concern for Leadership in the National Council
of Catholic Bishops' Program of Priestly Formation

1. Introduction

The impetus for this study of priest as leader in a U.S. context came
from the fourth edition of *The Program of Priestly Formation* (*PPF* IV),
approved by the United States Bishops in 1992. As noted above in Chapter One, the *PPF* IV refers to the leadership role of priests: for example,
«Priests provide leadership in the community of faith»; «As leaders of
the faith community [...] priests are called to provide vision, direction
and leadership»[1]. It was further noted that in describing priests as leaders
the *PPF* IV, in effect, brought together two epistemologically distinct
categories: Roman Catholic priesthood (a transcultural, theological reality) and leadership (a culturally-conditioned reality), thus suggesting a
process of inculturation. The Church's teaching on inculturation, then,
determined the methodology for exploring the ministerial priest as leader
in a U.S. context.

Before completing the last step of the process, that is, before putting
the findings from Chapters Two and Three into correlation and critical
dialogue with the conclusions from Chapter Four, in order to observe
the process of inculturation, it is necessary to focus briefly on the U.S.
Bishops' *PPF* which posited the assertion of priest as leader in the first
place. A brief consideration of the evolution of the *PPF* in U.S. seminary formation, as well as the development, structure, and content of
the *PPF* IV will help to establish the immediate context for articulating
a description of the priest as leader and thus naturally lead into the
third part of our examination of the process of inculturation, correlating

---

[1] *PPF* IV, 10-11.

and establishing a critical dialogue between the theological and cultural terms of the equation, and evaluating the fidelity and adequacy of such a description to Church teaching and authentic cultural values.

2. Priestly Formation in the U.S. After Vatican II

2.1 *The Sacred Congregation for Catholic Education's* «*Ratio Fundamentalis Institutionis Sacerdotalis*»

The Second Vatican Council's «Decree on Priestly Formation», *Optatam Totius*, enunciated an important principle that led to the development of the U.S. Bishops' first *PPF* and its subsequent revisions:

> Since the variety of peoples and places is so great, only general rules can be legislated. Hence in each nation or particular rite a "Program of Priestly Formation" should be undertaken. It should be drawn up by the Episcopal Conferences, revised at definite intervals, and approved by the Apostolic See. By it, universal laws are to be adapted to the special circumstances of time and place, so that priestly formation will always answer the pastoral needs of the area in which the ministry is to be exercised (*OT* 1).

Archbishop Gabriel-Marie Garrone, appointed by Pope Paul VI as «pro-prefect» of the Sacred Congregation of Seminaries and Universities in 1966, provided important assistance to the various Episcopal Conferences in developing «Programs of Priestly Formation» in their countries. That Congregation issued a letter in October of 1966 that authorized seminaries to begin experimenting with seminary reforms in line with the principles articulated in *Optatam Totius*[2].

At the First International Synod of Bishops, held at Rome in 1967, Garrone proposed that the newly constituted Sacred Congregation for Catholic Education draft a plan for seminaries, in the spirit of *Optatam Totius*, that would assist the Episcopal Conferences in developing their various programs of priestly formation. The Synod Fathers approved Garrone's proposal and he then gathered a committee which drafted the *Basic Plan for Priestly Formation* or *Ratio Fundamentalis Institutionis Sacerdotalis* (hereafter *Ratio*). After a long process of revision and amendment, in consultation with the various national Episcopal Confer-

---

[2] For a description of the process of implementing the seminary reforms mandated by the Second Vatican Council, see J. M. WHITE, *The Diocesan Seminary in the United States*, 405-430. White notes that in the general curial reorganization of 1967, the Sacred Congregation of Seminaries and Universities was renamed the Sacred Congregation for Catholic Education and that Garrone, who became a cardinal in 1967, was named Prefect of the Congregation in 1968. Cf. ID., *The Diocesan Seminary in the United States*, 415.

ences, the plan was approved by Pope Paul VI on December 10, 1969[3], and issued on March 16, 1970[4].

The 1970 *Ratio* was composed of three parts: 1) preliminary remarks describing its development and the principles that the Congregation followed in drafting it; 2) an introduction that stressed the necessity of seminaries, described the dispositions of young people in today's world, and articulated the Catholic concept of priesthood as the goal of seminary formation; 3) and the basic plan itself, the longest part of the document, consisting of seventeen sections which closely parallel the sequence of ideas in *Optatam Totius*. In the introductory notes to the edition of the *Ratio* published by the U.S. Conference of Catholic Bishops, T. William Coyle remarked that the *Ratio* combined conciliar innovations with traditional understandings of priestly formation:

> Some will criticize it for being too traditional; others for being too progres-
> sive. Perhaps the fact that it will be criticized from both extremes is a test of
> its balance. Only by retaining what is valid in the past and courageously
> accepting what is valid in the new can the Council's desired renewal of semi-
> naries be brought about[5].

As an example of this balance, the *Ratio* highlights the de-centralization of authority from the Holy See to Episcopal Conferences and emphasizes the need for dialogue at all levels of formation, while also stressing the importance of a seminary rule book approved by the bishop, a traditional feature of seminary life[6]. In order to assist Episcopal Conferences in drawing up their own national programs of priestly formation, the *Ratio* delineated the basic, constitutive elements that are to be part of all seminary programs. The individual seminaries, in turn, are to comply with the plan written by the Episcopal Conferences of their respective countries[7].

---

[3] Cf. J. M. WHITE, *The Diocesan Seminary in the United States*, 416.

[4] At a press conference releasing the *Ratio*, Garrone described it as «[...] a sort of draft law wherein the Conferences would find the guidelines for their work, and which would serve as a basis for the control to be exercised by the Congregation. [...] Its only *raison d'être* is to provide an instrument for the Episcopal Conferences. On many points it lends itself to choices, and even suggests a variety of possible options. It is intended to help progress, not paralyze it. However, and along these lines, it is stamped with the spirit of the Council: its pastoral orientation, its desire to remain in contact with reality, its respect for legitimate individual initiatives», *Ratio*, 4-5.

[5] T. W. COYLE, «Introductory Notes», *Ratio*, 7-12.

[6] Cf. T. W. COYLE, «Introductory Notes», *Ratio*, 8-9.

[7] Cf. J. M. WHITE, *The Diocesan Seminary in the United States*, 416.

In 1985 the Sacred Congregation for Catholic Education revised the *Ratio* in order to comply with the 1983 *Code of Canon Law*. The structure of the revised *Ratio* is essentially the same as that of the 1970 version, except that, instead of preliminary remarks describing the development of the document and the operative principles behind its composition, there is a preface explaining the reasons for the revision[8]. With the exception of adjustments to some footnotes, the Introduction and the Basic Plan itself remain substantially the same as in the 1970 version.

2.2 *The Development of the U.S. «Program of Priestly Formation»*

2.2.1 «Interim Guidelines for Seminary Renewal» – 1968

In response to the Sacred Congregation of Seminaries and Universities' letter of October, 1966, which authorized seminaries to begin experimenting with seminary reforms in line with the principles articulated in *Optatam Totius*, the United States Bishops began the process of seminary reform. This was even before the Synod of 1967 had mandated the Sacred Congregation for Catholic Education to draw up the *Ratio*. At their November, 1966 meeting, the U.S. Bishops established the Committee on Priestly Formation which began to develop interim guidelines for American seminaries[9]. The guidelines set broad goals and objectives for seminary formation on the theologate, college, and high school levels: «Avoiding excessive detail, they leave room for adaptation in seminaries with differing local situations or apostolic orientations. They

---

[8] For the rationale behind the decision to revise the *Ratio*, see CCE, «Basic Norms for Priestly Formation», vol. 1, 17: «Since, nevertheless, in the new Code of Canon Law [...] all the pedagogical and disciplinary material dealing with seminaries and priestly formation was reordered *"ex integro"*, the "Basic Norms", treating the same material, has been deprived of its juridical value. In some way Bishops and Educators have been found bereft of a very good working document which they previously enjoyed in the fulfillment of their tasks.

«Moreover, [...] very many "Programs of Priestly Formation" were deeply rooted in the "Basic Norms" (often quoting verbatim various of its paragraphs), and ecclesiastical Superiors themselves readily refer to the same document whenever they must consider or resolve questions not explicitly contained in the new Code.

«In consideration of this, the Congregation for Catholic Education has judged it opportune to revise the aforesaid "Basic Norms for Priestly Formation" after the promulgation of the new Code of Canon Law, and to include in it some, indeed, very few emendations, as new circumstances require. As is apparent at the first glance, the new adjustments pertain to footnotes, abundantly enriched in various places, rather than to the text itself of the document which is substantially the same as it was when produced along with the help of the Episcopal Conferences».

[9] Cf. J. M. WHITE, *The Diocesan Seminary in the United States*, 415.

clarify the responsibility of educators to continue constant improvement»[10]. The *Interim Guidelines for Seminary Renewal* were approved by the U.S. Bishops and by the Sacred Congregation for Education and then issued to the U.S. seminaries[11].

2.2.2 The Program of Priestly Formation First Edition – 1971

In the preface to *PPF* I, Bishop Thomas J. Grady, the Chairman of the Bishops' Committee on Priestly Formation, observed that there is notable harmony between the U.S. *PPF* I and the universal Church's *Ratio*[12], not only because the *PPF* I represented a serious application of the *Ratio's* directives, but because it was developed by the U.S. Bishops at the same time that the *Ratio* was being developed. As part of the development of the *Ratio,* the Sacred Congregation for Catholic Education circulated draft texts to the various Episcopal Conferences, thus enabling the U.S. Bishops to shape the *PPF* I in conformity with the *Ratio*. After a lengthy process of refinement and revision, the NCCB accepted the *PPF* I in November of 1970, and the Sacred Congregation of Catholic Education approved it on 18 January 1971, for a period of five years[13].

---

[10] BCPF, *Interim Guidelines for Seminary Renewal*, Part 2, 6.

[11] Cf. In the preface to *Interim Guidelines for Seminary Renewal*, part 1, Bishop Loras Lane, the first chairman of the Bishops' Committe on Priestly Formation, observed that «[...] extensive consultation with people engaged in seminary work, of both the diocesan and religious clergy, preceded the formulation of the guidelines. [...] Perhaps the reason why seminary people will find little that is startling here is the very fact that those actively engaged in the seminary experience helped so profoundly in the formulation of the reports», BCPF, *Interim Guidelines for Seminary Renewal*, part 1, 3. Bishop James A. Hickey, Bishop Loras' successor as chairman of the Bishops' Committee on Priestly Formation, outlined the process leading to approval of the guidelines in the introduction: «The Bishops' Committee on Priestly Formation has been established as the instrument of the Episcopal Conference to develop the American program for seminary renewal. The National Conference of Catholic Bishops has authorized the publication of these guide-lines for interim use. For full juridic force, however, the guidelines approved by the NCCB require the final approbation of the Holy See», ID., *Interim Guidelines for Seminary Renewal*, part 2, 6. White observes, «The guidelines reflect the implementation of the spirit of the Council and the practices found in the leading American seminaries», J. M. WHITE, *The Diocesan Seminary in the United States*, 416.

[12] Bishop Grady wrote that while the creation of the *PPF* was in progress, «[...] draft texts of the *Ratio Fundamentalis* were being circulated to the various national conferences and the United States *Program* was constantly compared with the *Ratio* for congruence. Each section of the *Program* approved by the NCCB was submitted to the Sacred Congregation for Catholic Education and authorized for interim use», *PPF* I, xii.

[13] Cf. *PPF* I, xii-xiii.

The *PPF* I is divided into four major parts: 1) professional formation (theologate); 2) college formation; 3) high school formation; 4) religious priest's formation. There are also five appendices focusing on model curricula, relation of philosophy and theology, observations about high school seminaries, pastoral care of vocations, and a list of those bishops who served on the NCCB's Committee on Priestly Formation during the years when the *PPF* I was being developed. Very clearly, the major focus of the *PPF* I is the theologate, which receives more extensive coverage than both the college and high school seminaries.

White observed that the *PPF* I is innovative and groundbreaking in a number of its aspects:

> A major emphasis is that the seminary constitutes a community which in its human, faith, apostolic, and academic dimensions provides the most effective basis for priestly formation. This aspect is a decisive reversal of the older tendencies of the seminary as a kind of aggregation of individuals pursuing personal holiness and whose internal discipline and enforced silences kept seminarians apart from each other[14].

In addition to the *PPF* I's emphasis on community, White noted its attention to the seminary's administrative structure; its articulation of general principles for students' admission, evaluation, and endorsement; its rooting of spiritual formation in personal, Scripture-based prayer and the celebration of the Eucharist; its emphasis on service; its updating and balancing of the academic curriculum; and its emphasis on the pastoral goals of all formation efforts[15].

Bishop Grady observed that the *PPF* I is both extrinsically and intrinsically authoritative: extrinsically because it has the force of law, but, more importantly, intrinsically because of the broad consultation and authentic experience upon which it is based. He stressed that it is a whole, integral, organic program whose individual parts can only be adequately understood in relation to the whole[16].

2.2.3 The Program of Priestly Formation, Second Edition – 1976

The *PPF* II is very similar to the original one in structure, style, and content. In a preliminary consultation with faculties and students of various U.S. seminaries, the Bishops' Committee on Priestly Formation learned that there was general satisfaction with the original edition of the

---

[14] J. M. WHITE, *The Diocesan Seminary in the United States*, 417.

[15] Cf. J. M. WHITE, *The Diocesan Seminary in the United States*, 417-418.

[16] Cf. *PPF* I, xiii.

PPF and that most felt that more time was needed to thoroughly test it[17]. Because of this, the second edition contains very few changes.

The document is divided into five major parts: 1) professional formation (theologate); 2) college formation; 3) high school formation; 4) religious priest's formation; and 5) seminary education in a multi-cultural and multi-racial society. The five appendices include two letters from the Sacred Congregation for Catholic Education, one concerning philosophy, the other canon law. The section on the theologate is substantially the same as in the previous edition; the most noticeable alteration was to shift the treatment of spiritual formation into a more prominent position in order to highlight its importance. The section on college formation highlighted the necessity of considering the psychological development of the college seminarian in all aspects of formation. The gradual growth and development of college seminarians, and a spiritual formation appropriate for college-age students was emphasized throughout the entire section. The section on high school formation was completely rewritten in the light of the profound changes in high school seminaries in the years immediately after the Council and up to the first edition of the *PPF* in 1971. Because the Conference of Major Superiors of Men was awaiting a statement from Rome concerning priestly formation for religious, it was decided to leave the section on the formation of religious priests unchanged from the first edition. The fifth section, on formation in a multi-cultural and multi-religious society, was added to the *PPF* II because of the desire of African-American, Hispanic, and Native-American communities to have more priests from their own cultures, as well as to acknowledge the global mission of the Church[18].

On 3 March 1976, the *PPF* II was approved for a period of five years by the Sacred Congregation for Catholic Education. In his letter of approval, the prefect of the Congregation, Cardinal Garrone observed:

> The new impetus that the Second Vatican Council intended to give to seminary training finds a basic foundation in the traditional anxiety of the

---

[17] The «Preface to the Second Edition» states that, because of the general satisfaction with the original *Program of Priestly Formation*, as well as the desire to test it more thoroughly, «[...] a decision was made at the very outset that this revision would not concern itself with the basic assumptions of the *Program*, that no changes would be made which would interfere with the existing philosophy of the document. This meant that the revision would be confined to introducing elements which were overlooked in the first edition, clearing up vague passages, and eliminating the few contradictions which had surfaced through the years in the original document», *PPF* II, ix.

[18] Cf. *PPF* II, ix-x.

Church that her priests be men of holiness and wisdom penetrated with apostolic zeal. This foundation, however, was skillfully brought, by the Council documents, into a fruitful encounter with the needs and reality of modern times[19].

A perusal of the *PPF* II reveals a genuine concern on the part of the bishops to offer a program of formation that is rooted in the tradition of the Church, yet cognizant of and responsive to the reality of the massive technological, sociological, and cultural changes of modern times which create an important context for priestly ministry.

2.2.4 The Program of Priestly Formation, Third Edition – 1981

In the «Preface» to the third edition, Bishop Michael J. Murphy, chairman of the Committee on Priestly Formation from 1978 until 1981, commented that preparation of the text took place over three and one-half years, following the same process used for the first two editions. In the initial consultations with personnel involved in priestly formation, the Committee detected basic satisfaction with the *PPF* II, as well as some desire for various modifications[20]. In addition to an expanded general introduction, the document is composed of five major parts and an appendix. Parts One, Two, and Three, like previous editions, focus on the theologate, college seminary, and high school seminary. Part Four deals with implications of a multi-cultural and multi-racial society for seminary formation. In Part Five are new formation programs for other ministries and their relation to the seminary program, while the section on the formation of religious priests is dropped[21].

The «General Introduction» to the third edition lists seven significant changes or innnovations in the *PPF*. In addition to the omission of the

---

[19] *PPF* II, vii.

[20] Cf. *PPF* III, 1.

[21] In a critique of the changes in the formation of religious priests that have taken place in the United States, J. W. O'Malley, commenting on the *PPF* III, writes, «[...] the third edition (1981) dropped this section on religious priests because, according to the "Statement from the Conference of Major Superiors of Men" (p.3): "Religious and diocesan priests share an increasingly pluriform priesthood; their needs for priestly formation as such do not differ. [...] Thus the Conference of Major Superiors of Men adopts the program of priestly formation as the one program for all United States religious seminarians". It is not altogether clear, however, that this statement in fact perfectly reflects the reasons why the CMSM urged or conceded the dropping of Part Four. The statement should not in any case be taken as reflecting a fully matured theological position on the underlying issues», J. W. O'MALLEY, «The Houses of Study of Religious Orders and Congregations», 44.

section on the formation of religious priests, the *PPF* III acknowledges the variety of seminary structures or models operative in the U.S., all of which must encompass the constitutive elements of the *PPF*[22]. As noted above, the third edition acknowledged the variety of ministries in the Church — both lay and ordained — and the need for the formation and education of non-ordained ministers. Although it may be necessary to use the seminary resources for such training, the third edition stressed that the «[...] seminary maintain the integrity of the various components required for priestly formation, and the specific nature of priestly ministry be adequately presented to the students preparing for the priesthood»[23]. The third edition also acknowledged the stresses caused by the increased demands on seminarians in the post-Vatican II seminary. Because of this, it called for «[...] a development of a healthy rhythm of life that seeks balance and integration»[24]. The third edition also placed greater stress on a more adequate formation for celibacy, which includes addressing issues of human sexuality, relationships, intimacy, growth, and celibacy as it relates to other Christian virtues, especially obedience and poverty. The phenomena of older applicants for seminary, and those who lack a solid grounding in the traditions of Catholicism, along with the associated possibility of a longer period of formation, were also addressed in the third edition. Finally, the *PPF* III emphasized the importance of education for social justice at all levels of seminary formation[25].

In his introductory letter to the *PPF* III, Bishop Thomas J. Murphy, successor to Bishop Michael J. Murphy as Chairman of the Committee, noted that because of the apostolic visitation of United States seminaries to begin in 1983, the third edition was approved for an indefinite period of time, pending a review following the apostolic visitation[26], and also stressed the intimate connection between the *PPF* III and the universal Church documents on priesthood and priestly formation:

> While the program of the NCCB is the instrument which adapts the universal laws to the particular pastoral needs of the United States, it is always to be

---

[22] The third edition cited the traditional or free-standing seminary model: the supplemental model which provides the other aspects; the collaborative model which allows for the pooling and sharing of resources for priestly formation; three expressions of the collaborative model are the union, the federation, and the mixed model; Cf. *PPF* III, 7.

[23] *PPF* III, 8.

[24] *PPF* III, 8.

[25] Cf. *PPF* III, 9.

[26] Cf. *PPF* III, i.

understood in relationship to the entire official documentation related to priestly formation[27].

Because of this, the Bishops' Committee on Priestly Formation published a companion volume to the *PPF* III, containing a compendium of official Church documentation pertinent to priestly formation[28].

3. The Program of Priestly Formation, 4th Edition – 1992

3.1 *Introduction*

The creation of the fourth edition of the *PPF* was a three-year project initiated in 1989 by the Bishops' Committee on Priestly Formation. Even a superficial glance reveals significant differences from its predecessors in structure and style. Although, like them, it is rooted in the documents of the Second Vatican Council, the *Ratio*, and the various documents and letters from Vatican Dicasteries that pertain to seminary formation, three important events occurring after the publication of the *PPF* III had a great influence on the development of the *PPF* IV: the apostolic visitation of the U.S. seminaries; the 1990 Synod of Bishops on «The Formation of Priests in the Circumstances of the Present Day»; and publication of Pope John Paul II's Apostolic Exhortation, *Pastores Dabo Vobis*, «The Forma-tion of Priests in the Circumstances of the Present Day». Each event provided important perspectives that were taken into consideration in developing the *PPF* IV. Because the 1990 Synod and *Pastores Dabo Vobis* have already been extensively examined in Chapter Three, only the apo-stolic visitation of U.S. seminaries will be considered here.

3.1.1 The Apostolic Visitation of U.S. Seminaries

In 1981 Pope John Paul II, in collaboration with the United States Bishops' Conference, mandated an apostolic visitation of all college seminaries and theologates in the United States, including those for training religious. To coordinate and oversee the visitation[29], the Holy See appointed Bishop John Marshall of Burlington, Vermont, who estab-lished a process whereby designated teams — most consisting of two bishops, a religious superior, and two seminary leaders[30] — visited each

---

[27] *PPF* III, ii.

[28] NCCB, *NPF*.

[29] Cf. J. ROACH, «Study of U.S. Seminaries Launched», 263-264.

[30] Cf. «Marginalia», 315-316: «In all, 38 American bishops, 25 religious order representatives and 65 seminary professionals (rectors, spiritual directors, professors,

seminary and conducted extensive interviews with faculty, staff, and students to determine how well the teachings of the Second Vatican Council were being implemented[31].

In a 1986 letter to the U.S. Bishops, Cardinal Baum, Prefect of the Congregation for Catholic Education, expressed his observations on free-standing diocesan seminary theologates, based on visitation team reports[32]. A similar letter was sent from the Sacred Congregation for Catholic Education to the U.S. Bishops regarding college seminaries in 1988[33], and a joint letter on the formation of religious candidates was sent from the Congregation for Catholic Education and the Congregation for Institutes of Consecrated Life and Societies of Apostolic Life to the the U.S. Bishops and Religious Provincials in 1990[34]. Because the *PPF* IV focuses on diocesan candidates at the theologate level, our comments will be limited to the first letter about free-standing theologates, whose tone is generally positive and supportive of seminary efforts, recognizing good leadership and example on the part of rectors and seminary staffs, as well as efforts to offer balanced formational programs in their spiritual, academic, and pastoral dimensions. But Cardinal Baum notes:

> Our most serious recommendations have been about the need to develop a clearer concept of the ordained priesthood, to promote the specialised nature of priestly formation in accordance with Vatican II's affirmation of seminaries, to deepen the academic formation so that it becomes more properly and adequately theological (with more convinced and convincing attention to the Magisterium in some courses), and to ensure that the seminarians develop a good grasp of the specific contribution that the priest has to make to each pastoral situation. There are some confusions, lacunae and staffing inadequacies, but there are more strengths and accomplishments[35].

---

directors of field education, deans, etc.) served on the visitation teams. At the conclusion of each visit, an oral report was made to the bishop or religious superior responsible for the seminary, the rector, and the faculty. Later, the team prepared a written report which was reviewed by seminary representatives for factual accuracy before being forwarded to the Congregation for Catholic Education in Rome».

31 Cf. «Marginalia», 315.

32 Cf. CCE, «Letter to the Bishops of the United States Concerning Free-Standing Seminaries», vol. 2, 221-240.

33 Cf. CCE, «Letter to the Bishops of the United States Concerning College-Level Formation of Diocesan Candidates», vol. 2, 241-250.

34 Cf. CCE – CICL, «Letter to the Bishops of the United States and Religious Provincials on the Formation of Religious Candidates for the Priesthood», vol. 2, 251-262.

35 Cf. CCE, «Letter to the Bishops of the United States Concerning Free-Standing Seminaries», vol. 2, 223.

As the examination of the *PPF* IV will show, the Congregation's recommendations were taken seriously and included in the revision.

3.2 *The PPF* IV – *Continuity and Development*

As noted above, the *PPF* IV, like its predecessors, is rooted in the conciliar documents that provide a normative understanding of presbyteral office, the *Ratio*, and the various documents of Roman Dicasteries that have a bearing on seminary formation. It thus «[...] builds on previous editions of this document and on the experience of priestly formation in the United States during the past two decades»[36]. Like the previous editions, the *PPF* IV contains sections on theologate, college, and high school seminaries; it addresses spiritual, intellectual, and pastoral formation at all levels of seminary education; it offers guidelines for seminary administration and faculty; it deals with ecumenism, multiculturalism, and issues of peace and justice; and it addresses the area of admission requirements and evaluation of students. In covering these areas and addressing associated concerns, the document retains, to a large degree, the content of the previous edition[37].

The fourth edition is decidedly different, however, in format, style, and certain points of emphasis. As noted above, the apostolic visitation of U.S. seminaries, the 1990 Synod, Pope John Paul II's *Pastores Dabo Vobis*, and various seminary documents issued by Roman Dicasteries and the National Conference of Catholic Bishops, took place or were published in the years between the publication of the third and fourth editions, and all had an impact on the creation of the fourth. A simple glance at the footnotes in the two editions is revealing. The third contains a total of thirty-one footnotes, while the fourth contains 220. Of the 220 footnotes in *PPF* IV, 101 are from *Pastores Dabo Vobis*, enabling the authors to claim that «[...] *Pastores Dabo Vobis* provides significant emphasis for this edition» of the *PPF*[38]. Thus, although the fourth edition builds on and retains much of the earlier content, it is also quite different because of the impact of events that transpired in the intervening years.

---

[36] *PPF* IV, 3.

[37] Cf. *PPF* IV, 6.

[38] *PPF* IV, 3. In addition to 101 citations of *PDV*, the fourth edition cites Pope John Paul II's *Christifideles Laici* five times, the documents of the Second Vatican Council fifty times, the 1983 Code of Canon Law twenty-two times, the 1985 Extraordinary Synod three times, Sacred Scripture seventeen times, and numerous citations of Roman Curial documents pertaining to seminary formation, seven of which were published after the *PPF* III.

As the *PPF* IV itself acknowledges, «The first and most obvious [new] emphasis concerns the priesthood itself»[39]. The entire first chapter, subdivided into four articles, focuses on articulation of the meaning of the ministerial priesthood: doctrinal understanding of the ministerial priesthood; the spiritual life of diocesan priests; priesthood within the context of religious life; and a concluding reflection on the necessity of a thorough human, spiritual, intellectual, and pastoral formation for the ministerial priesthood. This new section on the meaning of the ministerial priesthood reveals the influence of both *Pastores Dabo Vobis* and recommendations stemming from the apostolic visitation.

In the 1986 letter to the U.S. Bishops from the Congregation for Catholic Education, Cardinal Baum wrote:

> Every seminary should have a very clear idea of the priesthood as the guiding concept of the seminary's enterprise. This idea needs to be not only modelled explicitly on Jesus Christ and hence be theologically correct but also expressed in a way that is intelligible to the student even as he begins his study of theology. [...] we would urge that all seminaries ensure that their seminarians understand the distinctiveness and complementarity of the ordained priesthood and the priesthood of all the faithful while devoting themselves confidently to the formation of the former. This requires a sound knowledge of the nature, purpose, and uniqueness of the Sacrament of Holy Orders in relation to and service of the many members of the Body of Christ[40].

Pope John Paul II also stressed the importance of sound doctrinal understanding of the ministerial priesthood as the basis of priestly formation:

> This problem [of priestly formation in present-day circumstances] cannot be solved without previous reflection on the goal of formation, that is, the ministerial priesthood, or, more precisely, the ministerial priesthood as a participation, in the Church, in the very priesthood of Jesus Christ. Knowledge of the nature and mission of the ministerial priesthood is an essential presupposition, and at the same time the surest guide and incentive towards the development of pastoral activities in the Church for fostering and discerning vocations to the priesthood and training those called to the ordained ministry (*PDV* 11).

The fourth edition's rather extensive articulation of the Church's doctrinal understanding of the ministerial priesthood and its associated spirituality is thus born of a wider Church concern that the formation programs

---

[39] *PPF* IV, 3.

[40] CCE, «Letter to the Bishops of the United States Concerning Free-Standing Seminaries», 224.

of all seminaries be rooted in a clear and common understanding of the
the ministerial priesthood, the goal of formation[41].

The *PPF* IV also introduces a new section on pre-theology programs
that offer both academic and spiritual preparation to enable candidates to
achieve an adequate level of readiness for the spiritual, intellectual, and
pastoral formation that takes place at the theologate level[42]. The rationale
for such a program is based on the variety in age, cultural background,
religious heritage, and personal experience that candidates might exhibit:
«Diverse issues — facility in language, training in philosophy and the
liberal arts, a grounding in Catholic tradition and religious education,
matters of personal and spiritual maturity — must be addressed before
candidates are ready to begin theological studies and appropriate an
authentic priestly identity»[43]. Although the establishment of pre-theology
programs is an innovation of the *PPF* IV, the roots of the issue lie in the
previous *PPF* which also acknowledged the challenges that a less homo-
geneous body of candidates presents to seminary formation programs[44].

---

[41] This is not to say that the previous editions were not grounded in a correct,
doctrinal understanding of the priesthood, but rather that it was necessary to more clearly
highlight this understanding and emphasize it as the foundation for programs of priestly
formation. In the previous *PPF* documents, the common doctrinal understanding of the
ministerial priesthood was clearly implicit in the various guidelines and norms. The
fourth edition, however, is different in that it highlights the doctrine by devoting an entire
chapter to it, and emphasizes its foundational nature by placing it in the first chapter. In
its «Introduction» the fourth edition stresses that such emphasis provides «[...] sure
guidelines for diocesan bishops, religious ordinaries, and seminary leadership in the
challenging task of priestly formation. This same clarity about priestly identity also offers
direction and support for seminarians in the course of formation. From many points
of view, clear priestly identity and sound priestly formation are necessary correlates»,
PPF IV, 3.

[42] Cf. *PPF* IV, 4.42-47.

[43] *PPF* I, 4.

[44] See especially *PPF* III, 73: Regarding older candidates and those who have not
had benefit of a growing-up in a traditional Catholic «culture», the third edition
emphasizes, «Bishops, seminaries, and vocation directors are to recognize that additional
time will usually be necessary to prepare for priestly ordination in the areas of spiritual
formation, philosophical education, and theological education». Cf. CCE, «Letter to
the Bishops of the United States Concerning Free-Standing Seminaries», especially
227-230, which addresses the issue of the great diversity among seminary candidates
and how theologates should respond programmatically to such diversity; see also,
CCE, «Letter to the Bishops of the United States Concerning College-Level Formation of
Diocesan Candidates», 246: «There is a growing conviction among the leadership of the
seminary community in the United States that candidates for entry who already possess a
college degree should have two years of pre-theology rather than one, and that these two
years concentrate on philosophy and on Catholic culture and piety».

Another point of emphasis in the fourth edition is formation for celibacy, with two reasons cited: the social climate of the United States which can often impede an individual's capacity for lifelong commitment, as well as erode the support system on which such commitment depends, and a widespread tolerance for sexual behavior contrary to Church teaching. Both factors foster an atmosphere which makes celibacy both less intelligible and more difficult to practice[45]. It was thus decided to give more extensive attention to it in the fourth edition. Although the topic of celibacy is treated more extensively in the *PPF* IV, it is not necessarily a «new» point of emphasis as implied in the «Introduction». The previous *PPF* also put significant stress on formation for celibacy[46]. Like its successor, it cited the pressures of U.S. culture which render celibacy difficult for people both to understand and to practice, hence the necessity for sound education in celibacy. Perhaps what is significant in the fourth edition is that the spiritual-theological underpinnings of celibacy are treated in more depth and are included in a substantive way in Chapter One, Article Two, «Spiritual Life of Diocesan Priests», and Chapter Three, Article Two, «Spiritual Formation», especially the section titled «Formation for a Priestly Way of Life»[47]. Although it emphasizes the positive dimensions of celibacy and its theological and spiritual underpinnings, the fourth edition does not put as much emphasis on education in Christian sexuality as a context for celibacy as did its predecessor. For instance, in its treatment of celibacy, *PPF* III states:

> rectors and directors of formation in seminaries cannot assume that seminarians have a healthy Christian appreciation of the positive meaning and purpose of sexuality, or a mature, Christ-centered acceptance and direction of their own sexuality. Education in the realities of human sexuality is needed for seminarians. This education should deal specifically with such topics as the nature of sexuality, growth toward sexual maturity, marital and celibate chastity, the single state, premarital and extramarital sexual relationships, and homosexuality. Those who provide this education should seek to present clearly the Christian virtues of chastity and modesty in accordance with the teachings of Jesus[48].

The third edition also stressed that this dimension of seminary formation cannot be assumed to be adequately addressed only in personal spiritual

---

[45] Cf. *PPF* IV, 4.
[46] Cf. *PPF* III, especially 8-9.24-26.
[47] Cf. *PPF* IV, 16-17.55-58.
[48] *PPF* III, 24.

direction, the Sacrament of Reconciliation, or a single theology course[49].
The fourth edition seems to go in a different direction; it says very little
about the relation of sexuality and celibacy and stresses spiritual direction
as the primary forum for addressing the related issues of sexuality and
celibacy. Although the two editions do not contradict each other, the *PPF*
IV's seeming de-emphasis of the importance of education in the realities
of human sexuality seems a rather significant omission in the light of its
very clear acknowledgement of the detrimental impact of the U.S. social
climate on matters sexual, not to mention the spate of sexual scandals
involving priests that have been so much in the public eye in recent
years[50].

---

[49] Cf. *PPF* III, 25.

[50] One of the general editors of the *PPF* IV, Howard Bleichner, SS, collaborated
with Robert Leavitt, SS, and Archbishop Daniel Buechlein, OSB, Chairman of the
Bishops' Committee on Priestly Formation during the writing of the fourth edition, to
produce an excellent paper addressing the topic of celibacy. The paper, in booklet form,
helps to understand the perspective from which the fourth edition approached the topic.
In the paper the authors evaluate the current state of the issue and elaborate on the
background of and rationale for priestly celibacy. Their concern was to clearly present the
Church's theological and spiritual rationale for priestly celibacy in an atmosphere in
which the topic is distorted by controversy. Cf. H. BLEICHNER et al., *Celibacy for the
Kingdom*, 9: «The discipline of celibacy in the Roman Catholic Church is a complex
matter. There are indeed layers of issues and concerns to be considered. Certainly,
celibacy as a phenomenon must be studied from a psychological, sociological, anthropological, and political point of view. Information and objective data are vital to
understand it. Certainly, as well, abuse must be frankly acknowledged. But such voices
have struck the principal notes which have filled the recent silence and while they remain
important, they are not primary. On such a complex topic, perspective or balance is
everything and this is what has been lost. *In our view, the positive case for celibacy has
not been made much lately. That case is essentially theological and spiritual. If it is
missing, then nothing makes sense. If it is present, then all other ways of studying or
examining the celibate life fall into perspective. Simply put, celibacy is essentially a
religious commitment. This is the voice which first must be heard* [emphasis added]».
This seems to have been the perspective that guided the fourth edition's approach to
celibacy. As such, it represents a positive improvement over previous editions of the
PPF. Although it is a sound, helpful, and much-needed approach, it would have been
strengthened by incorporating a stronger emphasis on the need for a thorough education
and formation in a Christian understanding of sexuality which was one of the strengths
of the third edition. For other influences on the the fourth edition's approach to celibacy,
Cf. CCE, «Letter to the Bishops of the United States Concerning Free-Standing
Seminaries, 232; JOHN PAUL II, *Pastores Dabo Vobis* 29, quoting Proposition 11 of
the 1990 Synod: «The Synod would like to see celibacy presented and explained in the
fullness of its biblical, theological and spiritual richness, as a precious gift given by God
to his Church and as a sign of the Kingdom which is not of this world, a sign of God's
love for this world and of the undivided love of the priest for God and for God's People,
with the result that celibacy is seen as a positive enrichment of the priesthood».

Another important development in the *PPF* IV is the integration of certain themes into all sections, some of which were treated separately in previous editions of the *PPF*: namely, 1) the changing ethnic and racial fabric of the Church in the U.S.; 2) issues of peace, justice, and respect for life; 3) ecumenism and interfaith relations; and 4) collaboration. The rationale for this integration is stated as «[...] a desire to introduce these subjects into all phases of priestly formation, because each represents a value central to the life of the Church in the United States and the future ministry of priests»[51].

Previous editions of the *PPF* indeed included sections on seminary education in a multi-racial and multi-cultural society, with a strong emphasis on education for justice because, as both *PPF* II and *PPF* III state, «In nearly every instance this question of justice involves the relationship between a dominant majority and a minority group that is poor, oppressed, and very often either Black, Brown, or whose native language is not English»[52]. Also emphasized was the importance of promoting vocations in the various ethnic and racial groups and the necessity for seminaries to make adjustments in order to assist those coming from different racial and ethnic backgrounds. While the fourth edition maintains the same concerns as its predecessors, it weaves the topics into the entire document, rather than treating them discretely. Regarding the racial and ethnic diversity of the U.S., the *PPF* IV states, «Candidates for the ministerial priesthood are called to serve a multiracial, multiethnic Church. [...] This changing face of the Catholic Church in the United States should have a significant effect on seminary formation»[53]. Similarly, in addressing the topic of peace and justice, it cites the significant statements from the U.S. Bishops on various topics and asserts, «In a world that seeks to privatize religious commitment, seminary education should appropriately emphasize the social dimension of the Gospel, its concern for human life, justice in the marketplace, and peace in the world»[54]. The issues of multiculturalism, peace and justice, and respect for life, therefore, are integrated into all the various dimensions of priestly formation as articulated in the *PPF* IV.

In a similar manner, the topic of ecumenism was treated separately in previous editions of the *PPF*. In both the second and third editions

---

[51] *PPF* IV, 5.
[52] *PPF* II, 133; *PPF* III, 139.
[53] *PPF* IV, 5.
[54] *PPF* IV, 5.

it formed a chapter entitled «Ecumenical Dimension in Theological Education» in the section on the theologate. The fourth edition dropped the separate chapter on ecumenism, stressing that since the Second Vatican Council ecumenism has become an important dimension of priestly formation «[...] that should be integrated into all phases of seminary formation»[55].

Finally, in terms of thematic integration, the *PPF* IV introduces a new theme — collaboration — which, it stresses, should also be integrated into all aspects of seminary formation:

> All baptized persons are called to collaborate in Christ's mission. The distinctive quality of the laity is its "secular character", its unique capacity to witness to "the significance of the earthly and temporal realities in the salvific plan of God" beyond the Church. The ministerial priesthood attests to "the permanent guarantee of the sacramental presence of Christ, the Redeemer". According to duty, talent, and hierarchical responsibility, priests and laity collaborate together in all dimensions of the Church's life and mission. Priestly formation should model this collaborative spirit[56].

Although the previous edition of the *PPF* emphasized the conciliar ecclesiology of the People of God as the context in which priesthood is exercised[57], the fourth edition explicitly names collaboration as an integral aspect of priestly identity and activity. Because collaborative situations are characteristic of ministry in today's Church, it stresses that seminary formation must both model this spirit and train seminarians to be able to work effectively in these situations. The *PPF* IV thus attempts to integrate the theme of collaboration into all aspects of seminary formation. In stressing collaboration, the fourth edition highlights a leadership theme common to both the ministerial priesthood and popular U.S. approaches to leadership.

Another significant addition to the fourth edition is a brief section on priesthood in the context of religious life. This topic had been included in the first two editions of the *PPF*, but dropped in the third edition for reasons cited above. The topic is re-introduced in the fourth edition and

---

[55] *PPF* IV, 5.

[56] *PPF* IV, 6.

[57] Cf. *PPF* III, 4: «Sacramental priesthood relates to the total community of believers through its mission of ministerial service to that community and its hierarchical responsibility of forming and governing the priestly people who constitute the Church in the world today. [...] The renewal efforts of the Church today must be especially evident in the formation and education of those called to share an ordained ministry with the People of God».

focuses on «[...] the diverse, yet authentic, ways in which religious priests live and discern the one priesthood of Jesus Christ according to the Church's doctrinal understanding of the presbyteral office»[58]. Acknowledging the traditional difference between formation for religious life and formation for diocesan priesthood — which still holds today — the *PPF* IV stresses that religious candidates must be schooled in both the tradition and charism of their own institution or society, and the theology of the priesthood[59].

Finally, the fourth edition differs from its predecessors in format, which it has rearranged for purposes of clarity, brevity, and practicality. An example of this streamlining can be seen in the treatment of pre-theology programs, high school seminaries, and college seminaries. All three are included in Chapter Two, «Paths to the Theologate», whereas in previous editions they were treated in separate, lengthier chapters. Like the previous editions, the theologate is once again the main focus of the document and comprises the lengthiest chapter. Instead of addressing the topic of seminary administration and faculty at each level of seminary — high school, college, and theologate — as the previous editions did, the fourth edition devotes one chapter to the topic. Admission and evaluation of seminarians is covered in a similar manner. A new accent in the fourth edition is a brief chapter devoted to the continuing formation of priests, a very strong concern expressed by Pope John Paul II in *Pastores Dabo Vobis*. In addition the *PPF* IV adds «norms» to many sections of the document in order to spell out elements that should be par of every formation program. This is a departure from previous editions, which articulated very few norms, and marks the new *PPF* as more prescriptive in nature than its predecessors.

4. Concern for Leadership in the PPF

4.1 *Interim Guidelines for Seminary Renewal*

In the *Interim Guidelines for Seminary Renewal* the description of the ministerial priesthood mirrored the teaching of the Second Vatican Council. For example, at the beginning of the section on spiritual formation in the seminary, the *Guidelines* quoted the Council's «Decree on Priestly Formation» to describe the kind of priest the seminary must seek to form: «[...] the entire training of the students should be oriented to the

---

[58] *PPF* IV, 6.
[59] Cf. *PPF* IV, 21-23.

formation of true shepherds of souls after the model of our Lord Jesus
Christ, teacher, priest and shepherd» (*OT* 4)[60]. Later in the same section
the *Interim Guidelines for Seminary Renewal* added, «[...] the people
of God need wise and holy pastors, men close to the heart of Christ
and consumed in His work of salvation. It is the seminary's task, under
God, to prepare men for this ministry of service. The goal encompasses
three basic areas: ministry of the Word; ministry of Sacrament; pastoral
ministry»[61].

Like the Council documents on priesthood, the *Interim Guidelines for
Seminary Renewal* did not explicitly use the language of leadership but
it clearly described a leadership role for the priest. The leadership is
described in terms of the threefold ministry of Word, Sacrament, and
Pastoral Care in service to the Church's unity:

> Not only must he communicate God's message of unity-through-love, and
> make the Lord's saving action present sacramentally; his pastoral service
> involves personal knowledge of the Christian layman in the latter's vocation
> of restoring all things in Christ. Above all, priestly service looks towards
> effecting unity in one fold. Thus the priest must strive to form communities,
> opening people to the shared cooperative effort and profound sense of
> union that the Spirit of God's love inspires[62].

The *Interim Guidelines for Seminary Renewal*, then, very closely
followed the conciliar understanding of the ministerial priesthood.

In a significant paragraph, however, it referred to the impact that U.S.
culture has on the exercise of the ministerial priesthood, an impact that
has implications for the leadership role of priests:

> In an American seminary, virtues should reflect the values prized among
> Americans, such as: personal freedom and initiative, teamwork and respect for
> democratic processes, adaptability, tolerance of another's faults and limita-
> tions, and a talent for organization and implementation[63].

Later, in a similar vein, the *Interim Guidelines for Seminary Renewal*
stressed:

> The priest, perhaps more today than at any time in the Church's history must
> develop a fine sensitivity to people, their needs and aspirations, their circum-
> stances of life, their attitudes towards God and man. Only if the candidate
> develops this sensitivity and awareness will he be able to enter fruitfully into

---

[60] Cf. *Interim Guidelines for Seminary Renewal*, part 2, 27.
[61] Cf. *Interim Guidelines for Seminary Renewal*, part 2, 28.
[62] *Interim Guidelines for Seminary Renewal*, part 2, 31.
[63] *Interim Guidelines for Seminary Renewal*, part 2, 42.

that "dialogue with men" which the "Decree on Priestly Formation" urges upon him (n. 19)[64].

Although not using the explicit language of leadership, it is nonetheless clear that the *Interim Guidelines for Seminary Renewal* was concerned about the leadership function of the priest, and particularly that the ministerial priest would be prepared to effectively carry out a priestly ministry of leadership in the cultural context of the United States.

4.2 *PPF* I

In the spirit of the Council's «Decree on Priestly Formation» and building on the *Interim Guidelines for Seminary Renewal,* the *PPF* I described the goal of seminary education: «[...] to form true pastors of the People of God after the model of our Lord Jesus Christ, teacher, priest, and shepherd»[65]. In the introduction to the document, however, the impact of the American cultural context on the exercise of the ministerial priesthood was acknowledged:

> Response to God's call to serve His People has always been the object of this [priestly] formation. In the past this service was usually exercised in clearly defined areas of priestly competence. *Today, because of our rapidly evolving understanding of man, the world and the Church, and because of the characteristic pluralism of American society, the education of our priests must be broader, more flexible and more creative*[66] [emphasis added].

The *PPF* I also retained the section, quoted above, concerning values prized by Americans that should be reflected in U.S. seminary education[67].

In the section on promotion to Sacred Orders, the *PPF* I spelled out specific qualities that should be present in a candidate:

> a) a knowledge of, and a fidelity to the Word of God and the authentic teaching of Christ's Church; b) charity, zeal for souls, and lifelong dedication signified by celibacy according to the tradition of the Western Church; c) *competence in pastoral skills*, especially in the proclamation of God's Word and in leading divine worship; d) *a sense of responsibility and commitment to the people entrusted to him and an ability to communicate with them; e) personal initiative and capacity for courageous leadership*

---

[64] *Interim Guidelines for Seminary Renewal*, part 2, 46.

[65] *PPF* I, 5.

[66] *PPF* I, 1.

[67] Cf. *PPF* I, 44.

together with prudence and decision in action; f) willingness to subordinate personal preferences in the interest of cooperative effort[68] [emphasis added].

Here the document specifically singled out leadership as a quality for ministerial priesthood in the United States. It similarly stressed the theme of competence — the ability to communicate, collaborate, and take personal initiative — all qualities associated with leadership in any sphere, but here particularly connected to the ministerial priesthood. The first edition of the *PPF*, then, included the concerns of the *Interim Guidelines for Seminary Renewal* about priestly leadership in a U.S. context, but took them a step further and explicitly named leadership as one of the characteristics, qualities, or functions essential for the effective exercise of the ministerial priesthood in the culture of the United States.

4.3 *PPF* II

As indicated above, with a few exceptions the second edition of the *PPF* is essentially the same as the first. In Chapter Three, however, which deals with the seminary's academic program, the *PPF* II added a significant subsection entitled «Pastoral Leadership and Counselling» to the section on Pastoral Studies. This subsection emphasized the importance of the leadership dimension of priestly ministry and of offering education to develop such leadership:

> Such priestly work as guiding the Christian community as a group and the individual members of the community makes it important that the curriculum include training to fulfill these needs. The task of leadership in the parish and community requires knowledge of how to approach people as a group and work with them. The areas of group dynamics, management techniques, and organizational development provide resources for this task. [...] The student should come to understand that the priest is ordained to serve a priestly people, to assist this people to grow in their own gifts of the Spirit, not to dominate but to inspire and guide[69].

The *PPF* II thus built on the previous *PPF* as well as the *Interim Guidelines for Seminary Renewal*, in that it explicitly recognized leadership as part of the identity and work of the ministerial priest, and that the peculiarly U.S. context requires a certain amount of training in the areas of group, organization, and management theory, although not to be divorced from the theological perspective. To prevent such an under-

---

68 *PPF* I, 55.
69 *PPF* II, 38.

standing the same section emphasizes that such training «[...] should be so organized that the student does not merely learn prescribed routines of ministry but becomes sensitive to human needs and skilled in finding theologically sound solutions to pastoral problems»[70]. Yet the emphasis on training for pastoral leadership indicates an acknowledgement that the particular cultural context of the U.S. does partially shape how such leadership is to be understood, thus how one is to be trained for it.

4.4 *PPF* III

The «General Introduction» to the third edition made a significant statement about priestly leadership which built on and developed what was contained in the previous documents:

> The vitality of any structure in society will depend on its present and future leadership. Those sharing the sacrament of ordained ministry have a special responsibility to exercise the needed leadership for the Church to continue the mission of Christ as Priest, Prophet, and King, a mission shared with the entire People of God. Seminaries have been established by the Church to prepare students for such leadership and ministry which will contribute to the life of the Church now and in the future. Tomorrow's leaders of the Catholic faith community are involved now in a program of seminary formation and education. [...] Seminary formation and education must strive for ever-increasing growth in the quality of the program to equip future leaders to serve the People of God as ordained ministers of Word and Sacrament[71].

This is perhaps the most significant statement, thus far, of the *PPF*'s concern for leadership connected to the identity and role of the ministerial priest. Ordained ministry, as described here, includes leadership as a constitutive dimension. The statement does not equate leadership with a particular aspect of the threefold office of Priest, Prophet, and King. Priestly, or presbyteral, leadership transcends all three dimensions of ministry: the ordained leadership continues the mission of Christ as Priest, Prophet, and King and makes it possible for the entire Church to take part in this mission. It also implies that when the priest engages in ministry he is necessarily engaging in leadership, and that the seminary is preparing him for such «leadership and ministry». Finally, the statement identifies ministerial priesthood with leadership when it says that «[...] tomorrow's leaders of the Catholic faith community are involved now in a program of seminary formation and education», and

---

[70] *PPF* II, 38.
[71] *PPF* III, 10.

that the seminary's task is «[...] to equip future leaders to serve the People of God as ordained ministers of Word and Sacrament».

The remainder of the *PPF* III contains essentially what was in the previous editions. However, in the chapter on pastoral formation in the theologate, the section on supervised field education experiences offers some important insights into how the priest is to exercise leadership vis-à-vis other parish ministers:

> Seminarians should understand and make use of the dynamic of shared responsibility in the development of the parish community and of cooperative team effort if they are to appreciate their role as animators and coordinators of those who will work along with them in their ministry as priests. Special attention should be given to an orientation on the rightful role of the various ecclesial ministries, including the nature and role of the permanent diaconate[72].

Such emphasis makes it clear that although the priest exercises a leadership role in the community by virtue of his ordination, he does so in the context of other ministers and leaders. His leadership is thus to be characterized by collaboration, shared responsibility, and cooperative team effort.

In order to develop the leadership skills and identity of seminarians, the third edition strongly encouraged that seminarians be involved in implementing the goals of the seminary. It stressed that the best way to achieve this is by allowing «[...] some form of student participation in the decision-making process»[73]. Such collaboration develops seminarians' «[...] potential for articulating community thought, [...] and permits members of the group to grow through participating in shared responsibilities and teamwork»[74]. This emphasis reflects the third edition's concern for leadership as an intrinsic dimension of priestly ministry that needs to be developed in the seminary so that the effectiveness of the future priest's ministry is enhanced.

4.5 *PPF* IV

As noted above, the fourth edition represents a significant development in style and format from the previous editions of the *PPF*. Although it does retain «[...] in large measure the content of the third edition»[75], it

---

72 *PPF* III, 59.
73 *PPF* III, 76.
74 *PPF* III, 76.
75 *PPF* IV, 6.

nuances and alters certain themes that were present in the previous editions, for example, the theme of leadership. Absent in the fourth edition is the previous explicit identification of seminarians as the future leaders of the Church[76]. This is not to say that the fourth edition is not concerned with the leadership theme (in fact, the contrary is true). It simply points to the different way it treats certain themes from the previous editions.

An example of the fourth edition's strong concern for the role of priestly leadership is seen in Chapter One, «The Foundations of Priestly Formation». In its articulation of the Church's doctrinal understanding of the ministerial priesthood, this chapter devotes an entire subsection to priesthood described as «Pastoral Leadership in the Community of Faith». Before describing the nature of this leadership it stresses the complementarity of the laity and priests: «[...] priests and laity share a sacramental origin and a common purpose as disciples of Christ. These bonds imply a relationship of collaboration and mutual respect»[77]. This complementarity provides the context for priestly leadership:

> There is today an increased emphasis on the role of the laity, their gifts and the various ministries to which they are called. As leaders of the faith community, priests exercise a significant dimension of their shepherding role through the support they offer to the laity. As they encourage others to perform the tasks which are theirs by virtue of baptism, priests are called to provide vision, direction, and leadership. In doing so, they support the exercise of the gifts of the laity and encourage them to participate actively in building up the body of Christ[78].

The document goes on to emphasize that this leadership is carried out in the context of the threefold ministry of Word, Sacrament, and Pastoral Care, and that such ministry extends beyond the Church on behalf of all people. The exercise of the threefold ministry of leadership will have a profound impact on the spiritual life of the priest himself because, as the document stresses, Christ himself is present in and to priests in a special way in the exercise of their ministry[79].

In Chapter One, Article Two, «The Spiritual Life of Diocesan Priests», the document seems to make a subtle shift from its understanding of priestly leadership as transcending all three aspects of ministry, to an

---

[76] Cf. *PPF* III, 10.

[77] *PPF* IV, 11.

[78] *PPF* IV, 11.

[79] Cf. *PPF* IV, 11.

identification of leadership with the Kingly office, or the ministry of pastoral care:

> Diocesan priests continue the proclamation of the kingdom by preaching, sanctifying, and *leading* God's people, fulfilling the roles to which they were especially commissioned at ordination[80] [emphasis added].

It shows a similar shift in understanding when it speaks of the sacramental relationships established by ordination as the deepest source of the priest's spiritual life:

> These sacramental relationships to Christ and the Church find their active expression in the threefold ministry of preaching, sanctifying, and *pastoral leadership*, thereby establishing the inseparable unity of priestly identity, ministry, and spirituality[81] [emphasis added].

It immediately stresses, however, the connectedness of the threefold ministry which enters deeply and powerfully into the personal lives of priests:

> The Church repeatedly underscores this connection. Priests preach the Word of God first by living it. In the ordination rite, they are challenged to imitate in their own lives the sacramental mysteries they celebrate. *Leadership without the witness of holiness, asceticism, and personal integrity lacks authenticity*[82] [emphasis added].

Thus, even if the document does tend at certain points to equate leadership with the third of the threefold ministry, that ministry transcends and is expressed in the other two, and they are expressed in it. In other words, when a priest is explicitly engaging in the ministry of Word or Sacrament, he is in effect, exercising his role of leadership; similarly, when he is exercising his leadership role in other situations, the ministry of Word and Sacrament is being exercised, even if only implicitly[83].

It was noted previously that the *PPF* IV strongly emphasizes collaboration, an important leadership theme. In fact this theme was present in the previous edition; the fourth edition, however, significantly expands it by stressing that the theme of collaboration should be integrated into seminary formation at every phase[84]. Such collaboration is rooted in an

---

[80] *PPF* IV, 12.

[81] *PPF* IV, 13.

[82] *PPF* IV, 13.

[83] Cf. above, p. 105, n. 183, on the inadequacy of *exclusively* equating the «kingly office» with leadership.

[84] Cf. above, p. 266; *PPF* IV, 6.

ecclesiology of communion which stresses the complementarity of laity and priests noted above, and it reflects the description of leadership that was stressed above in Chapters Two, Three, and Four: leadership cannot be seen as a relationship of superiority over others, but can only be properly understood as a relationship of service.

Chapter Three of the *PPF* IV, concerning «The Theologate», describes the community life of the seminary as the context in which the skills of leadership are developed:

> The give-and-take between those who share the same vocational goal provides mutual support and promotes increased tolerance while allowing fraternal correction to take place. Community life affords the opportunity for the development of leadership skills and individual talents. It can also motivate seminarians to develop a sense of self-sacrifice and a spirit of collaboration[85].

Thus, although the fourth edition does not explicitly identify seminarians as future leaders, it clearly does see the seminary as the place where they can acquire the leadership skills needed for their future ministry.

The *PPF* IV drops the recommendation of previous editions that the seminary's academic curriculum include training in leadership skills. The previous editions connected pastoral leadership with counselling as a distinct area of pastoral studies, but the fourth edition simply offers the following norm: «Pastoral studies should include pastoral counselling and provide an introduction to initiation rites for adults and children»[86]. Thus, the fourth edition places the acquisition of leadership skills in the context of field education which «[...] helps seminarians appropriate their role as spiritual leaders and public persons in the Church»[87].

> Theological field education provides an opportunity for seminarians to exercise leadership in the Church and to learn the priestly dimension of pastoral ministry. [...] learning by example and identification, an aspect of education often used in other professions, is of great importance in the pastoral formation of seminarians[88].

This shift of leadership formation from a setting of academic emphasis to an exclusively pastoral formation de-emphasizes the theoretical knowledge of group dynamics, management techniques, and organizational

---

[85] *PPF* IV, 59-60.
[86] *PPF* IV, 72.
[87] *PPF* IV, 74.
[88] *PPF* IV, 75.

development necessary for the priestly leadership, stressed in previous editions, and instead focuses on its more practical dimensions.

Finally, the *PPF* IV emphasizes the importance of leadership in Chapter Four, «Seminary Administration and Faculty», when it stresses that seminary administrators «[...] have a unique opportunity to serve as models of leadership for seminarians»[89] by fostering initiative and responsibility through collaboration with them. However, *PPF* IV did not include a significant section from the *PPF* III describing the ways in which seminarians can learn the skills of collaboration: the third edition stressed the importance of students' participation in the decision-making process of the seminary:

> Effective understanding and collaboration in carrying out decisions can best be achieved by some form of student participation in the decision-making process: a) it permits open exchange and more understanding between faculty and students in areas of concern to both and shows the value of both authority and freedom; b) it encourages more ready acceptance of decisions on the part of all participants; c) it selects the leaders of the group and develops their potential for articulating community thought; d) it permits members of the group to grow through participating in shared responsibility and teamwork; e) it permits a progressively broader scope of responsibility as the students advance; f) it enables seminarians to understand the stages of prudential judgement and action.[90].

Although the *PPF* IV neglected to include an important description of how the seminary can inculcate the practice of collaboration, it does affirm the importance of including seminarians in the decision-making process: «Direct involvement and participation by the seminary community, including seminarians themselves, should be characteristic of policy making in seminaries»[91]. Later, in Chapter Five, «The Admission and Continuing Evaluation of Seminarians», the *PPF* IV asserts that candidates for Holy Orders should be able to show evidence of having interiorized their seminary formation. Among the evidence of such interiorization it names qualities also articulated in past editions, such as the «[...] capacity for courageous and decisive leadership»[92]. The fourth edition fuses the «collaboration» theme to a previously articulated criterion as evidence of interiorization: the «*ability to work in a collaborative, professional manner with men and women, foregoing personal*

---

[89] *PPF* IV, 83.
[90] *PPF* III, 76.
[91] *PPF* IV, 85.
[92] Cf. *PPF* IV, 103; *PPF* III, 75.

preference in the interests of cooperative efforts for the common good»
[italics added to show new point of emphasis][93].

As this survey has demonstrated, the various editions of the U.S. *PPF*
all show evidence of a concern for leadership as a constitutive dimension
of priestly identity and ministry. The ministerial priest is repeatedly
identified as a leader; such leadership is shaped, not only by ecclesial
realities, but by cultural ones, as the frequent references to the influence of U.S. culture on priestly identity and ministry stress. Thus it is
clear that in the identification of the ministerial priest as a leader in the
various editions of the U.S. Bishops' *PPF*, a description largely absent in
universal Church documents, a process of inculturation is at work, a
process that seeks to keep the priesthood firmly rooted in the Church's
tradition, while at the same time enabling it to flourish, grow, and be
effective in a particular culture, that of the U.S.

5. Review of Chapters One Through Four

The remainder of the chapter will review the methodology of inculturation established in Chapter One, the Church's teaching on priesthood
from the perspective of leadership, which was examined in Chapters Two
and Three, and the U.S. cultural understanding of leadership explored in
Chapter Four. Such a review will make it possible to proceed to our final
chapter which will demonstrate the process of inculturation at work in
identifying the ministerial priest as leader in a U.S. context, and offer
indications that such an understanding of priesthood has for the spirituality of priests living and ministering in the U.S. cultural context.

5.1 *Methodology of Inculturation*

As indicated in the discussion on inculturation in Chapter One, the faith
of the Church does not exist as a disembodied reality but is enfleshed and
lived by people in particular cultures. Faith and culture, therefore,
encounter each other and are influenced by one another. The goal of faith
is the penetration and transformation of culture by the Gospel. As the
research has shown, Church doctrine stresses that the Church is to be
open to and make use of all that is true and good in a culture in order to
deepen the penetration of the culture by the Gospel. In this process the
Church is inevitably affected by the culture. Thus while the Church
transforms a culture, it is at the same time influenced by the culture.

---

[93] *PPF* IV, 103.

As an essential part of the Church's structure, the ministerial priest-hood does not escape this process. Although primarily a theological reality, it too is lived out in concrete cultural circumstances and is influenced by cultural realities. This influence can be seen in the various editions of the U.S. Bishops' *PPF* which explicitly correlate the ministerial priesthood with leadership, a correlation that is largely absent in universal Church documents. Theological and cultural categories are brought into play in the *PPF* and they must be approached in such a way that their own methodological peculiarities are respected. In other words, each component of the inculturation equation must be approached on its own terms: an exploration of priest as leader must be done in such a way that both the theological nature of priesthood and the cultural understanding of leadership are examined and highlighted before the two are brought into correlation.

Because the culture and the Church mutually influence each other, the methodology of inculturation requires that such mutual influence be critically examined[94]. Such a critical examination requires three steps: 1) it must focus on the relevant data; 2) it must reflect critically on the data; and 3) it must evaluate every instance of inculturation in order to determine its faithfulness to the Gospel and to authentic cultural values[95].

Chapter One described Carrier's criteria for evaluating particular instances of inculturation: 1) «distinguishing faith's proper role» stressed that the Gospel and the Church cannot be exclusively identified with any culture, but also that such distinction does not preclude deep interaction and association with cultures; the challenge is to encourage creative interaction between faith and culture without collapsing the two; 2) «building the Church according to its identity» emphasized the historical nature of the Church which has been enriched down through the ages by various cultural expressions of the faith, and that, because such expressions contribute to the Church's identity in both its unity and catholicity, the cultural experience of local Churches need to be harmonized with the universal Church; 3) «reconciling unity and pluralism» highlighted the Church as a communion that needs to respect and integrate whatever is of positive value in the world's various cultures;

---

[94] Cf. P. J. DRILLING, *Trinity and Ministry*, 20. For Dermot Lane, the «... mutually critical correlation between human experience and Christian tradition» is the first step of a methodology of inculturation; Cf. D. LANE, «The Challenge of Inculturation», 13. For a description of some of the methodological elements involved in inculturation, see above, pp. 50-55.

[95] Cf. above, pp. 54-55; P. J. DRILLING, *Trinity and Ministry*, 21.

4) finally, «discernment and investigation» is necessary to successfully implement the previous three criteria[96].

In the light of these considerations a methodology was delineated that allowed for the three steps of critical examination to be carried out in a way that respects the epistemological differences of the two categories being studied. Thus far in our study, the first two steps have been completed. In Chapters Two and Three the ministerial priesthood was examined from the perspective of leadership. As we have seen, the ministerial priesthood is a transcultural, ecclesial reality that is rooted in the Church's tradition and articulated in its teachings. The Second Vatican Council's «Decree on the Ministry and Life of Priests», *Presbyterorum Ordinis*, and Pope John Paul II's Post-Synodal Apostolic Exhortation, *Pastores Dabo Vobis*, are of particular importance for understanding the ministerial priesthood. Both of these documents and also three pertinent related documents — *Lumen Gentium* 10 and 28, *Optatam Totius*, *Christus Dominus*, and the 1971 Synodal document *The Ministerial Priesthood* — were examined thematically from the perspective of leadership in order to yield a particular understanding of the universal Church's teaching on the ministerial priesthood. Thus the first two steps of analyzing the process of inculturation — attentiveness to the data and critical reflection for understanding — have been carried out with regard to one aspect of the «priest as leader» equation, namely the ministerial priesthood.

In Chapter Four the second part of the equation — leadership as popularly understood in a United States cultural context — was examined, leading to the contention that the specific cultural context profoundly shapes and influences how leadership is understood. It showed that there is a vast body of literature on leadership by American authors, making it necessary to focus on a limited number of widely popular authors in order to arrive at a general description of leadership as it is popularly understood in the United States. Chapter Four then examined popular and influential works by Warren Bennis, Peter F. Drucker, James M. Kouzes, Burt Nanus, and Barry M. Posner, and from this examination offered conclusions about leadership as popularly conceived in the United States. As in Chapters Two and Three, the first two steps of analyzing the process of inculturation — attentiveness to the data and critical reflection for understanding — were carried out with regard to the cultural aspect

---

[96] Cf. above, pp. 47-50; H. CARRIER, *Evangelizing the Culture of Modernity*, 73-81.

of the «priest as leader» equation, namely leadership as understood in a U.S. context.

In order to complete this examination, the third step of the process, namely a correlation and critical dialogue between the two parts of the equation, must take place in order to determine their faithfulness to Church teaching and authentic cultural values. As noted in Chapter One, the conclusions of Chapters Two and Three regarding priesthood from a perspective of leadership, as articulated in Church documents, and the conclusions of Chapter Four, regarding a popular U.S. cultural under-standing of leadership, must be placed in critical dialogue and correlation with each other. This dialogue and correlation takes place in the context of the U.S. Bishops' *Program of Priestly Formation* which identified priesthood in the United States with leadership and was the impetus for this study. Such an interaction will help clarify a particular instance of inculturation: the *PPF*'s identification of the ministerial priesthood with leadership. In addition to showing how such an example of inculturation is faithful to both Church teaching and to cultural values, it will also show the inadequacies and potential pitfalls of such an understanding. Finally, it will identify some implications and challenges both for semi-nary formation and for a more effective living-out of priesthood that is faithful to the Gospel and Church tradition and adequate to the cultural understanding of leadership.

5.2 *Review of Church Teaching on Priest as Leader*

In Chapters Two and Three, teaching on the ministerial priesthood in the conciliar and postconciliar Church was examined from the perspec-tive of leadership. Using Cooke's rather general description of leadership as a key, the texts were approached in order to discover how they illu-mined an understanding of the ministerial priest as leader. As the research revealed, the Church's teaching on the ministerial priesthood is built upon a foundation composed of ecclesiological, christological, and pastoral elements. The salient points which emerged from that research will now be briefly reviewed.

5.2.1 Significant Ecclesiological Themes

a) *Trinitarian Ecclesiology as Context*

The ecclesiology of the Second Vatican Council, synthesized by Pope John Paul II in *Christifideles Laici* as mystery, communion, and mission, sets the context for understanding the ministerial priesthood and any theme associated with it. Of particular importance in conciliar ecclesiology is the aspect of communion (cf. *PDV* 12). In examining an ecclesiology of communion, Chapter Three stressed that the dynamism of the communion of the Church and its ministries mirrors that of the Trinity and is characterized by equality, distinction, and mutuality. In the Trinity there is a radical equality by which each person of the Trinity can be described as fully divine, a distinct identity constituted by relationship to the other two persons, and an absolute mutuality expressed in complete self-giving. Similarly, in the Church and its ministries there is, rooted in Baptism, a radical equality in the dignity of all members which does not take away from each member's unique and distinct identity; these equal but distinct members exist together in mutuality as a community in which each member offers his or her gifts in service and receives the gifts of the others in return.

The trinitarian dynamism of communion is at the heart of conciliar and post-conciliar ecclesiology and sets the broader context for understanding the ministerial priesthood. Pope John Paul II described the priesthood as «fundamentally relational» and stressed that «[...] the nature and mission of the ministerial priesthood cannot be defined except through this multiple and rich interconnection of relationships which arise from the Blessed Trinity and are prolonged in the communion of the Church» (*PDV* 12). Any consideration of the ministerial priest as leader, if it is to be true to conciliar and post-conciliar Church teaching, must begin with this «fundamentally relational dimension of priestly identity», a dimension that is rooted in the communion of the Church. An understanding of priestly leadership, then, must remain firmly anchored in conciliar ecclesiology, which is to say that, although the priest's distinctiveness is rooted in his sacramental configuration to Christ the Head and Shepherd which marks him as a leader, such distinction is conditioned by the radical equality he shares with all of the baptized, as well as by the self-giving love with which it must be exercised if it is to be authentic priestly leadership.

b) *The Priesthood: Ministerial and Hierarchical,*
   at the Service of the Common Priesthood,
   in Collaboration with the Bishop and Presbyterate

In context of the ecclesiology articulated above, a number of important themes emerged. First, the Council's affirmation of the common priesthood emphasized the profound unity that marks the Church because all of its members have been baptized into the one priesthood of Christ, have an active role in the Church's mission, and are called to a holiness characterized by the sacrificial gift of self. The ministerial priesthood and the common priesthood, although distinct, are ordered towards each other.

The Council used the terms ministerial and hierarchical to describe the relation of the ordained and common priesthood. Acknowledging the ordained priesthood as hierarchical indicates that it has a role of sacred authority or leadership vis-à-vis the common priesthood; to say that it is ministerial is to say that sacred authority or leadership must be understood as a service. Thus early in the research into the ecclesiological underpinnings of the ordained priesthood, the reality of leadership began to emerge. Although different «in essence and not only in degree» (*LG* 10), the ordained priesthood is profoundly ordered to the common priesthood, an interrelation characterized by the sacred authority that the ordained priest exercises as a service in promotion of the common priesthood. To describe the ordained priesthood as ministerial and hierarchical, then, is to affirm that leadership exercised as service is one of its constitutive dimensions, rooted in its very sacramental structure.

In addition to the relation of the ministerial and common priesthood as fundamental to an understanding of the priest as leader, the research into the ecclesiological foundations of the ordained priesthood revealed two other important themes for understanding priest as leader: the ordained priest's relation to the bishop and his membership in a presbyterate. Vatican II's teaching on the priesthood's dependent relation to the bishop stressed that the priest exercises his ministry of leadership collegially and with accountability, always at the service of the unity of the Church. The Council's designation of the ministerial priest as presbyter carries with it an inherent understanding of leadership which, by definition, emphasizes collegiality: the priest belongs to a body of presbyters, a college of «elders» or leaders, under the leadership of the bishop.

In conclusion, the ecclesiological underpinnings of the ministerial priesthood stress the ministerial priest's membership in a Church characterized by a trinitarian dynamism, thus radically relational. Within the Church, the ministerial priesthood is found profoundly oriented towards the common priesthood. Under the collegial leadership of the bishop and in collaboration with other presbyters, the ministerial priesthood is invested with a sacred authority which, at least in part, is to be exercised as a service for the growth and life of the common priesthood. Because of the wider ecclesial context, priestly leadership is relational, communitarian, and exercised as part of a collective work. Leadership is thus a constitutive dimension of the ministerial priesthood.

5.2.2 Significant Christological Themes

a) *The Priesthood: Sacramental Representation of Christ*

Although the ecclesiological perspective sets the wider context for articulating the doctrine of the ministerial priesthood, study of conciliar and post-conciliar documents, most notably *Presbyterorum Ordinis* and *Pastores Dabo Vobis*, revealed that the christological perspective is at the heart of the Church's understanding of the ministerial priesthood: «Reference to Christ is thus the absolutely necessary key for understanding the reality of the priesthood» (*PDV* 12). The christological perspective, therefore, is crucial for filling out a description of the leadership aspect of priesthood, which the ecclesiological investigations revealed to be a constitutive component.

Research into the christological foundations revealed that the Church documents adopted a fundamentally sacramental hermeneutic for understanding the priesthood, emphasizing that «[...] priests are a sacramental representation of Jesus Christ the Head and Shepherd» (*PDV* 15; cf.*LG* 28 and *PO*2); in other sections, *PDV* stressed the priest's configuration to Christ the Head, Shepherd, and Spouse of the Church. Configuration to Christ is foundational for every aspect of the priest's life; thus it can be said that his ministry and spirituality is inscribed in this prior relation to Christ. The research into the christological foundations of the priesthood revealed that just as Christ was consecrated by the Father and sent forth in mission in service to the Kingdom of God, so too, the ministerial priest shares in the same dynamic: he is consecrated for mission. There is thus a profound symbiosis between who he is and what he does. It was pointed out that, as sacramental representations of Christ, priests are to embody and prolong Christ's presence to the Church. Such a sacramental understanding is crucial for understanding the leadership aspect of the ministerial priesthood because it reinforces what was seen above in the ecclesiological section, namely, that leadership is an intrinsic, constitutive aspect of the priesthood, part of the sacramental structure itself, and not an extrinsic accretion or designation.

b) *Configured to Christ the Head, Shepherd, and Spouse*

Sacramental configuration to Christ the Head, Shepherd, and Spouse establishes possibilities and sets limits on an understanding of priestly leadership. Configured to Christ, and thus the instrument of Christ, the priest stands towards the Church in a permanent relation of love, solicitude, and service. Such configuration, traditionally described by the term sacramental character, denotes not only the priest's relationship to Christ but Christ's enduring fidelity and love for the Church. Christ must always be present to his body, vivifying it and uniting it to himself. For this reason, ministerial priests are instruments not only of Christ's headship but also of his pastoral care and spousal love. The priest's sacramental representation of Christ, therefore, has direct implications for both priestly ministry and spirituality, thus for priestly leadership. The priest, as a sacramental representative of Christ the Head, Shepherd, and Spouse, is to embrace and mirror, as best he can, the attitudes and characteristics of Christ: self-emptying, obedient service, radical availability, and the complete gift of self in love to Christ and to the Church. As Christ's instrument, the ministerial priest's life is to be characterized by service (Christ the Head), pastoral solicitude (Christ the Shepherd), and spousal love (Christ the Spouse). Priestly leadership, therefore, is to always point beyond the priest himself to the person of Christ whom the priest represents sacramentally.

c) *Continuing the Ministry of Christ the Priest, Prophet, and King*

Concretely, the ministerial priest's configuration to Christ also determines his activities, which in turn shape an understanding of the kind of leadership he is to exercise. The research revealed that the Church chose to emphasize the ministry of Christ as characterized by preaching, sanctifying, and guiding the People of God. His threefold ministry is bound up with an expressive of the consecration and mission he received from the Father. By anchoring the ministerial priesthood in Christ's threefold office through sacramental configuration to Christ, the Church situated the priesthood at the heart of the mystery of Christ, which has ramifications for understanding priestly leadership. Identification with Christ, in his person and in his work, is the foundation upon which priestly leadership is built. It is rooted in the mystery of Christ and expressed in the threefold ministry of Christ which gives content and definition to the kind of leadership the priest is to offer in the Church, namely a leadership that is expressed in the service to word, sacrament, and pastoral care.

5.2.3 Significant Pastoral Themes: Functional and Relational Aspects of Ministerial Priesthood

The research in conciliar and post-conciliar documents, including *Pastores Dabo Vobis*, revealed that the pastoral dimension of the ministerial priesthood is rooted in both the ecclesiological and christological components, and so touches on many of their main themes. Within the pastoral perspective, however, these themes are approached from a different angle, one that considers some of the more practical and existential ramifications of the christological and ecclesiological themes in the ministry and life of the priest, particularly the priest's functions and relationships. In terms of priestly leadership, the primary activities are comprised of the threefold ministry of Christ the Priest, Prophet, and King. In order to engage in these activities after the example of Christ, the documents emphasized that the priest must interiorize Christ's three-fold mission by allowing himself to experience the power of the Word and reality of the Paschal Mystery in his own life to be able to effectively engage in the ministry of pastoring God's people. Although stressing different points of emphasis, the research showed that because the three-fold ministry is constituted by an intrinsic unity and profound integra-tion, each aspect must be understood in relation to the others. Thus, when the priest engages in any aspect of the threefold ministry of Christ, he is expressing leadership; it is not exclusively tied to any one function. In *Pastores Dabo Vobis*, Pope John Paul II developed this theme by stressing the ministerial priest as the leader of the «new evangelization». Such leadership is not tied solely to the ministry of the Word, but includes all aspects of the threefold ministry.

In addition to specific functions, certain relationships also condition an understanding of priest as leader. The documents revealed that the minis-terial priesthood is lived out in the context of relationships with the bishop, other priests, and lay people, relationships in which priestly leadership is to be accountable, collegial, collaborative, and always to be exercised in service to the unity of the Church. *Pastores Dabo Vobis* added an important clarification in terms of understanding the priest's relationships by stressing that, configured to Christ the Spouse, the priest stands *towards* the Church, a stance characterized by spousal love. *PDV* also stressed the Evangelical Counsels as a means to enhance the pastoral life of the priest; in addition to expressing and deepening his configu-ration to Christ, they help to create the interor dispositions and freedom he needs to put himself entirely at the service of the Church, thus offering a leadership that gives witness to his relationship to Christ and is characterized by the pastoral charity of Christ. Finally, *PDV* stressed that the priest's functions and his relationships are lived out in the context of a particular Church. The priest relates to a particular bishop, belongs to a particular presbyterate, and serves a particular people. The reality of the particular Church thus shapes the exercise of the priest's leadership.

5.2.4 Conclusions

In the light of the extensive research into the conciliar and post-conciliar documents concerning the ministerial priesthood, particularly *Presbyterorum Ordinis* and *Pastores Dabo Vobis*, a number of conclusions concerning the Church's understanding of the leadership role of the ministerial priest can be articulated.

First, priestly leadership is anchored in the Sacrament of Ordination which permanently configures the priest to Christ the Head, Shepherd, and Spouse of the Church. The ability to be a sacramental representation of Christ the Head, Shepherd, and Spouse does not come from community designation, but from God through the sacrament. Lest such an exalted understanding of the ministerial priesthood lead to an exclusivist interpretation, it is crucial to immediately add that the Church, mirroring the trinitarian dynamism of radical equality, distinctiveness, and mutuality, sets the context for the exercise of priestly leadership. The priest is not in a position of superiority vis-à-vis the Church. He is in the Church and exists for the Church, and because of his configuration to Christ, can only genuinely exercise his leadership as love for and service to the Church (the common priesthood). Because his sacramental leadership is a sign of Christ's fidelity to the Church, it participates in and must be motivated by the «pastoral charity» of Christ the Good Shepherd in order to be authentic. This points to the importance of an interior life, rooted in Christ, that seeks to appropriate the attitudes of Christ, expressed by the Evangelical Counsels, in order to be a more effective minister. The priest's leadership is concretized by his participation in the threefold ministry of Christ, a ministry of word, sacrament, and pastoral care. Because he exercises his ministry of leadership in the Church, a complex web of relationships, the priest's leadership is accountable, collegial, and collaborative, always exercised in service to the unity of the Church. The research has shown that the portrait of priest as leader that emerges from the study of pertinent Church documents, is fairly nuanced and complex because leadership is not something extrinsic to the ministerial priesthood or associated with one dimension of it, but rather is rooted in its theological and spiritual foundations.

5.3 *Review of U.S. Cultural Understandings of Leadership*

5.3.1 Transformational Leadership

Chapter Four traced and examined major points in the development of leadership theory in the U.S., showing that leadership theory has evolved from a traits approach, to a functional or behavioral approach, to a situational approach, and finally to the transformational approach, which incorporates and builds upon previous schools of thought but moves beyond them in its emphasis on engaging people's higher needs and motivations to bring about a change in thinking that will translate into a change of behavior in the pursuit of a common goal. As noted above, Burns was the first to describe transformational leadership:

> The transforming leader recognizes and exploits an existing need or demand of a potential follower. But, beyond that, the transforming leader looks for potential motives in followers, seeks to satisfy higher needs, and engages the full person of the follower. The result of transforming leadership is a relation-ship of mutual stimulation and elevation that converts followers into leaders and may convert leaders into moral agents[97].

Transformational leadership, then, engages people in such a way that they are raised to higher levels of motivation and morality.

The research showed that various theorists after Burns associated certain factors or characteristics with transformational leaders. They are described as charismatic, inspirational, intellectually stimulating, and considerate; they are creative, interactive, visionary, empowering, and passionate[98]. Bass stated that «[...] the transformational leader sharply arouses or alters the strength of needs which may have lain dormant. [...] It is leadership that is transformational that can bring about the big differences and big changes in groups, organizations, and societies»[99]. The transformational model of leadership has become the most popular contemporary approach, and the authors considered in Chapter Four represent, in varying degrees, this school of thought.

The authors whose works were examined in Chapter Four, Drucker, Bennis, Nanus, Kouzes, and Posner, were chosen on the basis of their expertise in the field, wide popularity, and representativeness. A synthe-tic analysis of a representative sample of their works was offered and general themes pertaining to leadership were highlighted. The key to synthesizing their works was based on Garry Wills' observation that leadership is tripartite; that is, «Leaders, followers and goals make up the three equally necessary supports for leadership»[100]. Hence, three basic

---

[97] J. M. BURNS, *Leadership*, 4.

[98] Cf. above, p. 207; B. M. BASS, *Bass and Stogdill's Handbook of Leadership*, 218; M. Z. HACKMAN – C. E. JOHNSON, *Leadership*, 63-65.

[99] B. M. BASS, *Leadership and Performance Beyond Expectations*, 17, quoted in M. Z. HACKMAN – C. E. JOHNSON, *Leadership*, 63.

[100] G. WILLS, *Certain Trumpets*, 17.

questions were asked of the literature: What does it say about the leader? What does it say about followers? What does it say about goals or vision? A synopsis of the findings is offered here in order to set the stage for a «dialogue», or correlation, between the U.S. cultural understanding of leadership and priestly leadership as it emerged in the Church documents studied in Chapters Two and Three, and was summarized above.

5.3.2 Significant Leader Themes

As noted in Chapter Four, each of the authors put strong emphasis on the person of the leader and the qualities a leader needs in order to be effective. The leader's character is of central importance and determines his or her success or failure as a leader. Drucker's question about a leader's character typified all of the authors' approaches to the topic: «If I had a son or a daughter would I be willing to have him or her work under this person?»[101]. In other words, because followers tend to model themselves on a strong superior, that person's character is very important, and nothing is more destructive to an organization than a corrupt leader. Drucker also emphasized the importance of character by insisting on congruence between a leader's actions and his or her professed beliefs. Such consistency is necessary if the leader is to engender trust among the members of the organization. In a similar way, Bennis and Nanus stressed the fundamental importance of a leader's character and named four virtues that are essential in this regard: integrity, dedication, magnanimity and openness. For Bennis and Nanus the leader's character is foundational for everything else. As Nanus stressed, «Nothing is noticed more quickly — and considered more significant — than a discrepancy between what executives preach and what they expect their associates to practice»[102]. Similarly, Kouzes and Posner accented the importance of a leader's character and stressed that credibility — the product of honesty, competence, the ability to inspire and to look forward — is the key to character. For all of the authors, congruence between the leader's shared values and his or her behavior is critical and is a sure gauge to reveal the leader's character.

In addition to character, the authors stressed the importance of self-development in a leader. It is only by developing themselves that leaders assure continued effectiveness. To stress this theme Drucker identified five practices; Bennis and Nanus offered four strategies; and Kouzes

---

101 P. F. DRUCKER, *The Effective Executive*, 86.
102 B. NANUS, *The Leader's Edge*, 102.

and Posner articulated five practices, ten commitments, and six disciplines — all designed to help leaders develop personal strengths and skills for maximum effectiveness. Perhaps the statement that best sums up all of the authors' approaches to self-development is that of Kouzes and Posner who compared leadership to an art whose primary instrument is the self: «The mastery of the art of leadership comes with the mastery of the self»[103].

5.3.3 Significant Follower Themes

Although all of the authors emphasized that leadership consists in a relationship that must be characterized by trust in order to be effective, Kouzes and Posner most clearly developed the theme of the importance of followers in the process of leadership. Rooted in the conviction that «leadership is in the eye of the follower», they devoted an entire book to approaching leadership from the perspective of followers. In their research they discovered that leaders earn credibility — and the loyalty of their followers — by practicing certain behaviors that accent other-centeredness: responsiveness to the needs of others, an ability to look beyond themselves, showing of appreciation, affirmation and development of others, and showing trust in them. These behaviors display a leader's belief in the intrinsic self-worth of others and emphasize the relational nature of leadership. Similarly, Bennis described qualities in leaders — constancy, congruity, reliability, and integrity — that engender trust and loyalty in followers. For Bennis and Nanus, «Trust is the lubrication that makes it possible for organizations to work»[104], and they stressed that such trust can only be established when the leader consistently holds up the collective vision before the followers, establishing a permanent niche for the vision. Bennis stressed that the effect of good leadership on followers is empowerment, which is reflected in four basic attitudes of followers: significance, competence, community, and enjoyment. Like the other authors, Drucker too, emphasized the importance of trust, adding that without it «[...] there won't be any followers — and the only definition of a leader is someone who has followers»[105]. In addition to trust, Drucker consistently stressed the importance of building upon followers' strengths and appraising them based on objective criteria of performance. Drucker also emphasized the

---

[103] J. M. KOUZES – B. Z. POSNER, *The Leadership Challenge*, 298.
[104] W. G. BENNIS – B. NANUS, *Leadership*, 43.
[105] P. F. DRUCKER, *Managing for the Future*, 122.

centrality of the organization's mission or goal as the determining factor of leader-follower interaction. Within this broader framework it is the leader's role to establish opportunities for followers to develop their skills and strengths.

5.3.4 Significant Vision/Goal/Mission Themes

As noted in Chapter Four, the terms «vision», «mission», and «goals» were often used interchangeably by the authors. They all put a strong emphasis on the importance of a central, clarifying vision or mission for the life of an organization; additionally, they stressed the leader's crucial, although not exclusive, role in articulating and developing the vision. Drucker stressed that the key to the relationship between leader and followers is the vision; the vision must reflect the values of the organization, express its strengths, respond to a real need, and be communicated clearly so that both leader and followers can commit themselves to it. Bennis and Nanus also stressed the importance of the vision and the leader's role in developing and articulating it. They argued, however, that the vision does not necessarily originate in the leader but may come from many sources, including followers. It is important, therefore, that the leader be a listener and pay close attention to other sources that will enable him to develop and articulate the vision. Leaders must take into consideration data from the past and present, as well as well-founded speculation about the future, and then be able to interpret the information received during this consideration; collaboration is thus crucial in development of vision.

Nanus delineated certain properties of transforming visions: they are appropriate for the organization and the times; they set high standards and reflect high ideals; they clarify purpose and direction; they inspire enthusiasm and commitment; they are clearly articulated and easily understood; they reflect the uniqueness of the organization; and they are ambitious. Bennis and Nanus stressed that vision is crucially important for an organization because only a clear, shared sense of purpose and direction will enable the members to have a sense of their own roles in the organization and to work effectively for the overriding vision. This is especially true during times of great change and in a complex environment. For Kouzes and Posner, vision is a future-oriented, concrete image that expresses both the ideals and the uniqueness of an organization, and it is a principal task of the leader to enlist followers to invest in the articulated vision. In order to do this, Nanus and Bennis insisted that the leader must be the social architect who manages the meaning of the organization by effectively articulating the vision. Such an understanding also reflects Drucker's point of view regarding vision.

5.3.5 Conclusions

As noted above, because leadership necessarily entails the involvement of leaders, followers, and goals, Garry Wills described it as tripartite in nature. He emphasized that the three aspects are not simply juxtaposed to each other, but are intrinsically connected. For leadership to exist, a leader and followers must join together in pursuit of a common goal, vision, or mission. Although they may have little else in common, the goal brings them together and establishes a leader-follower relationship.

As leadership theory has evolved, it has become clearer that the leader-follower-goal relationship is rather complex and involves more than meets the eye. Although the leader's personal traits, skills, and behaviors are still important in the process of leadership, research has shown that the context, or situation, is also crucial; this includes the followers, the nature of the group, and the common goal that brings them together. Additionally, research has shown that the most effective leadership involves more than an appeal to the lower human needs for safety and sustenance, and instead seeks to engage higher needs of self-fulfillment and human growth. Thus, leadership is seen as more than a transactional, *quid pro quo* relationship and instead has the potential to be transformational.

Transformational leadership theory, then, is the most popular understanding of the process of leadership in the U.S. today, and the authors examined in Chapter Four represent, in varying degrees, that school of thought. As Hackman and Johnson observed, transformational leadership is interactive, involving a reciprocal relationship between followers and leader; it is visionary, submitting itself to an overarching goal, vision, or mission that gives direction to both leaders and followers and shapes concomitant behavior; it is empowering, encouraging both leader and followers to take initiative and develop their potential in order to maximize their contribution; it is creative, risking even failure in its willingness to innovate; it is passionate, showing a love for and commitment to both the task and the other people involved[106]. In addition to Hackman and Johnson's observation, the research revealed that transformational leadership is grounded in a relationship of trust, which in turn is dependent in large part on the character and integrity of the leader.

---

[106] Cf. M. Z. HACKMAN – C. E. JOHNSON, *Leadership*, 63-67.

Having examined the concern for priesthood and leadership in the various editions of the *PPF*, and having completed a review of the salient themes of Chapters One through Four, we can now proceed to the «critical dialogue» and moment of resonance between the ecclesial and cultural data in the final chapter, «The Inculturation of a Spiritual-Theological Theme of Priesthood in a U.S. Context: A Spirituality of Priest as Leader».

CHAPTER VI

The Inculturation of a Spiritual-Theological Theme
of Priesthood in a U.S. Context:
A Spirituality of Priest as Leader

1. Introduction

In the previous chapter the various editions of the United States
Bishops' *Program of Priestly Formation* were examined and their
concern for understanding the priest as leader was highlighted. Additionally, the salient points of Chapters One through Four, concerning
inculturation, the Church's teaching on the ministerial priesthood from
the perspective of leadership, and U.S. cultural approaches to leadership
were reviewed and highlighted. Following the methodology of inculturation established in Chapter One, this final chapter will bring the various
elements of the research into a critical «dialogue» with each other, a
dialogue that will culminate in an articulation of a spirituality of the
priest as leader in a U.S. context. Such a spirituality will most aptly integrate the various elements of the research of the previous chapters and
illustrate a genuine process of inculturation.

It was noted in the previous chapter that the first two steps of a
methodology of inculturation — 1) consideration of relevant data and 2)
critical reflection on the data — have already been carried out in
Chapters Two through Five. The third step — an evaluation of the data
in order to determine fidelity to the Gospel and to authentic cultural
values — can now completed. Such an evaluation entails two parts. The
first is a correlation and evaluation of the data. Important as such a
correlation and evaluation is, it alone does not express the full process of
inculturation, but merely acculturation, which is only a part, albeit an
important part, of the process. Such a step is essential for setting the
stage for genuine inculturation. Chapter One indicated that genuine

inculturation must also include a moment of «liberating praxis» or «truth» or «resonance» which is the basis for action. Thus the second part of the third step will take the data from the correlation and gather it into such a moment of resonance or liberating praxis: the articulation of a spirituality of priest as leader in a U.S. context. Finally, we will conclude with implications and challenges that such an understanding of priest as leader poses for seminary formation in the U.S. today.

2. Acculturation: The Correlation of Salient Themes

A caveat or proviso seems necessary at the beginning of the correlation of spiritual-theological and cultural themes. The research has shown that the ministerial priesthood is a constitutive dimension of the Church which cannot be properly understood apart from that context: it must be first and foremost an ecclesial reality rooted in ecclesiological, christological, and pastoral foundations. The process of inculturation, as described in Chapter One, does not seek to rob it of its theological and spiritual richness by reducing it to an exclusively cultural category. Affirming the *semina Verbi* present in creation and in culture, it demonstrates the possibilities and limits of a particular cultural category, in this case a U.S. understanding of leadership, for enhancing the understanding and practice of priesthood as lived out in the cultural context of the United States. The process of inculturation also shows how the Church's understanding of the priesthood can influence the U.S. cultural understanding of leadership, so there is no question of collapsing two epistemologically distinct categories into each other. With this proviso in mind, certain complementary themes or points of convergence from both categories will be correlated (stage of acculturation) to set the stage for describing a spirituality of priest as leader in a U.S. context (stage of inculturation).

2.1 *Ecclesiological and U.S. Cultural Themes*

The examination of the ministerial priesthood from an ecclesiological perspective demonstrated that an ecclesiology of communion is a crucial context for understanding the priesthood[1]. Mirroring the Trinity,

---

[1] In correlating the themes we are following the same order established in Chapters Two and Three. Chapter Two noted that because the ecclesiological perspective was the lens through which the Second Vatican Council's teaching on the ministerial priesthood was developed, the ecclesiological perspective needed examination first, then the christological and pastoral perspectives. Chapter Three noted that *PDV*'s doctrinal exposition of the priesthood moved from the ecclesiological to the christological to the

members of the Church, although unique and distinct as individuals, are radically equal in virtue of baptism and exist in relationships of mutuality and love. The ecclesiology of communion, a «multiple and rich interconnection of relationships which arise from the Blessed Trinity» (*PDV* 12), assures a relational understanding of priesthood, a starting point for understanding the priest as leader: rooted in the communion of the Church, the priest is fundamentally relational, and although distinct, his distinctiveness as a leader does not diminish the radical equality he shares with all baptized, nor remove him from the mutuality that characterizes all members of the Church in virtue of their common baptism.

The ecclesiological perspective can be correlated with findings from the research into the U.S. cultural understanding of leadership. First, Wills' statement about the intrinsically threefold nature of leadership, that it simply cannot exist without leaders, followers, and goals, points to a context for understanding leadership that involves more than the person of the leader. Kouzes and Posner emphasized the importance of the wider context: «Followers determine whether someone possesses leadership qualities. [...] Leadership is in the eye of the follower»[2]. Drucker echoed this by emphasizing that «[...] the only definition of a leader is someone who has followers»[3]. Thus both the ecclesial and popular U.S. cultural approach to understanding of leadership emphasize the importance of the wider context for the exercise of leadership. For priesthood the wider context is the Church, the community of the baptized; for a secular leader it is the group made up of followers or constituents. Both understandings stress that leadership is fundamentally and essentially relational.

Another ecclesiological theme was that of the ordained priesthood as ministerial and hierarchical, that is, as service and leadership. While the priest is certainly a leader within the community of the Church, such leadership can only be understood in the context of service. It was stressed that the ministerial priesthood exists in a relationship of service

---

pastoral perspectives. We will follow the same order in this correlation of themes. As emphasized throughout the chapters, however, the christological perspective is primary and central to a proper understanding of the ministerial priesthood.

[2] J. M. KOUZES – B. Z. POSNER, *The Leadership Challenge*, 15. This correlation does not imply that priestly leadership is something designated by the community. It has already been demonstrated that priesthood, and thus priestly leadership, is rooted in the sacramental structure of the Church and is not dependent upon community election or approval. The correlation simply points to the necessity of the ecclesial context for understanding priestly leadership, just as the group context is necessary for understanding secular leadership.

[3] P. F. DRUCKER, *Managing for the Future*, 122.

and leadership to the common priesthood, in order to help the common priesthood to actualize itself in terms of self-giving and worship. The theme of service has also become increasingly important in secular understandings of leadership, particularly the transformational approach. In fact, the key to greatness or success as a leader is servanthood: the leader must be seen as a servant first and foremost, and out of this sense of being a servant, he or she will be an effective leader. One of the basic understandings of transformational leadership is that it is more than transactional; that is, it appeals to the higher human needs of self-actualization and meaning. Thus according to the theory, in the process of pursuing a common goal both leader and followers are transformed, and move to higher levels of achievement and satisfaction. Leadership is thus understood as service to both the lower and higher human needs in the process of serving organizational needs. Indeed the secular authors stressed the importance of understanding leadership as a responsibility, thus as service to the people and purposes of an organization. Here again, the understanding of priestly leadership as servanthood within the Church corresponds to the transformational approach, which understands secular leadership in terms of servanthood relative to the goals, the common good of the group, and individuals' personal needs within the group.

Related to the emphasis on service or servanthood, the ecclesiological perspective stressed the priest's fundamental relation to the bishop and presbyterate, assuring that priestly leadership is accountable, collaborative, and collegial. The priest is not «superior» to the people he serves, nor does he exercise his leadership as an «independent agent». Similarly, research into the understanding of leadership in the context of U.S. culture has shown that leadership is profoundly interactive and focused on the other members of the group or enterprise. The leader is accountable to his or her organization and serves the organization (not vice-versa); he or she must be focused on the followers, acting in ways that win trust and loyalty, empowering followers to develop themselves in the process of furthering the cause of the enterprise or organization. For both priestly and secular leadership, collaboration, encouragement, empowerment, and accountability are key ingredients.

2.2 Christological and U.S. Cultural Themes

The sacramental hermeneutic is at the heart of the Church's teaching on the ministerial priesthood: as a sacramental representation of Christ, the priest is configured to Christ the Head, Shepherd, and Spouse of the Church. Such configuration, traditionally understood as priestly character, not only reveals the priest's relationship to Christ, but more importantly, Christ's enduring fidelity to the Church. As the research has shown, priestly ministry and life are inscribed in the priest's relationship with Christ. The priest's configuration to Christ touches the priest on the level of his being, is prior to all else, and determines the kind of life the priest is to lead, the ministry he is to do, and the leadership he is to exercise. The priest exercises a leadership characterized by service, solicitude, and love for the Church in the concrete activities of preaching the Word, celebrating the sacraments, and caring for the People of God. The attitudes and activities of Christ are to determine how the priest serves as a leader; again, the prior relation to Christ defines the priest's ministry and life, including his leadership. As the research in Chapter Three has shown, «pastoral charity» is at the core of Christ's attitudes and activities, and thus at the heart of the ministerial priesthood.

The secular literature studied in Chapter Four stressed the importance of character as foundational for leadership[4]. Because of the christological centrality of priestly identity and ministry, it is more difficult to correlate themes from a popular understanding of leadership, but some indications can be made. Each author stressed the necessity of congruence between a leader's expressed beliefs and values and his or her activities. Such congruence is necessary if the leader is to have credibility with his or her followers and so build up a relationship of loyalty rooted in trust. The character of the effective leader was described by words such as integrity, magnanimity, dedication, openness, constancy, reliability, and congruity. In an analogous way, the character of the priest must express a similar congruence between his explicitly articulated beliefs and values and his activities. The sacramental hermeneutic demands that the priest live out what his public commitment proclaims: he is to enflesh the service, solicitude, and love of Christ in his activities of word, sacrament, and pastoral care. The prior relation to Christ, then, determines priestly activity. If priestly leadership is to be effective, there must be congruence between what he proclaims and how he lives. Integrity is just as crucial for a priest as it is for a secular leader. For the ministerial priest, however, the integrity is determined by the demands, possibilities, and limits set by sacramental ordination which determines the priest's particular configuration to Christ.

---

[4] This is not to be confused with the sacramental character associated with Holy Orders.

The research in Chapter Four highlighted the importance of vision as a dimension of the leadership process, in which the leader and followers come together in service to a common vision or goal that determines their activities. The vision must be clearly articulated and expressive of the values and purpose of the group or organization. Although the source of the vision is not necessarily the leader — there can be a variety of sources — it is the leader's task to articulate the vision in such a way that it guides the activities and purpose of the group. Similarly, the priest as leader does not originate the vision that guides that portion of the Church entrusted to his care. The vision is rooted in Christ, as expressed by the Church in Sacred Scripture, tradition, liturgy, and in the lived experience of the People of God in all of its diversity and unity. Thus the articulation of the Church's vision necessarily takes place through a process of dialogue, listening, prayer, and study: that is to say, through profound collaboration carried out in the context of the Church. The research stressed that the priest, in order to be true to his sacramental configuration to Christ, must be deeply immersed in the scriptures, the sacramental life of the Church, and the lives of the people he serves, if he is to properly serve and lead in the Church. He must also be motivated by a profound missionary spirit that is able to look beyond the boundaries of his own particular Church. In this way the priest articulates not his own vision, but the vision of Christ as expressed by the Church. Like secular leaders, the priest is responsible for articulating the guiding vision, but he does not create the vision; it is rooted in Christ and the Church and is arrived at collaboratively.

Additionally, the secular literature and Church documents stress self-development. The priest needs skills in order to exercise his ministry effectively; hence the Church encourages his ongoing formation and development as a person and as a priest. The priest's self-development, however, is more than a matter of the mere acquisition of skills. As noted above, the priest's sacramental representation of Christ is both a challenge and an invitation to an ongoing deepening of his configuration to Christ. Again, this takes place through immersion in the sacramental life of the Church and the Scriptures. In his sacramental representation of Christ the Head, Shepherd, and Spouse — appropriating the pastoral charity of Christ by engaging in the threefold ministry and embracing the Evangelical Counsels — the priest most effectively and convincingly acts as a leader. Thus the theme of self-development, which is so prominent in the popular secular literature, takes on a particular christological resonance when applied to the ministerial priest: like a deepening spiral, his self-development must flow out of and lead into his configuration to Christ. The implications of this for priestly spirituality of leadership will be described in more detail below.

2.3 *Pastoral and U.S. Cultural Themes*

The research in Chapters Two and Three demonstrated that the pastoral elements of the ministerial priesthood flow out of the ecclesiological and christological elements, and emphasize the more practical and existential ramifications of the priest's grounding in Christ and the Church. The research focused on the functions and relationships that are consequential to the priest's sacramental ordination. In terms of functions, it was shown that the priest continues the threefold ministry of Christ, the Priest, Prophet, and King; that the leadership exercised by the priest transcends — and is transcended by — each of these three aspects of ministry; and that it is not exclusively tied to any single function. The leadership of the priest, concretely expressed in the actions of the threefold ministry, is entirely at the service of the Church, and is aimed at the empowerment and actualization of the common priesthood. It was stressed above in the Christological section, that the priest does not simply engage in superficial activities, but is to interiorize the threefold ministry of Christ through his own immersion in the Sacred Scriptures and the Paschal Mystery as celebrated in the sacraments.

In addition to the priest's activities, the research showed that he exercises ministry within the context of the Church, characterized by a web of relationships that includes the bishop, fellow priests, and the laity. Church teaching stressed that the ministerial priesthood is dependent upon the bishop who possesses the fullness of Orders. It also showed that ordination situates the ministerial priest in a presbyterate, a body of elders, or leaders, with the bishop as its head. Finally, the doctrine on priesthood stressed that ordination puts the ministerial priest into a particular relation of service to the common priesthood, the laity. Thus the ministerial priesthood is characterized by a «radical relationality» that demands it to be lived out accountably, collegially, and collaboratively.

Focusing on the functional and relational aspect of the ministerial priesthood, some correlations can be made with findings from the study of U.S. cultural understandings of leadership. As noted above, the authors studied in Chapter Four all stressed the relational, interactive dimensions of transformational leadership and that the activities and functions of the leader are at the service of the relationships that exist for the pursuit of a common goal. The vision, or goal, defines both the activities and the relationships of the leader. On the practical level, the leader must demonstrate other-centered behavior that reveals his belief in the intrinsic value and worth of the other members of the group. He must demonstrate a certain congruity between his expressed beliefs and his behaviors. Finally, he must be open to self-development and growth so that he can improve his ability to serve the common vision and empower the members of the group to grow in their own competence and skills.

In the practical arena of functions and relationships, the importance of skills and competence for effective priestly leadership begin to emerge, suggesting correlations with a more secular understanding of leadership. Although the priest's relation to Christ is prior to all else, he still needs practical skills, just as a secular leader does. He needs to be committed to find ways to improve his effectiveness and thus offer better priestly leadership that enables the other members of the Church to live out their faith more fully. Preaching, presiding at sacraments, collaborating with people at various levels in his ministerial activities, require that the priest have a certain measure of leadership qualities and skills. His capacity to lead, as has been emphasized, is rooted in the sacrament itself; but by developing himself and enhancing his skills and abilities, the ministerial priest will improve his effectiveness as a priest and as a leader. In this sense, it is every bit as necessary for the priest as it is for the secular leader to find ways of self-development in order to improve his leadership skills. This is not a matter of self-indulgence or self-centeredness, but of service to the Church. Such self-development is an example of the priest's commitment «[...] to serve the People of God who are the Church and to draw all mankind to Christ» (*PDV* 12).

2.4 *Adequacy of Correlating Priesthood and Leadership*

Having correlated the spiritual-theological and cultural themes according to the methodology of inculturation established in Chapter One, the question can be asked: «Is the *PPF*'s identification of the ministerial priesthood with leadership faithful to the Church's understanding of the priesthood, and is it adequate to leadership as it is popularly understood in the culture of the United States?». The research indicates that the initial answer would seem to be an unqualified «yes». Using Cooke's generic description of leadership as a key, it was demonstrated that leadership is an intrinsic dimension of the ministerial priesthood, built into the Sacrament itself, and shaped by its ecclesiological, christological, and pastoral foundations. But it was also shown that the theme of leadership, connected to priesthood, most *explicitly* emerges in the U.S. *PPF* documents, not in universal Church documents. It was also shown that leadership, as it is popularly understood in the U.S., takes on particular, culturally-conditioned accents which were highlighted in the study of popular U.S. authors. To identify the ministerial priest as leader is true enough, but to identify the priest as leader in a U.S. context is to bring two different categories together. The answer to the question requires clarification.

Insofar as the ministerial priest is understood, as defined and described by Church teaching, he can be defined as a leader, indeed a transformational leader, as delineated by the U.S. authors studied in Chapter Four. The correlations described above showed a great deal of convergence between priestly leadership themes and transformational leadership themes — for example: the fundamental relationality of the ministerial priest and the interactional nature of the transformational leader; the ministerial priesthood understood as a leadership of service to Christ and to the Church, and transformational leadership understood as service to the group; the ministerial priesthood as serving, in part, the actuation of the common priesthood, and transformational leadership understood as seeking to empower the members of a group to achieve not only the group goals, but to develop as human beings; the accountable, collaborative nature of both the ministerial priesthood and transformational leadership; the need for congruence between personal behavior and professed values on the part of both ministerial priests and transformational leaders, or «character» as understood non-theologically; the importance of self-development in both priests and transformational leaders in order to better serve the goals and needs of the people they serve/lead; the importance of a common vision that shapes and guides the leadership of both priests and transformational leaders.

In the light of the many correlations between the ministerial priesthood as understood by Church teaching, and transformational leadership as described by U.S. authors, it can be asserted that within certain limits and respecting the epistemological distinction of the two categories, the identification of priest as leader in a U.S. context is faithful to both Church teaching and to U.S. cultural values. It can even be asserted that the priest is a transformational leader, as it is popularly understood in the U.S. cultural context, and that such an understanding can be an aid to the priest in developing priestly leadership skills and practices; but such assertions, must immediately be nuanced and put into larger context, since the identification of priesthood with leadership in a U.S. context also suffers from certain inadequacies to be described below.

2.5. *Inadequacy of Correlating Priesthood and Leadership*

Although the correlations between priestly leadership themes and U.S. secular leadership themes reveal many points of convergence that can help the ministerial priest in developing his competence as a leader, transformational leadership alone, as understood in a U.S. cultural context, cannot adequately describe or define the priesthood. It has been repeatedly stressed that the ministerial priesthood is fundamentally an ecclesial reality; that is to say that it is rooted in the sacramental structure of the Church and can only be properly understood in terms of its ecclesiological, christological, and pastoral foundations. Hence the Church's spiritual-theological tradition, as articulated in its doctrines, is the only adequate starting-point for understanding the ministerial priesthood. To describe the priesthood in terms of a cultural category such as leadership, although helpful, is secondary to the theological understanding.

Related to the fundamental inadequacy described above are a number of other cautions. First, as pointed out in Chapter Four, the fundamental paradigm for transformational leadership is business and management[5]. Although the exigencies of parish life often require priests to have business and management skills, the priest is not first and foremost a businessman or manager. Removed from an understanding of the ecclesial and theological moorings of the priesthood, the purely U.S. cultural «leadership» description risks reducing the priest to a caricature of a businessman or office manager.

Second, it was noted in the critique of contemporary U.S. leadership theory in Chapter Four that authors tend to create a kind of phantom leader that does not really exist. The literature put heavy emphasis on the traits, talents, skills, and behaviors of leaders, with very little acknowledgement of leaders' flaws and weaknesses and how to deal with them. Such emphasis tends to convey that the source of leadership is completely within the person and solely dependent on his or her self-development. Although the ministerial priest, like the secular leader, needs to actuate

---

[5] Bennis claimed that «[...] our culture [U.S.] is currently dominated and shaped by business», W. BENNIS, *On Becoming a Leader*, 4. Drucker observed, «What explains the tremendous interest in business ethics — in the media, in business schools, in business itself? It's not because there has been any sharp change in the behavior of business people. What has happened is that the behavior of business and business people has acquired a different meaning in the industrialized world. It suddenly *matters*», P. F. DRUCKER, *Managing for the Future*, 113. Cf. above, pp. 244-245, for examples of how the business/management paradigm dominates the popular U.S. concept of leadership.

his capacity to lead by developing his talents and abilities, the source of his leadership does not lie within himself but within the sacrament of Orders. In other words, as important as his skills and dispositions are, much more important is the fact that the ministerial priesthood represents Christ and not an idealized image that the priest might have of himself Such an understanding leaves room for the work of grace and avoids what would be a rather Pelagian understanding of priestly leadership if understood only in terms of transformational leadership.

Finally, as the reseach in Chapter Four indicated, leadership, as it is understood in a U.S. cultural context, is a rather fluid, evolving concept. In this century alone, four major paradigms for leadership have been delineated. As long as these models contain positive values — *semina Verbi* — they can indeed help to enhance and develop an understanding of priestly leadership in the U.S. But it is impossible to predict how the concept will evolve in the future; there is always the possibility that it could contain elements that are inimical to the Church's faith and its understanding of priesthood. It is important, therefore, to continually evaluate this instance of inculturation, that is, priest as leader, so that fidelity to the Church's teaching on priesthood is maintained.

2.6 *Conclusions*

As noted above, the third step of the methodology of inculturation, the evaluation of the data in order to determine fidelity to the Gospel and to authentic cultural values, entails two parts. The first part is a correlation and evaluation of the data which has been carried out above. The correlation of themes revealed that it is both adequate and inadequate to describe the priest as a leader. The understanding of transformational leadership, as described by the authors studied in Chapter Four, can be very helpful for assisting the priest in developing his own leadership skills and indicating how to exercise such skills with maximum effect in the culture of the U.S. However, as the research has shown, the ministerial priesthood is more than leadership, whether transformational or otherwise. Hence, the designation of the priest as leader, while helpful, does not exhaust his identity. In order to be adequate to U.S. culture and faithful to Church teaching, such leadership must surely be understood in terms of U.S. culture, but primarily it must be understood within the sacramental matrix that determines the identity of the priest. Thus in describing the priest as leader in a U.S. context, both terms of the equation have been respected and kept intact. Because they are epistemologically distinct, they cannot be collapsed into each other without diminishing either the Church (ministerial priesthood) or the culture (leadership). This correlation and evaluation, however, is not the final step in the process of inculturation.

Although such a correlation and evaluation is important, alone it is incomplete, sterile, and extrinsic; it does not express the full process of inculturation, but merely acculturation which sets the stage for genuine inculturation. Thus it is necessary to move to the second part of the third step, which takes the data from the correlation — including both their adequacies and inadequacies — and gathers them into a moment of resonance or liberating praxis: the articulation of a spirituality of priest as leader in a U.S. context. This moment of resonance is at the heart of inculturation and allows the interpenetration of Church and the *semina Verbi* present in the culture to come into bold relief. The key to such resonance between the ministerial priesthood and a popular U.S. understanding of leadership will be «pastoral charity» as articulated in *PO* and fully developed in *PDV*. «Pastoral Charity» will allow the two epistemologically distinct categories of priesthood and transformational leadership to come together in a moment of resonance and integration, thus suggesting possibilities for a more effective living out of the priesthood in the context of the culture of the United States.

3. Inculturation: Spirituality of Priest as Leader in a U.S. Context

3.1 *Pastoral Charity*

As noted in Chapter Three, Pope John Paul II identifies pastoral charity as «[...] the soul of priestly ministry» (*PDV* 48) — «[...] the internal principle, the force which animates and guides the spiritual life of the priest inasmuch as he is configured to Christ the Head and Shepherd» (*PDV* 23), and moreover the foundation for understanding the relationship between the spiritual life of the priest and the exercise of his ministry (cf. *PDV* 24). John Paul II's understanding of the centrality of pastoral charity in the ministry and life of the priest both echoes and develops the conciliar understanding, which described pastoral charity as the bond of perfection that brings into unity the various aspects of the priest's ministry and life (cf. *PO* 14). John Paul II also emphasizes that because of the priest's configuration to Christ the Head and Shepherd, effected in the sacrament of Orders, the priest receives from the Holy Spirit the gift of pastoral charity, which is no less than a participation in Christ's own pastoral charity. Such a gift is also a call which demands the priest's free response and commitment (cf. *PDV* 23). Pastoral charity, then, is at the core of priesthood: rooted in the sacrament itself, it is the heart of the ministry and spiritual life of the priest, and thus at the heart of understanding the priest as leader. As such it is the integrating core of ecclesial and cultural data that have been correlated in the previous section, thus enabling the process of inculturation — in terms of priestly leadership — to achieve its fullest expression. As demonstrated below, pastoral charity is the key to integrating the correlations listed above, and to reconciling certain inadequacies that were observed. Such allows artic-ulation of a spirituality of priestly leadership that is intrinsic to the Church's teaching on priesthood and to U.S. cultural understanding of leadership, enabling us to move beyond an extrinsic correlation (mere acculturation) to a genuinely intrinsic inculturation of a spiritual-theo-logical theme of priesthood in a U.S. context.

3.2 *Pastoral Charity: Spirituality of the Cross*

According to Pope John Paul II, pastoral charity sums up «[...] the way of thinking and acting proper to Jesus Christ, Head and Shepherd of the Church (*PDV* 21). As noted in Chapter Three, the headship of Jesus, as well as his role as shepherd, are expressive of his servanthood. His servanthood, in turn, can only be properly understood in terms of the Cross, and indeed *PDV* stresses the intrinsic connection among pastoral charity, servanthood, and the Cross:

> Jesus' service attains its fullest expression in his death on the Cross, that is, in his total gift of self in humility and love. "He emptied himself, taking the form of a servant, being born in the likeness of men. And being found in human form, he humbled himself and became obedient unto death, even death on a cross [...]"[6].

Pastoral charity is properly understood in terms of the mystery of the Cross, a connection repeatedly stressed throughout *PDV* and reflecting the understanding of *PO* as well. The model for the pastoral charity of the priest is Jesus Christ «[...] who brought his pastoral charity to perfec-tion on the Cross with a complete exterior and interior emptying of self» (*PDV* 30). Rooted in the spirituality of the Cross, the salient features of pastoral charity are obedience and the gift of self.

---

6 *PDV* 21, quoting Phil 2,7-8; Cf. *PO* 15.

3.2.1 *Pastoral Charity and Obedience*

Both *PDV* and *PO* cite passages from the Gospel of John that emphasize the obedience of Jesus: «Doing the will of him who sent me and bringing his work to completion is my food» (Jn 4,34); «I cannot do anything of myself. I judge as I hear, and my judgement is honest because I am not seeking my own will but the will of him who sent me» (Jn 5,30); «[...] it is not to do my own will that I have come down from heaven, but to do the will of him who sent me» (Jn 6,38)[7]. Similarly, the Letter to the Hebrews stresses obedience as a key characteristic of Christ's earthly life and ministry: «Son though he was, he learned obedience from what he suffered; when perfected, he became the source of eternal salvation for all who obey him» (Heb 5,8-9). In a presentation on diocesan priestly spirituality, Herbert Alphonso emphasized that the obedience of the priest mirrors that of Christ and thus is not a mere following of superior's orders, but is rather the foundation for the inner-freedom needed to choose God's will, in order to perfect one's life:

> Not obedience merely to the orders of superiors, [...] but the obedience of all times and all moments — that ceaseless dispossession of self that makes one docile and pliable, yes, to the orders of superiors, but also to events, things and persons as they come along: to failure and success, to health and sickness, to difficult and easy human relations [...] in a word, free for and open to the God who comes ceaselessly into our lives to redeem and transform them[8].

An essential component of any spirituality of the Cross, then, is the obedience of Christ in embracing and following the Father's will and the implications that follow from such obedience.

Such an understanding of obedience points the intrinsic relationship between the priest's exercise of authority and the dialogue of discernment that must take place between the priest and those associated with his ministry. The research in Chapters Two and Three highlighted the relational, collaborative nature of the ministerial priesthood. Such an understanding coincides with the obedience associated with pastoral charity. Priestly authority is to be permeated with the spirit of obedience. That is to say that, not only does the priest seek to discern God's will in the voice

---

[7] See, for example, *PO* 15: «Among the virtues most necessary for the priestly ministry must be named that disposition of soul by which priests are always ready to seek not their own will, but the will of him who sent them (cf. Jn 4,34.5,30.6,38)». Cf. *PDV* 28.

[8] H. ALPHONSO, «The Spirituality of the Diocesan Priest Today», 9.

of the bishop or the Church's magisterium, but also in the voices of the people to whom he ministers. His authority, then, is not exercised in isolation but relationship, which requires a spirituality of obedience: that is, «[...] that ceaseless dispossession of self» that allows the priest to enter into dialogue with the people and events of life in order to discern God's will. The priest's exercise of authority, then, is intrinsically connected with obedience and is only properly exercised within the context of this dialogue of discernment.

3.2.2 Pastoral Charity and the Gift of Self

Closely related to the obedience of Christ is the complete gift of self that characterizes his pastoral charity. As emphasized in Chapters Two and Three above, the most remarkable characteristic of the priesthood of Christ is the complete gift of himself, culminating in his sacrifice on the Cross: «The Son of man came not to be served but to serve, and to give his life as a ransom for many» (Mk 10,45)[9]. The Exhortation uses shepherd and spousal imagery to explicate and unfold the meaning of Christ's complete gift of himself on behalf of the Church. Both images, and the scripture passages used to exemplify them, stress the love-unto-death of Christ for the Church. The Cross is thus at the heart of an accurate understanding of both images because they signify the complete and total gift of self (cf. *PDV* 22).

The pastoral charity of Christ, then, is intrinsically connected to and expressive of his complete obedience to the Father and to the complete gift of himself on behalf of the Church, which in turn can only be properly and fully understood in terms of their culmination in his death on the Cross. The pastoral charity of Christ is thus an eloquent expression of his way, which is the way of the Cross that opens up for us a spirituality of the Cross. Pastoral charity is at the very core of Christ's role as Head, Shepherd, and Spouse of the Church; it unifies his threefold ministry; it expresses the purpose of his consecration and mission; and it is the source of his power and authority. The pastoral charity of Christ, as *PDV* stresses, is at the heart of priestly spirituality and thus the center of a spirituality of priest as leader.

---

[9] Cf. *PDV* 21.

3.3 *Personalization of the Pastoral Charity and Mission of Christ as the Basis for Leadership*

Because the ministerial priesthood carries on the mission of Christ, the Head and Shepherd of the Church, the spiritual exigencies of the priesthood require the priest to personalize the office and mission of shepherd and head of the community. Such personalization includes assiduous study and contemplation of the Word (prophetic office), a manifestation in the priest's own life of the Paschal Mystery (priestly office), and a Christ-like exercise of authority through service and self-giving (cf. *PDV* 46-49)[10]. In the light of John Paul II's teaching on the inherent association of pastoral charity with the priestly mission, such personalization would necessarily include pastoral charity, which as noted above, is «[...] the internal principle, the force which animates and guides the spiritual life of the priest inasmuch as he is configured to Christ the Head and Shepherd» (*PDV* 23). Alphonso observes, however, that such personalization, in and of itself, is not enough:

> In all this personalization of his triple office as prophet, priest and king, the ministerial priest must make evident the personalization of his *specific* role in the Church — that is, he must, inasmuch as he participates in Christ's role as Shepherd and Head of the flock, stand out as *leading, inspiring, shining witness* of this personalization of mission, thus becoming an incentive and urge to the Christian community to fulfill its own mission in and to the world[11].

Here can be seen a clear articulation of priest as leader, indeed priest as *transformational* leader. In Chapters Two and Three, Cooke's generic description of leadership as «[...] a capacity to inspire and direct and support a social group as it moves towards some goal»[12] was used as a key to interpreting Church teaching on priesthood. It is the priest's manifestation of his personalization of the roles of head and shepherd of the community, his intrinsic identification with Christ in his role as Head and Shepherd — in other words, the clear, specific and inspiring manifestation of his pastoral charity — that thrusts priesthood into the realm

---

[10] Cf. *PDV* 21, 4-5. Alphonso stresses that such personalization mirrors that of Christ: «What is specifically new [...] in Jesus Christ is precisely the identification of Person and Mission — or, in other words, the *Personalization of Mission*: the complete coincidence, we might say, between ministry and life, between sacrifice and self-gift», H. ALPHONSO, «The Spirituality of the Diocesan Priest Today», 2.

[11] H. ALPHONSO, «The Spirituality of the Diocesan Priest Today», 5.

[12] B. COOKE, *Ministry to Word and Sacrament*, 209.

of transformational leadership and allows the priest to be an inspiration and incentive to the Christian community as it seeks to achieve its goal of fulfilling its mission in and to the world.

Connected to the personalization of the priest's mission as shepherd and head of the community is the realization that such personalization is culturally specific: that is, it is only genuinely realized in a concrete cultural context. In Chapter One, the teaching on inculturation stressed that the Incarnation of Christ (the basis for the theology of inculturation) was culturally specific. Christ did not simply become a «generic» human being but belonged to a specific culture in a specific country at a specific time — all factors that influenced the unfolding of his life and ministry. Similarly, one does not become a «generic» priest, but rather a priest who lives out his ministry in a particular cultural context, which has a profound influence both on how the priest understands and exercises his priestly ministry.

The priest's manifestation of his personalization of pastoral charity in the exercise of his mission — the basis for effective priestly leadership — takes place, then, within a particular cultural context which, in turn, influences how such leadership is carried out. Pastoral charity demands that the priest seek out the *semina Verbi* already present in his culture and allow them to grow in accord with their own nature and through the preaching of the Gospel. Pastoral charity thus shapes and characterizes the priest's approach to culture. Even more, pastoral charity, with its components of obedience and self-gift, requires the priest to embrace as his own — and to make use of — those *semina Verbi* that will assist him in accomplishing his mission. Here is the basis not not only for a spirituality of priest as leader, but for a spirituality of priest as *transformational* leader, that is, leadership as it is understood in the cultural context of the U.S. In order to be effective in a U.S. context, the priest must not only be faithful to the exigencies of the ministerial priesthood as articulated in Church teaching, he must do so in a way that allows those exigencies to be recognizable and efficacious in the U.S. culture. Such an undertaking requires more than a mere adaptation of external forms and practices; it is not simply an instance of the Church putting on a particular cultural «garb». It requires, rather, a deep love and respect for — and immersion in — the culture, incorporating those aspects of the culture that are compatible with the Gospel and Church teaching; in this case one of those *semina Verbi* is the theory of transformational leadership. In this way the ministerial priesthood will emerge within the context of a specifically U.S. culture, clearly recognizable as

distinctively Catholic, rooted in and faithful to the Church's doctrine on
the priesthood, but at the same time clearly recognizable as distinctively
American and capable of serving the common priesthood as it seeks
to further the Church's mission in a U.S. context. The personalization of
pastoral charity and mission allows the correlation of ministerial priesthood themes and U.S. leadership themes, carried out above, to come
together — coalesce, as it were — and unfold as a specific instance of
inculturation.

3.4 *Ministerial Priesthood as Transformational Leadership*

A distorted preconciliar understanding of the ministerial priesthood
accented the priest's separateness: his ordination marked him as one who
was superior to the rest of the baptised. It was almost as if he were
in possession of an arcane knowledge and power that others did not
possess; he was thus to be respected and obeyed and kept at a distance,
because of his knowledge and power. A person set apart, his difference
from the rest of the people was emphasized and very little attention was
focused on his connectedness to the faithful. In a similar way, early
understandings of leadership focused on traits or characteristics that
distinguished leaders and set them apart from followers. Very little
attention was paid to the larger context of the situation and the leaders'
interactions with and dependence upon followers.

As the research has shown, both the Church's understanding of priestly
leadership and a U.S. cultural understanding of leadership have under-
gone profound changes. Both now stress the wider context and the intrinsically relational nature of both priesthood and leadership. The Church
has stressed an ecclesiology of communion, thus a spirituality of communion, which marks the priest as no longer remote and removed, but
inherently relational and dependent upon the larger body of the Church
for the exercise of his ministry. Contemporary leadership theory has
stressed its transformative nature in that it seeks to engage people in such
a way that they — both leaders and followers — are transformed and
made more human in the process; thus leadership too is essentially relational and can no longer be understood in isolation from its wider
context. Such an emphasis on relational and communitarian dimensions
enables us to move beyond a mere correlation of themes and affirm that
the ministerial priest *is* a transformational leader. It also allows the
importance of pastoral charity to come into clearer focus: such leadership
can only be effective if it is motivated by a clear willingness to put
oneself at the disposal of others — the gift of self — and to dialogue with

and listen to them — obedience — in order to move toward the articulated goal. Pastoral charity, the basis for a spirituality of communion, thus intrinsically unifies the ministerial priesthood and transformational leadership. In a U.S. context, the priest who is genuinely motivated by pastoral charity will necessarily seek to be a transformational leader in order to be effective in that particular culture.

Stress on the ministerial priesthood as dependent upon the bishop, belonging to a presbyterate, and fundamentally ordered to the common priesthood, has emphasized that the priesthood is accountable, collegial, and collaborative. The priesthood exists and is lived out in the context of a web of relationships so that it can no longer be seen or properly understood in isolation from these other realities; because «[...] the priest is a man of communion, in his relations with all people he must be a man of mission and dialogue» (*PDV* 18). Such an understanding highlights the priest's interdependence, precluding a «lone ranger» type of approach to priestly ministry. It moreover serves as a reminder that Jesus handed his mission to the entire Church and that specific aspects of the Church's mission can only be arrived at through listening and dialogue: in short, the process of collaboration. Similarly, transformational leadership theory has stressed the necessity of collaboration. The leader does not make decisions in isolation from followers. Just as specific aspects of the Church's mission are arrived at through a process of collaboration, so in transformational leadership, the vision or goal that guides an organization is determined collaboratively with other members of the group. The leader must articulate and give himself over to the vision, to be sure, just as the priest must articulate and give himself over to the Church's mission But the vision originates in something larger than the person of the leader. Because of the common emphasis on accountability, collegiality, and collaboration, the ministerial priest exercises a style of leadership that can best be described as transformational, which is neither easy nor simple. It requires a certain obedience, a receptivity and openness to others and their contribution to the process; it also requires generosity of spirit and the willingness to give oneself over to the demands that such a process requires. It is interesting to note that the English word «obedience» is rooted in the Latin «*oboedio, oboedire* — to give ear to; to listen to»[13]. Such «obedience» is the basis for collaboration. In a word, effective priestly leadership that is true to the identity of the priesthood and to its exercise in the U.S. culture must be transformational, requiring

---

[13] *CLD.*

a spirituality of communion that will blossom in collaborative leadership. Once again, pastoral charity, with its foundations of obedience and self-gift, is the basis for such a spirituality.

It was repeatedly stressed that the ministerial priesthood can only be properly understood in terms of service. The teaching of the Church is that the ministerial priesthood is ordered to the common priesthood and the nature of this relationship is one of service. The ministerial priesthood exists to actualize and build up the common priesthood. The description of the priest's configuration to Christ, the Head and Shepherd of the Church, emphasizes that the priest is a servant. *PDV* 21 states, «The authority of Jesus Christ as Head coincides then with his service, with his gift, with his total, humble and loving dedication on behalf of the Church». It then goes on to add that the priest's spiritual life «[…] receives its life and inspiration from exactly this type of authority, from service to the Church […]». The word «authority» has its roots in the Latin «*augeo, augere, auxi, auctum* — to make grow, to increase»[14], thus perfectly expressing the nature of the relationship between the ministerial and common priesthood: it is a service of leadership for the life and growth of the Church. Similarly, transformational leadership theory has stressed that the leader is actually a servant who exists and acts for the life of the group. He has genuine authority insofar as he is able to build up the group — and individuals within the group — helping it to achieve its potential. Indeed, the original definition of transformational leadership expresses this authority of service:

> the transforming leader looks for potential motives in followers, seeks to satisfy higher needs, and engages the full person of the follower. The result of transforming leadership is a relationship of mutual stimulation and elevation that converts followers into leaders and may convert leaders into moral agents[15].

Servanthood, then, is a salient feature of transformational leadership as it is of the priesthood. The transformational leader seeks to serve the goals of the group and the personal growth and increase of the members as well. Once again, the themes move beyond mere correlation and allow for designating the ministerial priesthood as a particular example of transformational leadership that is motivated by pastoral charity and thus characterized by service, selflessness, and a deep sensitivity to and respect for, not only the members of the common priesthood, but all humanity.

---

14 *CLD*.

15 J. M. BURNS, *Leadership*, 4.

In examining some of the inadequacies in correlating the ministerial priesthood and transformational leadership, it was pointed out that the literature on transformational leadership theory emphasized the positive traits of leaders, with very little acknowledgement of their weaknesses and flaws. When weaknesses were acknowledged, the stress was on the importance of self-development and acquisition of skills in order to overcome them, the implication being that the source of leadership was almost completely within the person of the leader himself, and that if he or she followed certain steps or acquired certain skills, weaknesses would be diminished and strengths would be augmented. Because the source of the priest's leadership lies in his sacramental configuration to Christ, the theme of self development takes on a particular christological inflection. Although the acquisition of certain skills and abilities may help the priest in certain aspects of his ministry of leadership, his primary source of self-development will lie in his ever-deeper personalization of the pastoral charity and mission of Christ.

Unlike the self-development of leaders as emphasized in transformational theory, which tended to gloss over personal weaknesses and deficiencies, the christological context explicitly acknowledges the importance of weakness for self-development in the image of Christ. Two of the scripture passages cited above exemplify this paradox: «He emptied himself, taking the form of a servant, being born in the likeness of men. And being found in human form, he humbled himself and became obedient unto death, even death on a cross [...] » (Phil 2,7-8); and «Son though he was, he learned obedience from what he suffered; and when perfected, he became the source of eternal salvation for all who obey him» (Heb 5,8-9). Once again, pastoral charity shows itself to be at the heart of the priesthood and at the heart of the priest's self-development. Because it is in weakness — the emptying of himself, complete obedience to the Father, giving himself completely over to the Father's will — that Jesus «develops» or perfects himself, such weakness will also be the most powerful pattern for the ministerial priest's self-development.

St. Paul shows a deep understanding of such «self-development» in his letter to the Christians at Corinth:

About this man [Christ] I will boast; but I will do no boasting about myself unless it be about my weaknesses. [...] But I refrain, lest anyone think more of me than what he sees in me or hears from my lips. As to the extraordinary revelations, in order that I might not become conceited I was given a thorn in the flesh, an angel of Satan to beat me and keep me from getting proud. Three times I begged the Lord that this might leave me. He said to me, "My grace is enough for you, for in weakness power reaches perfection". And so

I willingly boast of my weaknesses instead, that the power of Christ may rest upon me. Therefore I am content with weakness, with mistreatment, with distress, with persecutions and difficulties for the sake of Christ; for when I am powerless, it is then that I am strong (2Cor 12,5-10).

For Paul, then, as for Christ himself, self-development, or perfection, did not consist of skills-development or self-aggrandizing activities, but rather in an honest acknowledgement and acceptance of weakness so that the power of God might be allowed to work and bring him to perfection. Such an understanding of «self-development» — emphasizing weakness as the source of true power — echoes an earlier Pauline passage which posited the absurdity of the Gospel:

Since in God's wisdom the world did not come to know him through "wisdom", it pleased God to save those who believe through the absurdity of the preaching of the Gospel. Yes, Jews demand signs and Greeks look for "wisdom", but we preach Christ crucified — a stumbling block to the Jews and an absurdity to Gentiles; but to those who are called, Jews and Greeks alike, Christ the power of God and the wisdom of God. For God's folly is wiser than men, and his weakness more powerful than men (1Cor 1,21-25).

For Paul, «power» also enters a specifically Christian context and is completely transformed in the process.

Klaus Hemmerle has observed that, from a secular perspective, power is normally understood as self-assertion or the successful imposition of one's own will over others[16], a notion redeemed by the Cross:

Supreme love, in Jesus' death, accepts self-abandonment to the will of the Father on behalf of many, to be confirmed and manifested by the Father in the resurrection as the supreme power of the Son. [...] the cross of power involves for the Christian not only readiness for self-sacrifice, but willingness to accept power in its vulnerable earthly conditions[17].

The understanding of power from a Christian perspective has profound implications for understanding the priest as leader in a U.S. context. Although the priest and the leader are invested with a certain power or powers, such from a Christian perspective can only appropriately be understood as love. (From the perspective of transformational leadership, power is associated with the ability of the leader to care for members of the group, calling forth the best within them; although it may not be explicitly designated as love, it is certainly not inimical to, and even complements, the Christian understanding of power.) As articulated

---

[16] Cf. K. HEMMERLE, «Power», vol. 5, 72.
[17] Cf. K. HEMMERLE, «Power», vol. 5, 72.

above, such love reaches its fullest expression in Christ's obedient gift of self on the Cross. For the priest, self-development is most clearly expressed in deepening his identification with, or personalizing, the «power» of Christ. Pastoral charity, rooted in the Cross, is the only proper foundation for a spirituality of the priest as transformational leader, and the basis for his self-development as a leader. Although this *kenotic* approach to life is to be the pattern of perfection for all Christians, it takes on a particular resonance in terms of the ministerial priesthood because of the intense personalization emphasized above. Because of his sacramental configuration to Christ the Head and Shepherd, the ministerial priest is to be a shining witness of the power of Christ at work in his life, perfecting him and transforming his weaknesses. This is the source of his power and effectiveness as a leader. Thus the priest must be involved in ever-deepening identification with Christ and personalization of his pastoral charity and his mission.

Self-development, then, a key theme in transformational leadership theory, must enter into a christological context when applied to priestly leadership. Such a context emphasizes pastoral charity — obedience to the will of God and the complete gift of self on behalf of the Church — as the essential dynamism of priestly self-development. This christologically centered approach to priestly self-development does not gloss over weaknesses or look upon self-development solely in terms of the acquisition of skills, but rather in terms of an honest acknowledgement of utter weakness and dependence upon God, obedience to God, and the giving of oneself over to the will of God, so that the pastoral charity of Christ becomes more and more an integral part of the priest's life. In this way the priest's «self-development» will be most effectively manifest and he will show himself to be a most effective and powerful leader who serves the members of the common priesthood by assisting them to live out their own priesthood more deeply and effectively. Pastoral charity thus shows itself to be the force or dynamism capable of integrating the Church's understanding of the ministrial priesthood with a U.S. cultural understanding of leadership, allowing the priest to be designated a transformational leader in the fullest sense of the term.

Closely related to the Christian context for the self-development of the priest is the importance of «character», which is such a prominent theme in the literature on transformational leadership. The secular authors stressed the importance of congruence between the leader's articulated beliefs and the manner of his or her life. Such congruence is necessary if the leader is to be a credible model and example for his or her followers. Without this credibility the leader would be unable to inspire the followers in the pursuit of their common goal(s). This emphasis on character and credibility reveals that leadership is not simply a set of behaviors that are extrinsic to the person of the leader, but rather that it is inherently rooted in the person and life of the leader. Without such credibility and integrity, all the skills in the world would not be able to render the leader effective and transformative.

As noted above, such congruence and integrity is also essential for the priest to be an effective leader. But pastoral charity is the integrating core that establishes congruence between his actions and his articulated beliefs. Although pastoral charity is a gift bestowed in ordination, it is also a task and a call (cf. *PDV* 23) that demands an ongoing, life-long personalization. Such a commitment will bring integrity to the life of the priest, establishing him as one who is trustworthy and able to offer effective leadership to the People of God entrusted to his care. In effect, it will render him a transformational leader who, because of his identification with the pastoral charity and mission of Christ, is able to inspire the common priesthood to a deeper and fuller actuation of its own love and worship, furthering the Church's mission in the world. Pastoral charity, then, the internal principle and integrating core of the ministerial priesthood, is also the force that enables the priesthood to be understood as a very specific instance of transformational leadership in a U.S. cultural context. It is the basis of the priest's life as a servant, collaborator, and inspirer; and it determines a proper understanding of priestly power and authority. The source of priestly integrity, it determines both the specific ministerial activities of the priest and the very life of the priest, leading him to an ever-deeper embrace of the Evangelical Counsels, so that in his personalization of the pastoral charity and mission of Christ — both in who he is and what he does — he reveals the power of Christ at work in him, the only power capable of making him a transformational leader who stimulates and inspires the faithful, in the cultural context of the U.S., to actualize their own priesthood and so promote the Church's mission to transform the world in the image of Christ.

4. Conclusion: Implications and Challenges
for Seminary Formation

In his introduction to *PDV*'s chapter on the formation of candidates for the priesthood, Pope John Paul II quoted the «Final Message of the Synod Fathers to the People of God», a message underscoring the centrality of pastoral charity in the life of the priest and in the life of the seminarian:

To live in the seminary, which is a school of the Gospel, means to follow Christ as the Apostles did. You are led by Christ into the service of God the Father and of all people, under the guidance of the Holy Spirit. Thus you become more like Christ the Good Shepherd in order better to serve the Church and the world as a priest. In preparing for the priesthood we learn how to respond from the heart to Christ's basic question: "Do you love me?" (Jn 21,15). For the future priest the answer can only mean total self-giving (*PDV* 42).

Pastoral charity, whose essential content is the gift of self (*PDV* 23), thus is to be the response of the seminarian to Christ's call. Immediately after quoting this «Final Message of the Synod Fathers to the People of God», the Pope went on to stress the importance of the local context for shaping how this response of pastoral charity, the total gift of self, is carried out:

What needs to be done is to transfer this spirit, which can never be lacking in the Church, to the social, psychological, political and cultural conditions of the world today, conditions which are so varied and complex, as the Synod Fathers have confirmed, bearing in mind the different particular Churches (*PDV* 42).

Here John Paul II articulates the basis for looking upon the seminary as a locus where the process of inculturation unfolds.

Pastoral charity is at the heart of the ministerial priesthood, but it has been noted that the ministerial priesthood is a transcultural reality incarnated in the various world cultures, each having an influence on how the priesthood is lived out. In the U.S. context, priesthood has been explicitly described in terms of leadership. Leadership in a U.S. cultural context, in turn, is understood in terms of transformational theory. As noted in the previous section, pastoral charity, the heart of the ministerial priesthood, is also at the core of the priest as leader in a U.S. context and the integrating core for establishing a spirituality of transformational leadership. Thus seminaries, in order to be faithful to the Church's teaching on priesthood and adequate to the challenges posed by the culture of the U.S., must take seriously both the Church's teaching and U.S. cultural realities, and so seek to form priests who will be transformational leaders in the cultural context of the U.S. For this to happen most effectively, the seminary must be, as Pope John Paul II has indicated, a school of the Gospel and a place where seminarians can begin to learn and personalize the pastoral charity of Christ in ways that will enable them to be effective priests, indeed transformational leaders, in the particular cultural context of the U.S. In *PDV*, Pope John Paul II delineated four areas of priestly formation during seminary preparation: human, spiritual, intellectual, and pastoral formation[18]. Each of these four areas is essential for introducing the seminarian to the pastoral charity that is at the heart of the ministerial priesthood and also the foundation for a spirituality of transformational leadership. The four areas will be approached from the perspective of the implications and challenges that a spirituality of transformational leadership poses for seminary formation.

4.1 *Human Formation*

Asserting that the importance of human formation is most clearly perceived when related to the receivers of the priest's mission, Pope John Paul II states that «[...] in order that his ministry may be humanly as credible and acceptable as possible, it is important that the priest should mould his human personality in such a way that it becomes a bridge and not an obstacle for others in their meeting with Jesus Christ the Redeemer of man» (*PDV* 43). In order to be a «bridge» that facilitates others' encounters with Christ, priests must attain a certain level of affective maturity that will endow him with the capacity to relate to others and to be «a man of communion» (*PDV* 43). Such maturity is the product of an education in love: «A love for Christ, which overflows into a dedication to everyone, is of the greatest importance in developing affective maturity» (*PDV* 44). Such love is also the condition for the development of pastoral charity in the life of the seminarian/priest (cf. *PDV* 25).

As articulated by Pope John Paul II, the importance of human formation for the development of a spirituality of transformational leadership can be readily seen. It has been repeatedly stressed that the priest must be capable of a collaborative style of leadership. Such leadership is not simply a luxury or an option, but is rooted in the very sacrament of Orders, and necessary if the priest is to be the kind of transformational leader who is able to be effective in the context of U.S. culture. It is therefore incumbent on seminaries to offer the kind of human formation that enables seminarians to develop the affective maturity that in turn enables them to be «bridges» — leaders capable of relating to others and who can facilitate the actualization of the common priesthood in its efforts to continue Christ's mission in the world.

To facilitate such a human formation, *PDV* stresses the importance of education in sexuality, friendship, freedom, and conscience, and also the

---

[18] Citing the «[...] intimate connection between human and spiritual formation», the *PPF* decided to treat the two areas under the one heading of spiritual formation. Cf. *PPF* IV, 115, n. 105.

the importance of knowledge of and obedience to the truth of one's own being and the meaning of one's existence (cf. *PDV* 44). Emphasis on human formation is particularly important in the light of what has been said about the necessity of self-development in leaders and in priests. It was noted that such self-development, specifically applied to priests, enters into a Christian context and includes a recognition of one's weakness and failure as the condition for the power of Christ to «perfect» the priest. The pattern of the Paschal Mystery, then, is at the center of priestly self-development and is the foundation for transformational leadership in the priest. For the seminarian, the truth of one's own being necessarily includes the acknowledgement and acceptance of his weakness, sinfulness, and faults. Such honesty establishes the possibility for the grace of Christ to then transform the weaknesses into strengths. Human formation is not simply a matter of the seminarian coming to a knowledge of himself through the enumeration of his strengths and talents, although this is important, but even more a matter of acknowledging his weakness and utter need for Christ, so that the power of Christ can begin to transform him: a power, which we have seen, can only be understood as love. In this way the seminarian begins the process of coming to the knowledge of the truth of his being and the meaning of his existence (cf. *PDV* 44), thus establishing a foundation for being a man of communion, a «bridge» who is able to facilitate others' encounters with Christ.

4.2 *Spiritual Formation*

It was stressed above that pastoral charity is rooted in a spirituality of the Cross, its most notable features obedience and the gift of self. Pope John Paul II, quoting *Optatam Totius*, states, «Those who are to take on the likeness of Christ the priest by sacred ordination should form the habit of drawing close to him as friends in every detail of their lives. They should live his Paschal Mystery in such a way that they will know how to initiate into it the people committed to their charge» (*PDV* 45; cf. *OT* 8). Formation in pastoral charity, then, is a crucial component of the spiritual formation of the seminarian and an important aspect of preparing the seminarian for future leadership in the Church.

As noted in Chapters Two and Three, because the Church's teaching on the ministerial priesthood emphasizes the priest's configuration to Christ the Head and Shepherd of the Church, it would be easy to distort this understanding, painting an exalted, inflated image of the priest as someone superior to other members of the Church. Because the priest is distinct within the community and holds a position of authority and leadership, it is always a temptation to shed the Christian context to embrace a more «worldly», self-aggrandizing approach to authority and power. The spirituality of pastoral charity prevents such a distorted approach, affirming that the priesthood is indeed an exalted calling, but exalted in the manner of Christ, which necessarily includes embracing the Cross and patterning one's life on the dynamic of the Paschal Mystery.

Thus it is crucial that the spiritual formation of seminarians emphasize that the ministerial priest is first and foremost a servant of Christ and the Church. His service is to the common priesthood, helping it to achieve its fullest expression, and his authority as priest must be understood in this perspective of service. The priest's authority consists in building up and increasing the Church, and the power of the priest can only be adequately understood in terms of his weakness, which allows the love of Christ to come in and transform his life. Power, then, enters into a specifically Christian context and can only be understood as love. Spiritual formation thus introduces the seminarian into a life of paradox. Power is weakness; authority is service; perfection is imperfection; self-development is self-emptying — all so that the seminarian can begin the lifelong process of personalizing the pastoral charity and mission of Christ, a personalization whose vivid and clear manifestation will mark the priest as a person of integrity, thus a transformational leader capable of inspiring other members of the Church to a deeper and fuller commitment to Christ and to the mission of the Church.

4.3 *Intellectual Formation*

Both the *PPF* IV and *PDV* have stressed that it is essential that seminaries offer a clear doctrinal understanding of both the ministry and spirituality of the ministerial priesthood, which is especially important in the light of the research that has been carried out above. Chapter Two referred to the crisis in priesthood that occured following the Second Vatican Council, and in some places continues today. The research indicated that part of the reason for the crisis was a fuzzy, unclear concept of the meaning of the ministerial priesthood. A clear understanding and appropriation of the Church's teaching on the priesthood is therefore crucial, so that the seminarian or priest can understand how to integrate leadership into his prior identity as priest. The teaching on priesthood, with its ecclesial, christological and pastoral accents, forms the more basic context for developing and integrating the identity connected with leadership. Without this grounding in a clear understanding of the priesthood, there is danger of collapsing the fundamentally ecclesial category of priesthood into the cultural category of leadership.

The importance of appreciating the values at work in U.S. culture was stressed in some versions of the *PPF*, but less so in the fourth edition. The *Interim Guidelines for Seminary Renewal* and first three editions of the *PPF* noted the following:[19] «...virtues should reflect the values prized among Americans, such as: personal freedom and initiative, teamwork and respect for democratic processes, adaptability, tolerance of another's faults and limitations, and a talent for organization and implementation». Such «virtues» form the wider context within which the various U.S. leadership theories have developed. Even though the fourth edition highlights the challenges of American culture and society to priestly formation[20], it says very little about what is positive in American culture that can contribute to the development of a seminarian or priest[21].

Although it is necessary to criticize cultural values that are inimical to Church teaching, it is equally necessary to name those elements in a culture — those *semina Verbi* — that are conducive to a deeper penetration of the culture by the Gospel. Such a critical approach to culture, recognizing both its positive and negative aspects, is especially necessary for the intellectual formation of seminarians in order to prepare them to be effective leaders. Previous editions of the *PPF* have cited the cultural values, as well as the pluralism and rapidly changing character of U.S. society, as important factors in priestly formation that require a seminary education which is «[...] broader, more flexible, and more creative»[22]. Thus a deeper understanding of U.S. culture and its influence — both negative and positive — on the priesthood, is a necessary aspect of intellectual formation in U.S. seminaries if they are to prepare seminarians to be priests who are able to offer leadership to the

---

[19] *Interim Guidelines for Seminary Renewal*, part 2, 42. Cf. *PPF* I, 44; *PPF* II, 22; *PPF* III, 34.

[20] Cf. *PPF* IV, 4, for example: «The social climate of the United States can often hinder individual capacity for lifelong commitment and undermine the social support system on which it depends. This has a direct bearing on the permanent commitment asked of priests in the sacrament of Orders. Combined with a widespread tolerance of sexual behavior contrary to Catholic teaching, the above factors create an atmosphere that renders the celibate commitment less intelligible and its practice more difficult».

[21] The *PPF* IV does acknowledge the enriching presence of a variety of racial and ethnic groups that make up the Church in the U.S. (cf. *PPF* IV, 5), but there is no emphasis on values or qualities in American culture that can make a contribution to the exercise of priestly ministry.

[22] Cf. *PPF* I, 1; *PPF* II, 2; *PPF* III, 5-6.

Church in the context of a specifically U.S. culture. This intellectual formation is especially crucial in the light of the new evangelization which is to have priests as its leaders (cf. *PDV* 2).

Pope John Paul II, quoting the *Instrumentum Laboris*, stresses that such intellectual formation is closely related to and must be integrated with «[...] a spirituality marked by a personal experience of God. In this way a purely abstract approach to knowledge is overcome in favor of that intelligence of heart which knows how "to look beyond", and then is in a position to communicate the mystery of God to the people» (*PDV* 51)[23]. Emphasis on a personal experience of God accents the intense personalization of Christ's pastoral charity and mission which is necessary if the priest is to be a transformational leader. Here again, pastoral charity is seen as the integrating core of the priest and the foundation for priestly transformational leadership.

4.4 *Pastoral Formation*

In addition to intellectual formation in all of its aspects, some theoretical and practical preparation in the area of leadership theory would benefit the pastoral formation of future priests. The second and third editions of the *PPF* stressed the theoretical training in addition to practical field experience, singling out education in pastoral leadership:

> The task of leadership in the parish and community requires knowledge of how to approach people and work with them. The areas of group dynamics, listening skills, management techniques, and organizational development provide content for this. Pastoral courses and experiences should be organized so that the students do not merely learn prescribed routines of ministry but become sensitive to human needs and skilled at finding theologically sound solutions to pastoral problems even in complex and novel situations[24].

Although the fourth edition highlights the leadership dimension of priesthood in the section on field education, a more theoretically-grounded approach would be helpful in complementing the practical approach, giving the seminarian a more thorough grounding in and understanding of the dynamics of leadership.

It must be stressed, however, that education in leadership theory must be grounded in the human, spiritual, and intellectual formation described above. It is not enough to describe the priest as a leader or

---

[23] Cf. *Instrumentum Laboris*, 39.
[24] *PPF* III, 49; Cf. *PPF* II, 38.

to offer the seminarian training in leadership theory and practice. Such education must be integrated into the foundational teaching on the ministerial priesthood and the pastoral charity that is at the heart of the priesthood. Unless this integration takes place, the seminarian is in danger of understanding the leadership he is to offer in merely secular terms, divorced from the more fundamental Christian and priestly context.

4.5 *Conclusions*

In his introduction to *Pastores Dabo Vobis*, Pope John Paul II stressed the Church's responsibility to «[...] propose clearly and courageously to each new generation the vocational call, help people to discern the authenticity of their call from God and to respond to it generously, and give particular care to the formation of candidates for the priesthood» (*PDV* 2). In the same paragraph he singled out the formation of future priests as one of the most crucial tasks for the future of the Church's mission of the evangelization of the world:

> Today [...] the Church feels called to relive with a renewed commitment all that the Master did with his Apostles, urged on as she is by the deep and rapid transformations in the societies and cultures of our age, by the multiplicity and diversity of contexts in which she announces the Gospel and witnesses to it, by the promising numbers of priestly vocations being seen in some Dioceses around the world, by the urgency of a new look at the contents and methods of priestly formation, by the concern of Bishops and their communities about a persisting scarcity of clergy, and by the absolute necessity that the "new evangelization" have priests as its initial "new evangelizers" (*PDV* 2).

Seminary priestly formation, then, is at a crucial point in its history, requiring it to remain faithful to and rooted in an understanding of the priesthood as it has been passed down through the centuries of Church tradition, but at the same time cognizant of and responsive to the new cultural and societal contexts that are characterized by rapid change, if it is to form priests who can effectively lead the Church in its mission of evangelization of the world today. This interaction between faith tradition and the various cultures of the world highlights the necessity of inculturation for a thorough and effective evangelization to take place. Exploration of such inculturation has been the starting point of the present study, with an understanding of its effective implementation the overarching goal.

The concern for priestly leadership in the United States, which emerged in the various editions of the U.S. Bishops' *Program of Priestly*

Formation, led to the investigation of the Church's teaching on the ministerial priesthood from the perspective of leadership, an investigation of leadership as it is understood in the cultural context of the United States, and the interaction between the two. The interaction between the leadership themes present in the Church's teaching on the ministerial priesthood, and transformational leadership as it is understood in a U.S. cultural context, has moved beyond a mere correlation of themes to a critical dialogue, and then to a moment of resonance or inculturation: a spirituality of transformational leadership for the ministerial priesthood in the United States. Such a spirituality is needed today if priests are to be effective leaders of the Church in the United States as it pursues its mission to evangelize and transform U.S. culture in the image of Christ, and also challenges and demands seminaries to prepare priests who are capable of such transformational leadership. All aspects of seminary formation, then — human, spiritual, intellectual, and pastoral — must have as a common goal the formation of priests who are imbued with a spirituality of pastoral charity that equips them to be persons of service, of communion, and ultimately of self-giving love. As noted above, a lifelong commitment to personalize the pastoral charity and mission of Christ, in the particular cultural context of the United States — and all that such a context implies, according to the exigencies of the sacrament of Orders — will enable priests in the U.S. to become not only leaders in the new evangelization, but transformational leaders who are capable of inspiring the People of God to deepen their own commitment to give their lives, as sharers in the priesthood of Christ, in service of one another, and in worship of God. Such transformational priestly leadership is a moment of genuine inculturation that is both faithful to Church teaching and adequate to the realities of American culture.

ABBREVIATIONS

AA	SECOND VATICAN COUNCIL, *Apostolicam Actuositatem* [«Decree on the Apostolate of the Laity»]. *AAS* 58 (1966) 837-864.
AAS	*Acta Apostolicae Sedis* [official gazette of record for Papal and Vatican curial documents].
AA.VV	Various authors
Acts	Acts of the Apostles
AfER	*African Ecclesial Review*
AG	SECOND VATICAN COUNCIL, *Ad Gentes* [«Decree on the Church's Missionary Activity»]. *AAS* 58 (1966) 947-990.
Ang.	*Angelicum*
AnGr	Analectica Gregoriana Series
APs	*American Psychologist*
art., arts.	Article, articles
ASMS	American Society of Missiology Series
ASQ	*Administrative Science Quarterly*
BCPF	Bishops' Committee on Priestly Formation
BTAS	The Boston Theological Institute Annual Series
BThAf	*Bulletin de théologie africaine*
CA	JOHN PAUL II, *Centesimus Annus*, Encylical Letter on the Hundredth Anniversary of *Rerum Novarum*. *AAS* 83 (1991) 793-867.
CB	Congregation for Bishops
CC	Congregation for the Clergy
CCC	*Catechism of the Catholic Church*, London 1994.
CCE	Congregation for Catholic Education
CD	SECOND VATICAN COUNCIL, *Christus Dominus* [«Decree on the Bishops' Pastoral Office in the Church]. *AAS* 58 (1966) 673-701.
CDF	Congregation for the Doctrine of the Faith

CDV	VORMGRIMLER, H., ed., *Commentary on the Documents of Vatican II*, New York 1989[2].
CELAM	Conferencia del Episcopado Latinoamericano [Conference of Latin American Bishops]
Cf.	*Confer* (Compare, See also)
chap., chaps.	Chapter, Chapters
ChCul	*Church and Cultures*
CICL	Congregation for Institutes of Consecrated Life and Societies of Apostolic Life
CivCatt	*Civiltà cattolica*
CL	JOHN PAUL II, *Christifideles Laici*, Apostolic Exhortation on the Vocation and the Mission of the Lay Faithful. *AAS* 81 (1989) 393-521.
CLD	*Cassell's Latin Dictionary*, New York 1968[5].
CleR	*The Clergy Review*
CMSM	Conference of Major Superiors of Men
ColEun	Collana euntes
Conc.(GB)	Concilium [Great Britain]
Conc.(US)	Concilium [United States]
Cor	Letter(s) to the Corinthians
CSL	Canadian Studies in Liturgy
CT	JOHN PAUL II, *Catechesi Tradendae*, Apostolic Exhortation on Catechesis. *AAS* 71 (1979) 1277-1340.
CTPS	Collection théologie pastorale et spiritualité
DCSoTh	DWYER, J., ed., *The New Dictionary of Catholic Social Thought*, Collegeville 1994.
DCSp	DOWNEY, M., ed., *The New Dictionary of Catholic Spirituality*, Collegeville 1993.
DFT	LATOURELLE, R. – FISICHELLA, R., eds., *Dictionary of Fundamental Theology*, trs. R. Barr et al., New York 1994.
diss.	Dissertation
DM	*Dizionario di missiologia*, Pontificia Università Urbaniana, [Published] Bologna 1993.
DMLP	CONGREGATION FOR THE CLERGY, *Directory on the Ministry and Life of Priests*, Vatican City 1994.
DoLi	*Doctrine and Life*
DomAsh	*Dominican Ashram*
DSaWo	FINK, P., ed., *The New Dictionary of Sacramental Worship*, Collegeville 1990.

DT	RAHNER, K. – VORMGRIMLER, H., *Dictionary of Theology*, New York 1985.
ed., eds.	Editor, editors
EeT	*Église et Theologie*
EeV	*Esprit et vie*
EN	PAUL VI, *Evangelii Nuntiandi*, Apostolic Exhortation on Evangelization in the Modern World. *AAS* 68 (1976) 5-76.
EnTh	RAHNER, K., ed., *Encyclopedia of Theology*. The Concise Sacramentum Mundi, New York 1975.
Eph	Letter to the Ephesians
etc.	et cetera
Ez	Ezekiel
FaCu	Faith and Culture Series
FCSCa	ARMAGOTHE, J. R., *La formación de los sacerdotes en las circunstancias actuales*. XI Simposio internacional de la Universidad de Navarra, ed. L. F. Matteo-Seco et al., Pamplona 1990.
FJP	MCGREGOR, B. – NORRIS, T. eds., *The Formation Journey of the Priest*. Exploring «*Pastores Dabo Vobis*», Dublin 1994.
FoiTe	*La Foi et le temps*
Fs.	*Festschrift*
gen. ed., eds.	General editor, editors
Gr.	*Gregorianum*
GS	SECOND VATICAN COUNCIL, *Gaudium et Spes* [«Pastoral Constitution on the Church in the Modern World»]. *AAS* 58 (1966) 1025-1120.
Heb	Letter to the Hebrews
HeyJ	*The Heythrop Journal*
ID.	Idem
IRAPs	*International Review of Applied Psychology*
ITC	International Theological Commission
IThQ	*Irish Theological Quarterly*
JCB	*Journal of Contemporary Business*
JeDh	*Jeevadhara*
Jn	Gospel of John
JAPs	*Journal of Applied Psychology*
JPs	*Journal of Psychology*
JSI	*Journal of Social Issues*
JTD	*Journal of Training and Development*

Lat.	*Lateranum*
LDiv	Lectio divina
LG	SECOND VATICAN COUNCIL, *Lumen Gentium* [«Dogmatic Constitution on the Church»]. *AAS* 57 (1965) 5-71.
LiLi	*The Living Light*
Lk	Gospel of Luke
LouvSt	*Louvain Studies*
LThK	*Lexikon für Theologie und Kirche*
Lv(L)	*Lumière et vie* (Lyon)
MD	*La Maison-Dieu*
Mk	Gospel of Mark
MP	SYNOD OF BISHOPS (1971), «The Ministerial Priesthood», in *Norms for Priestly Formation. AAS* 63 (1971) 898-922.
Mt	Gospel of Matthew
n., nn.	Note, notes
NA	SECOND VATICAN COUNCIL, *Nostrae Aetate* [«Declaration on the Relationship of the Church to Non-Christian Religions»]. *AAS* 58 (1966) 740-744.
NCCB	National Council of Catholic Bishops [U.S.]
NCDVD	National Conference of Diocesan Vocational Directors
NCEA	National Catholic Education Association
NCW	*New Catholic World*
no., nos.	Number, numbers
NPF	NATIONAL CONFERENCE OF CATHOLIC BISHOPS, *Norms for Priestly Formation*, 2 vols., Washington 1994.
NRTh	*Nouvelle revue théologique*
NT	New Testament
NTR	*New Theology Review*
OmTer	*Omnia terra*
op. cit.	*Opere citato* (in the same work cited)
OR	*L'Osservatore Romano* [Citations refer to the weekly editions in English.]
ORQ(20)	Quademi di *L'Osservatore Romano*, ed. M. Agnes, vol 20, Vatican City 1992.
OT	SECOND VATICAN COUNCIL, *Optatam Totius* [«Decree on Priestly Formation»]. *AAS* 58 (1966) 713-727.
p., pp.	Page, pages
par., pars.	Paragraph, paragraphs
PBC	Pontifical Biblical Commission

PCTSA	CATHOLIC THEOLOGICAL SOCIETY OF AMERICA, Proceedings of Annual Meeting, ed. G. Kilcourse: vol. 39, Louisville – Mundelein 1984; vol. 40, Louisville – Mundelein 1985; vol. 45, Louisville –Silver Springs 1990.
PDV	JOHN PAUL II, *Pastores Dabo Vobis*, Apostolic Exhortation on the Formation of Priests in the Present Day. *AAS* 84 (1992) 657-804.
Phil	Letter to the Philippians
PO	SECOND VATICAN COUNCIL, *Presbyterorum Ordinis* [«Decree on the Ministry and Life of Priests»]. *AAS* 58 (1966) 991-1024.
PPF	NATIONAL CONFERENCE OF CATHOLIC BISHOPS, *Program of Priestly Formation*, Washington, 1971, 1976[2], 1982[3], 1993[4].
PrDi	*Prêtres diocésains*
PrPas	*Presenza pastorale*
PrPe	*Priest and People*
Ps	Psalms
PSp	*The Pope Speaks*
Pt	Letter(s) from Peter
RAMi	*Rivista di Ascetica e Mistica*
Ratio	CONGREGATION FOR CATHOLIC EDUCATION, *Ratio Fundamentalis Institutionis Sacerdotalis* [«Basic Program for Priestly Formation»]. *AAS* 62 (1970) 321-384.
RCI	*Rivista del clero italiano*
Rev	Revelation to John
RM	JOHN PAUL II, *Redemptoris Missio*, Encyclical Letter on the Permanent Validity of the Church's Missionary Mandate. *AAS* 83 (1991) 249-340.
Rom	Letter(s) to the Romans
RR(StM)	*Review for Religious*
RVS	*Rivista di vita sprituale*
SA	JOHN PAUL II, *Slavorum Apostoli*, Encyclical Letter in Commemoration of the Eleventh Centenary of the Evangelizing Works of Saints Cyril and Methodius. *AAS* 77 (1985) 779-813.
Sal.	*Salesianum*
SC	SECOND VATICAN COUNCIL, *Sacrosanctum Concilium* [«Constitution on the Sacred Liturgy»]. *AAS* 56 (1964) 97-138.
SacDot	*Sacra dottrina*
sec., secs.	Section, sections
SemD	*Seminaries in Dialogue*

SemN	*Seminary News*
serm.	Sermon
SM	RAHNER, K. ed., *Sacramentum Mundi*. An Encyclopedia of Theology, New York 1968.
SNEvan	DAL COVOLO, E. – TRIACCA, A. M., eds., *Sacerdoti per la nuova evangelizzazione*. Studi sull'Esortazion e apostolica «*Pastores Dabo Vobis*» di Giovanni Paolo II, Roma 1994.
SpTo	*Spirituality Today*
S.T.D.	Doctor of Sacred Theology
StDVE	Studi, riserche, documenti, di vita ecclesiale
StEa	Studi Sull'Esortazione apostolica
StSp	Studi di spritualità
TDNT	FRIEDRICH, G. – KITTEL, G., eds., *Theological Dictionary of the New Testament*, Grand Rapids 1971.
Ter.	*Teresianum*
ThHis	*Théologie historique*
ThLS	Theology and Life Series
ThMin	*Théologie du ministère*
ThTo	*Theology Today*
Tim	Letter(s) to Timothy
Tit	Letter to Titus
tr., trs.	Translator, translators
tr. ed., eds.	Translation editor, editors
TS	*Theological Studies*
UNESCO	United Nations Educational, Scientific, and Cultural Organization
UnSa	Unam Sanctum
USCH	*U.S. Catholic Historian*
v., vv.	Verse, verses
vol., vols.	Volume, volumes
Way	*The Way*
WpLFC	*Inculturation*. Working Papers on Living Faith and Culture Series.
WSup	*The Way Supplement*

BIBLIOGRAPHY[1]

AA.VV., «Evangelii inculturatio. Possibilitates et limites», *Seminarium* 32 (1992) 3-191.

AGNES, M., ed., *Vi darò pastori secondo il mio cuore*, ORQ (20), Vatican City 1992.

AHERN, N., «Seminary Education According to the Second Vatican Council and *Pastores Dabo Vobis*», in *FJP*, 142-161.

AIXALÁ, J., ed., *Jesuit Formation and Inculturation in India Today*. Final Report of the Inculturation Commission and Conclusions of the Jesuit Conference of India, Anand 1978.

ALPHONSO, H., «Discernment and Careful Nurturing of the First Seeds of Priestly Vocation», *Seminarium* 33 (1993) 322-333.

——— , The Spirituality of the Diocesan Priest Today». Paper presented at a meeting of seminary rectors, Roma 1994. Photocopy.

AMALADOSS, M., «Inculturation and Ignatian Spirituality», *WaySup* 79 (1994) 39-47.

AMALORPAVADASS, D. S., «Approach: Meaning and Horizon of Evangelization». Theological orientation lecture, All-India Consultation on Evangelization, Bangalore, 4 October 1973. Photocopy.

——— , Réflexions théologiques sur l'inculturation», *MD* 179 (1989) 57-66.

AMBROSIANO, A., «"Pro eis sactifico me ipsum" (Gv 17:19). Consacrazione e missione dei presbiteri», *Lat.* 56 (1990) 503-544.

ANTÓN, A., «Postconciliar Ecclesiology. Expectations, Results, and Prospects for the Future», trs. L. Raymond – E. Hughes, in *Vatican II, Assessment and Perspectives*. Twenty-Five Years After, ed. R. Latourelle, vol. 1, New York 1988, 407-438.

ARANDA LOMEÑA, A., «El sacerdocio de Jesucristo en los ministros y en los fieles. Estudio teológico sobre la distinción "essentia et non gradu tantum"», in *FCSCa*, 207-246.

---

[1] Documents of Vatican II are not listed in the «Bibliography», since they are cited in full under «Abbreviations»: *AG* (*Ad Gentes*), *GS* (*Gaudium et Spes*), *LG* (*Lumen Gentium*), *NA* (Nostrae Aetate), *OT* (*Optatum Totius*), *PO*, (*Presbyterorum Ordinis*), *SC* (*Sacrosantum Concilium*).

ARBUCKLE, G. A., «Inculturation, Community, and Conversion», *RR(StM)* 44 (1985) 835-855.

―――, «Inculturation Not Adaptation. Time to Change Terminology», *Worship* 60 (1986) 511-520.

ARMAGOTHE, J. R., «Acerca del sacerdote. Por una revaloración de las funciones ministeriales», in *FCSCa*, 69-79.

ARNALDO, P., «I preti del Duemilla. Esortazione apostolica *Pastores dabo vobis*», *RCI* 46 (1992) 586-606.

ARRUPE, P., «Father General's Letter on Inculturation to the Whole Society», in *Jesuit Formation and Inculturation in India Today*. Final Report of the Inculturation Commission and Conclusions of the Jesuit Conference of India, ed. J. Aixalá, Anand 1978, 181-189.

ASTELL, A. W., ed., *Divine Representations*. Postmodernism and Spirituality, New York 1994.

AUMANN, J., *Spiritual Theology*, London 1980.

AZEVEDO, M., «Inculturation and the Challenges of Modernity», in *Inculturation*, WpLFC 1, Roma 1982, 1-63.

―――, «Inculturation and the World Church», in *PCTSA*, vol. 39, 122-128.

―――, «Inculturation: I. The Problem», in *DFT*, 500-510.

BACIK, J. J., «The Practice of the Priesthood Working Through Today's Tensions», *Church* 9 (1993) 5-12.

BADARACCO, J. L., Jr., – ELLSWORTH, R. R., *Leadership and the Quest for Integrity*, Boston 1989.

BARRON, R. E., «Priest as Bearer of the Mystery», *Church* 10 (1994), 10-13.

BASS, B. M., *Bass and Stogdill's Handbook of Leadership*. Theory, Research, and Managerial Applications, New York 1990[3].

BAUM, G., «Appendix: A Message on the Priesthood», in *Priests*. Identity and Ministry, ed. R. J. Wister, Wilmington 1990, 149-157.

―――, «Modernity. A Sociological Perspective», in *The Debate on Modernity*, eds., C. Geffré – J.-P. Jossua, Conc(GB) 1992/6, London 1992, 3-9.

―――, *Theology and Society*, New York 1987.

―――, «Two Question Marks. Inculturation and Multiculturalism», in *Christianity and Cultures,* eds. N. Greinacher – N. Mette, Conc(GB) 1994/2, London 1994, 101-106.

BEAUCHESNE, R. J., «Worship as Life. Priesthood and Sacrifice in Yves Congar», *EeT* 21 (1990) 79-100.

BELLAH, R. N., «Leadership Viewed from the Vantage Point of American Culture», *Origins* 13 (1990) 217-223.

BELLAH, R. N. et al., *Habits of the Heart*. Individualism and Commitment in American Life, New York 1985.

―――, *The Good Society*, New York 1992.

BENNE, K. D. – SHEATS, P., «Functional Roles of Group Members», *JSI* 4 (1948) 41-49.

BENNIS, W. G., *On Becoming a Leader*, Reading 1989.

BENNIS, W. G. – NANUS, B., *Leaders*, New York 1985.

————, *Why Leaders Can't Lead*. The Unconscious Conspiracy Continues, San Francisco 1989.

BENSIMON, E. M. – NEUMANN, A. – BIRNBAUM, R., *Making Sense of Administration*. The «L» Word in Higher Education, Washington 1989.

BERGAMELLI, F., «Configurarsi a Cristo Sacerdote e Pastore. Prospettive di sintesi», in *Sacerdoti per la nuova evangelizzazione*. Studi sull'Esortazione apostolica *Pastores Dabo Vobis* di Giovanni Paolo II, eds. E. dal Covolo – A. M. Triacca, Roma 1994, 347-354.

BERGER, P., *Facing Up to Modernity*. Excursions in Society, Politics and Religion, New York 1977.

BERNARD, C. A., *Introduzione alla teologia spirituale*. Introduzione alle discipline teologiche 13, Casale Monferrato 1994.

————, *Teologia spirituale*, Cinisello Balsamo 1982³.

BERNARDIN, J. L., *Called to Lead, Called to Serve*. Reflections on the Ministerial Priesthood, Cincinnati 1981.

————, «Celibacy and Spirituality», *Origins* 20 (1990) 300-302.

————, «The Parish. Reflections for Priests», *Origins* 21 (1992) 782-787.

————, «Relationships and Relational Life in Seminary Formation», *Seminarium* 33 (1993) 334-340.

BERTOLA, C., *I Have Called You Friends*. Sacramental, Theological, and Existential Aspects of Priestly Fraternity, New York 1989.

BERTONE, T., «Il presbitero di fronte alle sfide del mondo attuale», in *SNEvan*, Roma 1994, 13-26.

BESNARD, A.-M., «Tendencies of Contemporary Spirituality», tr. A. C. Bourneuf, in *Spirituality in Church and World*, ed. C. Duquoc, Conc(US) 9, New York 1965, 25-44.

BIERNATZKI, W. E., «Symbol and Root Paradigm. The Locus of Effective Inculturation», in *Inculturation*, WpLFC 9, Roma 1987, 50-68.

BISHOP, P., «Sacramental Character», in *DSaWo*, 176-177.

BISHOPS' COMMITTEE ON PRIESTLY FORMATION, *Interim Guidelines for Seminary Renewal*, parts 1 and 2, May and December, Chicago 1968.

BISHOPS' COMMITTEE ON PRIESTLY LIFE AND MINISTRY, *As One Who Serves*. Reflections on the Pastoral Ministry of Priests in the United States, Washington 1977.

————, *A Shepherd's Care*. Reflections on the Changing Role of Pastor, Washington 1987.

BLEICHNER, H. et al., *Celibacy for the Kingdom*. Theological Reflections and Pastoral Perspectives, ed., R. Ruckmann, Baltimore [no date].

BLOCK, P., *Stewardship*. Choosing Service Over Self-Interest, San Francisco 1993.

BORNKAMM, G., «*Presbyteros*», in *TDNT*, vol. 6, 651-683.

BOUCHAUD, C., «A propos de l'exhortation apostolique *Pastores Dabo Vobis* sur la formation des prêtres dans les circonstances actuelles», *EeV* 102 (1992) 321-336.

BRENNAN, N., «A Breakthrough for Ministry», *AfER* 35 (1993) 27-36.

BROWN, R., *Biblical Exegesis and Church Doctrine*, New York 1985.

—————, *Priest and Bishop*. Biblical Reflections, New York 1970.

BUECHLEIN, D., «The Sacramental Identity of the Ministerial Priesthood», in *Priests*. Identity and Ministry, ed. R. J. Wister, Wilmington 1990, 139-148.

BURNS, J. M., *Leadership*, New York 1978.

BUTLER, S., «The Ordination of Women. Responses to Bishop Kenneth Untener», *Worship* 65 (1991) 263-268.

—————, «The Priest as Sacrament of Christ the Bridegroom», *Worship* 66 (1992) 498-517.

CACHIA, N., «"*I Am the Good Shepherd. The Good Shepherd Lays Down His Life for the Sheep*" *(Jn 10,11)*. The Image of the Good Shepherd as a Source for the Spirituality of the Ministerial Priesthood», S.T.D. dissertation, Pontifical Gregorian University, Roma 1994.

CALLAHAN, K. L., *Effective Church Leadership*. Building on the Twelve Keys, San Francisco 1990.

CAMELI, L. J., «Diocesan Priesthood. The Commitment to Mystery», Speech, NCDVD, Portland 1993. Photocopy.

—————, *Ministerial Consciousness*. A Biblical-Spiritual Study, AnGr 198, Roma 1975, 198.

—————, «Origin and Promise. Perspectives on Human Formation for the Priesthood», Presentation, NCCE, Cincinatti 1995. Photocopy.

CANDON, C., «Ongoing Formation. Questions and Suggestions», in *FJP* 210-214.

CAPRILE, G., «Il celibato sacerdotale al Sinodo dei vescovi 1990», *CivCatt* 143/4 (1992) 488-501.

—————, «Un dono del Papa ai sacerdoti. L'esortazione apostolica post sinodale *Pastores dabo vobis*», *CivCatt* 143/2 (1992) 284-292.

—————, «L'VIII assemblea generale ordinaria del Sinodo dei vescovi. Part 1: I lavori; Part 2: Gli argomenti affrontatti», *CivCatt* 141/4 (1990) 378-387.486-495.

—————, «Problemi del clero negli Stati Uniti», *CivCatt* 138 (1987) 273-281.

CAPRILE, G., *Il Sinodo dei vescovi*. Ottava assemblea generale ordinaria, Roma 1991.

CAPRIOLI, M., *Il decreto conciliare «Presbyterorum Ordinis»*. Storia, analisi, dottrina, 2 vols., Roma 1989-1990.

————, «Esortazione apostolica postsinodale *Pastores dabo vobis*», *Teresianum* 43 (1992) 323-357.

————, *Sacerdozio e santità*. Temi di spiritualità sacerdotale, Roma 1983.

————, *Il Sacerdozio*. Teologia e spiritualità, Roma 1992[3].

————, «Spiritualità sacerdotale. Valutazione della bibliografia 1965-1990», *Teresianum* 42 (1991) 435-473.

CARRIER, H., «The Contribution of the Council to Culture», tr. L. Wearne, in *Vatican II. Assessment and Perspectives Twenty-Five Years After, (1962-1987)*, ed. R. Latourelle, vol. 3, New York 1989, 442-465.

————, *Evangelizing the Culture of Modernity*, ed. R. J. Schreiter, FaCu, [no number], Maryknoll 1993.

————, *Gospel Message and Human Cultures*. From Leo XIII to John Paul II, Pittsburgh 1989.

————, «Inculturation: II. Inculturation of the Gospel», in *DFT*, 510-514.

————, *Lexique de la culture*. Pour l'analyse culturelle et l'inculturation, Tournai – Louvain-la-Neuve 1992.

CASTELLUCCI, E., *Dimensione cristologica ed ecclesiologica del presbiterato*. Ricerca sul Concilio Vaticano II in dialogo con la teologia postconciliare, S.T.D. diss., Pontifical Gregorian University, Roma 1988.

————, «L'identità del Presbitero in prospettiva cristologica ed ecclesiologica», *Seminarium* 30 (1990) 92-139.

————, «L'istituzione del presbiterato», *SacDot* 35 (1990) 156-194.

Catechism of the Catholic Church, London 1994.

CHARLES, H. J., «Three Images of Priesthood», *RR(StM)* (1992) 614-624.

CHIRICO, P., «Pastoral Ministry in the Church in Light of the Critical Priest Shortage», *SemD* 13 (1986) 2-10.

CHOSSONNERY, C., «Toute église est en inculturation permanente», *BThA* 6 (1984) 128-136.

CHRISTIAN, R. R., «Priestly Formation for a New Evangelization«, *Seminarium* 31 (1991) 118-134.

CLARK, K. E. – CLARK, M. B., eds., *Measures of Leadership*, West Orange 1990.

CLARK, T. E., «To Make Peace, Evangelize Culture», *America* 150 (1984) 413-417.

CLAVER, F., «The Basic Ecclesial Community. Vehicle Par Excellence for Inculturation», *Discovery* 3 (1993) 15-28.

————, «Jesuits and International Mission», *Discovery* 3 (May 1993) 1-13.

CLEMENT, A., «Société technicienne et éducation à la vie intérieure», *Seminarium* 31 (1991) 410-430.

CLOVER, W. H., «Transformational Leaders. Team Performance, Leadership Ratings, and Firsthand Impression», in *Measures of Leadership*, eds. K. E. Clark – M. B. Clark, West Orange 1990.

COCHINI, C., *Apostolic Origins of Priestly Celibacy*, tr. N. Marans, San Francisco 1990.

COLEMAN, J. A., *An American Strategic Theology*, New York 1982.

———, «Choosing a Metaphor for Ordained Ministry Today», *Origins* 20 (1991) 603-609.

———, «Dimensions of Leadership», *Origins* 20 (1990) 223-228.

———, «Discipleship and Citizenship. From Consensus to Culture Wars», *LouvSt* 17 (1992) 333-350.

———, «Inculturation and Evangelization in the North American Context», in *PCTSA*, vol. 45, 15-29.

———, «The Situation for Modern Faith», *TS* 39 (1978) 601-632.

———, «The Substance and Forms of American Religion and Culture», *NCW* 230 (1987) 106-111.

COLES, R., *The Call of Service*. A Witness to Idealism, Boston 1993.

COLETTI, D., «Il ruolo delle istituzioni (seminari, università, scuole) per la "nuova evangelizzazione"», *Seminarium* 31 (1991) 148-161.

———, «Il seminario maggiore», *Seminarium* 32 (1992) 561-574.

COLSON, J., *Ministre de Jésus-Christ ou le sacerdoce de l'Evangile.* Etude sur la condition sacerdotale des ministres chrétiens dans l'Eglise primitive, ThHis 4, Paris 1966, 4.

COMBLIN, J., «Secularization. Myths and Real Issues», tr. J. Drury, in *Sacralization and Secularization*, ed. R. Aubert, Conc.(US) 47, New York 1969, 121-133.

CONGREGATION FOR BISHOPS, *Directory on the Pastoral Ministry of Bishops*, Ottawa 1974.

CONGREGATION FOR CATHOLIC EDUCATION, «The Basic Plan for Priestly Formation (*Ratio Fundamentalis Institutionis Sacerdotalis*)», *AAS* 62 (1970), 321-384.

———, «The Basic Plan for Priestly Formation (*Ratio Fundamentalis Institutionis Sacerdotalis*)», (1985), in *NPF*, 15-60.

———, «Letter to the Bishops of the United States Concerning College-Level Formation of Diocesan Candidates», (1988), in *NPF*, 241-250.

———, «Letter to the Bishops of the United States Concerning Free-Standing Seminaries», (1986), in *NPF*, 221-240.

———, «Letter to the Bishops of the United States and Religious Provincials on the Formation of Religious Candidates to the Priesthood», (1990), in *NPF*, 251-262.

CONGREGATION FOR THE CLERGY, *Directory on the Ministry and Life of Priests*, Vatican City 1994.

CONGREGATION FOR THE DOCTRINE OF THE FAITH, «Letter to the Bishops of the Church on Some Aspects of the Church Understood as Communion», *OR* (17 June 1992). Original, *AAS* 85 (1993) 838-850.

CONTI, L., «Elementi per l'itinerario formativo al sacerdozio ministriale», *Lat.* 56 (1990) 645-651.

COOKE, B., *Ministry to Word and Sacrament*. History and Theology, Philadelphia 1976.

CORDES, P. J., *Inviati a servire. Presbyterorum ordinis*, storia, esegesi, temi, sistematica, tr. L. B. Tosti, Casale Monferrato 1990.

COSTA, R. O., ed., *One Faith, Many Cultures*. Inculturation, Indigenization, and Contextualization, BTAS, vol. 2, Maryknoll 1988.

COSTELLO, T., «The behavioral sciences in priestly formation», *DoLi* 42 (1992) 29-33.

———, «The Use of Psychology as an Aid to Priestly Formation», *Seminarium* 32 (1992) 629-636.

COUNCIL OF TRENT, Session 7, «Decree on the Sacraments», Canon 9, in *The Christian Faith in the Doctrinal Documents of the Church*, eds. J. Neuner – J. Dupois, London 1983, 372.

COVEY, S. R., *Principle-Centered Leadership*, New York 1992.

———, *The Seven Habits of Highly Effective People*. Restoring the Character Ethic, New York 1990.

CUNNINGHAM, A., *The Bishop in the Church*. Patristic Texts on the Role of «Episkopos», *ThLS* 13, Wilmington 1985.

———, «Elements for a Theology of Priesthood in the Teaching of the Fathers of the Church», in *Priests*. Identity and Ministry, ed. R. J. Wister, Wilmington 1990, 30-53.

D'SOUZA, A., *Leadership*. A Trilogy on Leadership and Effective Management, Nairobi 1989.

DAL COVOLO, E. – TRIACCA, A. M., eds., *Sacerdoti per la nuova evangelizzazione*. Studi sull'Esortazione apostolica *Pastores Dabo Vobis* di Giovanni Paolo II, Roma 1993.

DANNEELS, G., «The Priest. Sign of the Eternal in a Culture of Consumerism», in *FJP*, 29-39.

DE BOVIS, A., «Le Presbytérat, sa nature et sa mission d'après le Concile du Vatican II», *NRTh* 89 (1967) 1009-1042.

DEEGAN, A. X., *The Priest as Manager*, New York 1969.

DENAPOLI, G. A., «Inculturation as Communication», in *Inculturation*, WpLCF 9, 71-98.

DENAUX, A., «Le synode des évêques sur la formation des prêtres (October 1990)», *FoiTe* 21 (1991) 419-440.

DEVILLE, R., «Formation des prêtres et vie d'Église. Quelques étapes importantes», *FoiTe* 20 (1990) 318-339.

DIVARKAR, P., «*Evangelii Nuntiandi* and the Problem of Inculturation», *Relevance* 7 (1977) 5-12.

The Documents of Vatican II, English translations, gen. ed. W. M. Abbott, tr. ed. J. Gallagher, New York 1989.

DOLPHIN, B., «Human Formation, the Basis of Priestly Formation», in *FJP*, 70-82.

DONAHUE, J. R., «"The Foolishness of God". New Testament Foundations for a Spirituality of Priesthood», *Worship* 66 (1992) 517-536.

DONDERS, J. G., «Inculturation and Catholicity in Relation to the Worldwide Church», in *PCTSA*, vol. 45, 30-40.

DONOVAN, D., *What Are They Saying about the Ministerial Priesthood?*, New York 1992.

DRENNAN, M., «Special Issues in Human Formation», in *FJP*, 83-98.

——, «The Word of God. Radical Source of Christian Formation», in *FJP*, 55-69.

DRILLING, P. J., «Common and Ministerial Priesthood. *Lumen Gentium*, Article Ten», *IThQ* 53 (1987) 80-87.

——, «Fellow Pilgrim and Pastoral Leader. Spirituality for the Secular Priest», *SpTo* 35 (1983) 319-335.

——, «The Priest, Prophet and King Trilogy. Elements of its Meaning in *Lumen Gentium* and for Today», *EeT* 19 (1988) 179-206.

——, *Trinity and Ministry*, Minneapolis 1991.

DRUCKER, P. F., *The Effective Executive*, New York 1993. [First published by Harper and Row, 1966.]

——, *Managing for the Future*. The 1990's and Beyond, New York 1993.

——, *Managing the Non-Profit Organization*. Principles and Practices, New York 1990.

——, *The New Realities*. In Government and Politics; In Economics and Business; In Society and World View, New York 1989.

——, *The Practice of Management*, New York 1986.

DUCCI, E., «Formazione ed educazione nella dinamica della vita umana e cristiana. Presupposti per la formazione sacerdotale», *Lat.* 56 (1990) 431-439.

DUFFY E., «"Common Things Raised Up to Angelhood". Priestly Formation Then and Now», in *New Beginnings in Ministry*, ed. J. H. Murphy, Dublin 1992, 160-180.

DUFFY, E., «Toward What Kind of Priest?», *Furrow* 44 (1993) 208-214.

DULLES, A., «Catholicism and American Culture. The Uneasy Dialogue», *America* 162 (1990) 54-59.

DULLES, A., «The Emerging World Church. A Theological Reflection», in *PCTSA*, vol. 39, 1-12.

——, «The Four Faces of American Catholicism», *LouvSt* 18 (1993) 99-109.

——, «Models for Ministerial Priesthood», *Origins* 20 (1990) 284-289.

DUMONT, C., «La "charité pastorale" et la vocation au presbytérat. À propos de l'Exhortation post-synodale *Pastores Dabo Vobis*», *NRTh* 115 (1993) 211-216.

DUNN, P., *Priesthood*. A Re-Examination of the Roman Catholic Theology of the Presbyterate, New York 1990.

DWYER, J., ed., *The New Dictionary of Catholic Social Thought*, Collegeville 1994.

EDWARDS, P., «The Theology of the Priesthood», in *ThTo*, ed. E. Yarnold, Dublin 1974, 32.

EGAN, G., *Adding Value*. A Systematic Guide to Business-Driven Management and Leadership, San Francisco 1993.

ELLIS, J. T., ed., *The Catholic Priest in the United States*. Historical Investigations, Collegeville 1971.

ESQUERDA BIFET, J., «The Priest's Missionary Spirituality. *Pastores Dabo Vobis*», *OmTer* 27, English edition, (1993) 24-28.

——, «Renovación eclesial misionera para una nueva evangelización», *Seminarium* 31 (1991) 135-147.

——, *Teologia de la espiritualidad sacerdotal*, Madrid 1991².

EVANS, M., «*In Persona Christi* – The Key to Priestly Identity», *CleR* 71 (1986) 117-125.

——, «Priesthood. Something Worth the Sacrifice», *PrPe* 6 (1992) 180-184.

FAGIOLO, V., *La spiritualità del prete diocesano*, ColEun 6, Roma 1993.

FAHEY, M. A., «Church», in *Systematic Theology*. Roman Catholic Perspectives, eds. F. Schüssler-Fiorenza – J. P. Galvin, vol. 2, Minneapolis 1999, 1-74.

FASCHING, D., «Culture», in *DCSp*, 242-245.

FAVALE, A., «La formazione teologica e l'identità del presbitero», *Lat.* 56 (1990) 441-483.

——, *Il ministero presbiterale*. Aspetti dottrinali, pastorali, spirituali, StSp 7, Roma 1989.

——, *Spiritualità del ministero presbiterale*, StSp 6, Roma 1985.

FIEDLER, F. E. – GARCIA, J. E., *New Approaches to Effective Leadership*. Cognitive Resources and Organizational Performance, New York 1987.

FINK, P., ed., *The New Dictionary of Sacramental Worship*, Collegeville 1990.

——, «The Priesthood of Jesus Christ in the Ministry and Life of the Ordained», in *Priesthood*. Identity and Ministry, ed. R. J. Wister, Wilmington 1990, 71-91.

FINN, D. et al., *Theology of Priesthood and Seminary Formation*. Issues of Assembly II, Washington 1989.

FISCHER, J. A., *Priests*. Images, Ideals, and Changing Roles, New York 1987.

FORTE, B., *The Trinity as History*. Saga of the Christian God, tr. P. Rotondi, New York 1989.

FRANSEN, P., «Orders and Ordination», no tr. given, in *SM*, vol. 4, 305-327.

FRISQUE, J. – CONGAR, Y., eds., *Les Prêtres*. Décrets «Presbyterorum Ordinis» et «Optatam Totius», UnSa 68, Paris 1968.

GAIDÓN, M., «Amitiés sacerdotales et célibat», *Seminarium* 33 (1993) 77-87.

GAINE, M., «The State of the Priesthood (Since Vatican II)», in *Modern Catholicism*. Vatican II and After, ed. A. Hastings, New York 1991, 246-255.

GALLAGHER, M., «Leadership, Liturgy, and Identity. Parish Priorities», *Church* (1993) 17-22.

GALLO, L., «Il presbitero nella Chiesa, mistero, communione e missione», in *SNEvan*, Roma 1994, 94-95.100.103-109.111.

GALOT, J. *The Theology of the Priesthood*, tr. R. Balducelli, San Francisco 1985, 99-116.

GAMBINO, V., *Dimensioni della formazione presbiterale*. Prospettive dopo il Sinodo del '90 e la *Pastores Dabo Vobis*, Leumann 1993.

————, «La formazione spirituale del presbitero. Configurazione a Cristo e carità pastorale», in *SNEvan*, Roma 1994, 171-196.

GARDNER, J. W., *On Leadership*, New York 1990.

GEERTZ, C., *The Interpretation of Cultures*. Selected Essays, New York 1973.

GEFFRÉ, C. – JOSSUA, J.-P., eds., «Towards a Theological Interpretation of Modernity», in *The Debate on Modernity*, Conc.(GB) 1992/6, London 1992, vii-xi.

GERARDI, R., «La "caritas pastoralis" nella formazione e nella vita del pensiero», *Lat.* 56 (1990) 553-567.

GIAMMANCHERI, E., «Vocazione e libertà nella *Pastores Dabo Vobis*», *RCI* 74 (1993) 299-305.

GLEESON, G. P., ed., *Priesthood*. The Hard Questions, Newtown 1993.

GOERGEN, D. J., ed., *Being a Priest Today*, Collegeville 1992.

GONDA, I., «La nouvelle évangélisation d'après *Pastores Dabo Vobis*», *PrDi* (1993) 357-362.

GOZZELINO, G., «Il presbitero continuazione di Cristo. Natura e missione del sacerdozio ministeriale», in *SNEvan*, 83-98.

GREELEY, A., *The Catholic Priest in the United States*. Sociological Investigations, Washington 1972.

GREEN, T. J., «Particular Churches and Their Groupings», in *The Code of Canon Law*. A Text and Commentary, eds. J. A. Coriden et al., New York 1985, 316.

GREENLEAF, R. K., *Servant Leadership*. A Journey into the Nature of Legitimate Power and Greatness, New York 1977.

GREMILLION, J., ed., *The Church and Culture Since Vatican II*. The Experience of North and Latin America, Notre Dame 1985.

GRESHAKE, G., *The Meaning of Christian Priesthood*, tr. P. MacSeumais, Dublin 1988.

GRILLMEIER, A., «Chapter I, The Mystery of the Church, Article 2», in *CDV*, 138-152.

———, «Chapter II, The People of God, Article 10», in *CDV*, 153-185.

———, «Chapter III, The Hierarchical Structure of the Church with Special Reference to the Episcopate, Article 28», in *CDV*, 218-226.

GROOME, T. H., «Inculturation. How to Proceed in a Pastoral Context», in *Christianity and Cultures*, eds. N. Greinacher – N. Mette, Conc.(GB)(US) 1994/2, London – Maryknoll 1994, 120-133.

GUINDON J., ed., *The Integral Human Formation of Candidates for the Priesthood*, tr. T. Prendergast, Sherbrooke 1993.

HACKMAN, M. Z. – JOHNSON, C. E., *Leadership*. A Communication Perspective, Prospect Heights 1991.

HAIGHT, R. D., «The "Established" Church as Mission. The Relation of the Church to the Modern World», *Jurist* 39 (1979) 4-39.

HARVANEK, R. F., «"Decree on the Training of Priests", *Optatam Totius*», in *Vatican II and Its Documents*. An American Reappraisal, ThLS 15, ed. T. E. O'Connell, Wilmington 1986, 91-107.

HASTINGS, A., *A Concise Guide to the Documents of the Second Vatican Council*, London 1968.

———, «Mission», in *EnTh,* New York 1975, 967-969.

———, ed., *Modern Catholicism*. Vatican II and After, New York 1991.

HATER, R. J., «Priestly Identity. A Changing Focus», *Priest* 49 (1993) 19-22.

HEHER, M., «Future of Pastors. Woe or Wonder?», *Church* 9 (1993) 32-35.

HEMMERLE, K., «Power», no tr. given, in *SM*, vol. 5, 70-72.

HEMRICK, E., «The Priesthood in the Third Millenium», *Priest* (1993) 22-24.

HERSEY, P. – BLANCHARD, K., «Life-Cycle Theory of Leadership», *TDJ* 23 (1969) 26-34.

———, *Management of Organizational Behavior*. Utilizing Human Resources, Englewood Cliffs 1988[5].

HERSKOVITS, M. J., *Man and His Works*, New York 1952.

HOGAN, R. – CURPHY, G. J. – HOGAN, J., «What We Know about Leadership. Effectiveness and Personality», *JAPs* (1994) 493-504.

HOLLANDER, E. P., «On the Central Role of the Leadership Process», *IRAPs* 35 (1986) 39-52.

HOLLANDER, E. P., «Relational Features of Organizational Leadership and Followership», in *Measures of Leadership*, eds. K. E. Clark – M. B. Clark, West Orange 1990.

HOLLANDER, E. P. – OFFERMAN, L. R., *Leadership Dynamics*, New York 1978.

HOLLENBACH, D., «The Church's Social Mission in a Pluralistic Society», in *Vatican II, The Unfinished Agenda*. A Look to the Future, eds. L. Richard et al., New York 1987, 113-128.

HOUSE, R. J., «A Path-Goal Theory of Leader Effectiveness», *ASQ* 16 (1971) 321-338.

HOUSE, R. J. – DESSLER, G., «*The Path-Goal Theory of Leadership*. Some Post Hoc and A Priori Tests», in *Contingency Approaches to Leadership*, eds. J. Hunt – L. Larson, Carbondale 1974.

HOUSE, R. J. – MITCHELL, T. R., «Path-Goal Theory of Leadership», *JCB* 3 (1974) 81-97.

HUERGA, A., «Carácter sacramental e identidad sacerdotal», in *FCSCa*, Pamplona 1990, 256-267.

HURLEY, D. E., «Bishops, Presbyterate and the Training of Priests (*Christus Dominus*; *Presbyterorum Ordinis*; *Optatam Totius*)», in *Modern Catholicism*. Vatican II and After, ed. A. Hastings, New York 1991, 141-150.

IMODA, F., «Aspetti psicologici nella formazione al celibato sacerdotale», *CivCatt* 144/3 (1993) 359-372.

INCULTURATION COMMISSION FOR JESUIT FORMATION IN INDIA, «Interim Reports of the Inculturation Commission for Jesuit Formation in India», Delhi 1977.

INTERNATIONAL THEOLOGICAL COMMISSION, «Faith and Inculturation», *Origins* 18 (1989) 800-807.

———, «The Priestly Ministry», tr. J. Dupuis, in ITC, *Texts and Documents, 1969-1985*, ed. M. Sharkey, San Francisco 1989, 3-87.

JEANROND, W. G., «Leadership and Authority», *Way* 32 (1992) 187-195.

JOHN PAUL II, «Ad membra Pontificae Commissionis Biblicae, una cum Em.mo Francisco S.R.E. Cardinali Seper coram admissos» [«Address to the Pontifical Biblical Commission»], *AAS* 71 (1979) 606-609.

———, «Ad Patres Cardinales et Curiae Romanae Pontificalisque Domus Praelatos, imminente Nativitate Domini coram admissos» [«Address to the Roman Curia»], *AAS* 76 (1984) 477-487.

———, «Ad sodales Pontificii Consilii pro hominum cultura coram admissos» [«Address to the Pontifical Council for Culture»], *AAS* 75 (1983) 383-389.

———, *Catechesi Tradendae*. Apostolic Exhortation on Catechesis, London 1979. Original: *AAS* 71 (1979) 1277-1340.

JOHN PAUL II, *Centesimus Annus*. Encyclical Letter on the Hundredth Anniversary of *Rerum Novarum*, Vatican City 1991. Original: *AAS* 83 (1991) 793-867.

————, *Christifideles Laici*. Apostolic Exhortation on the Vocation and the Mission of the Lay Faithful in the Church and in the World, London 1988. Original: *AAS* 81 (1989) 393-521.

————, «Closing Address to the Synod», *Origins* 20 (1990) 378. Original: *AAS* 83 (1991) 494-499.

————, «John Paul II Institutes Pontifical Council for Culture», *OR* (28 June 1982). Original: *AAS* 74 (1982) 683-688.

————, *Pastores Dabo Vobis*. Apostolic Exhortation on the Formation of Priests in the Circumstances of the Present Day, Vatican City 1992. Original: *AAS* 84 (1992) 657-804.

————, *Redemptoris Missio*. Encyclical Letter on the Permanent Validity of the Church's Missionary Mandate, Vatican City 1991. Original: *AAS* 83 (1991) 249-340.

————, *Slavorum Apostoli*. Encyclical Letter in Commemoration of the Eleventh Centenary of the Evangelizing Works of Saints Cyril and Methodius, Washington 1985. Original: *AAS* 77 (1985) 779-813.

————, *Sollicitudo Rei Socialis*. Encyclical Letter on Social Concern in Commemoration of the Twentieth Anniversary of *Populorum Progressio*, Vatican City 1987. Original: *AAS* 80 (1988) 513-586.

KASPER, W., Ministry in the Church. Taking Issue with Edward Schillebeeckx», *Communio* 10 (1983) 185-195.

————, «A New Dogmatic Outlook on the Priestly Ministry», in *The Identity of the Priest*, ed. K. Rahner, Conc.(US) 43, New York 1969, 20-33.

KENNEDY, E. C. – HECKLER, V. J., *The Catholic Priest in the United States*. Psychological Investigations, Washington 1972.

KILMARTIN, E. J., «Bishop and Presbyter as Representatives of the Church and Christ», in *Women Priests*. A Catholic Commentary on the Vatican Declaration, eds. L. Swidler – A. Swidler, New York 1977, 295-302.

————, *Church, Eucharist and Priesthood*. A Theological Commentary on «The Mystery of the Most Holy Eucharist», New York 1981.

KILROY, B., «Priestly Development for Collaboration in Ministry», *DoLi* 43 (1993) 287-294.

KINAST, R. L., «A Tale of Two Synods. Laity and Clergy Formation», *RR(StM)* 53 (1994) 711-723.

KLEINMAN, S., *Equals Before God*. Seminarians as Humanistic Professionals, Chicago 1984.

KLOPPENBURG, B., *The Ecclesiology of Vatican II*, tr. M. J. O'Connell, Chicago 1974.

————, «, *The Priest*. Living Instrument and Minister of Christ, the Eternal Priest, tr. M. J. O'Connell, Chicago 1974.

KOESTENBAUM, P., *Leadership*. The Inner Side of Greatness, San Francisco 1991.

KOMONCHAK, J. A., «The Ecclesial and Cultural Roles of Theology», in *PCTSA*, vol. 40, 15-32.

KOUZES, J. M. – POSNER, B. Z., *Credibility*. How Leaders Gain and Lose It, Why People Demand It, San Francisco 1993.

————, *The Leadership Challenge*. How to Get Extraordinary Things Done in Organizations, San Francisco 1987.

KRESS, R., «We the People. The American Transformation of Roman Catholicism from Established State Church to Voluntary Free Church», *NTR* (1993) 63-88.

LACUGNA, C. M., *God for Us*. The Trinity and Christian Life, San Francisco 1991.

LAGHI, P., «La formazione dei sacerdoti alla luce della *Pastores Dabo Vobis*», *Seminarium* 33 (1993) 124-134.

————, «The Identity and Ministry of the Priest», in *FJP*, 22-28.

————, «*Pastores Dabo Vobis*. Presentazione», *Seminarium* 32 (1992) 505-517.

————, «Le principali chiavi di lettura», in *Vi darò pastori secondo il mio cuore*. Testo e commenti, ORQ, vol. 20, Vatican City 1992.

LAMBERT, C., «Leadership in a New Key», *Harvard Magazine* 97 (1995) 28-33.

LANE, D., «The Challenge of Inculturation», *LiLi* 29 (1992) 3-21.

LANE, T., «Person, Face, Presence, Voice. A Context for Ordained Ministry», in *New Beginnings in Ministry*, ed. J. H. Murphy, Dublin 1992, 107-127.

————, *A Priesthood in Tune*. Theological Reflections on the Ministry, Dublin 1993.

LANGAN, T., «Accommodating Cultures Without Dissolving the Unity of the Faith», in *Inculturation*, WpLFC 8, Roma 1986, 41-53.

LAPLANTE, A., *La Formation des prêtres*. Genèse et commentaire du décret conciliaire *Optatam Totius*, CTPS 23, Paris 1969.

LARKIN, E. E. – BROCCOLO, G. T., eds., *Spiritual Renewal of the American Priesthood*, Washington 1973.

LATOURELLE, R., ed., *Vatican II, Assessment and Perspective*. Twenty-Five Years After (1962-1987), 3 vols., New York 1988.

LATOURELLE, R. – FISICHELLA, R., eds., *Dictionary of Fundamental Theology*, tr. R. Barr et al., New York 1994.

LÉCUYER, J., «History of the Decree [on the Ministry and Life of Priests]», in *CDV*, 183-210.

LEGRAND, H., «Crises du clergé. Hier et aujourd'hui», *Lv(L)* 33 (1984) 90-106.

LEMAIRE, A., *Les ministères aux origines de l'église*. Naissance de la triple hiérarchie: évêques, presbytres, diacres, LDiv 68, Paris 1971.

LINSCOTT, M., «Leadership, Authority, and Religious Government», *RR(StM)* (1993) 166-193.

LOGAN, V., «An Overview of Priestly Formation», in *FJP*, 188-195.

LOPEZ-GAY, J., *Storia delle missioni*. Schemi per un corso triennale, Notes for Students' Use, Roma 1994.

LOVE, J. R., *Liberating Leaders from the Superman Syndrome*, Lanham 1994.

LUZBETAK, L. J., *The Church and Cultures*. New Perspectives in Missiological Anthropology, ASMS 12, New York 1988.

LYNCH, R., *Lead!* How Public and Nonprofit Managers Can Bring Out the Best in Themselves and Their Organizations, San Francisco 1993.

MACIEL, M., *Integral Formation of Catholic Priests*, tr. S. Fichter, New York 1992.

MANATHODATH, J., *The Inculturation of the Local Churches According to the Teaching of Pope Paul VI*, S.T.D. diss., Pontifical Gregorian University, Roma 1984.

MARLIANGEAS, B. D., *Clés pour une théologie du ministère*. «In persona Christi; In persona ecclesiae», *ThMin* 51, Paris 1978.

MASLOW, A., *Motivation and Personality*, New York 1954.

MASSON, J., «L'Église ouverte sur le monde», *NRTh* 84 (1962) 1032-1043.

MATEO-SECO, L. F., «El ministerio: fuente de la espiritualidad del sacerdote», in *FSCa*, Pamplona 1990, 383-427.

MATEO-SECO, L. F. et al., eds, *La formación de los sacerdotes en las circunstancias actuales*, XI Simposio internacional de teologia de la Universidad de Navarra, Pamplona 1990.

MCAREAVEY, J., «Celibacy. A Gift of Pastoral Charity», in *FJP*, 99-117.

MCGOLDRICK, P., «Sacrament of Orders», in *DSaWo*, 896-908.

MCGREGOR, B., «The Missionary Identity of the Priest», in *FJP*, 196-209.

MCNAMARA, K., *The Church*. A Theological and Pastoral Commentary on the «Constitution on the Church», Dublin 1983.

METZ, J.-B., «Unity and Diversity. Problems and Prospects for Inculturation», tr. F. McDonagh, in *World Catechism or Inculturation?*, eds. J-B. Metz – E. Schillebeeckx, Conc(GB) 204, Edinburgh 1989, 79-87.

MEYER, C., «Ambassadors of Christ», *RR(StM)* 50 (1991) 759-766.

————, *Man of God*. A Study of the Priesthood, Garden City 1974.

MIGLIARESE, S. R., *The Ministry of the Word as* Primum Officium. An Understanding and Application to Priestly Formation, S.T.D. diss., Pontificia Universitas a S. Thoma Aq. in Urbe, Roma 1978.

MITCHELL, N., *Mission and Ministry*. History and Theology in the Sacrament of Order, Wilmington 1983.

MÖRSDORFF, K., «Hierarchy», tr. not given, in *SM*, vol. 3, 27-29.

——, «Decree on the Bishop's Pastoral Office in the Church». tr. H. Graef, in *CDV*, vol. 2, 165-300.

MUELLER, J. J., «Second Stage Inculturation. Six Principles of the American Mind», *RR(StM)* 53 (1994) 658-674.

MULLIGAN, J. J., «The Presbyterate in *Pastores Dabo Vobis*». Parts 1 and 2, *Priest* 49 (1993) 29-35.30-35.

MUSZYNSKI, H., «Overview of Synod Proposals», *Origins* 20 (1990) 353-355.

——, «Il sacerdozio e i "tria munera"», in *Vi darò pastori secondo il mio cuore*. Testo e commenti, QuadOR, vol. 20, 217-224.

NANUS, B., *The Leader's Edge*. The Seven Keys to Leadership in a Turbulent World, Chicago 1989.

——, *Visionary Leadership*. Creating a Compelling Sense of Direction for Your Organization, San Francisco 1992.

NARDI, C., «Prete e popolo nell'antichità cristiana», *RAcMi* 16 (1991) 362-374.

NATIONAL CONFERENCE OF CATHOLIC BISHOPS, *Norms for Priestly Formation*, 2 vols., Washington 1994.

——, *Program for Priestly Formation*, Washington 1971, 1976², 1982³, 1993⁴.

NEUMAN, M., «Pastoral Leadership. Beyond the Managerial», *RR(StM)* (1992) 585-594.

NEUNER, J., «Decree on Priestly Formation», tr. J. Neuner, in *CDV*, vol. 2, 371-404.

NEUNER, J. – DUPUIS, J., eds., *The Christian Faith in the Doctrinal Documents of the Catholic Church*, London 1983.

NICHOLS, A., *Holy Order*. The Apostolic Ministry from the New Testament to the Second Vatican Council, Dublin 1990.

NIEDERAUER, G., «A Ministerial Spirituality. Reflections on Priesthood», *Church* (1991) 23-27.

NOLAN, B. M., «What Difference Does Priestly Ordination Make?», in *New Beginnings in Ministry*, ed. J. H. Murphy, Dublin 1992, 128-159.

NORRIS, T., «Intellectual Formation. Understanding the Faith», in *FJP*, 162-174.

«La nuova evangelizzazione», No author given, *CivCatt* (1994/3) 351-363.

NYGREN, D. J. et al., «Religious-Leadership Competencies», *RR(StM)* (1993) 390-393.

O'BRIEN, D. J., «Catholic Evangelization and American Culture», *USCH* 11 (1993) 49-60.

O'BRIEN, D. J. – STEINFELS, M., «The Laity and the Leadership Crisis», *Commonweal* (10 September 1993) 8.16-20.

O'CONNELL, T. E., «"Decree on the Ministry and Life of Priests" *Presbyterorum Ordinis* (7 Dec. 1965)», in *Vatican II and Its Documents*. An American Reappraisal, ThLS 15, Wilmington 1986, 197-215.

O'CONNOR, J., «A Bishop Reflects on Pope John Paul II's *Pastores Dabo Vobis*», Address given on 10 March 1993 at the North American College in Roma. Unpublished booklet.

O'DONNELL, J. – RENDINA, S., *Sacerdozio e spiritualità ignaziana*, Roma 1994.

O'MALLEY, J. W., «Diocesan and Religious Models of Priestly Formation. Historical Perspectives», in *Priests*. Identity and Ministry, ed. R. J. Wister, Wilmington 1990, 54-57.

————, «The Houses of Study of Religious Orders and Congregations. A Historical Sketch», in K. SCHUTH, *Reason for the Hope*. The Futures of Roman Catholic Theologates, Wilmington 1989, 29-45.

————, «Priesthood, Ministry, and Religious Life. Some Historical and Historiographical Considerations», *TS* 49 (1988) 223-257.

————, *Tradition and Transition*. Historical Perspectives on Vatican II, ThLS 26, Wilmington 1989.

O'MEARA, T., «The Ministry of the Priesthood and Its Relationship to the Wider Church», *SemD* 11 (1985) 1-8.

————, *Theology of Ministry*, New York 1983.

ORR, D., «The Giving of the Priesthood to the Faithful», in *Priesthood*. The Hard Questions, ed. G. P. Gleeson, Newton 1993, 61-77.

OSBORNE, K., *Priesthood*. A History of Ordained Ministry in the Roman Catholic Church, New York 1988.

L'Osservatore Romano, Weekly Editions in English, «Statement by General Secretary on *Instrumentum Laboris*», 23 July 1990; «VIII Synod Opens on Formation Topic», 1 October 1990; «Major Themes Emerge from Synod Discussions» and «Language Groups Elect Moderators», 15 October 1990; «English Groups Report», 29 October 1990; «*Pastores Dabo Vobis*. Program for Renewal», 8 April 1992.

PADOVANO, A., «American History and Catholic Ecclesiology», *NCW* 230 (1987) 112-116.

PARISE, M., «Management, Discipleship and the Priesthood», *Priest* (June 1992) 36-38.

PATRICK, A. E., «Inculturation, Catholicity, and Social Justice», in *PCTSA*, vol. 45, 41-55.

PAUL VI, «Counsels for the City Priest. Address to Pastors and Lenten Preachers of Rome», *PSp* 13 (1968) 113-117. Original: *AAS* 60 (1968) 214-219.

————, «E.mis Patribus Cardinalibus et Exc.mis Praesulibus, qui "Episcoporum Symposio" ex universa Africa in urbe Kampala habito interfuerunt» [«Kampala Address»], *AAS* 61 (1969) 573-578.

PAUL VI, «E.mis Patribus Cardinalibus et Exc.mis Praesulibus, qui "Episco-porum Symposio" ex universa Asia orientali in urbe Manila habito interfuerunt» [«Address to the Bishops of Asia»], *AAS* 63 (1971) 21-27.

————, *Evangelii Nuntiandi*. Apostolic Exhortation on Evangelization in the Modern World, Vatican City 1975. Original: *AAS* 68 (1976) 5-76.

PEELMAN, A., *L'Inculturazione*. La Chiesa e le culture, Brescia 1993.

PÉNOUKOU, E-J., *Église d'Afrique*. Propositions pour l'avenir, Paris 1984.

PETERS, T. J. – WATERMAN, R. H., JR., *In Search of Excellence*. Lessons from America's Best-Run Companies, New York 1982.

PHILIPS, G., «Dogmatic Constitution on the Church. History of the Consti-tution», tr. K. Smyth, in *CDV*, vol. 1, 105-137.

PICKEN, E. J., «Forum: If Christ Is Bridegroom, the Priest Must Be Male?», *Worship* 67 (1993) 269-278.

PITTAU, G. – SEPE, C., eds., *Identità e missione del sacerdote*, Roma 1994.

PONTIFICAL BIBLICAL COMMISSION, *The Interpretation of the Bible in the Church*, trs. J. Kilgallen – B. Byrne, Roma 1993.

PONTIFICAL COUNCIL FOR CULTURE, «Inculturation. Papal Visit to the U.S.A.», *ChCul* 9 (1988) 7-8.

PONTIFICAL COUNCIL FOR THE LAITY, *The Formation of Priests in Circum-stances of the Present Day*. Lay Contributions, Vatican City 1990.

PORTIER, W., «Inculturation as Transformation. The Case of Americanism Revis-ited», *USCH* 11 (1993) 107-124.

POULAT, E., «Catholicism and Modernity. A Process of Mutual Exclusion», tr. J. Bowden, in *The Debate on Modernity*, ed. C. Geffré – J-P. Jossua, Conc.(GB) 1992/6, London 1992, 10-16.

POWER, D. N., *The Christian Priest*. Elder and Prophet, London 1973.

————, *Ministers of Christ and His Church*. The Theology of the Priesthood, London 1969.

————, «Representing Christ in Community and Sacrament», in *Being a Priest Today*, ed. D. J. Goergen, Collegeville 1992, 97-123.

POZO, C., «Sacerdocio ministerial y radicalismo de los consejos evangélicos», *Seminarium* 32 (1992) 550-560.

RADCLIFFE, T., «Inculturation», Address delivered to the Second Joint Confer-ence of Dominican major superiors and formators at Nagpur, India, on 21 October 1993, *RR(StM)* 53 (1994) 646-657. [Originally published in *DomAsh* 12 (1993) 149-159.]

RAHNER, K., *Bishops*. Their Status and Function, tr. E. Quinn, Baltimore 1964.

————, «Chapter III [of *Lumen Gentium*], The Hierarchical Structure of the Church, with Special Reference to the Episcopate, Articles 18-27», tr. K. Smyth, in *CDV*, 186-218.

RAHNER, K., ed., *The Identity of the Priest*, various trs., Conc.(US) 43, New York 1969.

————, *The Priesthood*, tr. E. Quinn, New York 1973.

————, «Priestly Existence», in *Theological Investigations*, tr. K. Kruger – B. Kruger, vol. 3, New York 1967, 239-262.

————, *Servants of the Lord*, tr. R. Strachar, New York 1968.

RATZINGER, J., «Biblical Foundations of Priesthood», *Origins* 20 (1990) 310-314.

————, *Ministers of Your Joy*, Ann Arbor 1989.

————, «Priestly Ministry. A Search for its Meaning», tr. D. Roy, *Emmanuel* 76/11,12 (1970) 442-453.490-505.

RATZINGER, J. – MESSORI, V., *The Ratzinger Report*, San Francisco 1985.

RAUSCH, T. P., «Forming the Priest for Tomorrow's Church. The Coming Synod», *America* 162 (1990) 168-172.

————, *Priesthood Today*. An Appraisal, New York 1992.

REISER, W., «Inculturation and Doctrinal Development», *HeyJ* 22 (1981) 135-148.

RICHARD, L., «Inculturation», in *DCSoTh*, 481-483.

————, «Mission and Inculturation. The Church in the World», in *Vatican II, The Unfinished Agenda*. A Look to the Future, eds. L. Richard et al., New York 1987, 93-111.

RICHARDS, M., «Servants of the Word, Shepherds of the People. The Ordained Ministry After Trent and After Vatican II», *CleR* 64 (1979) 239-246.

————, «Hierarchy and Priesthood», *PrPe* 7 (1993) 228-232.

————, *A People of Priests*. The Ministry of the Catholic Church, London 1995.

ROACH, J., «Study of U.S. Seminaries Launched». Letter of Archbishop Roach to the U.S. Bishops, *Origins* 11 (1981) 263-264.

ROEST CROLLIUS, A. A., «What Is So New about Inculturation?», *Gr.* 59 (1978) 721-738. Reprinted in *Inculturation,* WpLFC 5, Roma 1984, 1-18.

————, «Inculturation and the Meaning of Culture», *Gr.* 61 (1980) 253-274. Reprinted in *Inculturation*, Wp LFC 5, Roma 1984, 33-54.

————, «Inculturation. From Babel to Pentecost», in *Inculturation*, WpLFC 8, Roma 1986, 1-7.

————, «Inculturazione», in *DM*, Bologna 1993.

————, *Teologia dell'inculturazione*. Notes for Students' Use, Roma 1994.

RONCO, A., «Formazione umana di base del futuro pastore», *Sal.* 55 (1993) 263-270.

ROSATO, P. J., «The Spirituality of the Diocesan Priest», *WSup* 39 (1980) 83-96.

ROSATO P. J., «Priesthood of the Baptized and Priesthood of the Ordained. Complementary Approaches to Their Interrelation», *Gr.* 68 (1987) 215-266.

ROSINSKI, G. – MANNION, M. F., «Getting Down to Cases. Conflicting Styles of Parish Leadership: Two Responses», *NTR*, 6 (1993) 95-101.

ROSSI DE GASPERIS, F., «Continuity and Newness in the Faith of the Mother Church of Jerusalem», in *Inculturation*, WpLFC 3, Roma 1983, 17-69.

RUSSELL, A., «Sociology and the Study of Spirituality», in *The Study of Spirituality*, eds. C. Jones et al., London 1992, 33-38.

RYPAR, F., «La *Pastores Dabo Vobis* alla luce del pensiero conciliare sul sacerdozio e la formazione sacerdotale», *Seminarium* 32 (1992) 530-549.

SAINT JUSTIN, MARTYR, «The Second Apology», *The Writings of St. Justin, Martyr*, tr. and ed. T. B. Falls, in *The Fathers of the Church. A New Translation*, ed. L. Schopp, New York 1948, 119-135.

SARAIVA MARTINS, J., «La formazione missionaria dei sacerdoti alla luce del Sinodo 1990», *Seminarium* 31 (1991) 332-352.

――――― , «La formazione missionaria dei sacerdoti alla luce della *Pastores dabo vobis*», *Seminarium* 32 (1992) 575-599.

――――― , «Il progetto sacerdote-pastore nella Chiesa peregrinante», *Seminarium* 33 (1993) 135-144.

SARTAIN, J. P., «The Challenge of Priestly Leadership», *RR(StM)* 53 (1994) 675-693.

SAYLES, L. R., *Leadership*. Managing in Real Organization, eds. F. Luthans – K. Davis, New York 1989[2].

SCANNONE, J. C., «The Debate about Modernity in the North Atlantic World and the Third World», tr. F. McDonagh, in *The Debate on Modernity*, eds. C. Geffré – J-P. Jossua, Conc.(GB) 1992/6, London 1992, 78-96.

SCHAEFER, M. M. – HENDERSON, J. F., *The Catholic Priesthood*. A Liturgically Based Theology of the Presbyteral Office, CSL 4, Ottawa 1990.

SCHILLEBEECKX, E., *The Church with a Human Face*. A New and Expanded Theology of Ministry, New York 1985.

――――― , *Ministry*. Leadership in the Community of Jesus Christ, New York 1981.

SCHINELLER, P., *A Handbook on Inculturation*, New York 1990.

――――― , «A Method for Ministry», *Emmanuel* 87 (1981) 137-144.

――――― , «Ten Summary Statements on the Meaning, Challenge and Significance of Inculturation as Applied to the Church and Society of Jesus in the United States, in Light of the Global Process of Modernization», in *Inculturation*, WpLFC 2, Roma 1983, 53-87.

SCHNEIDERS, S. M, «Spirituality in the Academy», *TS* 50 (1989) 676-697.

SCHNEIDERS, S. M., «Theology and Spirituality. Strangers, Rivals, or Part-
    ners?», *Horizons* 13 (1986) 253-274.

SCHOENHERR, R. – YOUNG, L., «The Catholic Priest in the U.S. Demographic
    Investigations», *Origins* 20 (1990) 206-208.

SCHOTTE, J. P., «Perché un Sinodo sulla formazione sacerdotale?», *Seminarium*
    30 (1990) 47-68.

SCHREITER, R. J., *Constructing Local Theologies*, Maryknoll 1986.

———, «Inculturation of Faith or Identification with Culture?», in *Christi-
    anity and Cultures*, eds. N. Greinacher – N. Mette, Conc(GB)(US)
    1994/2, London – Maryknoll 1994, 15-24.

SCHÜSSLER, F. – GALVIN, J. P., *Systematic Theology*. Roman Catholic Per-
    spectives, 2 vols., Minneapolis 1991.

SCHUTH, K., *Reason for the Hope*. The Futures of Roman Catholic Theolo-
    gates, Wilmington 1989.

SCHWARTZ, R., *In Christ and In the Church*. An Ecclesial Spirituality for
    American Priests Founded on the Magisterium of the Bishops of the
    United States, S.T.D. diss., Pontifical Gregorian University, Roma
    1987.

———, «Ordained Ministry. Sign of Leadership and Unity in the Great Sacra-
    ment of the Church», in *Priests*. Identity and Ministry, ed. R. J.
    Wister, Wilmington 1990, 92-103.

———, «Responding to the Laity's Mission», *Origins* 20 (1990) 76-78.

———, «Search for Identity in a Church of Many Ministers», *Origins* 20
    (1990) 73-76.

———, *Servant Leaders of the People of God*. An Ecclesial Spirituality for
    American Priests, New York 1989.

SECONDIN, B., «La spiritualità contemporanea e la sfide delle nuove culture», in
    Esperienza e spiritualità, Fs. C. A. Bernard, Roma 1995, 209-240.

SECONDIN, B. – GOFFI, T., eds., *Corso di spiritualità*. Esperienza, sistematica,
    proiezioni, Brescia 1989.

SEGURA, P. B., «L'initiation, valeur permanente en vue de l'inculturation», in
    Mission et cultures non-chrétiennes. Rapports et compte rendu de la
    29e Semaine de Missiologie, Louvain 1959.

SENIOR, D., «Biblical Foundations for the Theology of Priesthood», In *Priests*.
    Ministry and Identity, ed. R. J. Wister, Wilmington 1990, 11-29.

SEPE, C., «La dimensione dei ministri ordinati nell'esortazione post-sinodale»,
    PrPas 7-8 (1992) 31-38.

SHEETS, J. R., «The Nature and Meaning of Priesthood in *Pastores Dabo
    Vobis*», *Priest* (1993) 33-37.

SHIH, J., *La catechetica missionaria*. Notes for Students' Use, Roma 1993.

SHORTER, A., *Toward a Theology of Inculturation*, Maryknoll 1988.

———, *Evangelization and Culture*, London 1994.

SLIPEK, L., *La spiritualità del sacerdote diocesano dopo il Concilio Vaticano II*, S.T.D. diss., Pontifical Gregorian University, Roma 1982.

STACKHOUSE, M. L., «Contextualization, Contextuality, and Contextualism», in *One Faith, Many Cultures*. Inculturation, Indigenization, and Contextualization, ed. R. O. Costa, Maryknoll 1988, 3-13.

STARKLOFF, C. F., «Inculturation and Cultural Systems». Parts 1 and 2, *TS* 55 (1994) 66-81.274-294.

STENICO, T., ed., *Il sacerdozio ministeriale nel magistero eclesiastico*. Documenti (1908-1993), Vatican City 1993.

STOGDILL, R. M., «Personal Factors Associated with Leadership. A Survey of the Literature», *JPs* 25 (1948) 35-71.

SUDBRACK, J., «Spirituality, I», tr. not given, in *SM*, vol. 6, 147-153.

SWAIN, B. F., *Liberating Leadership*. Practical Styles for Pastoral Ministry, San Francisco 1986.

SYNOD OF BISHOPS, (1985), «Final Report. The Church, in the Word of God, Celebrates the Mystery of Christ for the Salvation of the World», *Origins* 15 (1985) 444-450.

———, (1990), *Instrumentum laboris*. The Formation of Priests in the Circumstances of the Present Day, Roma – Washington 1990.

———, (1990), *Lineamenta*. The Formation of Priests in the Circumstances of the Present Day, Roma – Washington 1989.

———, (1971), «The Ministerial Priesthood», in *NPF*, vol. 1, 293-313. Original: *AAS* 63 (1971) 898-922.

SZCZUREK, J., *La cristologia nella prospettiva sacerdotale secondo l'insegnamento del Concilio Vaticano II*, S.T.D. diss., Pontifical Gregorian University, Roma 1989.

TARTRE, R. A., *The Postconciliar Priest*. Comments on Some Aspects of the «Decree on the Ministry and Life of Priests», New York 1966.

TERRIEN, L., «Theology and Spirituality of the Priesthood in *Pastores Dabo Vobis* and *The New Catechism of the Catholic Church*», *SemN* 32 (1994) 11-22.

TETLOW, J. A., «The Inculturation of Catholicism in the United States», in *Inculturation*, WpLFC 2, Roma 1983, 15-50.

TETTAMANZI, D., ed., *La formazione dei sacerdoti nelle circostanze attuali*. Documenti ufficiali dell'ottava assemblea generale ordinaria del Sinodo dei vescovi; sintesi originali degli interventi e delle «proposte» dei Padri Sinodali, StDVe 10, Roma 1990.

THAYER, D., «Literature Survey on Priesthood». Report prepared for the members of the sub-committee and staff preparing the revision of the *PPF*, 6 February 1990. Photocopy.

THOMAS AQUINAS, *Summa Theologiae*, tr. and ed. D. Bourke, London 1975.

THOMPSON, W. M., «A Theological Reflection on Priesthood Today», *Priest* (1992) 46-53.

THURIAN, M., *L'Identità del sacerdote*, Casale Monferrato 1993.

TILLICH, P., *Systematic Theology*, Chicago 1963.

TRIACCA, A. M., «Lo Spirito Santo nella formazione sacerdotale», *Seminarium* 33 (1993) 305-321.

———, «Spirito Santo e "dinamismi" del ministero ordinato, in margine al linguaggio della *Pastores dabo vobis*», *Sal.* 55 (1993) 271-294.

TYLOR, E. B., *Primitive Culture*, 2 vols., London 1891.

VALADIER, P., «Opportunities for the Christian Message in Tomorrow's World», tr. J. Bowden, in *The Debate on Modernity*, eds. C. Geffré – J.-P. Jossua, Conc.(GB) 1992/6, London 1992, 107-114.

VAN ALLEN, R., «Catholicism in the United States. Some Elements of Creative Inculturation», in *Inculturation*, WpLFC 8, Roma 1986, 55-76.

VANDENBROUCKE, F., «Spirituality and Spiritualities», tr. K. Sullivan, in *Spirituality in Church and World*, ed. C. Duquoc, Conc(US) 9, New York 1965, 45-60.

VANHOYE, A., *Old Testament Priests and the New Priests, According to the New Testament*, tr. J. B. Orchard, Petersham 1986.

VANZAN, P., «*Pastores dabo vobis*. Chiavi di lettura ecclesiologico-trinitaria, cristologica, e pastorale» Parts 1 and 2, *CivCatt* 143/4 (1992) 233-343.353-361.

VELIATH, D., «The Crisis in Priestly Formation», *JeDh* 22 (1992) 310-317.

VORGRIMLER, H., ed., *Commentary on the Documents of Vatican II*, various trs., 5 vols., New York 1989[2].

———, «The Sacrament of Orders», in *Sacramental Theology*, tr. L. M. Maloney, Collegeville 1992, 237-282.

WARREN, M., «Questioning Culture», *NCW* 230, (1987) 100-105.

WEAKLAND, R. G., «Leadership Skills for the Church of the 90's», *LiLi* 26 (1990) 295-303.

WHITE, J. M., «The Diocesan Seminary and the Community of Faith. Reflections from the American Experience», *USCH* 11 (1993) 1-20.

———, *The Diocesan Seminary in the United States*. A History from the 1780's to the Present, Notre Dame 1989.

WILLS, G., *Certain Trumpets*. The Call of Leaders, New York 1994.

WINSTANLEY, M., «The Shepherd Image in the Scriptures», *CleR* 71 (1986) 197-206.

WISTER, R. J., ed., *Priests*. Identity and Ministry, Wilmington 1990.

———, «Reflection on the Priesthood in Contemporary America», *USCH* 11 (1993) 126-129.

WITHERUP, R. D., «The "Intellectual" Formation of Priests», *Priest* (1993) 46-52.

WOLANIN, A., *Teologia della missione*. Notes for Students Use, Roma (no date given).

WUERL, D., *The Catholic Priesthood Today*, Chicago 1976.

———, «The Lifelong Process of Formation», *Origins* 20 (1990) 306-307.

———, «The Third Synod of Bishops on the Priesthood», *Ang.* 51 (1974) 50-87.

———, «Toward the Year 2000. Priest and the Laity», *Origins* 19 (1990) 765-767.

WULF, F. et al., «Commentary on the Decree [on the Ministry and Life of Priests]», in *CDV*, vol. 4, New York 1989, 210-297.

YOUNG, G. C., «Priests», in *The Documents of Vatican II*, ed. W. M. Abbott, New York 1989, 526-531.

ZAGO, M., «Sacerdoti per la missione», in *Vi darò pastori secondo il mio cuore. Testo e commenti*, QOR, vol. 20, Vatican City 1992, 225-232.

ZIEGENAUS, A., «Identidad del sacerdocio ministerial», in *FSCa*, Pamplona 1990, 81-96.

ZIMMERMAN, J. A., «Priesthood and a Challenged Church», *EeT* 19 (1988) 149-157.

———, «Priesthood Through the Eyes of a Non-Ordained Priest», *EeT* 19 (1988) 223-240.

INDEX OF AUTHORS

TABLE OF CONTENTS

TESI GREGORIANA

Since 1995, the series «Tesi Gregoriana» has made available to the general public some of the best doctoral theses done at the Pontifical Gregorian University. The typesetting is done by the authors themselves following norms established and controlled by the University.

Published Volumes [Series: Spirituality]

1. D'DOUZA, Rudolf V., *The Bhagavadgītā and St. John of the Cross. A Comparative Study of the Dynamism of Spiritual Growth in the Process of God-Realisation*, 1996, pp. 484.

2. PONNUMUTHAN, Selvister, *The Spirituality of Basic Ecclesial Communities in the Socio-Religious Context of Trivandrum/Kerala, India*, 1996, pp. 360.

3. WINTERS, Bartholomew, *Priest as Leader. The Process of the Inculturation of a Spiritual-Theological Theme of Priesthood in a United States Context*, 1997, pp. 368

Riproduzione anastatica: 24 gennaio 1997
Tipografia Poliglotta della Pontificia Università Gregoriana
Piazza della Pilotta, 4 – 00187 Roma